W9-DGS-586

GOOD AMERICANS

POSTER FOR THE THIRD LIBERTY LOAN, APRIL-MAY 1918.

CHRISTOPHER M. STERBA

GOOD AMERICANS

* * * * * * * * * * * * * * * * * *

ITALIAN AND JEWISH IMMIGRANTS

DURING THE FIRST WORLD WAR **

CABRINI COLLEGE LIBRARY
610 KING OF PRUSSIA ROAD
RADNOR, PA 19087

OXFORD
UNIVERSITY PRESS

2003

#49576532

OXFORD
UNIVERSITY PRESS

Oxford   New York

Auckland   Bangkok   Buenos Aires   Cape Town   Chennai
Dar es Salaam   Delhi   Hong Kong   Istanbul   Karachi   Kolkata
Kuala Lumpur   Madrid   Melbourne   Mexico City   Mumbai   Nairobi
São Paulo   Shanghai   Taipei   Tokyo   Toronto

Copyright © 2003 by Oxford University Press, Inc.

Published by Oxford University Press, Inc.
198 Madison Avenue, New York, New York 10016

www.oup.com

Oxford is a registered trademark of Oxford University Press

All rights reserved. No part of this publication may be reproduced,
stored in a retrieval system, or transmitted, in any form or by any means,
electronic, mechanical, photocopying, recording, or otherwise,
without the prior permission of Oxford University Press.

Library of Congress Cataloging-in-Publication Data
Sterba, Christopher M.
   Good Americans : Italian and Jewish immigrants during the First World War /
Christopher M. Sterba.
      p. cm.
Includes bibliographical references and index.
ISBN 0-19-514754-5; ISBN 0-19-515488-6 (pbk)
1. World War, 1914–1918—United States.   2. World War, 1914–1918—Italian
Americans, 3. World War, 1914–1918—Jews.   4. Italian Americans—History—20th
century.   5. Jews—United States—History—20th century.   6. United
States—History—1913–1921.   I. Title.
D619 .S64 2003
940.373—dc21   2002067150

9 8 7 6 5 4 3 2 1

Printed in the United States of America
on acid-free paper

To my parents, Frank and Shirley

★　★　★

Acknowledgments

There are a great many people who helped me through the long process of writing this book. My first thanks are to my advisers, who read this study in its earliest forms and encouraged me to keep on going. I was blessed to have worked with three superb historians at Brandeis. For five years, Morton Keller provided exceptional commentary. Even more important, he helped reframe my thinking on issues of periodization in American history and encouraged me to work on a much larger playing field, with many more actors, than I had been prepared to do when I first arrived in Waltham a decade ago. Jacqueline Jones's solid support and critical readings were invaluable, and I've tried to follow her great example as a plain-speaking social historian. To Jane Kamensky I owe a huge debt. She made the publication of this book possible, and her excellent advice, sharp wit, and keen commentary on making the most of primary sources were a constant source of inspiration.

I was also very fortunate to have several careful readers. Christian Warren has been a terrific friend and colleague through it all, and I have benefited tremendously from swapping chapters and papers with him, unfortunately most of it long distance. Peter Carroll, Marjorie Feld, Lawrence Fuchs, Martha Gardner, Steve Lassonde, Ted Liazos, Wes Montgomery, Stephen Rice, Jonathan Sarna, and Stephan Thernstrom all provided helpful comments and criticism. I am deeply indebted to Martin Sklar for his many years of thoughtful and encouraging commentary on my work, as well as for his inspiring scholarship, which had a major influence on the shaping of this project. Susan Ferber at Oxford deserves special praise for her extremely thorough editorial guidance on the book. I would also like to thank the editors and reviewers of *The New England Quarterly* and the *Journal of American Ethnic History*, where portions of this manuscript have previously appeared as articles. Several other teachers and scholars have been important in helping me to shape the project, even if they did not advise me on the writing and research: thanks to Lolene Blake, Jon Butler, Ann Fabian, Michael Gelinas, David Hackett Fischer, David Montgomery, Peter Santos, and Sam Bass Warner.

There were many friends and family who read little if any of the manuscript, but whose advice and support helped just as much to keep the work moving over the last eight years: Mark Aronson; David Barquist; Judith Brown; Catherine Dana; Natalie Danner; Jacque Ensign; Michael Fein; Melissa Friedman; Miriam Greenburg; Juliette Guilbert; Talbot Imlay; David and Vivian McCracken; Ina Malaguti; Timothy Pieser; Raúl Ramos; Lucio, Marcia, and Vanessa Ruotolo; Marion Sandquist; Jim Sterba; Tom and Sue Wilson; and the incredible staff at BRIDGE Housing Corporation. Special thanks go to both Seth Garfield and Martin Berger for their sage counsel, generosity, and great sense of humor on many critical and not so critical occasions.

The accessibility and advice I enjoyed at a number of libraries and archives were crucial. I am indebted to the archivists and staff of the American Jewish Archives, American Jewish Historical Society, Connecticut State Library and Archives, Hoover Institution, National Museum of American Jewish Military History, New Haven Colony Historical Society, New Haven Free Public Library, New York Public Library, United States Military History Institute, Yale University's Sterling Memorial and Mudd libraries, and the interlibrary loan departments at Yale, Brandeis, San Francisco State University, the San Francisco Public Library, and U.C.-Berkeley. To quote a New York judge in 1917: "These people are on the job."

I owe an even greater debt to the generous financial support of Brandeis' Graduate School of Arts and Sciences, the Crown Fellowship program, the Rabbi Marc Tanenbaum Foundation, the History of American Civilization program, and the Garvan Furniture Study. Their assistance made this study possible.

My family has been a tremendous source of support—and healthy diversion. I feel very lucky to have been able to do my research so close to my sisters Beth and Melissa and to see their children Amber Ansari, Bill Ansari, and Samantha Sterba grow up. Living in New Haven also allowed me to cross paths with the most important person in my life, Cristina Ruotolo. For this reason alone, the book has been worth writing.

Contents

GOOD AMERICANS

Introduction

The Melting Pot Goes to War

✶ ✶ ✶ ✶ ✶ ✶ ✶ ✶ ✶ ✶ ✶ ✶ ✶ ✶ ✶ ✶ ✶ ✶ ✶

Private Abraham Krotoshinsky was in serious trouble on the night of October 7, 1918. A member of the famous "Lost Battalion" surrounded in the Argonne Forest, Krotoshinsky had made his way through enemy positions in a desperate attempt to find relief for his starving and casualty-ridden unit. By sprinting through machine-gun fire, inching along flat on his stomach, and even pretending to be a corpse, he had eluded capture for more than ten hours. "Then my real trouble began," he recalled, as he neared American trenches. "I was coming from the German lines and my English is none too good. I was afraid they would shoot me for a German before I could explain who I was." Deciding to call out "hello" several times, "since [the enemy] never used that expression when he tried to talk English," the young Polish Jew was able to convince nearby doughboys that he too was a U.S. soldier. Despite the fact that he had gone through the same process of training and combat duty as his American-born comrades, his eastern European background nearly cost him his life.[1]

The image of Krotoshinsky caught in the middle of No Man's Land suggests both the extent and the limits of the Great War as an acculturating experience for millions of southern and eastern European immigrants in the United States. These "New Immigrants," as they were popularly known, arrived in America between the 1880s and the outbreak of the World War in 1914. Among them were approximately 6 million Italians and eastern European Jews, who, compelled by poverty at home and lured by the tremendous industrial growth of the United States, left the social and economic turmoil of their home countries. The poverty and exploitation they endured in America are well documented. So are the bigotry and nativism they confronted, which considered them incapable of assimilating the culture and mores of the United States. To much of the native born public, these newcomers were much less desirable than the British, Irish, German, and Scandinavian immigrants of the so-called Old Immigration from northern and western Europe that had predominated up to the 1870s. As the country entered the war, America's Italians, Jews, Slavs, Greeks, and other southern and eastern European immigrants were very much in the process of breaking down social and political barriers. Much like Private Krotoshinsky, they still sought the recognition and acceptance of their American-born peers.

To gauge the effect of the war on the new immigrants' settlement in the United States, this study examines the experiences of two specific populations, the Italian *colonia* of New Haven and the eastern European Jewish enclaves of New York City. These two communities were the largest immigrant groups in their respective cities, and helped to produce two of the most compelling military units of the American war effort: an all-Italian machine gun company, and Private Krotoshinsky's own highly decorated organization, the so-called "Melting Pot" Seventy-seventh Division. Making such a significant contribution to the war effort both at home and abroad, these New Haven Italians and New York Jews offer a particularly vivid example of what it meant to be a European immigrant in America during the Great War.

In the late nineteenth and early twentieth centuries, these two groups developed strong communities with very little outside aid or interference. From scratch they had built an impressive range of religious institutions, mutual aid societies, newspapers, and ethnic businesses. Their contact with the federal government was minimal, unlikely to extend beyond Ellis Island, the post office, and an occasional census taker. But in the spring of 1917 they faced a barrage of appeals to participate in a conflict that had been raging in their homelands for three years, a war that had cut off the stream of migration that had brought them to America. In addition to providing soldiers like Private Krotoshinsky for military service, new immigrant men and women "did their bit" in dozens of other ways. They bought Liberty Bonds and War Savings Stamps, gave money to agencies like the Red Cross and Jewish Welfare Board, and obeyed the government's numerous demands for food and fuel conservation. Collectively these activities and others represented the first national experience that the "newest immigrant races" shared with the native-born public. Never again would they be as culturally and politically isolated as they were before 1917.[2]

Focusing on their experiences, I have asked three central questions of the years 1917–1919, each addressing an important weakness in our historical understanding of ethnicity in the early twentieth century. First, how did the American war effort confront the southern and eastern European immigrant communities of the United States? What were the points of contact, conflict, and consensus? Historians have focused on the repressive treatment of German Americans and immigrant radicals while neglecting the wartime experiences of other ethnic groups. Was that treatment the same for the Italians of New Haven, who solidly supported the war, and for the Jews of New York, whose attitudes were strongly divided? As important, given the rushed and haphazard character of America's military mobilization, how much of the war effort specifically targeted the nation's immigrants?

My second question focuses on the new immigrants' perspective on the war. How did they respond during the nineteen months of American belligerency? What level of support, resistance, or resignation did they demonstrate in response to the various calls for loyalty, soldiers, money, and industrial production? In the popular view, the American home front was extremely polarized, a struggle between an intolerant and even self-interested prowar crowd and a highly principled opposition movement. While the two immigrant groups of this study might have responded in similar ways, even more important was their continuing identification with their homelands. Italy was an ally of the United States and had been fighting the war since 1915. Czarist Russia, from which most of New York's Jews emigrated, disintegrated on the eve of American intervention, and the revolutionary governments that followed took the lead in asking for a negotiated end to the war. The conflict's destructiveness also boosted the Zionist movement for an independent Jewish state. How did these ethnic ties and concerns play out on the American home front? Did the American-born children of these immigrants view the war in similar terms?

The third and final question is the most critical. How should we understand the long-term significance of the war for the "New Immigration" to America? For the most part we continue to view the first decades of the twentieth century in bits and pieces, often defining them as "eras" and "periods" even though these successive events—the Progressive Era followed by the World War, the Red Scare, the Roaring Twenties, and the Great Depression—may have lasted just a few years in duration. But now that more than eighty years have passed since the end of the war, we should be able to step further back and see larger developments and trends that have shaped the meaning of American ethnicity and democracy through to the present day. The context I found most appropriate for this study is the first fifty years of the southern and eastern European immigrant experience in America. During that time, from roughly the mid-1880s to the mid-1930s, the nation's new immigrant communities rose from random groups of individuals struggling in a new country to a major political force during the New Deal years. What role, if any, did the "war to make the world safe for democracy" play in this transformation?

As these questions suggest, I see the need for new emphases in the interpretation of immigration and ethnicity in American life. The field of social and ethnic history has moved far from the filiopietism of its early, immigrant practitioners—perhaps too far. The first, mainly amateur historians of communities such as the Italian *colonia* of New Haven and the Jews of New York City were primarily concerned with how to document the lives of group members who had left the confines of their ethnic neighborhoods and played important roles in the making of American history and culture.

In sharp contrast, for the last three to four decades immigration historians have largely ignored national events, while focusing instead on topics such as occupational mobility, generational conflict, labor militancy, class structure, and the impact of consumerism and mass culture.[3] Rather than incorporating the country's myriad ethnic groups into a broader narrative of American history, this scholarship leaves its readers with the impression that the nation is only an "imagined community," that each of these populations lived, thought, and made history on their own independent terms and in isolation from one another.[4]

The ultimate goal of the present study is to bring national events and a concern for "contributions" back into the story, without asserting that cultural and political consensus ruled or should rule the land. It seeks to explore not only differences in thought and action between immigrants and their native-born peers, but also their mutual influence on each other. What I have found helpful is to view the immigrant experience as a series of events, both great and small. There are the private events of a person's life—getting married, having children, buying a house, starting a business—that helped bind immigrants to a new environment. There are the community events that are important in the life of an ethnic group—the construction of a synagogue or church, employment in a local industry, the election of "one of our own" to public office—that helped nurture a sense of belonging to a particular place. And then there are national events that have an even broader integrating effect, providing experiences that ethnic groups could share with the larger American public.

The First World War played such a role for the country's newest European immigrants. It offered opportunities for participating in American public life that did not exist prior to 1917. People of Italian and eastern European Jewish descent eventually helped to push the United States in a more cosmopolitan, internationalist, and social democratic direction by embracing and championing a new urban liberalism in the 1930s. The First World War greatly accelerated this process, and perhaps made much of it possible.

The new immigrants' story is told chronologically, with a running comparison between the Italian and Jewish experiences. In chapter 1, I survey the historical development of the two communities in order to gauge the level of settlement and social status each had achieved by the eve of America's entry into the war. An examination of their mass emigration, the employment and residential patterns they created in the new American environment, and the institutions and political influence they had developed by the spring of 1917 will provide a basis for evaluating the war's impact.

In chapters 2 and 3, I describe how these communities responded to the most contentious issue of any war, the recruitment of their young men to fight. Ethnicity played a major role in the mobilization of men both in New Haven and New York. A lackluster recruiting drive for the Connecticut National Guard enabled the Italian colony to make its presence felt. Its eagerness to form the "Italian machine gun company," a unit composed entirely of Italian-American volunteers, eliminated any potential criticism that the Italian *colonia* was not giving its all to win the war. In New York, the home of the Civil War draft riots, the first national attempt to conscript men deeply troubled the city's Jewish population. No other ethnic group contested the draft so vigorously, as immigrant memories of czarist conscription and the strength of the Jewish labor movement and antiwar socialism combined in full force during the summer of 1917. In both cities, federal policy drew the new immigrants into public life, expanding their contact with American institutions whether they supported the war or not.

The focus of chapters 4 and 5 is on the recruits who were pulled out of these communities, new immigrant men who felt the wartime demands of the federal government most keenly. The Italian machine gunners trained in France, while most New York Jewish draftees learned how to become soldiers at Camp Upton on Long Island. They encountered unique language and cultural difficulties, but they also endured military discipline with all doughboys regardless of ethnic background. Most important was the integrative and even liberating impact of the wartime state's most ambitious project, the creation of the National Army. Composed entirely of conscripts, it did not break the color line. But in placing a higher value on a white recruit's skills and performance than his class or immigrant background, it marked a major departure from previous military practice and pointed to the eventual desegregation of the armed forces three decades later.

In chapters 6 and 7, I look at the experience of Italian and Jewish immigrants "over here" during the war. Landmark events overseas and important developments on the home front forged a new relationship between new immigrant men and women and their adopted country. The Italian Army's collapse at Caporetto, the turmoil that raged in Russia, and the promise of a Jewish homeland in Palestine helped to diminish the importance of European local and regional ties, as community members increasingly identified themselves in collective terms as "Italian" and "Jewish" Americans. The government's domestic war effort, meanwhile, carefully cultivated the immigrants' support and offered them ample opportunities to participate. For the first time their activities in America received recognition and praise.

In chapter 8, I examine the "Great Crusade" from the perspective of the new immigrant soldiers who fought in it. The Italian machine gunners from New Haven and their Jewish colleagues in "New York's Own" Seventy-seventh Division experienced the worst the western front had to offer. Their heavy casualties would not be quickly forgotten. Though as a group they rarely made headlines after the war, their strong sense of entitlement and loyalty would be deeply felt by their families and neighborhoods through the middle decades of the twentieth century. These veterans represented an important new attitude toward a culture and society that they and their communities had known for less than two generations.

How Italians and Jews won only temporary recognition from the larger American polity, rather than sustained treatment as social, cultural, and political equals, is the subject of the Epilogue. The wave of nativism and anti-Semitism that engulfed the country in the early 1920s made it clear that their wish to be treated with respect and toleration was still far from being fulfilled. The new immigrants and their children did not respond by retreating back into their enclaves, however. Through the 1920s and into the early 1930s they consolidated their gains as residents and took an increasing interest in the public arena where issues of culture, rights, and citizenship were being played out on a national stage.

Private Abraham Krotoshinsky's dangerous mission in the Argonne Forest did not end when he reached the safety of the American lines. He immediately led a patrol back to help rescue the surrounded Lost Battalion. For his actions, the young immigrant received the Distinguished Service Cross, returned to New York City a celebrated war hero, and became a U.S. citizen.[5]

But Krotoshinsky's ethnic origins still figured very prominently in his thoughts and aspirations. He became a committed Zionist, and in the early 1920s a New York Jewish philanthropist sponsored him as a settler in Palestine. Krotoshinsky struggled as a farmer in a Jewish colony for several years before returning to New York a poor and forgotten man. Then, in 1927, his life took still another curious turn, when a newspaper reported that he was unemployed and penniless, with a wife and two small children to support. On the urging of Harlem Congressman Fiorello LaGuardia, President Calvin Coolidge personally signed an executive order giving the veteran a position as a clerk in a Manhattan post office. Krotoshinsky worked there the rest of his life and passed away in 1953 at the age of sixty.[6]

Millions of Jews, Italians, Slavs, and other new immigrants would go through a similar difficult process of permanent settlement in the United States, though in much less dramatic fashion. Their ties to homeland, region, and village, so strong during the first decades of the twentieth century and perhaps felt most poignantly during the conflagration of 1914–1918, would weaken in the interwar period and beyond. The closing of immigration, and the immigrants' new families, friendships, and responsibilities in their adopted country framed and completed the transplantation of a tremendous variety of cultural, religious, and social and political folkways to the United States.

This book will describe the role that the Great War played in this process and suggests that the themes of participation and inclusiveness, as well as prejudice and coercion, were critical elements of the twentieth-century immigrant experience. The story that unfolds here is one of struggle and sacrifice, of hope and achievement. It describes how the war effort, while temporarily curtailing civil liberties in the United States, would help expand the parameters of American democracy to include millions of immigrants and their children from southern and eastern Europe.

I The Heyday of the New Immigrant Enclave

⋆ ⋆ ⋆ ⋆ ⋆ ⋆ ⋆ ⋆ ⋆ ⋆ ⋆ ⋆ ⋆ ⋆ ⋆ ⋆ ⋆ ⋆

A merica's entrance into the war posed challenges for two populations that were very much in flux. By 1917, New Haven Italians and New York Jews had moved well beyond the initial stage of establishing their housing and employment niches and were now able to rely on a wide range of ethnic institutions. Observers regarded these settlements as foreign cities-within-the-city. The immigrants lived and worked mainly with their kinsmen, bought familiar homeland foods from ethnic grocers, and attended religious services and read newspapers (if they could read) in their own languages. The immediate prewar period was really the heyday of the New Immigrant enclave, when its roots in the American landscape were secure and the adult population was still overwhelmingly made up of immigrants.

Yet despite the fact that the *colonia* of New Haven and the eastern European Jewish communities of New York City were very well developed internally, their influence on the larger American settings was still minor. The two groups were the largest immigrant populations in their respective cities on the eve of the war, but their numbers did not translate into a commensurate level of political clout. For the most part, the two groups enjoyed only token representation on party tickets and did not hold other positions of public trust and authority on an important scale—as teachers, policemen, and professionals—let alone employment in the larger nonethnic businesses, banks, and newspapers that wielded power on the local scene. Though they had been in America for close to four decades, neither community had yet found its voice in mainstream public life.

The war thus came at an important moment for southern and eastern European immigrants and their children in the United States. It called for major, sustained participation in a national effort at a time when the communities were nearly ready to move to the next stage of their settlement, from standing largely outside of the mainstream American public arena to asserting a major role in the politics and society that now shaped their lives.

To understand the response of Italian New Haven and New York Jewry to the war, this chapter focuses on both communities' circumstances before 1917. Their rapid growth, internal diversity, and meager but improving social and political status highlight an important era in American urban history. As was true for the many immigrant groups that came before them, their migration not only created hardships but also cultivated a strong sense of achievement and affirmation. What distinguished the experiences of the southern and eastern European immigrants was the "Great Crusade," the most insistent call for citizenship and participation the nation had ever witnessed. Capping decades of Italian and Jewish "colonization," the world war helped to forge bonds of loyalty and affection toward the United States that even the repression and nativism of the postwar era could not break.

★ *The Italians of New Haven*

An excellent description of the rapid growth and development of new immigrant communities in America can be found in the book, *La Colonia Italiana di New Haven*, published by an Italian printer in 1921. Antonio Cannelli, an immigrant who settled in New Haven, provided the most extensive account of the city's Italian population ever written. His book was hardly a work of rigorous historical analysis. His purpose was simple: to commemorate the achievements of a vibrant ethnic community. With great care and obvious pride, he bound the book's three hundred glossy pages in a red cloth hardcover and decorated its Italian text with hundreds of illustrations. Cannelli describes the immigrants' origins and the struggles they endured in the early years of settlement. But the bulk of his narrative focuses on what he considered the most laudable aspects of Italian New Haven: not the colony's vast majority of laborers and factory hands but its handful of doctors and lawyers; not the hallowed institution of the Italian family but its churches, societies, and newspapers.[1]

What Cannelli does best is convey a sense of the *colonia*'s substantial roots in the city by the time the United States entered World War I. The first third of his book recounts New Haven's past before the Italians came, describing in detail the city's history, its most noteworthy residents, institutions, parks, and monuments. Only after establishing this American setting does he begin a parallel discussion of the Italian community. In this context the colony's statue of Columbus and its variety of ethnic institutions and businesses appear as worthy contributions to New Haven history. The biographies of men like banker Paul Russo and "theater king" Sylvester Poli strengthen the impression that Italians were actively participating in the city's continued growth. Whether they carried a shovel to work or delivered speeches in City Hall, thousands of Italians now viewed their residence in New Haven as permanent. Their personal pasts and futures had become intertwined with the history of the Elm City, as Cannelli's book vividly testifies.[2]

The federal census documents the growth that Cannelli describes in less analytical terms. In 1880 the census recorded only 102 persons of Italian descent in New Haven. By 1920 that number had increased to over 34,000, or more than a fifth of the city's entire population (see table 1.1).

These immigrants came mainly from the southern provinces surrounding Naples and to a lesser degree from Sicily and the north of Italy. The vast majority were from rural, agricultural backgrounds. Living in villages and towns, they worked the land as small landowners, tenant farmers, and casual laborers. The typical home was a one- or two-room stone building, which served as shelter for the family and their chickens and livestock. By the late 1800s, Italy's farming population was well accustomed to producing for a market, migrating considerable distances to find work, and learning whatever skills necessary to make ends meet. Men often supplemented their agricultural work by laboring as fishermen, miners, and building tradesmen, or by offering their services in town as tailors, barbers, and shoemakers. Women worked at home and in the fields, but also in small manufactures, and as dressmakers and laundresses. The Catholic parish was the most prominent local institution. Of increasing importance were the mutual aid associations that offered economic and even educational assistance. New forms of community behavior, fostered by poverty and diminishing prospects, preceded the big step of leaving the country altogether.[3]

Arriving in New Haven, the Italians were part of a wave of immigration and industrial growth that was transforming the city. New Haven doubled in size between 1890 and 1920, increasing from 81,298 residents to 162,537. By 1910 more than two-thirds of the population were either immigrants or American-born children of foreign or mixed parentage. The older wave of European ethnics, dominated by the Irish but also containing substantial numbers of Germans and other Britons, were primarily second- and third-generation residents. The Italians led the more recent arrivals, followed by a large Jewish community and smaller groupings of Poles, Hungarians, and French-Canadians. The city also had an established African-

Table 1.1   Italian-American Population of the City of New Haven[a]

Year	Italian American	New Haven Total	Italian % of Total
1890	2,330	81,298	2.87
1900	7,780	108,027	7.2
1910	21,919	133,605	16.41
1920	34,558	162,537	21.26

[a] Myers, "Time Differential Factor," 26–27.

American population, accounting for 2.7 percent of the population in 1910. New Haven Yankees, the descendants of New England's Puritan past, represented only a quarter of local residents when America went to war.[4]

Why the Elm City developed into such a polyglot city is best expressed by the slogan "What New Haven Makes—Makes New Haven." By 1918, eight hundred manufacturers of all shapes and sizes produced 155 different lines of goods. Local weapons, tool, and rubber goods makers were the city's industrial backbone, and firms like the Winchester firearms and Sargent hardware companies enjoyed international recognition. New housing, a variety of municipal projects, and the region's railroad network also provided thousands with construction jobs during the Progressive Era. Italians, like so many other groups, found a very heavy demand for their labor in New Haven.[5]

For the *colonia*, local employment defined three distinct stages of settlement. The first, pioneering stage was sporadic and transient. City directories from the 1860s through the early 1880s list an odd collection of laborers, street musicians, and peddlers. *Padrone*, the notorious labor bosses who exploited immigrants in search of work, lived in the area, controlling the labor of hundreds of Italians. Such a motley group of immigrants, whether "bonded" or free individuals, hardly made for a substantial population. A WPA study notes that they were referred to as "swallows." "A not inappropriate name," the report comments, "when we consider that most of them used to return to Italy for the winter months and come back the following spring."[6]

Yet some of these *pionieri* [pioneers] were able to secure jobs with major city firms, creating a beachhead for the mass migration that soon followed. This second phase of Italian settlement, which covered the high tide years of the late-1880s to 1910, was anchored to specific locations on both sides of the Atlantic. Early migrants linked family and neighbors to a handful of Italian-friendly New Haven companies, and particular towns and villages in the regions of Campania, Calabria, Molise, Abruzzi, and the Marches became the main source of Italian labor. As early as 1890, more than a third of the Sargent hardware company's one thousand shop hands were Italian, and in 1902 the New Haven Railroad employed ten thousand Italians. Thousands of "swallows" continued to arrive for seasonal work through the outbreak of World War I. But the great majority now traveled in well-defined paths with precise work destinations in mind.[7]

This second migration stage included many immigrants who came to provide services for the expanding population. Though most Italians were unskilled and semiskilled workers between 1890 and 1910, a substantial minority also ran their own businesses. By 1900, there were more immigrant proprietors per capita within the *colonia* than there were business owners for the city population as a whole. Among the Italian grocers, butchers, and restaurateurs who catered to homeland food and leisure-ways were those who had already diversified their activities, selling steamship tickets and handling

immigrant savings. Skilled urban workers, meanwhile, cut deeply into existing competition in the shoe repair and barber trades.[8] The tremendous sacrifices of migration notwithstanding, these proprietors and year-round workers laid the foundation for a solid local Italian presence that has persisted to
the present day.

In the last phase of Italian settlement prior to 1917, employment became more widely dispersed and immigrants began a meager but perceptible
degree of climbing on the occupational ladder. A number of food dealers
started up macaroni and bread-making companies, and several businessmen
opened ethnic banking and real estate firms. The G & O Radiator Company,
formed by two immigrant factory hands in 1915, was the only local Italian-
owned industrial firm before the war. For the overwhelming majority of
working-class Italians, upward mobility was limited to the movement to
semiskilled jobs. After working a few years and learning to speak adequate
English, many immigrants were able to escape the back-breaking life of the
day laborer and become machine operators, building craftsmen, and even
foremen. Allied demands for materiel before America entered the war accelerated this process. Italians and the other newer immigrant groups clearly
benefited when the Winchester, Maxim, and Marlin arms factories increased
their payrolls.[9]

These developments fundamentally reshaped the demographic makeup
of the *colonia*. The proportion of men to women and of immigrants to
American-born children showed the greatest change. Many immigrant men
chose to marry and raise families in New Haven, creating a core of settled
kin that not only included women who were wives or prospective wives, but
also sisters, mothers, and female cousins. Single women rarely emigrated on
their own to obtain work, usually coming over as family members or friends
planning to marry or help others maintain a home, keep lodgers, or run a
small business. With married couples came American-born children, who by
1920 outnumbered the first-generation *paesani*. "Many of these immigrants
had large families," recalled a resident; "it was not uncommon to find family
after family with eight or ten children." When America went to war, children
of Italian descent constituted the largest single group of students in the
public school system. In three schools they made up more than 95 percent
of the students enrolled. Most adult workers were still foreign-born, but a
small number of second-generation children with schooling and English
skills had begun to enter the work force. On reaching (what their fathers
claimed to be) the age of fourteen, they went straight to factories and construction sites or started learning trades alongside their parents. With steady
jobs, the first workers born in America symbolized the colony's growth better
than any immigrant success story.[10]

As the work force expanded in the *colonia*, so did its array of institutions.
No individual family, no matter how extended, could satisfy all of the pressing economic and social needs that came with settlement in a foreign country. Societies that offered sick and death benefits, churches that provided

spiritual care, and clubs that organized recreational and political activities sprouted up as soon as the newcomers could create them. Having only each other to rely on, Italians developed an impressive array of institutions to reduce the strain of emigration as much as possible.

The first institutions appeared between the mid-1880s and the early 1890s. Since the population was small, migrants from a variety of regions had to pull together. They named organizations after values and national symbols that were acceptable to diverse memberships. The first mutual benefit societies, La Fratellanza (the Brotherhood) and the Società Giuseppe Garibaldi, were established in 1884. Immigrants of the Wooster Square neighborhood, after attending Irish Catholic parishes and saving money for several years, purchased a vacant Lutheran church and renamed it St. Michael's in 1889. When the colony unveiled a statue of Columbus in 1892, the first local Italian newspaper heralded its importance. La Stella d'Italia's premier issue proclaimed: "Though our colony is small, the hearts of so many Italians beat strongly and in unison, giving proof that when it comes to honoring our homeland, all agree, all act without any hesitation." Early associational activity reflected much of this sentiment. Though immigrants might have preferred to create institutions along regional lines, their small numbers required united effort.[11]

With thousands of arrivals each year, the number of Italian organizations mushroomed. When a second Catholic church was needed, immigrant numbers were sufficient to finance its construction from scratch. St. Anthony's, established in 1904, ministered to residents of the "Hill," the other large Italian neighborhood. In 1910 the two Italian churches claimed to have more than twenty-eight thousand parishioners, and a third church was built in 1915. This population constituted a large newspaper audience as well. Several Italian weeklies, from four to eight pages in length, carried news from the old country and advice for making a livelihood here in America. By 1913 there were four in New Haven, each promoting its own political and social perspective. Il Corriere del Connecticut was the largest and supported the Republican party, while La Parola Cattolica addressed the colony's religious concerns.[12]

But immigrants were most active when creating institutions that affirmed their provincial origins. When populations from specific towns grew large enough, the number of mutual aid societies and clubs dramatically multiplied. Between 1898 and 1908, immigrants from Atrani, Amalfi, Castellamare, Scafati, and Minori formed societies named after their hometowns' patron saints. Membership in these organizations and dozens more like them was tightly restricted to people from the same locality in Italy. As finances became more secure, several groups sponsored social events and patron saints' festivals. The many circoli [clubs], meanwhile, whose hometown roots were just as strong, promoted a wide variety of cultural, educational, and political activities. Immigrants from Caserta province, for example, formed the Circolo San Carlino in 1897 and built a five-hundred-seat theater for plays and concerts. By 1917 New Haven was home to more than thirty clubs and mutual aid societies, representing clusters of immigrants from all over Italy.[13]

Within a span of roughly thirty years, New Haven's Italian population had grown from a pocket of random individuals to the largest ethnic group in the city. The *New Haven Register* remarked in 1915 that with so many parishes, shops, clubs, and newspapers, the Italians had "everything that would be necessary if they were a community by themselves."[14] Indeed, observers wondered if the immigrants had ever really left Italy. But the rise of the *colonia* was also manifest proof of their desire to settle permanently in the area. The decisions that immigrants were making—to buy homes, raise families, and donate hard-earned wages to ethnic institutions—constituted a commitment to life in America that their "foreignness" to a great extent disguised. With a definite future in their adopted country, they would be very receptive to the calls to service when America went to war. For many immigrants, the "war to make the world safe for democracy" represented an opportunity to express aspirations that outsiders simply did not recognize.

Despite their large presence in the area by 1917, the Italian population did not have a substantial voice in city affairs. Economic inequality and the prejudice it nurtured kept Italians out of positions of local power, while deep cultural, class, and generational divisions prevented the *colonia* from acting in a unified manner. When "American" New Haven threw its full resources into mobilizing for war, the Italian contribution was noticeably separate and unequal.

Of the many internal fissures that divided the *colonia*, none were more profound and debilitating than the regional differences the immigrants brought from Italy. Though they learned American work rhythms and decided on America as their future home, the Italians maintained and adapted as much of their homeland folkways as possible. The ways in which they made sense of their world and endured its severity had developed over countless centuries, in towns and villages that rarely experienced the centralizing influence of an outside power. Their localism only grew stronger in New Haven, where trust and aid were extremely valuable quantities, and close contact with immigrants from all over Italy made regional differences all the more obvious.

The different dialects Italian residents spoke and the variety of patron saints they worshipped demonstrate how resilient and divisive these folkways could be. Though the immigrants could understand Italian, their American-born children often learned just the provincial dialect spoken at home. The most basic building block for constituting a community—the ability of members to communicate with one another—was to a significant degree absent from Italian New Haven. The patron saints of homeland cities and towns were even more numerous than the different dialects. Adoration for these figures went well beyond a reverence for their martyrdoms. Inhabitants viewed them as protectors and benefactors who could grant favors large and small.[15]

Along with these distinctive loyalties and traits went a considerable provincial chauvinism, which was visible among immigrants at work and in everyday life. Plant foremen learned to hire only Italians from a single locality in their departments, and a social worker observed that women from different regions did not associate with each other even though they were neighbors. By the turn of the century, the immigrants had developed essentially three different neighborhoods. The Wooster Square enclave, nicknamed "Little Naples" because of its heavy concentration of immigrants from the province of Salerno, was by far the largest. Two smaller groupings resided in the "Hill" section of New Haven, one composed of northern Italians from the Marches region, and the other of southerners from the provinces of Caserta, Avellino, and Benevento. Not surprisingly, the energy and expense the immigrants poured into their regionally defined societies, clubs, and saints' festivals rarely supported communitywide campaigns.[16]

In addition to their provincial loyalties, the outlook of colony members differed according to their place in the social order and their length of residency in the United States. As historian John W. Briggs has noted, the "fluid population" of Italian enclaves made for "increasing complexity and variety as the colonies matured." Class differences within the colony were on a more concentrated scale than was true for the city population as a whole. The overwhelming majority of Italians fell somewhere between the ranks of hustling shopkeepers and lowly day laborers. In 1910, nearly one out of two Italian workers toiled in unskilled jobs. When combined with semiskilled employees, this total accounted for more than 70 percent of the Italian working population. Craftsmen, clerical employees, and shop owners who enjoyed a slightly better standard of living made up more than a quarter of employed Italians in 1910. But their incomes could hardly sustain much more than the hand-to-mouth existence of their unskilled neighbors, and on the eve of the war 90 percent of the Italian population still resided in what was considered the lowest strata of housing.[17]

The tiny minority who had the means and energy to pursue interests beyond making a living became the *colonia*'s most visible spokesmen. Professionals like Dr. William Verdi and attorney Rocco Ierardi constituted less than 1 percent of employed Italians in 1910. Yet they and a handful of businessmen and editors dominated the colony's political life. These *prominenti's* backgrounds were clearly exceptions to the rule. Sylvester Z. Poli, who owned a large chain of theaters, trained as a sculptor in Paris before coming to America. Paul Russo made use of his Italian education to open the colony's first grocery store, become Yale Law School's first Italian-American graduate, and establish the first Italian bank in the city. City sheriff Frank Palmieri, whose father was a mayor in southern Italy, became the first Italian to win a citywide election in New Haven in 1914.[18]

In such a heavily working-class population, it might seem surprising that a strong proletarian voice did not echo through the *colonia*. Except for a strike at the Sargent's factory and the publication of a prolabor newspaper in 1902, there is little evidence of a radical presence in the three enclaves. The local Socialist party attempted to attract Italians with little success. The Elm City was no Lawrence, Massachusetts, or Paterson, New Jersey, places where Italian labor unrest captured national headlines during the Progressive Era. Unlike these one-industry towns, New Haven had a booming and diverse economy that largely satisfied the newcomers' desire for security. The *New Haven Register* singled out the Italian community for its high level of home ownership and "Americanization." What was linked together in the editors' minds was in reality more a reflection of what Italians had come to the city for in the first place: to live and work in a community that provided a better life for themselves and their families.[19]

The lack of a strong, united community contributed to the Italians' minor influence on the affairs of the city at large. But so did the severe prejudice the immigrants encountered, based on their poverty as well as cultural distinctiveness. In the first decades of settlement, ethnic antagonism directed at Italians found expression in both word and deed. Antonio Cannelli reported that until the 1880s local Italians concealed their nationality from census takers to avoid harassment. "A few of our older residents," he reported, "recall with deep bitterness the frequent and terrible outbursts of racial hatred that took place." Many factories excluded Italians from employment, claiming the newcomers "were unfit or were troublemakers," and *paesani* who did find jobs continued to suffer verbal and even physical abuse.[20]

It was not until after the turn of the century that this open hostility began to fade. Because of the sheer weight of their growing numbers, Italians found themselves increasingly tolerated by employers, politicians, and newspaper editors. Italian leaders made much of this transformation possible. The colony's first newspapers and political clubs emerged largely in order to protest discrimination. As a result, New Haven had cleaned up its act to a fair degree by 1917, careful not to offend the Italian fifth of the population in public statements or actions.[21]

Italians nonetheless had little political influence in the Elm City. Tokenism best describes their political status, as both of the major parties wooed voters with favors and minor places on their tickets. With few naturalized citizens, Italians missed out on the patronage spoils that made political involvement so valuable during the period. In 1917, the city payroll included only five Italian clerical employees and teachers, one fireman, and no policemen. The city sheriff's office and a handful of lesser posts were all that the Italians' 21 percent of the population could claim as their own. It would take another, American-born generation to obtain significant power in the city.[22]

Acurious incident took place in March 1917, which highlighted the extent of the Italians' progress and foreshadowed what they would encounter during the war. A young man from New Haven was arrested on charges of espionage just a few days before the nation declared war on Germany. The police of Bristol, Connecticut, linked Leopoldo Cobianchi to several pieces of incriminating evidence. Detectives discovered among his possessions a map of Bristol marked with a drawing of a cannon. Finding calculations of the gun's firing range, they suspected Cobianchi to be one of a pair of men seen prowling about the city's factory district. Police were particularly interested in his button bearing the cryptic message "One of 1,000" and an essay defending the German policy of unrestricted submarine warfare. To the U.S. marshal who was called in to investigate, it looked as though the rising fears of sabotage were now a dangerous reality.[23]

Officials soon realized, however, that there had been a terrible misunderstanding. Cobianchi was a Sargent hardware factory employee who had been taking night classes to prepare for the Yale Law School entrance exam. Upon his instructor's recommendation that he take a break from his work and studies, Cobianchi went to Bristol, but continued to work on physics problems by using features of the local landscape. The mysterious button, which police thought meant "One of 1,000" plotters against the government, was the slogan of the New Haven Young Democratic Club, of which Cobianchi was a member. The young man's father was the publisher of the New Haven weekly *L'Indipendente*, and Leopoldo had written the paper on German submarines because his father insisted that he learn to argue both sides of an issue. With an explanation for each piece of evidence, the case against Cobianchi was quickly dropped.[24]

Cobianchi's arrest illustrates the leverage the Italian *prominenti* and newspapers could exert when sufficiently pressed. Leopoldo's father was able to meet personally with the U.S. district attorney and paid his son's five thousand dollar bail bond with a loan from a colony banker. Leopoldo himself visited the city's daily papers to give his side of the story. He was a rising star in local politics and would soon be elected as a city alderman. On the eve of the war, the colony had the means—newspapers, banks, and political connections—to cause quite a stir, if only on behalf of an individual with strong ties to the enclaves' leaders.[25]

But the case also demonstrated how tenuous an Italian's position could be when connections were not apparent. It is unclear whether Cobianchi's appearance or accent compelled the boarding-house keeper to contact authorities. But as Antonio Cannelli claimed, it was not uncommon to hear of "the small injustice, the minor act of retaliation, the poorly disguised outburst of rage, or at the very least, the unconscious prejudice against anything that is Italian." Cobianchi's ethnicity may have instantly made him an object of suspicion, the feared crime in this case being espionage. His family, education, and aspirations of "working hard to improve his future" mattered little, a demeaning experience that was regularly felt by most of the Italian population.[26]

Finally, the affair exemplified the circumstances that would mark ethnic life during the next nineteen months. The war demanded a new, if temporary, relationship between the individual and the state, even if that individual was not a citizen, and Leopoldo Cobianchi and the rest of the *colonia* were just beginning to get a sense of Uncle Sam's long, wartime reach. Campaigns calling for military mobilization and steadfast loyalty would soon sweep through the colony as they did every other American community. New Haven's enclaves were no longer to be ignored as they had been since the days of the swallows and the *pionieri*.

★ The Eastern European Jews of New York City

Approximately 1.5 million Jews lived in New York City in 1917. The vastness of this population was too great for any single author, like New Haven's Antonio Cannelli, to describe. A sixteen-hundred-page volume, *The Jewish Communal Register of New York City, 1917–1918*, probably the closest equivalent to Cannelli's book on the Italian *colonia*, was published by an organization, the Kehillah, or Jewish communal council, of New York City. A team of researchers examined the religious, social, and political life of New York Jewry, and more than thirty prominent Jews contributed feature-length articles.[27]

The *Communal Register*'s findings offer great insight into the character of New York Jewry on the eve of the war. By 1917, Gotham's Jews constituted fully half of the Jewish population of the United States and roughly 10 percent of all Jews living in the entire world. They worshiped in two thousand synagogues and belonged to thirty-six hundred mutual aid societies. The *Communal Register* estimated that 400,000 Jewish workers in New York were union members, and that the city's Yiddish press sold 300,000 papers daily. New York Jews were a study in contrasts, ranging in religious practice from Reformed and Conservative, to Orthodox and Hasidic; in politics from socialist and anarchist, to Tammanyite and Republican; and in national origins from German and Austrian, to Russian, Rumanian, and Turkish. But despite these differences, the minority status and discrimination they knew both in America and Europe fostered stronger ethnic ties than was true for other and far less internally diverse immigrant peoples.[28]

This tension, between diversity and union, also characterized New York Jewry's response to American intervention in World War I. The population's disparate groups initially took positions that ranged from enthusiastic support to outright opposition and expressed themselves effectively through an array of newspapers, institutions, and trade unions. Not until nearly a year after the American declaration of war did New York Jewry become united behind the Allied cause.

In contrast to the Italian experience in New Haven, sixty thousand Jews were already living in New York City when the New Immigration began to reach American shores in the early 1880s. These residents traced their origins to the wave of German emigrants who settled in the mid-nineteenth century. In contrast, the 2 million Jews who arrived in America between 1880 and the outbreak of World War I hailed mainly from eastern Europe. A variety of factors, including anti-Semitic violence, discriminatory laws, and the poverty of a region in economic turmoil, had induced one of the largest diasporas in human history (see table 1.2).

New York's favorable cultural milieu and its unique labor market compelled most eastern European newcomers to make the city their home. Over 100,000 came to Gotham in the 1880s alone, nearly tripling the city's Jewish population. Many local German Jews provided the immigrants with a major reason not to stray far from Ellis Island. Having already established themselves in the clothing industry, German Jewish manufacturers could hire the immigrants on terms that made the observance of many Orthodox practices possible. The industry soon became the main magnet for the eastern European exodus to America.

The city's unique manufacturing base also aided this migration, framing the work experiences of most incoming Jews even if they did not toil in the needle trades. By being the nation's commercial capital, its largest port, and its greatest source of cheap immigrant labor, New York became an unbeatable location for the finishing and marketing of small consumer goods. The ready-made garment industry was king of all city manufactures, and by 1910 Gotham produced over two-thirds of all women's and more than one-third of all men's clothing made in the United States. Cut and sewn in small factories, tiny shops, and crowded tenement kitchens, these garments were

Table 1.2   The Jewish Population of New York[b]

Date	Jewish Population	Total City Population	% Jewish
1880	60,000	1,911,698	3.1
1890	195,000	2,507,414	4.9
1900	500,000	3,437,202	14.5
1910	861,980+ (Yiddish speakers only)	4,766,883	18.1+
1920	1,643,012	5,620,048	29.2

[b] Jacob R. Marcus, *To Count a People: American Jewish Population Data, 1585–1984* (New York: University Press of America, 1984), 149–151; and Kenneth Jackson, ed., *The Encyclopedia of New York City* (New Haven, Conn.: Yale University Press, 1995), 921, 923.

the lifeblood of hundreds of thousands of Jewish immigrants and their families.[29]

The suffering these workers endured has become legendary. The tenement districts were honeycombed with men, women, and children assembling pieces of a finished product that they themselves could rarely afford to buy. Working long hours in poorly ventilated apartments, they struggled to put food on the table and avoid the ravages of illnesses like tuberculosis—which was called the "tailor's disease." These conditions did not go unchallenged. Waging a series of strikes from 1909 through to America's intervention in the war, the International Ladies Garment Workers, Amalgamated Clothing Workers, and other unions enrolled over 200,000 members, the vast majority of whom were eastern European Jews. From the tragedy of the Triangle Shirt Factory Fire to the heroism of the women's "Uprising of the 20,000," Jewish immigrants produced some of the greatest union triumphs of the Progressive Era.[30]

The efforts of "downtown" Jews to improve their economic and social position were certainly not limited to collective means. For a substantial minority, Old World skills and the business and educational opportunities available in New York also made individual advancement possible. Immigrant masons, carpenters, and painters found a great need for their talents during Gotham's twentieth-century building boom. At the same time, jewelers were able to carve out an important niche in New York, and printers obtained work in the expanding Yiddish book and newspaper industry. The strictures of Orthodox Judaism, meanwhile, created a colossal market for ethnic goods and services. Able to satisfy the dictates of the *kashrut* [dietary laws], Jews quickly came to dominate the city's meat and poultry trade. Five hundred bakeries, for example, met the heavy demand for challa bread and matzoh by 1910. Although an immigrant presence in the professions was small before the war, the number of Jewish doctors, dentists, and teachers was significant and growing. The best avenues to prosperity, however, were the many opportunities in clothes manufacturing, wholesale and retail trade, and real estate. Thousands made the move from pushcart vendor or tailor to owner of a gent's furnishings store, sweatshop, or tenement. For the immigrant generation that predominated before 1917, the rough-and-tumble world of business was the most direct and attractive means of individual mobility.[31]

This remarkable ascendancy in the city's economic order set Jews well apart from the other immigrant groups that settled in New York in the late nineteenth and early twentieth centuries. Thomas Kessner's study of Russian Jewish heads of households in 1905 is revealing.[32] Forty-five percent of the Jews in his sample were white-collar workers, though more often listed as clerks and peddlers than as physicians or manufacturers. Only 1.7 percent toiled in unskilled jobs. The ratio of nonmanual to manual Jewish workers was already close to parity as America went to war. The contrast with the Italians of New Haven was dramatic. New York Jews, with a collectivist impulse that matched individual aspirations, and with a hunger for the schooling and welfare they had long been deprived of in eastern Europe, were a very driven population indeed.

In the years before the war, the immigrants' residential patterns reflected their limited but increasing diversity of employment. Up until the turn of the century, the Lower East Side was the unrivaled destination of incoming Jews. Drawn to the garment district and its surrounding blocks of rundown apartments, the newcomers rapidly took the place of the Irish and Germans who had preceded them. Soon the area was a microcosm of eastern European Jewry, with distinct clusters of immigrants from the Russian Pale, Hungary, Rumania, and the Levant. The wave of single male boarders in the 1880s and 1890s sent for their families as soon as possible, resulting in a density of population that in 1900 topped an astonishing seven hundred persons per square acre in some East Side wards. Packed into buildings like the notorious dumbbell tenements, the newcomers averaged three to four occupants per room. During the early decades of settlement, the high incidence of evictions, fires, and crime made the downtown housing experience all the more arduous.[33]

When they did attain better incomes, however, and when their employment and business concerns no longer tied them so closely to downtown, Jewish immigrants moved to other sections of the city in large numbers. Between 1895 and 1910 Harlem attracted a Jewish population of more than 100,000. Before the war Jews in the Bronx numbered roughly 200,000, and in Brownsville, Williamsburg, and other neighborhoods of Brooklyn they totaled more than half a million. In a little more than a generation the geographical distribution of Jews had completely changed.[34]

As in the Italian *colonia* of New Haven, in New York City institutions rapidly emerged that served the immigrants' spiritual, material, and recreational needs. The discrimination Jews had experienced in Europe and the strict demands of their religious and cultural traditions made them accustomed to building a separate and more comprehensive institutional life. By 1917, the *Jewish Communal Register* could list hospitals, schools, and day nurseries, as well as loan associations and credit unions. Thousands of mutual aid societies and synagogues flourished, while dozens of union locals, political and Zionist clubs, and Yiddish theaters also affected the day-to-day lives of most immigrants. Of these organizations, their synagogues and Yiddish newspapers particularly demonstrate the increasing assertiveness of the population.

Orthodox religious institutions in the prewar decades were marked by conflict, decline, and only partial renewal. The immigrant rabbi's perspective best articulates this upheaval. In eastern Europe, religious leaders interpreted and enforced laws that determined how local Jews could eat, when they could work, what they were taught, how their public institutions operated, and how their civil conflicts should be resolved. But in New York these matters, if they were dealt with at all by any authority, fell under the jurisdiction of municipal agencies. The impact on Jewish Gotham was far-reaching. "The rabbis' traditional, communitywide functions atrophied," comments historian Arthur Goren. "Questions of prestige became acute, and petty intrigues divided them into factions which militated against any common endeavor." This "laissez-faire organization of Orthodoxy" as Goren aptly describes it, remained virtually unchallenged through the first decade of the twentieth century. Many rabbis lived in dire poverty, while men of very dubious religious training were also circulating in the city, tarnishing the reputation of a profession that before the 1910s was completely unregulated in New York. Without this authority in place, such services as religious instruction, the rite of circumcision, and the certification of kosher foods suffered all kinds of abuses.[35]

But while Orthodoxy at the institutional level staggered and splintered, at the level of popular observance it persisted, although in diluted form. When well-known cantors from Europe came to sing, their concerts attracted wild enthusiasm and overflowing crowds. Two of the city's largest Yiddish newspapers were Orthodox in orientation. The city's more than one thousand Orthodox synagogues, which ranged from elaborate temples to storefront rooms, continued to exhibit their regional origins well through the war years. Functioning more often as community centers than places of fervent worship, their attraction was certainly not limited to the most devout. Immigrant Jews, accommodating themselves to the secularism of American society, selectively abandoned the religious authority that had controlled much of their day-to-day existence in eastern Europe.

This process of secularization was especially visible in the rise of New York's *Yiddishkeit* culture, at the heart of which was the most successful ethnic press in America. Acting both as a means of popular communication and as a forum for intense political and intellectual discussion, more than 150 different Yiddish publications appeared in the city between 1885 and 1914. New York's Jewish newcomers had not only their own daily and weekly newspapers, but also magazines specializing in commerce, humor, literature, and science. These journals benefited greatly from the post-1900 migration stream of immigrants, which included prominent writers and scholars as well as activists who had participated in the political movements then raging in eastern Europe.[36]

The daily press was especially adept at addressing the immigrants' immediate interests as well as their old-country concerns and nostalgia. The papers also reflected the tension between the population's secular and religious impulses. The *Tageblatt*, founded as a weekly in 1885, and the *Morgen Zhurnal* (1901) were Orthodox journals that backed the Republican party. Their competition consisted of the socialist *Jewish Daily Forward* (1897), the dominant daily of the prewar years, the left-leaning *Der Tog/The Day* (1914), and the *Warheit*, or *Truth* (1905), which supported the Democratic party. Despite these differences, all of the papers exhibited American influences, relying heavily on distillations of the *New York Times* and the *Journal* for news copy, and frequently informing their readers of the laws, history, and cultural habits of their adopted country.[37]

At first confined to the garment industry and the Lower East Side, immigrant Jews soon staked out new places on the economic landscape and established a number of enclaves throughout the city's five boroughs. Taking advantage of the greater economic resources and civil liberties existing in America, New York's Jews transformed an ethnocultural identity that had endured for several centuries in eastern Europe. By 1917 they had created a durable, expanding, and increasingly vocal and influential ethnic presence in the city.

Though considerable, this development occurred largely outside of the main currents of American culture of the period. The newcomers created employment niches, formed institutions, and established enclaves with practically no interference or assistance from federal and local governments. Yiddish was still the dominant form of communication for this overwhelmingly first-generation group, and the trials of settlement were still their main preoccupation. With security their primary goal, and mutual dependence their chief means of achieving it, immigrant Jews were limited in their engagement with the larger American environment before the war.

As in Italian New Haven, this cultural insularity fostered a heightened awareness of internal ethnic differences. But the main fault line among New York Jews was based on neither provincial nor regional ties. The key distinction was between the eastern Europeans collectively and the German Jews who had preceded them. Although their divisive relationship had evolved and softened considerably since the 1880s, it still played a crucial role when America entered the war.

In fact, the German and eastern European migrations of Jews shared a good deal in common. German immigrants, arriving mainly from the 1820s through the 1860s, also settled in America's cities and pursued careers in trade, commerce, and clothing manufacture. But by the time the eastern Europeans began to emigrate en masse, America's German Jews had already made substantial accommodations to their adopted home. By the 1880s they had lived through the nationalizing experience of the Civil War, achieved perhaps the most rapid rate of social mobility of any single immigrant group in U.S. history, and in embracing Reform Judaism, greatly secularized their religious identities as Jews. They were much less resistant to assimilation than the Orthodox Jews who followed them. Taking great pride in the language and intellectual achievements of Germany, they shared much of the liberal-rationalist ethos of the western world.[38]

A very different set of experiences forged the eastern European immigrants' consciousness. For the majority from Russia and Poland, anti-Semitic persecution was far greater than what had existed in preunification Germany. Russian Jews faced the threat of mob terror in addition to discriminatory laws. In the decades of mass migration tens of thousands suffered the brutality of pogroms, mass arrests, and forced removal to the Pale of Settlement, and were extremely fearful of conscription into the czar's armies. The poverty of the regions they were leaving was also much more severe. If politically active, they were far more likely to advocate the era's ideologies of collectivism and class conflict than the liberalism of the West. They also held the empire they had left behind in utter contempt. Secular *Yiddishkeit* and Zionism were manifestations of a Jewish cultural consciousness that took tremendous pride in its own heritage and beliefs. Even though Orthodoxy weakened as a result of migration, few immigrants embraced the Reform faith of the German community.[39]

With such great disparity in attitudes, it is not surprising that relations between the "uptown" Germans and "downtown" eastern European Jews were fraught with tension. German Jews viewed their coreligionists with a mixture of scorn, sympathy, and self-preservation. Before the turn of the century, their English language press heaped abuse on the newcomers' customs and radical politics. It was the German community that coined the pejorative term "kike," derived from the-ski ending of many immigrant surnames. But they also feared being equated in the eyes of the larger American public with the newcomers' traditionalism and poverty. This anxiety, along with the knowledge of the immigrants' suffering both in Europe and America, compelled German Jews to set up a variety of charities, schools, hospitals, and even programs to help migrants settle outside of New York. In 1906 they organized the American Jewish Committee, the first major institution committed to defending and helping foster the acculturation of Jews on a national basis. Their desire to assimilate the eastern European Jew predated and was much stronger than non-Jewish Americanization efforts before the war.[40]

The fact that the newcomers lived in poorer neighborhoods and often knew their German predecessors as bosses made interaction all the more difficult. Gotham's newest Jews resented the didacticism and self-serving character of uptown philanthropy, and formed their own self-help organizations as soon as possible. But in periods of crisis, either within the Jewish population or in relations with the larger populace, downtown Jewry recognized the value of having prominent Jews of German descent who were willing to act on their behalf as arbiters and advocates. Regardless of their social class, religious denomination, or European origins, they were still Jews in an overwhelmingly Christian country. During the Progressive Era, attorney Louis Marshall and financier Jacob Schiff repeatedly served as spokesmen for all of New York Jewry.[41]

It was the trauma of the European war, however, that produced the most sustained period of Jewish unity up to that time. The Joint Distribution Committee, which focused on the wartime suffering of European Jews, served as the umbrella group for the German and eastern European Jewish relief organizations in the fall of 1914. The "Joint," as it was called, was a dramatic success in New York as well as across the nation. By 1918 it had channeled $20 million in aid to Europe and sponsored soup kitchens, clothing, medical supplies, and schools for nearly three-quarters of a million Jews. In these efforts, New York's Jews were able to put aside much of their antagonism.[42]

While internal issues may have occupied more of the newcomers' attention, their evolving interaction with the Gentile population of New York was also contentious. Politically, the behavior of eastern European Jewry resembled what we have seen in New Haven, but with several crucial differences. Most immigrant Jews did not become naturalized citizens before the war. A combination of political inexperience and a European heritage of fear and distrust of the state made many newcomers wary of obtaining their citizenship and voting rights. As in the case of New Haven's Italians, low electoral power meant meager representation in public office and on the city payroll. Tokenism was as prevalent in Gotham as it was in New Haven. Tammany Hall backed a Jewish candidate to represent the East Side in Congress as early as 1900 and helped elect a Jew as Manhattan borough president the following year. Placement in minor party roles was also visible in Jewish neighborhoods, though thinly parceled out and by no means independent of the bosses' control. For their part, Jews showed little enthusiasm for either Tammany or the GOP. Accustomed to relying on their own social services, most Jews were repelled by the corrupt nature of city politics and remained outside of its system of patronage.[43]

In a word, there was no consistent "Jewish vote" in the decades before the war. Generally speaking, Gotham Jews voted for Republicans in presidential and congressional races, and favored Tammany for city representation. Like all ethnic groups, they responded to politicians who appointed a fellow immigrant to an important post or championed an issue of community interest. But the eastern European Jews' profoundly moralistic conception of politics, their social democratic impulses, and their respect for leaders of intellectual backgrounds also led them to support independent candidates. Before the war, reformers such as Theodore Roosevelt and Woodrow Wilson inspired Jewish backing regardless of party membership.[44]

What most differentiated New York's Jewish voters from their Italian contemporaries in New Haven was the support they gave to the Socialist party. A large portion of the eastern European Jewish migration arrived in the city in the wake of the failed 1905 Russian Revolution and many immigrants were well versed in the tactics of mass movement politics and trade union organizing. By the mid-1910s, the downtown left had a solid union base and the backing of the *Jewish Daily Forward*, which reached at least 200,000 readers. Though only a small minority of Jews were committed socialists, they provided the party with the majority of its votes as well as its most successful candidates. The Lower East Side elected Meyer London, a labor lawyer born in eastern Europe, to serve as the nation's only Socialist congressman in both 1914 and 1916. This close identification of Jews with radical politics became especially significant when the nation went to war.[45]

Their political activity outside of the electoral arena also distinguished Gotham's Jews. As Melvyn Dubofsky has observed, "what politics accomplished for the Irish, trade-unionism promised New York's Jews." At first ignored by the American labor movement, Jewish men and women created their own powerful organizations, blending a political vision that emphasized education, social insurance, and upward mobility with a pragmatic reliance on arbitration and collective bargaining. In many ways, the Jewish-led garment unions pioneered political goals and methods that were later adopted by the CIO. Similarly, community activism and the "quiet influence" of uptown leaders were also important nonelectoral forms of political activity. Throughout the prewar period, immigrant Jews conducted rent strikes, food boycotts, and student protests. In sharp contrast, high visibility was precisely what established German Jews most wanted to avoid. Fearing an anti-Semitic backlash, uptown lobbied in private and was very successful in influencing legislation on matters of across-the-board Jewish concern. Tenement reform, immigration policy, and sanctions against czarist Russia were among the many issues that prompted their *shtadlones*, or intercessions. Uptown and downtown alike recognized their right to freedom of expression in America, and both groups regularly asserted their concerns.[46]

Gentile perceptions of this growing presence were complex. America lacked the centuries of religious conflict as well as the legal discrimination that characterized Christian-Jewish relations in the countries the immigrants left behind. Only ten thousand Jews lived in the United States as late as 1840, and even after the German wave of immigrants the population was still less than one-half of one percent of the 1880 American total. America's Christian majority was itself divided into a myriad of denominations, religious freedom being a keystone of the young nation's cultural and constitutional existence. Discriminatory laws against Jews from the colonial era had been removed by the early 1800s. New York in particular had been a polyglot city since colonial times, and its population had always included a sizable number of Jews.

Through the 1880s American Gentiles shared many of the stereotypes and prejudices prevalent in Europe in constructing their image of the Jew: the Jew as a Shylock, whose riches did not depend on the sweat of one's brow; the Jew as a mysterious figure, self-segregating and bearing loyalty to no nation; and the Jew as Christ-killer. But the small numbers and ease in assimilation that marked the Jewish population before the tidal wave from eastern Europe had kept Jews from becoming a major object of attention and scorn. In the nineteenth century, African Americans, Catholics, Mormons, and even Masons suffered far more slurs and physical attacks than America's Jews.[47]

But the social dislocation that accompanied the nation's "search for order" at the turn of the century compelled a variety of critics to point to immigrants and particularly Jews as scapegoats. Populists accused Jewish financiers of impoverishing the American farmer. Urban nativists feared an end to American morals and democracy, while trade union leaders viewed immigrant labor as undermining the living standards of native-born workers. Both the successful German Jews and the struggling eastern European immigrants suffered as a result of these sentiments. Discrimination did not come in the form of anti-Semitic legislation, but in informal barriers to Jewish upward mobility and a tightening of immigration policy. Nativist groups led several strong but unsuccessful campaigns to close the nation's borders to further immigration, using eastern European Jewry as a prime example of how the "newer immigrant races" would never assimilate.[48]

Still, anti-Semitism in America in the years before the war was a far cry from the persecution that Jews faced in eastern Europe. There was of course the day-to-day tension between Jews and other ethnic groups, but examples of cooperation are equally present in immigrant memoirs and literature. Jewish efforts to contest anti-Semitic propaganda and activities were also significant during the Progressive Era. The most famous organization of this kind, the Anti-Defamation League, began its long and effective career in 1913. On the eve of the war, anti-Semitism was present but still far from reaching any kind of critical mass in America, let alone in the city of New York.[49]

Two events in Manhattan evoke a keen sense of where Jewish immigrants stood at the beginning of America's wartime crusade. A small riot erupted during the speech of a soapbox orator on August 25, 1917. Russell Dunne, an Irish immigrant, had been attracting crowds with his viciously anti-Semitic tirades. He was infamous among city Jews, who showed up in great numbers for this particular meeting in Madison Square. When Dunne began his attack on "the long-nosed greasy vermin of a kike," a Jewish soldier demanded equal time. Fighting then broke out, and police rushed in to make several arrests. But the speaker, with the aid of a policeman, was able to escape. Only when a Jewish reporter recognized Dunne later that day did the orator face charges of inciting a riot. Dunne's trial generated even more fireworks, as thousands tried to attend the proceedings. In his testimony, Dunne claimed he never mentioned Jews in his speech. But several witnesses, including two stenographers and a Yiddish newspaper reporter, provided overwhelming evidence to the contrary. Most damaging was the testimony of Judge Leonard Snitkin, a Russian Jew who served on the municipal court. The night court magistrate openly sympathized with the prosecution and sentenced Dunne to one-month's hard labor. But the affair was not yet over. After the trial, two men followed Snitkin into a stairwell and beat him severely.[50]

These incidents reflect the assertiveness of New York's Jewish population in the face of prejudice. The hundreds who attended both events represented a cross-section of local Jewry. Among those arrested in Madison Square were a student from Queens, an East Side doctor, and a printer from the Bronx. Judge Snitkin had served on the bench since 1909. All of the city's Jewish papers pressed for action, while the American Jewish Committee investigated a larger anti-Semitic conspiracy. Non-Jewish leaders such as the mayor, police commissioner, and district attorney vowed to prosecute all those "who publicly incite one part of the population against another," and the city dailies strongly endorsed Dunne's conviction. The best statement of support came from the magistrate who sentenced Dunne. "Let this be a warning to you," he declared, "and to those like you who use your methods. We don't want men of your kind in this country."[51]

But Dunne's rhetoric also revealed how a more virulent form of anti-Semitism was emerging during the war. New in his tirades was the claim that Jews were disloyal to the nation, that they were more interested in making profits than supporting the country. "They are all slackers," Dunne claimed, presenting himself as a true patriot. His solution was drastic. He urged the "lovers of Christ" in his audience "to teach the foreigners the lesson they were taught in Russia." The fact that these remarks enjoyed popular support was particularly ominous. Dunne was not just a crank: he had given recruiting speeches for two predominantly Irish-American regiments. In Brooklyn, where he was most active, Jews sensed "a change in attitude toward them by their Gentile neighbors" and Jewish merchants were suffering "a partial boycott by [their] Christian customers." To be sure, the anti-Semitism Dunne was able to muster was limited in scope. But in melding bigotry to the wartime spirit of nationalism, his venom made for a dangerous combination—one that would become full-blown throughout much of the country in the postwar era.[52]

The Jewish soldier who contested Dunne's remarks represented another kind of voice created by the war. "I never made a speech before in my life," Joseph Friedlander declared. "But I'm going to tell you that my people have been defamed by this man and that I am loyal to the flag of the United States." Patriotism could cut both ways. Friedlander was not the only Jewish soldier in the crowd, and many more came in uniform to the trial that followed. The nation recruited and drafted perhaps as many as 200,000 Jews, men like Friedlander who could point to their military records as proof of their feelings toward their adopted country. A new segment of the population was beginning to emerge from the ghettoes and *colonie*. It is time now to turn to the shaping of these new "citizen-soldiers" and gauge the impact of their aspirations and behavior.[53]

I Your Country Needs You

✯ ✯ ✯ ✯ ✯ ✯ ✯ ✯ ✯ ✯ ✯ ✯ ✯ ✯ ✯ ✯ ✯ ✯

A long with the rest of the nation, New Haven Italians and New York Jews watched anxiously as the Wilson administration and Congress created a framework for fighting America's first major overseas conflict. Decisions on how to mobilize the country's industries, armed forces, finances, and many peoples for war had to be made very rapidly in the spring and summer of 1917. By far the government's most critical and controversial demand was for military manpower. The decision to send hundreds of thousands of young men to fight in Europe brought the tremendous burden of the war directly into every American home and community, regardless of ethnicity. For the New Haven *colonia* and New York Jewry, the call for soldiers provoked a great deal of debate and discussion. It also provided a unique opportunity for each population to voice their opinions publicly and make their significant presence in their cities known.

Each of the large European ethnic groups living in the United States responded to American intervention differently, as the conflict that ripped Europe into two warring camps resonated powerfully at home. Residents of German and Austrian descent, despite their feelings for their ancestral countries, could do little other than accept the government's orders, while Irish Americans who strongly supported the movement for Irish independence were also less than enthusiastic at the prospect of fighting alongside the British Empire. The nation's Polish, Czech, and Slovak immigrants, in stark contrast, dreamed of Allied victory and wanted above all else to see their homelands liberated from Austro-Hungarian rule. Greek, Armenian, Syrian, and Lebanese communities felt similarly toward the Ottoman Empire and endorsed the American war effort, while many immigrants from Scandinavia maintained the neutrality of their home countries.

European ties and allegiances also framed the thinking of America's Italians and Jews on the war. Of the largest immigrant groups in the United States, Italians had the most direct connection to any of the Allied powers. The Republic of Italy had been fighting on the western front since May 1915, and for immigrant communities like the New Haven *colonia*, participating in the American war effort became practically synonymous with supporting Italy. For eastern European Jewish immigrants and their children, the issue was much more complicated. Russia's hated czarist regime collapsed in March 1917, but the provisional government that took its place led the call for a negotiated peace. Many Jews also closely followed events in Palestine, where the possibility of creating an independent Jewish state free from Turkish rule seemed increasingly realizable.

While issues like these consumed the thoughts and efforts of each ethnic community, the federal government had to decide how it would mobilize an army of sufficient size to fight the war. On paper, the nation's armed forces in April 1917 were woefully inadequate for the task at hand. A year earlier, the United States had been humbly ranked as the seventeenth largest military power in the world, and at the time of the declaration of war its army consisted of only 128,000 officers and men.

Historically, the nation had raised the bulk of its armies through voluntary recruitment, and much of the country insisted on mobilizing for the Great War in the same way. But the tremendous scale and mechanized pace of the present conflict was unlike any war the United States, or any other country for that matter, had ever seen. To make a serious contribution to the Allied cause, an American army of several million had to be raised in a matter of months. The Wilson administration, with reluctant congressional support, decided early on that only a draft could accomplish this goal in a systematic manner with as little disruption to the national economy as possible. For World War I, the placement of a man in uniform had much less to do with his individual feelings about the conflict than with the manpower needs of the country as a whole.

New Haven's Italian colony and the eastern European Jewish population of New York, like communities across the country, had to provide these soldiers. By raising an all-Italian machine gun company made up of local volunteers, New Haven Italians linked the war aims of Italy and the United States, while following a community tradition that dated back to America's early colonial era. New York Jews, meanwhile, made headlines for their opposition to intervention and the country's first nationwide draft. A blend of old world loyalties and immigrant and second-generation desires for acceptance and recognition in their new country framed the response of both ethnic groups. Military mobilization also drew them into the public life of their cities, whether they supported the war wholeheartedly or not.

★ ★ ★ ★ ★ ★ ★ ★ ★ ★ ★ ★ ★ ★ ★ ★ ★

2 "Get in Out of the Draft"

Raising Volunteers and the Italian Response in New Haven

☆　☆　☆　☆　☆　☆　☆　☆　☆　☆　☆　☆　☆　☆　☆　☆　☆

James Ceriani's life represented one of New Haven's best-known Italian immigrant success stories. At the age of fourteen, he left his family in northern Italy to come to America. He settled in the Elm City and worked for several years as a waiter before raising enough money to purchase his own restaurant and cabaret. A talented businessman, Ceriani was one of the few Italian entrepreneurs to leave the confines of the *colonia*. His place, the Café Mellone, was only a block from the city green, and his regular advertisements in the daily papers showed a keen sense of the American market. Promoting his businessman's lunch in the spring of 1917, Ceriani noted an added attraction to the café's live music and good food: "The Spring Shopping brings down many of the fair sex these bright March days," his ads hinted, "and we notice our dining room filled with the ladies during the noon hours."[1]

Ceriani was also a two-year veteran of the Connecticut National Guard. When Woodrow Wilson called up the country's National Guard units for immediate service in late March 1917, the owner of the Café Mellone dropped everything and reported for active duty. Then thirty-nine years old, Sergeant Ceriani spent the next several months drilling with his unit at nearby training camps. He was also assigned to recruit new men for the company. Driving his car through the Elm City's Italian neighborhoods, he used his advertising savvy to persuade dozens of young men to "join the colors." By early June his "untiring efforts" had provided many of the fifty men that were needed to bring the unit up to the full combat strength of seventy-four soldiers. Virtually all of these men were of Italian descent.[2]

The "Italian machine gun company," as it came to be known throughout the city, had been in existence since 1915. City Sheriff Frank Palmieri, an immigrant who had built a prosperous real estate and insurance business in New Haven, was the main mover behind the outfit's creation. He rounded up fifty local Italian men to petition the state to become one of Connecticut's first machine gun squads.³ The unit followed a cherished volunteer militia tradition in New Haven. Elements of the Second Connecticut Infantry Regiment, to which the machine gun company belonged, dated back to the early colonial period. The machine gunners bore an especially close resemblance to the city's German-American and Irish-American rifle companies, which were formed during the Civil War. Like these immigrant units, the Italian machine gun company offered an alternative to the language and customs of an American outfit and provided the Italian community with a means to challenge nativist prejudices and demonstrate its loyalty to the United States.⁴ When America entered the war in the spring of 1917, *colonia* leaders and the city's Italian press threw their full support behind the company and its recruiting campaign. Jimmy Ceriani did not act alone in attracting recruits to the Second Connecticut's machine gun company, but received the vigorous encouragement of an immigrant population that wanted its patriotic endeavors recognized and respected.⁵

The mobilization of Sergeant Ceriani and the Italian machine gun company is an interesting story, both for what it had in common with national recruitment and for its ethnic distinctiveness. The men of this special unit were only one of sixteen different companies in the Second Infantry Regiment of the Connecticut National Guard. As with National Guard organizations in most states, the war necessitated a drastic expansion of the regiment's ranks and a new and pronounced obedience to the federal government. These circumstances, along with the training and various assignments that all guardsmen had to perform before they departed for France, were not unique to the all-Italian outfit.

What is of particular interest is the role the Italian community created for itself as the Second Infantry struggled to raise volunteers. Obtaining the required number of enlisted men became a very difficult task for the regiment and quickly blossomed into a full-scale effort in New Haven. Despite a barrage of successful civilian mobilization activities throughout Connecticut that spring, recruiting stood out as the only campaign to not achieve "over the top" results. This lackluster response created a sense of near crisis among many native-born New Haveners. The time-honored local and voluntary ways of raising an army were not sufficient, and federal power would soon completely take over the recruitment process. The Italian enclave recognized these concerns and devoted its greatest energies to promoting the loyalty of Ceriani and his fellow machine gunners. While the American population's patriotism generated white heat, New Haven's Italians developed their own formula for mobilization. By appealing to both homeland and New World sympathies, the *colonia* strongly endorsed a unit of volunteers whose symbolic importance eliminated any public criticism that Italians were not deeply committed to the war effort.

Over the next nineteen months the war would bring many new individuals, institutions, and communities into the foreground of American politics and society. Traditions that seemed to generations of Americans as integral to the way the nation functioned would be challenged and even eclipsed, and new sources of power and influence would emerge. As seen in the recruitment of the Italian machine gun company, the newest immigrant groups from southern and eastern Europe were not left out of this process, but played important roles as the country mobilized for war.

On March 25, 1917, just a week before America declared war against Germany, the Connecticut National Guard and other state militias from Vermont to Virginia were called on to protect munitions factories and public works from possible enemy sabotage. It was the first large-scale mobilization of American soldiers for service directly related to the world war.[6]

In responding to Woodrow Wilson's request for soldiers, the guardsmen of Connecticut were following guidelines that army reformers had struggled to obtain since the turn of the century.[7] Recent legislation prevented America's militiamen from throwing themselves directly "into the breach," as had been the case in all previous national crises. From colonial times through to the Spanish American War, local and state militias had acted with a great deal of independence if not complete autonomy in responding to military conflicts. For nearly three hundred years, these citizen-soldier militias had provided America with the vast majority of its fighting men. For World War I, however, all of the country's National Guardsmen were drafted into federal service as individuals whose first military allegiance was not to their states or communities, but to the armed forces of the United States government.

One of the thousands of National Guard officers who had to comply with these orders was Colonel Ernest L. Isbell. An attorney in peacetime, Isbell was commander of the Second Connecticut Infantry Regiment, headquartered in New Haven. At noon on March 28, 1917, he received word of the Second's mobilization through the chain of command that ran from Washington to the offices of the Connecticut governor and state adjutant general. Isbell deployed his own organization to call up the members of the regiment, sending the message "first through the majors, and from them to the captains down to the corporals whose job it was to round up their squads." The men of the regiment's sixteen companies, based in New Haven and other southern Connecticut cities, were to proceed to their home stations and await further orders.[8]

In New Haven, hundreds of militiamen immediately left their workplaces and hurried over to the Meadow Street Armory for roll call.[9] Joseph Cosenzo was working at the Winchester Arms plant when the order came through. "I always loved the army," he recalled in a postwar survey, "and when my call came I was almost first to be at the Armory." Local newspapers believed this to be the attitude of many men that afternoon, noting that "all seemed in high spirits and anxious for duty." Within a few hours of the noon call-out order, most of the Elm City's six hundred khaki-clad guardsmen were assembled before a large audience of friends and curious city residents.[10]

The men of the regiment spent the next four days fulfilling federal obligations and preparing for active duty. To remain in the Connecticut National Guard, they now had to pass federal physical examinations and take a new "dual" oath that demanded their military allegiance to the nation as well as the state of Connecticut for six years. Most important, before the guardsmen could take up any assignment they needed to be officially mustered into federal service. On March 30, three regular army officers barked out the names of each man and announced: "This command is hereby accepted into the service of the United States Army by the call of the President, Woodrow Wilson." Meanwhile, officers kept the men busy with drill and instruction exercises that lasted throughout the day. Local papers commented that the "streets of the city are constantly filled with soldiers," and that New Haven had taken on "quite a martial appearance."[11]

On April 2, the regiment received marching orders. Its rifle companies were to guard area munitions factories, bridges, and power plants. Sergeant Ceriani's unit, meanwhile, remained at the armory to await the arrival of pack animals for use in training. That morning the men cheered as one of their companies marched out to guard the Winchester Arms plant. It was the regiment's first step toward the battlefields of France.[12]

Even during these early days of mobilization, the Connecticut volunteers were frequently left in a state of uncertainty and at times even bewilderment. Until they received their official orders from the War Department, the men did not know whether they were going to defend property against sabotage or serve as a police force to suppress internal disorders. "Hearsay has it," reported the *New Haven Journal-Courier*, "that the men will be sent to South Framingham, Mass., and the Canal Zone, and many intermediate points." Officers and men alike were "all at sea" about their future duties. This confusion was certainly a far cry from the celebrated tradition of Connecticut's volunteers—of Yankees rushing out at a moment's notice to fight in King Phillip's War, and charging hard on the battlefields of Saratoga and Gettysburg.[13]

A much more pressing issue that haunted the regiment throughout the next four months was its tremendous need for new recruits. As soon as the men assembled for federal service, the state adjutant general's office declared the Second Regiment far below war strength. Many of its units did not even meet their prescribed peacetime levels, including the all-Italian machine gun company. Overall, the nine hundred guardsmen who responded to the call from New Haven and other southern Connecticut cities represented less than half of what the Second required for a wartime roster. The regiment consisted of twelve infantry companies, lettered A–I and K–M, each of which was to have enrolled 150 men; a sanitary detachment (requiring 50 men), a machine gun company (74), a supply company (74), and a headquarters company (60).[14]

The uncertainty generated by the unit's dependency on Washington and the need for heavy enlistment collided on the same day the men took up their first assignments. Along with the Second's marching orders, Colonel Isbell got word that guard outfits across the country had to halt their recruiting activities immediately. "The order was received by the Second regiment commanders today and dumbfounded them," a paper reported, "particularly because of the fact that they had been ordered to rush recruiting and had been doing so with all the powers at their command." Deeply puzzled, most officers undoubtedly thought that the order signaled the regular army's attempt to minimize the guard's role in the European war.[15]

As soon as the regiment began to turn away young men wanting to enlist, Washington dropped another bombshell. All guardsmen with dependent family members had to be discharged as soon as possible. The federal government had spent $4 million in aid to the dependents of men serving on the Mexican border the year before, and did not want to repeat this expense on a more massive scale. Within a week of the order, "scores of men" applied for their discharges, and the *Register* claimed that "it will not be surprising if the regiment loses a third of its strength." The Second was now in big trouble, and many members now wondered if they would ever make it to France.[16]

Of the various units that made up the regiment, the Italian machine gun company was the most accustomed to the vagaries of federal intervention. Company founder Frank Palmieri and his Italian volunteers were in fact indebted to the War Department for their outfit's creation. Washington ordered the Second Regiment in late 1914 to create a new machine gun company.[17] Since the Second's existing companies were as much social clubs as military organizations at this time, the other men of the regiment preferred to keep the status quo and remain Italian-free.[18] The federal government clearly aided the machine gunners in this case. But regular army standards also kept the men from having Italian-American officers. By 1915, demands to "professionalize" the guard's leadership limited commissions to men with considerable military experience and education, thus putting a captain's bars totally beyond the reach of men like Signor Palmieri. Coming so late to the game, the Italians were not able to choose their community leaders as their American counterparts had done for more than two centuries.[19]

On April 12, the War Department ended its suspension of National Guard recruiting activities, offering no explanation for the halt order. Officers at the Meadow Street Armory once again put up their enlistment signs and waited for the volunteers to pour in. But the expected rush to join the colors was not forthcoming. For the next three months, Colonel Isbell, his company commanders, and seemingly every public figure and institution in the city of New Haven labored intensively to convince several hundred men to enlist in the regiment.[20]

Efforts to enlist the area's youth for the Second Connecticut Infantry Regiment did not take place in a vacuum, but amidst a wide variety of other recruiting activities, fund-raising campaigns, and individual expressions of full-blown patriotism. On April 8, just as the regiment's dilemma was becoming apparent, the *New Haven Union* proclaimed that "the American eagle and Stars and Stripes have taken possession of the city." "Flags flew everywhere," from city buildings, stores, and houses. News shops displayed war maps, retailers posted flag-draped portraits of Woodrow Wilson, and clothing stores brought out " 'militaire model" suits. "The words 'prepare,' 'protect,' and 'defend' are used in many advertising schemes," observed the *Union*, and "little badges of red, white and blue are seen in men's button-holes, and on women's dresses everywhere." The newspaper also noted the proliferation of army and navy enlistment posters, whose "pithy phrases" grabbed the attention of passersby.[21]

The Second Regiment was not alone in seeking local men for service in the spring of 1917. Army and navy recruiters and two newly created civilian organizations, the Connecticut Home Guard and the Senior Service Corps, expanded "the call" to cover all age groups in New Haven's adult male population. In addition, an array of tremendously successful wartime registration and fund-raising campaigns, ranging from the state's own military census to the first Liberty Loan and Red Cross drives, demanded the participation of thousands and touched the lives of virtually every city dweller. In the month of June alone, city residents experienced the bombast and boosterism of the first Selective Service registration day, "New Haven Liberty Loan Week," "American Red Cross Week," and "National Army Recruiting Week."[22]

The sudden birth of so many new boards and committees required the aid of New Haven's established groups and businesses. And city leaders readily provided this assistance. Clergy spoke at loan rallies, urged compliance with the draft law, and took up Red Cross collections at church services. Major employers allotted huge sums for each fund drive, set up "associations" to help workers pay for bonds, and staged flag-raising ceremonies complete with bands and orators. Yale, the city's most renowned institution, purchased $100,000 worth of war bonds in the first Liberty Loan drive and became a veritable West Point almost overnight, with training activities dominating campus life throughout the course of the war.[23]

The press also made sure to keep the city war engine churning. New Haven's four daily papers, the main source of news and information for most residents, both fueled and facilitated the breakneck pace of the first war months.[24] The papers uniformly, and loudly, supported all of the local mobilization activities and depicted the European war as a struggle between a rapacious, immoral regime and a humane alliance of peace-loving democracies. Editorials seethed at the atrocities of "Kaiserism" and "Kultur," while news articles tauntingly reported affronts to the American government, its people, and its military capabilities. The allied nations, in stark contrast, were lauded for their tremendous sacrifices, their "brilliant" military leadership, and their reverence for the United States. Flooded with one-sided coverage, city residents had little information with which to object to the war boosters' emotional appeals. Boosterism in the city press was not limited

to the news and editorial sections. The papers' sports pages regularly celebrated the voluntary enlistment of star athletes. In lauding the enlistment
of Jewish boxing champ Benny Leonard, the *Register* blustered: "The man
who is physically fit to take a punch amounts to little these days unless he
is morally fit to take a bullet if need be." The funny pages also carried heavy
patriotic themes. "Everett True of East Haven," a *Times-Leader* strip character, routinely dealt with slackers, pacifists, and fund drive cheapskates by
bashing them over the head with his umbrella.[25]

It was in this heated and high-spirited context that the Second Connecticut Infantry Regiment labored to double its ranks to number 2,002
men. The energy and patriotic fervor that characterized the city's mobilization activities was also brought to bear on the Second's recruiting dilemma.
City leaders and private institutions supported the effort to secure volunteers
for the regiment. Yet through the months of April and May, New Haven's
young men were not so obliging when it came to fighting the war in Europe
themselves. The discovery of this "slackerism" provoked a great deal of in-
trospection and even resentment among the native-born population. It also
provided a unique opportunity for New Haven's Italian colony to make its
local presence emphatically felt and universally acknowledged.

With the lifting of the War Department's recruiting ban order, Colonel
Isbell wasted no time in planning an aggressive strategy to attract new volunteers. He ordered every company to form a recruiting party to comb the
city. The machine gun company's party included Sergeant James Ceriani
and Sergeant Alexander Bon Tempo, a New Haven-born salesman and one
of the Italian outfit's original members. Individual companies also put up
their own enlistment signs and displays. Company F, known as the Grays,
attracted a great deal of attention with its posters. "Young woman," a placard
asked, "is your sweetheart a slacker?"[26]

Meanwhile, city leaders took on an active role. Mayor Samuel Campner
formed a special committee to aid recruitment, with subcommittees concentrating on the area's factories, newspapers, railroads, and automobile owners.
Meeting with members of the Chamber of Commerce and the local branch
of the National Security League, the committee planned a large parade and
rally. Colonel Isbell, his municipal supporters, and the local press fully expected these activities to solve the frustrating recruitment situation.[27]

But the parade and mass meeting proved flops. "Every point known to
the speakers," one paper wailed, "every stage trick, every heart touching
sentence uttered by patriots of other days, calculated to stir the latent patriotism in the hearts of the 3,000 gathered in the armory last night and
cause them to enlist, failed and failed utterly." Instead of scores of new
recruits, the regiment gained a handful. On the following day Isbell announced a series of rallies in twenty area towns, apparently having written
off New Haven as a source of volunteers. To the dismay of local leaders,
New Haven looked more and more like a slacker city, even though voluntary
enlistment was more successful than in other states.[28]

Residents offered a variety of explanations for their young men's poor response. The reason most commonly given was that the high wages offered by New Haven's numerous (and very busy) munitions plants were more attractive than military service. Meanwhile, rally speakers felt that New Haveners simply did not understand the dangerous threat that Germany posed, an idea rejected by an anonymous letter to the editor. "I am of military age, a born American, neither German nor Irish," wrote 'Observer,' "and would willingly give my life for it, but I and millions of others will resist with force if necessary the attempt to send us or our sons to drive the Germans from European trenches." For this writer, and perhaps many more who remained silent, a clear divide existed between being a loyal American and fighting the Kaiser's faraway armies.[29]

Others were anxious, even bitter about what they saw in the current drive for soldiers. A circular mailed to all eligible men claimed voluntary enlistment was more manly and worthy of respect: "Enlist now," it urged. "Show your neighbor and your friends that you are not waiting for the draft." Several commentators cited a deep generational divide as the real crux of the problem. A former National Guard captain claimed that New Haven's young men cared "more for the spirit of a 'big beer' than the spirit of '76." Many New Haveners expected men to rush to the colors as their counterparts had done in the Civil and Spanish-American wars. When the young men did not live up to that ideal, long-time residents branded them as a soft, selfish, and even cowardly generation.[30]

Critics did not cite the reason that comes most readily to the present-day mind: that the war on the western front was senseless slaughter and that no sane person would volunteer to fight in it. New Haven, like the Wilson administration, encountered the pitfalls of being neutral for nearly three years, or as the president himself put it, of being "too proud to fight." The youth of the Elm City had seen newspaper reports and film footage of the trenches and knew of poison gas and horrific casualty figures. This noncommittal attitude would change in 1918, but in the summer of 1917 there was still a large gap between being an Ally and fighting like one.[31]

The presence of guardsmen on duty throughout southern Connecticut was not helping matters. The Second Regiment's rifle companies served mainly as sentinels for railway lines and bridges, and these assignments were not only dreary but highly visible.[32] The Italian machine gunners fared only slightly better, spending the first few weeks in the city armory. Though the old Meadow Street Armory provided the men with indoor quarters, conditions were so decrepit and crowded that a *Journal Courier* reader feared "the monotonous time there is likely to injure the morale of the young soldiers." Jimmy Ceriani and his fellow machine gunners were not allowed to leave the armory without written permission and had to keep their equipment in a constant state of readiness to respond to an emergency. Both veterans and rookies received instruction in flag signaling, along with, as a company member recalled, "the nomenclature, operation and functioning of the Benet-

Mercier guns thrown in for good measure." The city's Red Cross chapter eventually provided a victrola and sports equipment for the facility, but even with these amenities the men were glad to move out to a nearby farm in mid-April.[33]

Their new assignment, however, was in some ways even less attractive. The company now had to train, guard, and care for 150 army mules and horses arriving from Texas. The orders came as "a great surprise to most of the men," the *Times Leader* reported, "who believed their experience with mules, not the pleasantest in life, ended with leaving Arizona." The men had acquired this distaste for mule-handling during their six months of service on the Mexican border the year before. Sure enough, the animals bolted out of their new quarters soon after arriving in Connecticut. The gunners spent all of that first night and most of the following day rounding up the escaped mules, which had fled to nearby Hamden. In May, company members, then living in tents near the corral, started fitting the mules with packs and wagon harnesses. The *Register* claimed there was "plenty of excitement" at the farm and joked that "Sergt. Jimmy Ceriani has felt the power behind the kick of a mule on more than one occasion." The gunners ultimately spent over two months at the camp with their new, and very stubborn, Texan colleagues.[34]

Standing watch over railroad bridges and cleaning up after a hundred jackasses hardly encouraged recruitment. To make matters worse, the guardsmen had to wait a month for their first pay envelopes, compelling the mayor and the Red Cross to sponsor charity events for their families.[35] And federal orders continued to meddle with the regiment's traditional modus operandi. Since the unit was in federal service, recruiters had to be much more rigorous in examining volunteers, and many applicants who formerly would have been mustered in were now shown the door. Colonel Isbell also had to end the ancient and cherished custom that enabled company members to elect their own officers. State legislators had voted to make the militia more professional, and Isbell's promotions went to men with college degrees and military experience.[36]

In the midst of these difficulties, the enlistment drive continued "at a snail's pace," despite a variety of new tactics employed by recruiters, city leaders, and area women's groups.[37] At the end of May the regiment still needed seven hundred soldiers. Colonel Isbell would be lucky to have a complete roster by September. Notified that all National Guard units would lose their state affiliations and come under federal control on July 25, the regiment's officers knew that something drastic would have to happen if they were to maintain the integrity of their commands.[38]

It was the federal draft, and not the efforts of local leaders and institutions, that finally turned the tide in New Haven. The passage of the Selective Service Act on May 18, 1917, did not spark an immediate rush to the Meadow Street Armory. But as the first registration for the draft in June came closer, the number of volunteers suddenly began to mushroom. More than 160 men joined the regiment during the week of June 5, the day that all men between the ages of twenty-one and thirty-one had to register with the new Selective Service System. Only in the days before and after July 20, when the first draft numbers were called, did enlistment totals again approach this high figure. It was not because they were waiting to be conscripted that New Haven men had been so reluctant to join the guard. On the contrary, for the hundreds of volunteers who poured into the ranks in June and July, the draft was precisely the "something drastic" they wished to avoid.[39]

The regiment and its local support network became aware of these concerns and adapted their efforts accordingly. The appeals of April and May to masculinity and patriotism took a backseat to a new emphasis on the advantages of serving in a familiar New Haven institution. Promotions of the Second Infantry as "Your Regiment and My Regiment" contrasted sharply with the fire-and-brimstone demands not to be "cowardly slackers" or "men who could not be expected to defend their wives and sweethearts." The hometown ties of the Second were now asserted at every opportunity, as the uneasiness of many a draft-age man coincided with the anxiety of city leaders concerned with New Haven's patriotic reputation.[40] Block notices in the local papers lauded volunteering as "Good for Yourself and the Town You Live in." Orators stressed the Second's volunteer heritage, always depicting the militiamen of the past as defenders of the community who brought honor to the city name. Editorials contrasted this heroic past with the present-day specter of conscription. "Would it be unfortunate, would it not be even a disgrace," the *Register* clamored, if residents were taken for the draft while the Second remained understrength. "But how much better to have the regiment made up of New Haven men, or at least Connecticut men. The occasion for pride in this excellent Connecticut institution, closely identified with New Haven, has not passed. Stand by the Second."[41]

Emphasis on the regiment's local roots went a step further with the boosters' advice to "Get in Out of the Draft." Serving with the Second, men would be with friends, relatives, and neighbors when enduring the rigors of training and fighting "over there." With officers who were respected members of the local community, and city men who had belonged to the unit for several years, the Connecticut National Guard represented a known quantity versus the unknown of a vast national army being created from scratch. Playing off the inevitability of conscription, these appeals pitted a city institution with familiar faces against a federal juggernaut teeming with faceless millions.[42]

This draft-inspired approach proved effective with the area's eligible men, whose attitudes toward the war seem to have ranged from resignation to a gung-ho desire to live the "Great Adventure." New Haven, unlike some other American cities and regions, did not experience the agitation of pacifist groups. The hypersensitive city press, with no local rally hecklers, police raids, or counterdemonstrations to report, could only print stories on disloyal behavior in other parts of the country. Yale was not a source of antiwar activity, but a de facto military cantonment with over twelve hundred undergraduates in ROTC training. New Haven's young men, whether they were smothered into conformity by the bellicose atmosphere, or participants in its creation who objected to fighting themselves, did not rush to get married or flee the area to escape wartime service. If many held strong moral or ideological objections, they kept these quiet, while the most commonly criticized response to recruiting efforts was a blend of sheepishness and silence.[43]

Only when the national draft made military service appear completely unavoidable did hundreds of these men flood into the Second's enlistment offices. Company recruiters, assisted by area clergy (on "Second Regiment Sunday"), the Connecticut State Council of Defense (during "Second Regiment Recruiting Week"), and a long list of rally and band concert participants, harvested well over the seven hundred volunteers needed in June and July. By the time the War Department relieved the Second of sentry duty in mid-July, Colonel Isbell and his officers were finally in command of an infantry regiment operating at the required manpower level.[44]

It was just as the recruiting troubles were beginning to dissipate that the Italian machine gun company made its first major impression on the local scene. On June 10 the city press announced that the gunners were the first of the regiment's companies to recruit up to war strength. After all the urgency about "a young American's patriotic duty" and the heroism of the Yankee citizen soldier, it was a group of men whose roots in New Haven ran no deeper than two generations that most rapidly responded. This fact did not escape the Second's boosters, who claimed in a newspaper appeal that residents of foreign parentage were enlisting in greater numbers than American-born men. "Are the sons of Yankees," the notice taunted, "the men who fought and died that their country might be free and maintain the principles of Freedom, Justice, and Humanity, going to fall behind in their patriotic duty now?" The *Register* published a photograph of Jimmy Ceriani and a carload of Italian volunteers with the equally provocative question, "Who Says Recruiting Isn't Good?" Hailing the Italians' achievement became yet another way to get native-born men to enlist.[45]

But for the company's members and for the Italian community as a whole, the complete war roster meant much more. The immigrant and second-generation youths who piled into Sergeant Ceriani's sedan no doubt encountered the posters, parades, and mass meetings of the citywide campaign. But the real encouragement for men like Louis Popolizio and Antonio Esposito to join came from fellow residents of the *colonia*. In ethnically distinctive appeals, community members approached possible volunteers on two levels, addressing them as both men of Italian descent and as immigrants wanting to settle permanently in the United States.

An April 21 notice in the Italian language weekly *Corriere del Connect-icut* targeted the first of these two forms of national identity by appealing to homeland loyalties. "ITALIANS!" it shouted, "the MACHINE GUN COMPANY—composed entirely of Italians—needs men."[46] The advertisement echoed the stern challenges of the city's English-speaking campaign, but with an interesting twist: "It is shameful that with so many young men living care-free in New Haven not one has enlisted, and we may face the spectacle of seeing the remaining positions filled with Americans."[47] According to company boosters, a 100-percent *Italian* organization would be the best means "to show our true patriotism" and to reassert continuing sympathy and deep affection for the mother country. "Today all the world is in upheaval," the notice concluded, "and we Italians in America must demonstrate that we are not going to fail our brothers now fighting and dying to save Civilization." To immigrants well informed of the Italian army's terrible losses on the Austrian front, *pro patria* appeals like these carried a heavy emotional charge.

The owner of the Café Mellone most likely used similar pleas in his recruiting work. But Ceriani also recognized the new allegiance that men like himself felt toward the United States. He scoured the streets in a car bearing the ambiguous banner "Your Country Wants You" and encountered Italian immigrants whose loyalty to their adopted country left little room for doubt. After the war, Vincenzo Darrico, a laborer from Carpini, Foggia, and Naples-born teamster John Morno both cited a desire "to fight for USA" as their main motivation for enlisting. "To stand by and fight against any enemy of the United States of America" was the similar reply of immigrant Salvatore Liguore, a watchcase maker and one of the unit's original members.[48]

Many of these volunteers were undocumented aliens who understood little if any English, and the 1916 National Defense Act required that all foreign-born guardsmen be naturalized or at least have possession of their first citizenship papers. "How to get [these men] in was a problem," reported the *Times Leader*, "until suddenly Sgt. Ceriani conceived the idea of teaching them English." Tutored by another company member, Ceriani's recruits devoted much of their first days at the armory and corral learning the alphabet and writing and understanding simple messages. On April 16, five new machine gunners, again chauffeured by Ceriani, went to the city courthouse to declare their intention to become citizens. "Being able to sign their names and read English," one of the dailies enthusiastically reported, their applications were promptly approved. This tactic proved very effective, especially during the last days of the outfit's enlistment push. "City court business every day during the past week was held up for some time," noted the *Register*, "while the new recruits were making application for their first papers." For these men, who by the fact of their undeclared status could have easily avoided military service altogether, joining the American army and becoming U.S. citizens went hand-in-hand. A unique blend of Italian and American patriotic appeals thus helped frame the decision of *colonia* men to enter the company's ranks.[49]

The first national draft, however, may have weighed most heavily in this decision. In a postwar questionnaire, Louis Popolizio stated flatly: "When America entered the war I knew if I didn't go they would get me so I enlisted right away." Nearly half of the new gunners enlisted in the week surrounding the June 5 Selective Service registration day. Though their behavior paralleled the rush of hundreds of non-Italian men of draft age, Ceriani's June volunteers must have viewed the machine gun company in an especially favorable light. They would be serving with friends and neighbors who spoke the same language and shared the same cultural and religious traditions. The thought of military discipline in a vast conscript army probably played a critical role in the choice of enlistment by Italian Americans who regularly suffered the prejudice and often open hostility of their native-born peers.[50]

What also differentiated these men from the eligible non-Italian population was the fact that they had already been through a full-scale mobilization drive. America's call for soldiers was the second time a nation had demanded their wartime services: the Italian government had been urging immigrant men to return home for active duty since May 1915. At that time hundreds of New Haven men rushed to join the Italian army, including a young assistant priest. But most immigrants remained in the states, either to avoid military service or because they had already settled permanently in their new land. Those who stayed knew more about the fighting in Europe than their American peers, for the city's Italian press provided extensive war coverage. More influential than the immigrant papers' propagandistic reporting, however, was information received from families and friends in Italy. Just as a transatlantic network had informed prospective immigrants of jobs and conditions in the United States, the "uprooted" also received ample news of the struggle then raging in their homeland. Two years of civilian hardships and heavy casualties in Italy generated a very different perspective among *colonia* men than the exuberance and confidence expressed by the older native-born population in New Haven.[51]

The pool of available Italian men that Ceriani and Bon Tempo encountered was therefore doubly concerned about the American draft. Fully seventeen of the twenty-one volunteers they collected during the week of the first registration day were undeclared aliens—men who were also wanted for service in the Italian Army. Numerous articles in the local Italian newspapers reflected the population's anxieties over the Selective Service guidelines and negotiations between Italy and Washington over the status of immigrants. In May *Il Corriere* stated with irritation that it was responding "for the hundredth time" to inquiries as to whether the Italian army could induct area men. Draft board officials also recognized this unwillingness to fight in Europe, as many of the city's eligible immigrant and second-generation Italian-Americans claimed exemption from military service. Although at least six hundred *colonia* residents became U.S. Army conscripts during the war, thousands more remained civilians by presenting themselves as either undeclared aliens or munitions workers. The men who joined the machine gun company were thus a very select group, not only differing from their American comrades in the Second Regiment, but also from other young men in New Haven's Italian enclave.[52]

Two years before, when the Republic of Italy was on the eve of becoming a belligerent in the war, New Haven Italians were not in favor of intervention. "But the experience of the past is proof enough," a reporter noted in late May 1915, "that they will be loyal to the mother country, so far as their continuing obligations of citizenship require." Though the limited response to the Italian army's call for men partially disproved this prediction, the community's grave concerns and deep sympathies for the mother country were obvious. Following the May 1915 declaration of war, residents donated money, food, and clothing to the Italian Red Cross and spent thousands of dollars on the Italian National Victory Loan. As would be the case for all of New Haven two years later, the *colonia*'s most prominent individuals and associations immediately took the lead in forming committees and coordinating local campaigns. The city's immigrant papers, meanwhile, endorsed the Italian war effort with rhetoric that would have made even the most sensationalistic American papers blush. Long before their non-Italian neighbors plunged headlong into the war, the *colonia* had held concerts, raffle drawings, a benefit walk, and special masses to collect money for war relief.[53]

Still, the enclave's wartime support for Italy differed significantly from what took place in the "American" spring of 1917. Community residents, of course, did not own major businesses like the Marlin Arms Corporation, which purchased $1 million of the first Liberty Loan. Donations to the Croce Rossa Italiana amounted to a few thousand dollars by the time America went to war, a pittance compared to the New Haven Red Cross Chapter's one-week collection of close to $400,000. Though the colony's priests, businessmen, professionals, and handful of city officials pushed and prodded their Italian brothers and sisters, the earnings of immigrants could only go so far.[54] Since Italians wielded little if any influence on such bedrock institutions as city hall, the Chamber of Commerce, or Yale, the bulk of their associational support rested on the many mutual aid societies, churches, and social clubs.[55]

These circumstances definitely marked the community's response when the entire city of New Haven mobilized for American intervention. What also came into play, however, was the isolated and cohesive nature of *colonia* life—the desire to be with and to take care of "our own"—that had prevailed during peacetime. The same *prominenti* who had boosted homeland relief activities now formed a separate, all-Italian company of the Home Guard and an equally distinctive team of fund-raisers for the American Red Cross drive. Leaders like former city attorney Rocco Ierardi visited factories to encourage immigrant shop hands to subscribe to the Liberty Loan and served as draft board examiners and interpreters in the heavily Italian districts. Clubs and lodges again acted as springboards for prowar work, holding patriotic mass meetings, passing resolutions of loyalty to the United States, and sending telegrams of support to the governor and President Wilson. The societies also lobbied hard, though unsuccessfully, to have the visiting Italian War Commission come to New Haven. The *Corriere del Connecticut*, meanwhile, imbued the American campaigns with a special ethnic significance. According to the paper, the United States was fighting to bring to Europe the same freedoms that its immigrant peoples had come to enjoy, and the money Italians contributed to the Liberty Loan and American Red Cross would aid soldiers and war sufferers in Italy. The same network that backed the mobilization of 1915 quickly leaped to meet America's 1917 wartime needs, while putting a definite Italian spin on the newly expanded war situation.[56]

New Haven's native-born population gladly accepted and applauded these efforts, though it also preferred the Italians' "separateness" and often interpreted the newcomers' work as proof of the success of Americanization. Italy and the United States were now allies, and the daily press coverage of the Italian military campaigns and the various expressions of Italo-American solidarity helped to elevate the standing of the *colonia*. This increased recognition, however, clearly came at the expense of the city's German immigrant community. The many opportunities for Italian participation in the American crusade contrasted sharply with the U.S. attorney general's blunt message to German immigrants: "Obey the law; keep your mouth shut." All German aliens in the United States had to register with local authorities. Because of New Haven's many weapons plants, German immigrants faced a variety of restrictions on where they could work and live in the city.[57]

The treatment of German residents must have resonated with the city's Italians, who were also recent arrivals but whose desire to participate in the American war effort was roundly cheered by city leaders and the daily press. In effect benefiting from the demands for strict conformity as well as the calls for vigorous action, the colony soon recognized the importance of having an all-Italian, all-volunteer company in the United States Army. In an American city despairing over its lack of "red-blooded" Yankee sons, the machine gunners' readiness to serve their adopted country carried far more symbolic weight than any Red Cross donation or war bond subscription the Italians could offer.

After the company accepted its last needed volunteer on June 9, *colonia* leaders formed a committee to collect funds for farewell gifts and to organize a series of celebrations in honor of their favorite sons. Donations poured in from *prominenti*, the various societies, and factory departments with large numbers of Italian employees for purchasing a special American flag and individual golden crucifixes. "In this way," the committee's secretary noted, the unit "will have with them on the battlefield, where the fight is raging, the memory, the encouragement, the concern and the heartbeat of the entire

Colony."[58] This support differed drastically from the *colonia's* reaction to the mobilization of the machine gun company during the Mexican border crisis of 1916. At that time, company founder Frank Palmieri suffered "heaps of abuse and vituperation" from "irate Italian mothers" whose sons had been sent to the American Southwest. Palmieri later claimed that one mother threatened him with a knife as he lay sick in bed.[59]

But with the United States as Italy's ally, there was no such dissent. In two impressive and well-attended events, the Italian *colonia* paid tribute to its departing soldier sons, displaying the same blend of Italian and American themes that had marked the machine gun company's recruiting campaign. The outfit's flag presentation ceremony at Yale Field observed several Italian cultural traditions, while the farewell evening of live entertainment was a decidedly modern American affair. On July 22, 1917, a crowd of three hundred friends and family members watched as the gunners received an impressive American flag bearing the dedication "La Colonia Italiana alla Machine Gun Company." Mayor Samuel Campner and a host of city leaders were in attendance, listening to a Roma Olympia Band concert and orations in English and Italian by several *prominenti*. The pastors of the largest Italian Catholic churches, after offering sermons of spiritual guidance to the men, blessed the flag and the golden crucifixes that were inscribed with the name of each company member. Frank Palmieri and the special banner's "godparents" in turn presented the flag to the unit. It was the flag's "godmother," Miss Juliette Poli, daughter of theater chain owner Sylvester Z. Poli, who made the most memorable speech of the day. "Our race has found a sure refuge behind the Stars and Stripes," declared Poli, "and we feel that among all her sons who are striving to carry this banner to victory, none will bring enthusiasm and more steadfast loyalty than her sons of Italian blood." She and her sister, dressed in their high school graduation caps and gowns, concluded the event by placing small crosses about the neck of each soldier. Amid the cheers of the crowd, the machine gunners snapped into formation and marched around the field with their banner rippling in the summer breeze.[60]

The presentation of the company colors was a tradition observed by all American militia units. But the role played by the pastors and godparents gave the Italian ceremony an air of Old World solemnity. The crucifixes that each man would carry to France symbolized not only the concern of families and neighborhood friends but also the common cultural identity of soldier and civilian. They represented both the Italian community's faith in Catholicism and the immigrants' penchant for amulets that could bring good luck to those who wore them. The flag, donated "in behalf of our race in New Haven," linked these new American soldiers to a *colonia* only recently removed from its Italian homeland.[61]

Significantly, the Catholic pastors did not take part in a farewell extravaganza orchestrated by theater king Sylvester Z. Poli. On August 19 the city's largest theater, decorated profusely with the national colors of Italy and the United States, opened its doors to "the most representative audience that ever attended a benefit performance." A committee of one hundred Italian and non-Italian residents persuaded well-known entertainers to appear at a fund-raising gala. The cast provided the thrills, oddities, and prejudices that made American vaudeville so popular. Italian performers also appeared, but devoted only a small portion of their acts to pleasing the Old World crowd. Future opera diva Rosa Ponselle sang "O Sole Mio," but also "Swannee River," while the violinist Leonardi played classical Italian standards as well as guitar "in the Hawaiian style." The evening's pièce de résistance was a film of the flag presentation ceremony. The pastors blessing the company colors and the men receiving their golden crucifixes had become a movie. Though the gunners were courageous "sons of Italian blood," they were also tuned in to the mass culture of twentieth-century America.[62]

New Haven's dailies reveled in the ceremonies, printing numerous photos and praising the Italian community's loyalty to the United States. Unlike other cities, New Haven's opinion-makers did not accuse Italians of being indifferent to the national cause. Since the *colonia* represented nearly a third of the city population, insulting and nativist remarks were probably off-limits in any case. But for a town so greatly disappointed with the response of its own native-born sons to recruiting, the rapid enlistment of the machine gun company and its farewell ceremonies made a considerable impression. Less than a year later, after the guardsmen had suffered their first casualties in France, the *New Haven Register* editorialized, "In this country the Italians have been the first to volunteer for service in our army":

> Nor has there been any race who have more cheerfully responded to the requirements of the draft. Here in New Haven, with our large Italian population, there is no need to remind anyone that we are represented at the front by one company composed entirely of men of Italian birth, who in action have acquitted themselves with greatest credit.[63]

Sergeant Ceriani and his fellow machine gunners served their local community in more ways than one.

While the Italians bade farewell to their men in uniform, the War Department completed its plans to transform the Connecticut National Guard. The Second Regiment was finally relieved of its security obligations in late June, and by mid-July the various companies had set up camp on the fields surrounding the Yale Bowl. In August the Second's sister regiment, the Hartford-based First Infantry, joined its New Haven counterpart at "Camp Yale." Despite persistent rumors that the men were going to be sent to a cantonment in Maine or Cuba, there was no longer any doubt that their ultimate destination was the trenches of France. Colonel Isbell confidently prepared his full complement of two thousand men with rifle and grenade exercises.[64]

But Isbell could not prepare his men for the federal sledgehammer that fell on August 20, 1917. The War Department ordered that the new "102nd Infantry, 26th Division, United States Army" be created immediately. "The Second regiment is transferred wholly to the new organization," the orders read, "the additional strength required . . . will be obtained by the transfer of about 1,700 enlisted men from the 1st Connecticut." A captain commented that the merger came "in such an unexpected way, that company commanders stood gaping for hours afterward." Another officer assured the press: "It's the new 102nd, the old 1 and 2 with 'nothing' between, no animosities or jealousies, no rivalry any more,—just the desire to get to France and fight." But the unit historian later admitted the reorganization caused "a severe testing of morale."[65]

Commanders now had to oversee the combination of their outfits with corresponding companies in the First Regiment. Infantry Company A of the Second had to be merged with A-men of the First, and so on down the line. Many officers lost their commissions, though Colonel Isbell remained in charge of the new regiment. But even with the merger, the twenty-seven-thousand-man division to which the former Second now belonged ultimately took on several hundred recent draftees.[66]

It was the Italian company's members who felt the blow of the War Department order most keenly. Not only were their counterparts in the First Regiment Yankees with deep roots in Connecticut, but the new, expanded company had to incorporate men from all over the state. Now the Italians were not even a majority of their new unit, which with a full roster contained 178 men. A First Regiment veteran identified its Italian members only once in his brief history of the 102nd, which claimed to be "presented by the Regimental Machine Gunners." The pride of the New Haven colony now found themselves amidst men who knew little of the *Compagnia*'s local and ethnic significance.[67]

The mobilization experience of Sergeant Ceriani and his Italian-American comrades was an example par excellence of the transformation that all National Guard units went through in the summer of 1917. For all the emphasis on the local and voluntary character of America's militias, it was the federal government that acted as the final arbiter in the mobilization for World War I. The War Department reduced the distinctions between the traditional independence of the guard and the supposed abject dependency of the conscript army. Volunteers for the all-Italian machine gun company did not really "get in out of the draft"; they went into combat with many unfamiliar faces.

In the early morning hours of September 7, 1917, the members of the 102nd Regiment's machine gun company rolled up their packs and "with the utmost secrecy" slipped out of camp to make their way to a troop ship in Hoboken, New Jersey. On board the camouflaged S.S. *Adriatic*, as it

glided out past the Statue of Liberty, were a group of Italian-American soldiers who would be among the very first National Guardsmen to arrive in
France.[68]

To their American-born fellow soldiers, these seventy-four men must
have seemed like a very homogeneous lot. They were two inches shorter
than the typical American doughboy, averaging only five feet five. They were
almost all brown-haired and brown-eyed, and according to their enlistment
papers their skin complexion was more often "dark" than "ruddy" or "fair."
Their average age was twenty-three, and two-thirds of the gunners were not
born in the United States. Though they hailed from all parts of Italy, the
great majority came from the southern provinces of the Mezzogiorno. These
men were overwhelmingly working-class: thirty-five were either laborers or
factory shop hands, another eighteen had been barbers, clerks, and chauffeurs, while fifteen practiced a variety of building trades. Only Ceriani ran
his own business. They had little if any education, the majority probably
having attended schools in Italy or New Haven for just a few years. Most
also belonged to one if not several of the *colonia*'s numerous societies. Undoubtedly they formed a tight-knit group aboard the *Adriatic*, not only as
Italian-speaking friends and neighbors but as soldiers who had worked together in close quarters for more than three months.[69]

But the group also contained a variety of personalities and backgrounds,
men who would experience the war in different ways. There were the New
Haven–born Bon Tempo brothers, Alexander and James, who went through
each of the company's five offensives without a scratch, only to be wounded,
both of them, on the day before the armistice. Also aboard were Pietro
Massaro, whose mother still lived in Italy and whose brother was fighting
in the Italian Army; and the effervescent Louis Popolizio, who later recalled
enlisting "with my whole heart and soul." Some of these men would not
make the return voyage, while others found their lives transformed by war
injuries. Italian-born Alfonso Cappuccio, a twenty-three-year-old foreman,
was the only member of the original company to die in combat. Immigrants
Frank Giordano, the "star half-back" of an all-Italian football team, and
Antonio Dellacamera, a tailor and local boxer known as Battlin' Gal, would
both be severely wounded. Plumber Ralph Bove's injuries would prompt
him to seek Veteran's Bureau benefits and find a new trade after the war.[70]

Whether wounded or left unscathed by their military service, the men
whom Jimmy Ceriani brought together would remember the voyage to
France as a landmark event in their lifetimes. Enthusiastic as they were when
they departed, most of the gunners soon found reason to echo Noe Spinaci's
response to a postwar survey. When asked about the fighting, the Sicilian
replied, "I was scared to death."[71]

3 "Not as a Jew but as a Citizen"

The Draft and New York Jewry

✳ ✳ ✳ ✳ ✳ ✳ ✳ ✳ ✳ ✳ ✳ ✳ ✳ ✳ ✳ ✳ ✳ ✳

At the same time that Sergeant Jimmy Ceriani's troopship steamed out of New York harbor, Meyer Siegel was preparing for boot camp. An immigrant Jew, Siegel left the village of Czarmin in Russian Poland when he was in his early teens for New York, where he helped with his father's clothing store on the Lower East Side and attended public schools. He later found work in an attorney's office and was taking evening law school classes when the United States went to war.[1]

Siegel became a soldier in a very different manner than Ceriani. He had never been in the military and was drafted by the Selective Service System, a branch of the federal government that was younger than the American war effort itself. Like millions of other men, Siegel encountered a national bureaucracy capable of putting into uniform practically any young male living in the United States. Registered for Selective Service on June 5, 1917, examined by a draft board in August, and sent to a training camp in September, he was one of the first New Yorkers to be inducted into the new National Army. In his memoirs, Siegel recalls the astonishment that every draftee must have felt that fall: "Here I am: One day, a student of law; the next day, learning how to kill my adversary and be killed. Some change-over!"[2]

Siegel's "change over" sounds smooth and efficient on paper. But like the draft in New York City as a whole, it was not trouble-free. While waiting for his draft board physical, the young immigrant was arrested for, as he remembers, "resisting arrest, disturbing the peace, and causing nearly a riot—enough charges to put me in jail for the duration of the war." Standing in a long line with friends, he joked about the rough behavior of a nearby policeman. The officer came over and shouted "What did you say about me, you dirty kike?" Siegel protested the slur and was marched off to a police station. The young law student then quickly made use of his legal contacts. With their aid, not only was the case against him thrown out of court, but the policeman faced possible suspension. Siegel bowed to the pleas of his father and did not press the matter. He was inducted into the army soon after, on September 10, 1917.[3]

For much of the country the draft evoked sinister visions of an autocratic state—"the Prussianizing of America," as opponents on both the right and left called it.[4] But the Selective Service System relied extensively on the participation and initiative of individual communities. Although the all-volunteer Italian machine gun company lost its hometown identity, the draft incorporated much of the local character of the communities it confronted. Washington needed New Yorkers not only to fight, but also to inspire the public, staff draft boards, and enforce federal laws. In satisfying War Department needs, Gotham soon took pride in what it had created: a segment of the new army that was originally intended to be free of regional chauvinism.

Federal policy also had to deal with the history, economy, and class and ethnic makeup of each city and town. The prospect of a draft resonated especially strongly with New York officials and the city's 1.5 million Jews. The last attempt to conscript New Yorkers ignited the worst rioting in American history. At a critical moment in the Civil War, more than a hundred people were killed in a five-day conflagration of lynchings, arsons, and severe military repression. Among the city's Jews, fear of conscription stemmed from military service in czarist Russia, which had meant abuse, hunger, and a high mortality rate even in peacetime. Many Jews from the Russian Pale fled to America specifically to evade conscription. These recent memories, plus the fact that widespread Jewish support for the Allies was just beginning to emerge, posed a special problem for Gotham's established and more assimilationist Jews. Tensions between uptown and downtown Jewry over the war were most pronounced when Uncle Sam called for draftees.

The induction of men like Meyer Siegel was therefore no simple matter, but an event that generated a great deal of anxiety and debate among national legislators, local leaders, and individual ethnic groups. The stakes were high. The draft would not only make millions of men combatants in a distant and controversial war, but also subordinate them to a major institution of the American government for the first time in their lives.

To be a success, the induction process required action from each link in the chain that connected Siegel to the U.S. Army. Washington would have to formulate a wartime relationship between the state and society that appealed to the country's regionally and ethnically diverse population. New York officials would have to mobilize the city's resources and eliminate obstacles to make the draft run smoothly. Prowar Jewish leaders and institutions would have to overcome eastern European fears while emphasizing the duty of immigrants to protect the country that had become their haven. Finally, young Jews like Siegel would respond to the draft in ways that were ethnically distinctive and common to all draft registrants. As a prospective conscript, the law student had to consider family needs as well as personal convictions, fears, and aspirations. As an immigrant, a naturalized citizen, and a Jew, he also had to ponder his place in American society and how the war related to local and worldwide Jewish concerns. Woodrow Wilson's claim in his 1917 draft proclamation, that "it is not an army that we must shape and train for war, it is a nation," was far more than a rhetorical flourish. It effectively described how the draft compelled native-born Americans and immigrants alike to accept new responsibilities, new attitudes, and a new national system for fighting a war.

Wilson himself was a recent convert to the idea of a draft. He committed to the policy just days before asking Congress for a declaration of war.[5] On April 7, 1917, the administration presented its plan for a draft to Congress. It eliminated the bounties and substitutions that made the Civil War draft so explosive and proposed a network of thousands of local draft boards staffed by neighbors of the men it evaluated. The Wilsonian draft would thus embody such traditional American concerns as civilian control over the military, local self-government, and equal treatment before the law. It also called for an orderly process of mobilization, one that would select men in a manner that minimized disruption to the wartime economy. Advocating the legislation in the language of progressivism, Wilson later said that "the business now at hand is undramatic, practical and of scientific definiteness and precision."[6]

Congress proved an even more reluctant convert to the draft idea. The last previous government experience with the conscription of soldiers had occurred during the Civil War, and it netted only 6 percent of the Union army's troops. In April and May 1917, the desire to rely instead on volunteers was strongest among the southern and western elements of Wilson's own Democratic congressional majority. The House and Senate wrangled over amendments and alternative bills, displaying a clear regional divide, one that crossed party lines and pitted rural-agrarian opponents against urban-industrial supporters. Contemporary political issues mingled with longtime concerns over states' rights and individual liberty. Southerners wanted no federal interference with Jim Crow; agrarian congressmen wanted to impede the drain of farm labor to war industries and the armed forces; prohibitionists wanted to exclude prostitution and the sale of liquor from all areas that surrounded military facilities. Only when the bill incorporated these demands, and when mounting public pressure to field an army convinced many dissenters (including Theodore Roosevelt) to change their position was the legislation passed by both houses of Congress. On May 18, 1917, Wilson signed "An Act to Temporarily Increase the Military Establishment of the United States" into law.[7]

Legislators made revisions and expanded its scope during the course of the war. But the basic system remained intact and proved very effective. The May 18 act called for all men between the ages of twenty-one and thirty-one to register on June 5, 1917. It authorized the creation of 4,648 draft boards across the country to evaluate each registrant's eligibility. No military personnel were to serve on these bodies. Instead, local officials would review their neighbors' wartime usefulness and exemption claims. In this way, draft resistance would be decentralized, and the horrifying spectacle of soldiers combing neighborhoods to impress men for the state would not occur. The scheme worked well. The June 5 registration day, the July 20 drawing of the first Selective Service numbers, and the autumn draft notices sent out to men like Meyer Siegel provoked only small pockets of opposition and netted more than 300,000 recruits.[8]

There were several reasons for the draft's considerable but by no means unqualified success. Skillful presentation was key. Administration officials were well aware of the power of public awareness and participation. Throughout the war, the concept of "service" rather than conscription, of individual responsibility rather than coercion, pervaded draft rhetoric and activities. What gave these appeals their motivational drive was the fact that the country preparing to go "Over There" was a much different place than its Civil War era counterpart. Five decades of stunning industrial, urban, and population growth had eroded much of the provincialism that kept government small in scope and sustained a preference for isolation over international engagement. A large, urban-based portion of the population had become convinced that large-scale planning and coordination were the only real means to win a modern war. The forces of voluntarism and localism temporarily lost their hegemony during the wartime emergency, and the draft was the clearest manifestation of this shift in attitudes. By November 1918 nearly 80 percent of the men in the armed forces were conscripts, a total reversal of the nation's recruitment policies.[9]

Publicity and sweeping cultural change went only so far in securing the compliance of millions. Coercion also played a critical role. Failure to register and agitation against the draft were federal offenses subject to severe prison terms. The Selective Service System released the names of eligible men to the press, making it a matter of public record whether a man claimed exemption or failed to appear before his draft board. When American involvement escalated, the government expanded the registration to all men between the ages of eighteen and forty-five and issued a "work or fight" order that designated even more of the population as eligible. The administration also did not discourage the activities of patriotic groups whose vigilante character became increasingly pronounced as the war progressed. In the summer of 1918 the Justice Department conducted "slacker raids" in several cities, enlisting the American Protective League to patrol streets for draft resisters. Had the war not ended so quickly, manpower demands might have generated even greater hysteria and resistance. Despite the plan's impressive results— the registration of 24 million men, nearly 3 million of whom would serve in uniform—at least 300,000 evaded the draft altogether.[10]

Concerns over the nation's numerous immigrants also shaped the process that eventually plucked Meyer Siegel out of the Lower East Side and transported him to the frontline trenches of France. The first Selective Ser-

vice Act included provisions for handling these immigrants. Draft administrators classified naturalized persons and those who had declared their intention to become citizens as eligible for service, and exempted nondeclarants,
diplomats, and persons of "enemy alien" origins. A number of domestic and
international considerations led to this formulation. Washington made re-
ciprocal draft treaties with allied nations and redefined quotas at home to
accommodate areas with high concentrations of immigrant residents. By
these means, the government was able to manage its ethnically diverse conscript pool and avoid any political crises.[11]

A variety of politicians, newspapers, and patriotic organizations complained during the course of the war that draft-exempt "alien slackers" were
able to live comfortably in America while native-born men were risking their
lives in France. But the response of immigrants to the draft was overwhelmingly cooperative. "From my observation," a draft board representative
reported, "I believe all nationalities registered by this board were eager to be
of service to the United States Government and help win the glorious victory
which finally came." The provost marshal general's office concluded that
boards everywhere encountered this "general attitude." Among the 487,434
immigrant draftees, nearly 200,000 were nondeclared aliens who waived
their right of exemption in order to serve in the military; 280,000 foreign-
born soldiers also took advantage of the liberalized naturalization process
available to them and became American citizens. Though a few thousand
immigrants contested their conscription in court or requested aid from their
embassies, the vast majority of foreign-born draftees responded positively to
the Selective Service call.[12]

New York City's past as well as its present posed a significant challenge
to the mobilization plan. Shortly before the first registration day of the
draft on June 5, 1917, the New York Tribune printed a full-page history of
the city's Civil War draft riots. The paper's editors confidently predicted that
the new draft system would encounter little if any resistance. "The similarities between the two situations are theoretical; but superficial," the article
claimed. "The differences are fundamental." During the Civil War, men of
means could avoid conscription simply by paying a three-hundred-dollar
commutation fee, putting the burden on the working poor to fight and die
for the northern cause. But the Selective Service program that was about to
register 600,000 New Yorkers was an entirely different scheme, the newspaper argued. "The draft of 1917 is essentially democratic. Exemption cannot be bought. It must be for cause." Like most urban papers in the Northeast, the Tribune was a strong advocate of the modern draft, lauding the new
system's respect for individual circumstances rather than personal wealth.[13]

New York draft officials might have shared the Tribune's conviction. But
they also knew that the similarities between 1863 and 1917 were not so
"theoretical." The underlying political, class, and ethnic divisions that had
ignited the city in the wake of Gettysburg were present to a great degree on

the eve of the World War I draft.[14] In 1863, the local Democratic party was a major proponent of negotiating peace terms with the South, and the city population was weary of the war's heavy casualties. In 1917, New York's Socialist party and many other pacifist and left-wing organizations opposed the war, and city residents were by no means convinced that the Central Powers posed a direct threat to the nation. In 1863, the draft's inequities inflamed the resentments of city laborers and industrial workers who were no strangers to militancy. In 1917, the ability of underfed and overworked factory hands to organize and fight was well known, and several industrial unions opposed the war. Most seriously, the violence of 1863 exposed the ethnic and racial tensions that simmered in Gotham, as mainly Irish rioters lynched and beat to death black residents regardless of sex or age, burning their homes and businesses, even the city's Negro Orphan Asylum. In 1917, New York was even more of a melting pot, containing millions who traced their descent to both sides of the European conflict. How these various peoples would respond to an American draft was an open question.

The mammoth task of inspiring 6 million New York residents to accept conscription was therefore a twofold job. Mayor John Purroy Mitchel and city officials had to oversee thousands of registering sites and nearly two hundred draft boards. To avoid repeating the disaster of 1863, they needed to make as much of the population as possible participants in the draft. As important, they would have to secure order during the proceedings without alienating popular support.

It was the first step in the draft process, the registration day on June 5, that produced the most anxiety and conflict. Registration was the first grass-roots test of popular opinion toward the war, when the abstraction of diplomatic crisis became a concrete personal choice for hundreds of thousands of young men and their families. How would New York's diverse population respond? How strong and widespread would the opposition be? New York officials might well have agreed with General Enoch Crowder, the director of the Selective Service System, when he later claimed that June 5 "is destined to become one of the most significant days in American history."[15]

The great size of New York's population in itself was a challenge to Gotham leaders. Census estimates put the quota of eligible city residents at nearly 600,000. To handle this large number, Mayor Mitchel appointed a Central Board of Control and subordinate boards for New York's five boroughs. The Central Board employed the machinery of New York's election commission and a volunteer force of eight thousand registrars, clerks, and assistants to operate the city's more than two thousand registering sites, most of which had been polling places in the previous election. It also set up numerous information centers and held rallies to answer questions from draft-age men during the four days prior to registration. For June 5, the Mayor's Committee on National Defense planned concerts in parks, provided flags for each registration place, and instructed every school in the city to conduct a half-hour patriotic ceremony.[16]

"Can everyone lend a hand?" asked Central Board chairman Edward F. Boyle on the eve of registration. "Yes," he answered himself, "let every New Yorker, men and women, whether subject to the registration or not, constitute themselves as agents of the Government for the purposes of Registration Day." Municipal agencies got a great deal of support from private organizations and individuals. Public schools served as locations for only a quarter of the city's 2,123 registration sites; the rest were located in retail stores, barber shops, and ironically, even funeral parlors. In addition to the "army" of volunteer registrars, hundreds of Home Defense League and American Protective League members helped policemen direct eligible men to their proper registration places, and automobile owners donated their cars and services as chauffeurs to facilitate communication between the various boards.[17]

Private institutions also aided the city government in getting out the "vote." New York's Republican party and Tammany Hall machines "canvassed" precincts, provided speakers, and held rallies in their district headquarters. The National Security League, in charge of celebration activities, arranged for a variety of bands and singing societies to provide patriotic entertainment. Many employers made the occasion a work holiday so that their employees could more easily register. Churches and synagogues organized special June 5 services and urged their congregations to comply with the draft law, and the daily newspapers gave detailed instructions on how to answer the local boards' questions and printed numerous editorials on the fairness of conscription and the duty of young men to serve their country during wartime.[18]

A similar blend of municipal and privately sponsored activities elicited the participation of New York's immigrant communities. Central Board chief Edward Boyle saw in the city's ethnic diversity a potential obstacle to the success of registration. "We have countless numbers of aliens within our boundaries," he warned, "who know not our ways or customs as yet, many of them incapable of understanding us at all." Boyle made the presence of foreign language speakers a top priority. More than eight hundred interpreters, many of them naturalized citizens, volunteered to help. The Mayor's Committee on Aliens supplemented these efforts by holding fifty-four informational mass meetings "in the most densely populated sections" on the night before registration. The rallies were highly effective. "Patriotic demonstrations at some of them," the *New York Times* reported, "especially on the east side, were accepted as proof that by far the majority of the men within the prescribed age limits in the city were willing to do their duty."[19]

Setting up the draft machinery and inspiring the public represented only one facet of the city's preparations. At a May 28 planning meeting of the Mayor's Committee on National Defense, a member interrupted the discussion of registration day ceremonies with an emotional outburst. "The whole trouble right now," John Humphreys exclaimed, "is that we are at war and the people of New York do not seem to realize it. What's the use of talking about singing and buttons when we ought to be looking out for bullets?" Describing the Civil War draft riots, he believed "that such things might be repeated." The committee chairman had to remind Humphreys that his suggestions were out of order, and the subject of enforcement was dropped "almost immediately."[20]

Most New Yorkers accepted or at least were resigned to registration for the draft and did not openly agitate for or against it. Those who were most vocal on the issue were self-proclaimed patriots like Humphreys and the pacifist, progressive, trade union and radical organizations that opposed them. Though both of these camps' numbers were small in relation to the total city population, the resources behind the prowar position were infinitely greater. In the week before registration day the local press and the combined force of city, state, and federal enforcement agencies overwhelmed the draft opposition in New York.

Two aspects of this campaign against dissent are particularly significant. First, authorities and draft supporters rarely focused on "Deutscher agents" or sympathizers within the German-American population. Gotham's Germans, like those in New Haven, quietly obeyed wartime restrictions on their liberty and were not targeted as a dangerous element against mobilization. The *New York World* declared that radical activists were the main source of antagonism and needed to be silenced as soon as possible. "It is not necessary to assume that such brawlers are acting in behalf of the enemy," the paper claimed. "They are for the most part persons who habitually urge others to violate law. They preach resistance to the draft precisely as on other occasions, when strikes were in progress, they have advocated riot and pillage."[21] That many progressives, religious leaders, and trade unionists also were opposed to the draft did not concern New York hawks so much as the city's radical population.

A second and equally important aspect of this campaign was the makeup of the forces that watched, harassed, and arrested draft opponents in the week before registration. The New York Police Department played a far less prominent role in the enforcement drive than the federal government. The city's U.S. attorneys and marshals and dozens of Justice Department agents monitored antidraft activism in the most extensive federal investigation of criminal activity the city had ever witnessed. As visible were unauthorized defenders of the draft: servicemen acting on their own and members of the National Security League and American Protective League who provided vigilante services that the Mayor's Committee on National Defense did not discuss.[22] As in New Haven, the press constantly fueled the fire by printing stories on disloyal activities and citing the various ways "slackers" were avoiding the draft. Some papers even called for a clampdown on the "traitorous" opposition.

If any city had reason to be anxious over homegrown agitation, it was Gotham. The home of "two score" pacifist organizations, the nation's only socialist congressman, and several major left-wing periodicals, New York was

THE DRAFT AND NEW YORK JEWRY ★ 61

the greatest center of antiwar activity in America. Emma Goldman, the so-called "high priestess of Anarchy," had recently formed the No Conscription League, which held rallies, distributed thousands of leaflets, and used the journal *Mother Earth* as its mouthpiece. By early June the No Conscription League claimed to have five to eight thousand members in New York State alone and attracted an audience of at least three thousand to a meeting on the eve of registration. The Collegiate Anti-Militarism League, also based in New York, was especially active at Columbia University. On May 31, two Columbia students and "a Barnard girl" became the first New Yorkers arrested under the new draft law.[23]

Though not as extreme in their activities and rhetoric, a variety of socialists and progressives also opposed the war. Papers on the left such as the *Forward*, the *New York Call*, and *The Masses*, together with the garment workers' unions, reached the largest audiences. A range of reformers, academics, and clergy were active in smaller Gotham-based organizations such as the American Union Against Militarism and the Women's Peace party. A coalition of these groups invited delegates from across the nation to help launch a mass movement against the war. Meeting on May 30–31 at Madison Square Garden with thirteen thousand attendees, their convention established the People's Council of America for Democracy and Peace, the country's most significant peace organization.[24]

The lineup of prowar and pacifist forces in New York was indeed impressive. But the actual clash between them before June 5 amounted to very little. Only a dozen activists were arrested, all for handing out leaflets, and skirmishes between police and crowds at mass meetings were minor. Authorities did not ransack offices, round up party members, or arrest rally speakers. These tactics were not yet part of the domestic war effort. If anything, the press exaggerated the power and numbers of the antiwar movement and gave a great deal of coverage to Goldman and fellow anarchist leader Alexander Berkman, the most vilified opponents, including full transcriptions of their circulars and speeches.[25]

Benjamin Gitlow, a New York Socialist who opposed the war, identified a key reason for this lack of conflict. "The leaders of the anti-war movement," he claimed, "though they all loudly shouted against the war, were not ready to back up their defiance with action." The city's socialist politicians, union leaders, and press urged compliance on June 5. "Both young and old men should obey the law," urged Congressman Meyer London; "No republic can last unless the laws are obeyed." *Jewish Daily Forward* editor Abraham Cahan agreed. "The paper I represent preaches faithful and loyal citizenship . . . every man between the ages of twenty-one and thirty must do his duty tomorrow." The American Union Against Militarism set its sights on protecting conscientious objectors, and the Women's Peace Party planned to agitate for an early end to the war. Organizers of the People's Council Conference at Madison Square Garden were also careful not to provoke federal authorities in either speeches or resolutions. Goldman's No

Conscription League remained the sole organized voice against registration, and its members were subjected to the most harassment and arrests.[26]

What the preregistration period lacked in fireworks it made up with the ominous precedent for the repression of free speech during wartime. Federal authorities appeared with stenographers at most opposition rallies and compiled a list of activists they considered suspicious. But the most menacing group of enforcers were the soldiers and "patriotic citizens" who fought dissent on their own terms. At the final meeting of the Madison Square Garden conference, bands of soldiers abducted activists handing out No Conscription League literature. Only several hours later did they turn five persons over to the police, one man arriving at a station house with bruises on his face. On June 4, two hundred servicemen provoked a riot at a Goldman-Berkman assembly that led twelve activists to be arrested. Again the soldiers were not picked up. Vigilantism, though not a part of official policy, was condoned in the days before registration.[27]

That same day, Mayor Mitchel declared that no serious challenges would disrupt registration on June 5. Not taking any chances, all ten thousand of "New York's Finest" were on alert. Joining policemen at each registration site were members of the city's Home Defense League, and several hundred American Protective League and National Security League volunteers were ready to serve as complainants if any arrests were made. Nine thousand soldiers were also on alert at local bases. Finally, U.S. marshals deputized hundreds of private citizens to form an "emergency body" that could be "hurried to any part of the city" if rioting broke out. This combined force, the *World* exclaimed, was "prepared for anything short of an invasion." Behind the hoopla of decorations and street singing was a mighty preemptive arsenal ready to ensure that the 1863 riots would have no sequel.[28]

Officials kept close watch on particular sections of the city. Though authorities and the mainstream press never identified them as such, Jews made up large percentages of the areas considered to be trouble spots. On May 30 the National Security League held a special rally in the congressional district that covered Jewish Harlem, an area believed "to contain many pacifists." The *Herald* noted that Brooklyn's U.S. marshal was focusing his attention on Brownsville, Williamsburg, and East New York, "which are strongholds of the socialist party, and where agitation against the selective draft act has been conducted since its passage."[29]

The connection authorities made between dissent and Jewish neighborhoods was not without cause. Most of the persons arrested before registration day had Jewish names, being members of the No Conscription League or "rioters" apprehended after its ill-fated meeting in the Bronx.[30] As in the union campaigns of the prewar period, Jewish women were prominent activists. Most of the crowd that filled Madison Square Garden for the peace conference rally "came afoot out of the lower East Side" and "fully a third were women." On the night before registration, the Women's Anti-High Price League, an organization made up primarily of eastern European Jews, held a demonstration on behalf of mothers whose sons were of draft age. After speeches near the *Forward* newspaper building the crowd of several hundred marched to City Hall to be dispersed by the police. On June 5, Brooklyn authorities took the most extreme precautions, dispatching a machine gun unit and a squad of motorcycle patrolmen to the Brownsville neighborhood.[31]

Many of downtown Jewry's most influential figures and institutions opposed the war. Socialist politicians Meyer London, Morris Hillquit and Jacob Panken; Abraham Cahan's *Daily Forward;* the Jewish Socialist Federation; the Workmen's Circle; and the leaders of the United Hebrew Trades, Amalgamated Clothing Workers, and International Ladies Garment Workers unions were outspoken in their dissent. This position was not the sole preserve of downtown Jewry, nor of the left. Also taking antiwar stances were well-known progressives like Judah Magnes, the founder of the New York Kehillah, and social worker Lillian Wald. Although they distanced themselves from anarchists of Russian Jewish descent like Goldman and Berkman, these socialists and liberals were also very active in opposing mobilization.

No established politician or mainstream newspaper declared the city's Jews to be disloyal. That type of slander was left to soapbox orators like Russell Dunne. Still, many Jewish leaders who supported the war feared that the charge would become more pervasive. This segment of Gotham Jewry was as vocal as its antiwar rivals. At its forefront were established figures like Jacob Schiff, Louis Marshall, Cyrus Adler, Oscar Straus, Joseph Barondess, Congressman Isaac Siegel of Harlem, and *New York Times* publisher Adolph Ochs. Also supporting intervention were such key institutions as the American Jewish Committee, the Educational Alliance, the Young Men's Hebrew Association, and both the Anglo-Jewish and Orthodox Yiddish newspapers. They matched editorial for editorial, speech for speech, and rally for rally, and countered their opponents by asserting and inspiring Jewish loyalty to the United States.

The war and conscription issues inflamed what was always a sharply divided leadership. But even though the debate within the Jewish population was greater than in the city as a whole, most of Gotham's 1.5 million Jews did not agitate for either position. In the weeks before registration day, the support of this not-so-silent majority, most of whom hailed from eastern Europe, was actively sought by both sides on the issue. In the midst of this war of words, New York Jews confronted the national draft with their own, ethnically specific loyalties and beliefs.

As in the case of the New Haven *colonia*, New York Jews focused attention on the conflict then raging through their homelands. From the outbreak of war until American intervention, Jewish opinion was more concerned with events on the eastern front, on the fighting in and near the Russian Pale, than with the crisis facing France and Belgium. This initially put them at odds with the pro-Allied direction in which the United States was moving. Between 1914 and early 1917 the vast majority of New York

Jews wished above all else to see Germany crush the Russian czar and his army.

This was not so much a desire for German triumph as for Russian defeat. As historian Joseph Rappaport has claimed in his careful study of the wartime Yiddish press, "the pro-Germanism of America's immigrant Jews was an inevitable consequence of their Russophobia."[32] The possibility of a czarist government reinvigorated by nationalist fervor and military victory, and the even grimmer prospect of a Russian conquest of new territories inhabited by Jews, were sources of tremendous concern to New York Jews. So great was the anti-Russian feeling that even the internationalist Jewish left faltered. *Jewish Daily Forward* editor Abraham Cahan compromised ideology within the first months of the European conflict. "All civilized people [must] sympathize with Germany," he wrote. "Every victory she attains over Russia is a source of joy."[33]

The Jews' dark history of forced removal and pogroms in Russia blended with shocking contemporary reports from eastern Europe. The Jewish Pale of Settlement had quickly become the setting of a no man's land that extended for hundreds of miles. The scorched-earth policy conducted by the retreating Russian Army increased the area's devastation. Treated like a hostile population, at least 600,000 Jews were forcibly sent eastward by the czar's troops, their property and livelihoods lost overnight. Packed into communities incapable of handling such a massive number of refugees, they faced starvation and epidemics of cholera and typhoid. Convinced that the czars' reign would have to collapse if the welfare of Russian Jewry was ever to become secure, New York Jews gave generously to a series of relief campaigns.[34]

The tremendous casualties and domestic hardships of the Russian war effort finally forced Czar Nicholas II to abdicate on March 15, 1917. Gotham Jewry celebrated the news in mass rallies and wild street demonstrations. The allied powers were now all democracies, fighting the autocratic empires of Germany, Austro-Hungary, and Turkey. When the United States entered the war in early April, many American Jews had already swung their support to the much-admired French Republic, a Britain that would soon declare its approval of a Jewish homeland in Palestine, and a fledgling Russian government that needed aid and protection to ensure its survival. This reversal in Jewish sympathies became so pervasive that within a year it absorbed most of New York's Jewish left.

But the question of wartime allegiance was only one obstacle that had to be overcome if American mobilization was to have a receptive audience in Gotham's eastern European Jewish enclaves. Conscription was perhaps the most damaging weapon the czars had employed to undermine Jewish communal solidarity in Russia. Since the reign of Nicholas I (1827–1854), Jews were liable to the notoriously long and severe service terms of the imperial army. Underage recruitment, anti-Semitic abuse, and even Christian proselytization marked the experience of Jews in the Russian Army through much of the nineteenth century, and draft evasion was widespread up to the Great War. Far worse in Jewish minds was the complicity of their own *kehillot* (Jewish community councils) in the draft process. Jewish community leaders were responsible for meeting the army demand, and their selections singled out the very young and the poor. The draft generated a consciousness of class differences that the Jewish councils were never able to subdue.[35]

Why Jews were so opposed to the draft was of little interest to imperial authorities, who charged them with cowardice and even treason. But Jewish antagonism and fears were rooted in a much more profound realm than contemporary nationalism. Mary Antin, in her memoir *The Promised Land*, claimed that the four-year term of the modern Russian conscript was horrific not so much for its anti-Semitic abusiveness, nor for the dislocation it caused families and communities. "The thing that really mattered," she wrote, "was the necessity of breaking the Jewish laws of daily life while in the service." The army did not allow for *kashrut* (dietary laws) or proper religious observance. "When [the Jewish soldier] returned home," Antin claimed, "he could not rid himself of the stigma of those enforced sins. For four years he had led the life of a Gentile." For most Jewish youths, who had lived their entire lives in the culturally isolated villages of eastern Europe, the drastic step of leaving the country altogether was a far more attractive alternative than a term in the army. As significant as these religious concerns, however, was the lack of civil rights that military service reflected in Russian society as a whole. Draft evasion was in many ways a secular political act, a direct challenge to a government that cared little if at all for its considerable Jewish population. Russian Jews were not allowed to participate in civil society and therefore felt little obligation to perform the most serious requirement of citizenship. In peacetime the Russian draft was avoided at all costs, and as seen in immigrant memoirs, was a major reason for many Jews to come to the United States.[36]

Even if immigrant Jews had no memories of military service, the news from the eastern front quickly dispelled the excitement that framed most Americans' conceptions of the Great War. At least 400,000 Jews enlisted in the imperial army, the need to defend their communities being one among several concerns.[37] And the war machine they served suffered horribly. Although claims of Russian casualties vary widely, it is moderately estimated that 3 million soldiers died, were wounded, or were taken prisoner in the year 1916 alone. The reports of relief workers and the news conveyed in letters from Russia only increased the immigrant Jews' cynicism toward and disgust for the conflict. Whatever political attitude they took with regard to the war in the spring of 1917, they harbored few illusions about the fighting in Europe.[38]

The profound cultural significance of the first registration for the American draft was not lost on either opponents or advocates of the war within New York's Jewish population. As June 5 approached, both sides rooted their arguments in the context of eastern European concerns and memories.

But behind their heated political rhetoric, two very different forms of cultural self-identification were being proposed. Draft opponents implicitly asked Jews to renew their ties to eastern Europe, while supporters called for a complete break with the Old World and total acceptance of the ideals and war program of the United States.

For Jewish antidraft activists the country that was truly acting to "make the world safe for democracy" was not America, but the new, democratic Russia. In the months that followed the American declaration of war, Jewish war opponents stressed this distinction at every opportunity. They lauded the socialist-led Petrograd Soviet of Workers' and Soldiers' Deputies, the de facto government of Russia, which urged an end to the war that would prohibit annexations and indemnities, while promoting the national sovereignty of all oppressed peoples. They attacked the Wilson administration and Congress for not only expanding the conflict by intervention, but also seeking to conscript, censor, and repress the American people. "It is quite clear that the spirit of Romanovism has not died," the Amalgamated Clothing Workers' *Advance* declared on June 1.[39] "Having been expelled from Russia, it took refuge in the United States." The Amalgamated, the ILGWU, and the United Hebrew Trades supported the People's Council for Democracy and Peace, which was directly patterned after the Petrograd Soviet.[40]

At the May 30–31 Madison Square Garden conference that launched the People's Council, Kehillah leader Rabbi Judah Magnes and Socialist party secretary Morris Hillquit strongly endorsed the Russian example. Magnes, acting as conference moderator, repeatedly condemned the heavy police surveillance of the event and criticized the conscription of an army without a clear statement of American war aims. Only the Russians had discarded these marks of autocracy. "Russia wants above all things—what?" he called out. "Peace," his listeners shouted in reply, affirming their conviction that if the United States were a true democracy, it would never have entered the war. Hillquit, meanwhile, spoke most passionately when mocking the slogan that America "must take the place" of a Russia that was no longer capable of fighting. "Russia has dethroned her czar and destroyed autocracy, she has established the rule of democracy, freedom and reason. We are to take the place of old Russia." Both men urged their audiences to reject the American example of idealism abroad and repression at home, and follow the beacon of revolutionary Russia. "Let us not seek the ignominious place of the dark and despotic Russia under the czar," Hillquit concluded, "but rather let us make common cause with the people of the new, free and democratic Russia in forcing the world to end the terrible war."[41]

In stark contrast, Jewish advocates of the draft also invoked eastern Europe in their speeches and rallies, but cited Russia only for its abusive czarist past.[42] They stressed the great divide between Jewish life in Europe and in the United States, and identified America as "our country" whose rights and opportunities must now be defended. Dr. Cyrus Adler described emigration from czarist Russia as "the frantic and successful attempt to escape from the new Egyptian slavery." "Thank God this bondage is over," he intoned, "we pray never to recur." For Adler, aiding the American cause was the obligation of all transplanted Jews. "We owe this to our country and we owe it to our Jewish heritage." In a "Jewish patriotic rally," attorney Louis Marshall reminded his listeners of their immigrant roots: "The United States—which opened its arms to all the oppressed peoples of the world—to my father, to you and your fathers—will not call upon you in vain in this hour of her greatest peril." Rabbi Samuel Schulman made one of the strongest statements of the prodraft position. "Do not be sad if the names of your sons are to be drawn," he advised his congregants two days before registration. "Their privilege it is to be the first to respond to the call of the flag. We should teach our sons to think life cheap when their country demands their honorable service."[43]

Rabbi Stephen S. Wise, a former member of the American Union Against Militarism, articulated what he believed was the ultimate meaning of immigrant support for the draft in a letter to the *New York Times*. "Tuesday, June 5," he claimed, "will mark the burial, without the hope of resurrection, of hyphenism, and will token the birth of a united and indivisible country." Patriotism, expressed in a successful Selective Service drive, would dissolve the hyphenated loyalties of the ethnic-American and forge a "unity among all those peoples, which, together, make up the American nation." Wise did not single out immigrant Jews, but their response to registration was clearly in his mind. New York's Jews were now to relinquish their past loyalties and identify themselves as committed U.S. citizens ready to fight for their liberty. Echoing Wilson's conviction that it was a nation that had to be shaped and trained for war, leaders such as Wise saw the American crusade as a critical moment in the assimilation of immigrant Jewry.[44]

On the eve of the first major grass-roots test of American support for the war, both the Jewish population of New York and city officials viewed the draft from distinctive historical perspectives. How the new immigrants truly felt about the war, and to what extent the country could count on their participation, were questions that no one could really answer until after the first registration day of the American draft.

At 7:00 A.M. on June 5, 1917, a blaring chorus of church bells, ship horns, and factory whistles sounded the opening of registration sites in New York's five boroughs. Many families accompanied their men to the neighborhood boards, and newspapers reported the "spirit of the day" to be "one of good-humored unconcern," with "no evidence of gloom, despondency, or reluctance." Arrests were "few and far between," and there was no need for extra enforcement.[45]

Despite the anxiety leading up to it, registration in Gotham was a stunning success. The city exceeded the 573,000 men that the federal government had expected it to register. Indeed, the main difficulty encountered by New York officials was the unexpectedly high number of registrants. Several districts found themselves overwhelmed, requiring the Central Board to "draft" hundreds of municipal employees during the day to keep the process running smoothly.[46]

Many of these problems arose because board registrars had underestimated the large immigrant populations living in their districts. Long delays were most common in neighborhoods with predominantly foreign-born residents. Even officials who had a variety of foreign-language speakers on hand occasionally found themselves helpless when a member of an unrepresented nationality came in to answer questions about citizenship, birthplace, and employment status. Registrars then had to quickly locate a volunteer interpreter to help process these "members of the less numerous races."[47]

Board officials expressed satisfaction as well as surprise over the cooperative attitude of immigrants and second-generation ethnics. "The most remarkable thing is how well and willingly the foreign element has responded," commented the head of a registry board. "These people are on the 'job.' They seem anxious to serve the country of their adoption." Lines of up to four hundred men waiting for registrars to arrive were reported in several immigrant sections. The mainstream press delighted in telling anecdotes of this support. A patrolman walking his beat before dawn on the East Side found three young men fast asleep on the steps of a registering site, the trio wanting to be the first in their neighborhood to register. Police arrested two Italian immigrants for shoving people aside to be the first registrants at their election district. The *New York Times*, meanwhile, noted the treatment that immigrants encountered: "The foreigner who too often had been snarled at or ignored when looking for a job found an interpreter for use in case of need, an official who was willing to explain everything to him and to listen patiently to his own statements." The serious nature of the occasion caused many registrars to treat their immigrant neighbors with a new degree of respect and consideration.[48]

As impressive as these results were, any celebration of New York patriotism had to be qualified. Emma Goldman and the American Union Against Militarism immediately charged that many men had been denied the right to claim exemption. Whether or not these abuses were widespread, the number of registrants who requested exclusion from the draft was large. On June 8, the Central Board reported that close to half of the 610,000 registered men claimed exemption. In a telegram to Washington, board chief Edward Boyle commented that citizenship status was the defining factor in this tendency. Predominantly native-born neighborhoods were far less prone to exemption claims than their immigrant counterparts. Since the city had to fill a large quota for the draft, the exemption of aliens became a highly contentious issue throughout the rest of the war.[49]

Much to the chagrin of prowar New York, thousands of immigrants drew a clear line between compliance with the registration law and risking their lives in the trenches. This was certainly true in the case of the city's eastern European Jews. Even attorney Louis Marshall, who served on New

York's central review board and was the most prominent prowar Jewish spokesman in Gotham, admitted that Jews were avoiding the draft in large numbers. In November, after reviewing thousands of exemption cases, he remarked privately that there was a strong "slacker spirit on the part of our people. . . . I could write a chapter which would be very unpleasant reading to those who have heretofore been the champions of the Jew in this country."[50]

Much of this evasive response was not specific to Jewish immigrants. Like the rest of the American population, many Jewish males claimed exemption because of dependents: wives, children, extended family. Since the first draft took no one under the age of twenty-one, it was hard to find men who were not already breadwinners for their families. Immigrants who had never declared their intention to become citizens were also automatically excluded, and many understandably wanted to stay in America rather than go to war. As in the case of New Haven's Italians, this attitude was true for newcomers regardless of nationality and religion. Even a Bronx draft board that was highly critical of its district's Jews reported that three-quarters of their exemption claims were valid.[51] And despite all the agitation among Gotham Jewry, the board also admitted that "any opposition to the Government, if any there was, was covert." New York Jews, like other ethnic populations in America, were asserting their legal right not to be conscripted.

These attitudes had visible public consequences. No other ethnic group in the city gave as much support to the antiwar People's Council. None set up as many facilities for helping men fill out their exemption request forms.[52] Compounded by the anger over immigrants excluded because of their citizenship status, the distinctive behavior of New York Jewry opened the door for anti-Semitic attacks. Previously ignored, soapbox agitators like Russell Dunne found a more receptive audience in the months following registration day.

But as the comments of several Jews who did become soldiers make clear, memories of eastern Europe could also generate an idealistic identification with the American cause. The law student-turned-soldier Meyer Siegel described his enlistment in precisely these terms. One night in 1905, Russian soldiers without any notice demanded lodging in his home and, despite his mother's protests, threw the young family into the street. He arrived in New York City a year later and found life in the United States decidedly more open. Attending a debate during a presidential campaign, he delighted in the American political process:

How simple it was to receive and cherish the freedom we had and even to protect it from enemies outside. I then compared the freedom we had in America to freedom in Russia, where the Mendel Beilis trial was going on. Yes, we were excited to learn that Beilis was on trial as a Jew, charged with using blood to make matzoth.

What ridiculous nonsense! But it was no nonsense to a government like Russia.

Though an orthodox Jew, Siegel viewed his enlistment in the army in secular terms, as a civil responsibility. Accorded political rights in his adopted country, he felt very strongly about his military service. "I was aware of this: That as long as I am a citizen of the United States, I was ready for Uncle Sam, even in war. If you are satisfied with a country which looks out for your existence, you should show your appreciation by even giving your life."[53]

Men who had firsthand experience with the draft in eastern Europe shared these sentiments. Solomon Novin, an infantry private who came to New York at the age of twenty-one, emigrated to evade the Russian draft. "Being an only son, my parents tried to obtain a discharge for me. But because no such thing was forthcoming I ran away. I could write a book of all I went through, I was arrested three times before I finally escaped." Drafted into the American army in April 1918, Novin cited the difference between his experiences in Russia and the United States. "My life here in America is very brief because things [before the war] were running very smoothly here. Some day, when the world will be at peace, I will bring my parents here and have no further use for Russia." Morry Morrison, whose father was killed while fighting as a conscript in the Russo-Japanese War, emigrated with his mother when he was a young child. They eventually settled in New York's East Side. "Boy, were things different here—no fear, that's the difference, no fear, see." When the United States entered the war, Morrison volunteered to serve in a Brooklyn unit. "My mother, she didn't want me to go, see, 'cause she was thinking of my father, but I figured this country was different from Russia; it was worth fighting for."[54]

Many American-born sons of Jewish immigrants also felt a special desire to serve in the army, their knowledge of eastern Europe clearly affecting how they viewed their own role in the war. Michael Shalinsky, a Seventy-seventh Division draftee who would be captured by the Germans, recalled: "When my turn to be drafted came, it didn't bother me at all. As a matter of fact, if I hadn't been drafted, I think I would have gone anyway. Both my parents had been Jewish immigrants from Europe, and this country had been good to our family."[55] Jack Kovar, a New York native whose parents were from Russia, was killed in action. "I have a remarkable collection of letters from him," his brother commented in a postwar survey, "showing his patriotism, his Judaism and his lofty ideals. He fought, as he writes in one of his letters to me, so that the poor Jews in Russia and other European countries would be given the right to live and return to the Holy Land."[56] As immigrants, Americans, or committed Zionists, Jewish soldiers had an ethnically unique set of motivations for enlisting.

The rhetoric of prowar Jewish leaders, which emphasized allegiance to America as one's home, did not fall on deaf ears. A deep revulsion of the

THE DRAFT AND NEW YORK JEWRY ★ 71

oppressiveness of Russian rule and sincere appreciation of the civil liberties found in the United States figured largely in the perceptions of Meyer Siegel and perhaps thousands more like him.

With 600,000 New Yorkers and over 9 million other men registered nationwide, the next step in the draft process was to find out how many were eligible and physically fit for service. Wearing a blindfold, Secretary of War Newton Baker selected the first of 10,500 draft numbers from the Senate Office Building in Washington on July 20. The results were printed in newspapers across the country, and draft boards sent notification cards to the men they would examine. Through August and September doctors at each board checked the eyesight, hearing, and heartbeats of several hundred thousand men. Board officials then asked questions concerning each man's occupation, marital and family status, citizenship, education, and police record.

Selective Service chief Enoch Crowder later described how the new draft represented "the invasion of the home, the laying bare of personal pride and shortcomings, the severance of ties of love and affection, and the breaching of a deep-rooted American tradition." Instead of volunteering on an individual basis, young men now appeared before representatives of the federal government and submitted to a close scrutiny of their bodies and their personal circumstances. Conscription advocates like Crowder lauded the unity of purpose (and common fate) the draft brought with it. "The nation glimpsed a common interest," he claimed, "sensed a common understanding, in a thing that lifted to a single level class and race and creed and color and social status, and fused the spirit of a people in a single aspiration and the hope of a common success."[57]

Of course, the draft would reflect stark differences in the class, race, and social status of the soldiers it selected, and the "single aspiration" of many Americans was to stay completely out of the war. But Crowder's flair for the dramatic does convey the magnitude of what was clearly a landmark event in American public policy. In a population whose previous contact with the state had consisted essentially of the local post office, the events of the summer of 1917 represented a major departure. Two months after the drawing of the first draft number, the nation's Selective Service boards had examined well over a million young men, classifying nearly 700,000 as eligible for immediate training and eventual deployment overseas.

Of these prospective conscripts thirty-eight thousand were to come from New York City, and Gotham's particularly difficult set of local circumstances continued to be felt. The city diverged from Washington's plan in three key ways. First, authorities in New York acted more forcefully to control what was America's most important center of dissent. But this repression, like the draft itself, was selective, leaving the largest of the Jewish antiwar organizations free to continue their agitation. Second, in a metropolis so large and diverse, it was inevitable that the city's 189 draft boards experienced a variety of problems. Incidents of ethnic discrimination and graft, however, had an especially keen impact on the Jewish population. Third, and most important, New York's immigrant Jews continued to act in a manner that contrasted sharply with the rest of the city and the nation. Meyer Siegel's induction into the army, an event so unremarkable on paper, took place amid rising concerns over Jewish loyalty.

The task of curtailing dissent became much less uncertain for authorities through the summer. United States Marshal Thomas McCarthy and Police Commissioner Arthur Woods were no longer afraid that police or federal action might set off an explosion of hostility toward the war effort. Not only was there meager opposition on registration day, but other mobilization drives in June—Liberty Loan Week, Red Cross Week, Regular Army Recruiting Week, the state military census, enlistment campaigns for the New York National Guard—also were highly successful. Choosing to repress only the smallest, weakest, and most extreme of the antidraft groups, federal agents and local police acted more deliberately after the Selective Service registration was completed. On June 15, U.S. marshals arrested Emma Goldman and Alexander Berkman and raided the offices of the No Conscription League. By the end of the month, Goldman and Berkman, two other NCL members, and the pair of students from the Collegiate Anti-Militarism League had been convicted of conspiracy to disrupt the draft.[58] In July, the U.S. postmaster general tried to strip *The Masses* of its mailing privileges.[59] New York police were also much quicker to combat activists, arresting speakers from the Women's League to Repeal Conscription.[60]

Serious infringements on civil liberties though these events were, they did not constitute a sweeping crackdown on dissent. Organizations with large memberships that questioned the war, such as the local Socialist party and the Jewish-led unions, were not subject to arrests, raids, or police harassment. And that fall Morris Hillquit made a dramatic bid for mayor as an antiwar candidate. Gotham's debate over American intervention remained lively and vociferous. It was this restricted form of political freedom that allowed antiwar Jews and their organizations to become so well known. Suppression of the smaller groups received front-page coverage through the early summer. Five of the six persons to go to trial for conspiracy in June were Jewish, and their defense counsels, Harry Weinstein and Morris Hillquit, were prominent left-wing Jewish attorneys. Jacob Panken, who would soon win a place on the New York bench as a Socialist candidate, defended a draft resister in July.[61] Probably the most heavily publicized antiwar action that summer also involved local Jews. A rally of the Women's League to Repeal Conscription, a small Lower East Side-based group, degenerated into a "near riot" when police arrested one of its leaders. In condescending articles, the mainstream press described the activists as hysterical and wielding hairpins.[62]

But even the more prominent antiwar organizations were beginning to draw fire. As early as June 24 the *New York Times* claimed that the People's

Council, which thrived on Jewish immigrant support, took its ideas "from Russia" and was working for "a German peace." The garment unions also came under attack from the press and within the national labor movement. Publicity that centered on these groups, as well as the local Socialist party, overshadowed the compliance with mobilization characteristic of most of New York Jewry. In August the *World* openly identified immigrant Jewish radicals as a key pillar of the antiwar opposition, accusing them of working with German agents.[63]

Doubts about Jewish loyalty also arose from the problems that confronted the draft machinery in Gotham. Individual boards varied considerably in the size and makeup of their staffs, the methods of examination they employed, and their degree of flexibility in exempting candidates. It is not surprising that, with 189 different local boards operating in a city that was no stranger to ethnic prejudice and corruption, there would be great disparities in treatment and scrupulousness.

The best example of those broad discretionary powers was Manhattan's Local Board 129. Its examiners, situated in the Museum of Natural History, took the need for "scientific" classification very seriously. "Realizing a great opportunity," a postwar report enthused, the board "made careful anthropometric studies of about 600 registrants." The staff carefully noted a man's "ancestry and nationality" and the size and shape of his teeth, jaw, and "foot imprint." Examiners then took photographs and made forty different measurements of each candidate's body, head, and face. "The figures seem to indicate that the foreign born registrants were markedly less fit for service than the native born, but there is no marked difference between the native born of foreign parents and those of native American stock." In its own curious way, the board's preoccupation with ethnicity and race reflected the assimilationist attitudes of many Selective Service advocates. They believed that the draft, like a second-generation immigrant's exposure to the American environment, would help dissolve the fear that some populations were unassimilable.[64]

Most Jewish immigrants did not encounter such clinical treatment. Since examiners came from the same draft districts as the men they reviewed, Jews staffed many boards in heavily Jewish neighborhoods. Whether or not this made a difference in the way immigrants were handled is unclear. There is evidence, however, that some boards with native-born staffs were rough on immigrants and Jews in particular. The examiners at a Brooklyn district openly expressed their prejudice toward Jewish registrants in a widely publicized telegram to Woodrow Wilson. They complained that they were "overwhelmed" with the exemption claims of their mainly Russian Jewish pool of candidates, and that "the flower of our neighborhood is being torn from homes and loved ones to fight for these miserable specimens of humanity, who under the law may remain smugly at home and reap the benefit of the life work of our young citizens." One of the board's members was later removed after remarking at a rally "there are three epochs in the life of the

Jewish boy: first, at birth, circumcision; second, at 13, confirmation; third, at 21, exemption."[65]

Public statements like these were rare and met with immediate condemnation from Jewish leaders and newspapers. But one board's confidential report to Washington also singled out the behavior of Gotham Jewry. Local Board 13 from the Bronx, whose jurisdiction was "composed mostly of Russian Jews," examined three thousand men in the summer and fall of 1917. It found that prospective candidates were extremely well-informed of their rights and "took full benefit of all draft loopholes." The board called for "instilling into these foreign folk the fact that there is a crime known as perjury . . . that an oath is the calling upon our God (as well as their God) to witness the truth of what they say." Even the threat of federal prosecution was not enough. The examiners wished they could "have them swear before their rabbi or ordained minister on their Talmud or other things holy. They have only a sense of humor when swearing on the New Testament." The city's largest immigrant group continued to generate the most criticism, despite the fact that the East Side, Brownsville, and other Jewish neighborhoods quickly provided their full quota of soldiers.[66]

The disparity of the boards was not limited to their members' racial attitudes. Corruption among draft officials was not uncommon and involved Gentile and Jewish board members alike. But punishment of these crimes again fell most heavily on Jews. The only officials arrested on federal charges in the city were Jewish. A total of five board members serving on the East Side and in Brooklyn were apprehended for receiving thousands of dollars in exchange for granting exemption and were sentenced to prison terms at the federal penitentiary in Atlanta. Ironically, it was the same prison that housed Alexander Berkman and two other New York Jewish activists.[67]

Public officials did not identify the men as Jews or use the occasion to question the ethnic group's loyalty. But within the Jewish community the identity of the perpetrators was a subject of extensive commentary. Both pro- and antiwar Jewish newspapers distanced themselves from the accused. "The East Side still cannot get over the shock," wrote the *American Jewish Chronicle*.[68] The paper claimed the Manhattan officials were "unknown to the Jewish public, and as it seems, have been picked to serve . . . for purely political reasons." The socialist *Forward* also chastised the men for tarnishing the reputation of the immigrant community. The editors condemned the claims of one of the board members, that he was "acting in full accord with [what] the *Forward* was preaching," as an attempt to discredit the paper's principled opposition to the war, and characterized his plea as "an effort to throw dirt upon the entire East Side."[69]

The unanimity of this condemnation, coming from newspapers who fought incessantly with each other on the war issue, reflected a common preoccupation. The *American Jewish Chronicle* argued that the "Jewish East Side" was being "watched over with a thousand eyes." The "press during the first days of the draft forgot about Greater New York . . . and confined its observations to the East Side," the editors charged. Draft advocates and opponents within the Jewish population could agree with this assessment. Even though a close reading of the five main New York dailies proves this claim to be exaggerated, the strength of Jewish antiwar opposition and the federal convictions overwhelmingly of Jews spoke louder than words.[70] The immigrant population was thinking and behaving in a very different manner than the rest of the city, and both Jewish and Gentile leaders recognized this stark contrast.

Key events affecting the Jewish population during the draft selection process illuminate the sources and nature of this disparity. Conflicts within the Jewish labor movement, between proponents of an American Jewish Congress, and even among Jews who supported the war attracted as much internal attention and debate as the national draft. These events received little commentary from "outside" leaders and the mainstream press. But for the city's Jews, critical issues of heritage and religion were at stake. The politics of cultural identity eventually proved stronger than the politics of class conflict, which had characterized the Jewish response during the first several months of American belligerency.

The struggle within the Jewish left to capture the support of immigrant workers was certainly the most visible of these conflicts. The People's Council for Democracy and Peace began an ambitious program of agitation among the city's working class in June 1917. The council sought to remove the prowar leadership of the Central Federated Union, New York's main labor body, and eventually called a series of strikes to disrupt mobilization. The Jewish-led unions, the *Forward*, and the Socialist party were the council's chief supporters in the local labor movement, so the campaign had a definite ethnic character.[71]

This effort immediately drew the attention of the top levels of the American labor movement. American Federation of Labor President Samuel Gompers himself rushed to Gotham to help form an organization to combat the council's strategy. In late July the newly formed American Alliance for Labor and Democracy (AALD) launched a major counterattack, with a nationwide campaign to inspire worker support for the war. Jewish labor journalist Robert Maisel was the AALD's director, and much of his work focused on New York's immigrant Jews.[72]

Over the next several months a small group of prowar trade unionists and socialists in New York battled against the established institutions of the Jewish left. Maisel and the AALD, working with funds from the Committee of Public Information in Washington, distributed thousands of patriotic pamphlets in Yiddish, created a special Jewish Bureau on the East Side, and enlisted members of two new prowar organizations—the Jewish Socialist League and the American League of Jewish Patriots—as speakers and publicists.[73] The assault on the Central Federated Union was thwarted, and no strike wave ever gripped the city. But the leadership of the garment unions, the United Hebrew Trades, and the Socialist party remained opposed to the war. And despite Maisel's repeated claims that the *Forward* wielded a dangerous level of influence, the federal government allowed the paper to continue publication.[74] Most significantly, immigrant Jews enthusiastically supported Morris Hillquit and other Jewish socialists in the November municipal elections. During the summer and fall of 1917, the left was still able to dominate a prowar voice within its ranks.

But the election of an American Jewish Congress, which took place just four days after the June 5 registration, foreshadowed the eventual collapse of the left's opposition to the war. Prior to 1914, the idea of creating a congress—a representative body that would demand equal rights for Jews in all countries and a Jewish homeland in Palestine—was little more than a fantasy. But when the war escalated, the European empires began to show signs of disintegration and hopes for national independence among the peoples they ruled surged. The congress became not only a realistic possibility but also a compelling political necessity. The suffering of Russian Jewry, the stunning success of American Jewish relief efforts, and the moralistic neutrality of the United States inspired a variety of Zionist and non-Zionist organizations to press for a strong, international political voice. For two years, Jewish institutions of the left, right, and center held negotiations, bitterly argued, and finally agreed on a program for electing delegates to a nationwide congress. Such archrivals as the American Jewish Committee, the socialist National Workmen's Committee, and the moderate Zionist organization of Louis Brandeis had endorsed a general program in December 1916.[75]

This unprecedented demonstration of Jewish unity was short-lived. Less than a month before the June 1917 elections, the National Workmen's Committee called for a boycott of the event. They believed that the proposed organization was unnecessary now that the Russian czar had fallen and were also fearful they would have little representation in the congress. This proved to be a major mistake. Two years of heated debate and conferences had riveted the attention and fueled the aspirations of American Jews regardless of their social class or political affiliation. In New York City alone, eight nominating conventions for congress candidates were held in May, and the Yiddish press packed its pages with coverage of the upcoming election. On June 9–10, more than 300,000 Jews across the country voted for their representatives. Nearly half of the ballots were cast in Gotham, an estimated 75,000 by workers who ignored the socialist boycott. To its dismay, the left discovered how the war's nationalist passions had inspired the immigrant Jews it claimed to represent. By mid-1918, few leaders of the Jewish labor movement still marched behind the banner of antiwar internationalism.[76]

The left was not the only element within Gotham Jewry that had to confront demands for independent Jewish action. Assimilationist leaders faced a cultural challenge from their immigrant Orthodox colleagues, who were deeply concerned about the conditions that thousands of young Jews would face in the armed forces. Would there be enough Jewish chaplains?

Would Jews be able to observe dietary laws and worship on the sabbath and High Holidays? The conservative New York papers *Morgen Journal* and *Yiddishes Tageblatt*, hearing of the formation of a Jewish Legion in the British Army that would fight in Palestine, called for the creation of similar all-Jewish units in the U.S. Army. To make such a demand on the federal government would have been unthinkable among the country's Jewish population just a few years earlier.

Separatism on so large and visible a scale was of course anathema for Jewish war advocates who championed Americanization. "The Jewish citizen of this country," commented the *American Jewish Chronicle*, "when called upon to serve his country, does so not as a Jew, but as a citizen. There is no room for hyphenism in the trenches or on the battlefield." The *American Hebrew* also denounced ethnic regiments and argued that military service would reduce anti-Semitism. "The close association of our Jewish soldiers with their Gentile comrades will help bring about that appreciation of the Jewish character, bravery and undaunted patriotism which will tend towards a complete disappearance of the last traces of racial prejudice."[77]

The plea for Jewish regiments was especially disturbing, since a number of institutions had already formed an organization, the Jewish Board for Welfare Work (later named the Jewish Welfare Board, or JWB), to provide services for Jews in the military. The board was launched just three days after the American declaration of war in April to recommend rabbis for the military chaplaincy, distribute religious literature to the men, and lobby the government to offer kosher food and holiday furloughs. Most ambitiously, the Jewish Welfare Board planned to train its own "welfare workers" who would work at the army training camps as well as in France. The War Department recognized the JWB in September 1917, and the main Jewish relief agency gave it a donation of $900,000 that December. But the effort was still not enough to satisfy the demands of religious conservatives, and the JWB would be subject to criticism throughout the rest of the war.[78]

The summer and fall of 1917 was a turbulent period for New York Jewry. The creation of the American Alliance for Labor and Democracy, the election of the American Jewish Congress, and federal approval of the Jewish Welfare Board reflected the passions and hopes of an ethnic group that had the power to make itself heard nationally. More than their European past determined the manner in which New York's Jews responded to American mobilization. Organized political opposition to the war and the flourishing of Zionist aspirations were local developments, very much dependent on the cosmopolitan and comparatively open environment of the Empire City. Not surprisingly, these activities attracted the attention and increasing antagonism of many Gentile New Yorkers, whose hearts and minds had a more singular patriotic focus.

But viewed from a larger perspective, many of these distinctions diminish in importance. As with the Italian *colonia* of New Haven, the majority of the Jewish population attracted little attention because it accepted and

Samuel Goodman's military career was fairly typical of many New York Jews. A Russian immigrant who settled in Brooklyn, Goodman was among the first group of New Yorkers to be drafted. He rose to the rank of sergeant in the 77th Division and fought in four combat sectors before being temporarily blinded by mustard gas. Spending five months in military hospitals, he returned to the U.S. and was eventually able to resume his trade as a printer. Courtesy of American Jewish Historical Society.

participated in what was happening without fanfare. The distinctiveness of Gotham Jewry was a matter of proportion—its pro- and antiwar forces were much larger than in most American communities. But most Jews registered for the draft, waived or claimed their right to exemption, and in the process deepened their knowledge of American institutions. While internal struggles raged, Jewish neighborhoods held farewell celebrations for their men.[79]

Perhaps the most interesting assessment of how local Jews responded to the draft came from its New York City director Roscoe Conkling, a Manhattanite whose ancestry dated back to the days of New Amsterdam. More than any other official, he knew the factual basis of charges of Jewish disloyalty. But his knowledge did not lead to condemnation. Two decades later he wrote a novel praising the participation of New York Jewry during the war. In his view, the deep anxiety the draft caused among Gotham Jews and the anti-Semitism they faced made their response all the more remarkable.[80]

On August 31, 1917, Assistant Attorney General Conkling announced that the city's draft boards were ready to induct their full quota. Four days later, Manhattan, Brooklyn, and the Bronx held parades to honor these men, who were about to become the first soldiers of the new, all-conscript National Army. Seven thousand draftees marched up Fifth Avenue, still wearing civilian clothes, with only an armband bearing the insignia "N.A." to distinguish them from the rest of the population. With Mayor Mitchel in the lead, they paraded with their draft board officials and banners noting each district represented. In the parade's reviewing stand were Theodore Roosevelt, past presidential candidates Charles Evan Hughes and Alton B. Parker, and Provost Marshal General Enoch Crowder. A crowd of 400,000 lined the streets to watch; its "backbone," the *New York Times* reported, "formed of relatives and friends of individuals in the ranks."[81]

While Gotham cheered, President Wilson and members of Congress led a parade of Washington, D.C.'s, own draft contingent. On "the Day of the Selected Man," Wilson published an open letter to the soldiers of the National Army. "The eyes of the world will be upon you," he declared, "because you are in some special sense the soldiers of freedom. Let it be your pride therefore, to show all men everywhere not only what good soldiers you are but what good men you are, keeping yourselves fit and straight in everything and pure and clean through and through." Wilson's message was not idle rhetoric. The War Department would make every effort to introduce the men to middle-class standards and a prideful American nationalism.[82]

The Empire City asserted its own stake in this national effort. Public officials and the press claimed a special local significance for Gotham's drafted men, one that the city (and the soldiers themselves) would embrace throughout the rest of the war. The *New York Times* and other papers stressed the virtues of urban democracy and the symbolism of the melting pot, lauding the men "of every race, class, type, and color" who would soon go to Camp Upton, Long Island, for training. "[The parade] was composed of the rich and the poor," the *Herald* proclaimed, "the scholarly and the unlettered, the fashionably garbed and the ill-clad, the native American of Puritan or Cavalier stock and the American of recently naturalized origin, the Gentile and the Jew. Yes, even the Caucasian of purest strain tramped alongside negroes whose freedom from bondage was one of the fruits of an earlier war fought by freemen for world freedom."[83]

This cosmopolitan form of democracy would last no longer than the parade itself. The army immediately sent African Americans to segregated units and eventually selected most of the wealthy and well educated for officer training. The doughboys, the celebrated infantry soldiers of the Great War, were overwhelmingly white working-class men and nearly one out of every five was not even born in America.[84] But the realities of conscription were no match for the powerful image that New York affixed to its portion of the new army. This local pride was not limited to city boosters. When regular army officers chose an insignia for the Seventy-seventh Division, the organization to which most of the draftees were assigned, they decided that the Statue of Liberty was most appropriate.[85]

The "Melting Pot" Division, as it came to be known, captured the imagination of New Yorkers more than any other military unit the city sent to France. Identifying with the Seventy-seventh, Gotham assumed a degree of control over the government's impersonal system of classification. Residents filled the ranks after their neighbors selected them for service; the city itself was able to erase much of what lingered of a traumatic moment in its past. A year after the draft parades "New York City's Own" Seventy-seventh Division was fighting in the Argonne Forest, and Gotham followed its every move.

The conflict-ridden response of local Jewry to the selection process played a key role in casting a spotlight on the draft army. But the Jewish conscripts who paraded on September 4 evoked a new phase of wartime concern: hope that a loved one would return home safe and sound. Jews accounted for possibly as many as a third of this initial wave of thirty-eight-thousand New York draftees.[86] As in every community across the country, their absence from homes, workplaces, and neighborhoods in the months to come shaped people's attitudes toward the war more than any loan drive or patriotic rally.

Since the federal government did not record the religion of every soldier, it is not possible to provide a definitive description of this Jewish group of conscripts. But an American Jewish Committee survey conducted after the war gives at least some insight into who these men were.[87] The questionnaires reflect the preponderance of Russian immigrants, the hunger for education, and the occupational mobility that characterized the Jewish population up to 1917. Ninety-seven percent of these men were either immigrants or second-generation Americans, and three-quarters of them claimed roots in the Russian Pale. Nearly half had obtained more than an elementary school education by attending New York's many high schools, colleges, and vocational academies. The Jewish immigrants' ability to move "out of the sweatshop" and adapt to Gotham's commercial environment is also very evident. Over half of the respondents were engaged in business, either as shop owners, small manufacturers, clerks, or salesmen. The presence of students, public employees, and skilled tradesmen also is significant, accounting for more than a fifth of the survey. This mobility illustrates a major reason why return migration rates were so low among eastern European Jews. Permanent settlement in America went hand-in-hand with material achievement, and no doubt many of these men saw military service as a price one had to pay for living in the United States.[88]

The price the future Jewish members of the Seventy-seventh Division would pay in France was indeed a high one. Among the survey respondents were Manhattan native Irving Goldberg, who spent four months in a German prison camp. Immigrant barber Abraham Krotoshinsky, later applauded as "New York City's Greatest Hero of the War," would suffer from the poison gas he inhaled in the trenches for the rest of his life. Salesman Julius Klausner answered his questionnaire from a hospital bed. He listed

his injuries: "High Explosive Shell—Gunshot Wound and Compound Frac-
ture—Left Leg. Gunshot Wound in Mouth breaking Five teeth—Three
Gunshot Wounds in Right Arm." Emma Goldman's nephew David Hochstein would make "the supreme sacrifice." The violinist, who played in Carnegie Hall before the war, "was killed one month before Armistice Day, in
the prime and glory of his youth."[89]

But in the fall of 1917 the young men receiving their draft notices could
only speculate on what they would encounter overseas. Whether or not
Meyer Siegel marched up Fifth Avenue is not known. But there is no doubt
he received a small red card in the mail that same week. "From the date
herein specified," the card read, "you will be in the military service of the
United States and subject to military law." Like hundreds of thousands of
other American men, Siegel learned of his "change over" from civilian to
soldier via the Government Printing Office in Washington, D.C. For the
next year and a half, he would be subject to the discipline and cultural
preoccupations of one of the largest federal institutions ever created in the
history of the United States—the new National Army.[90]

II Training the New Immigrant Soldier

* * * * * * * * * * * * * * * * * *

Mobilized for federal service, the Italian volunteers from New Haven and the Jewish draftees of New York were now ready for intensive training. In the fall and winter of 1917–18 they began to learn the rudiments of trench warfare—of artillery barrages, bayonet attacks, and full-scale assaults in no man's land. Training respectively in Landaville, France, and at Camp Upton, the members of the Twenty-sixth National Guard and Seventy-seventh National Army divisions rushed to become combat ready. Like millions of other enlisted men in camps on both sides of the Atlantic, these ethnic soldiers were discovering what the war would be like "over there."

Their training experiences deserve close attention for two reasons. First, the men spent most of their time at training areas rather than at the front. The Italian machine gunners were in federal service for nearly a year before spending eight months in a variety of combat sectors. For New York's conscripted Jews, the ratio of instruction to frontline duty was almost two to one. Second, the same blend of federal control and local voluntarism that had shaped their mobilization also affected the training process. The Italian guardsmen had to undergo a new course of instruction, one that satisfied both the needs of modern warfare and the demands of a highly critical regular army. In sharp contrast, the green conscripts of the Seventy-seventh Division knew no other form of training and relied heavily on their own initiative and their city for support. Despite the government's desire to mold the training process to a single standard, the experiences of the National Guard and the draft army continued to diverge.

Preparation for war had a sustained and complicated influence on the ethnic soldiers. For the New Haven Italians, the conservative outlook and laissez-faire character of the all–New England Twenty-sixth Division played a critical role. When the officers of the Twenty-sixth selected an insignia, they chose the letter Y superimposed on a letter D, a navy blue symbol set against an olive drab background. The emblem, signifying "Yankee Division," reflected the organization's plain and austere New England heritage. Past traditions, and the need to uphold them, served as a constant organizing principle and source of inspiration for the Twenty-sixth. The soldiers were urged to see themselves as a link between the past and present, maintaining the historical pride of their units while defending their hometown communities in the here and now.

But this emphasis on tradition and community also blunted whatever acculturating effect the war may have had on the division's ethnic members. It reinforced a parochial and romanticized view of the war, in conflict with the modernizing impulses the army needed to embrace to be effective on the western front. The proud Yankee Division made little effort to emphasize or celebrate the diversity of its ranks. The institutional culture of the division harked back to the colonial Minuteman, not the recent immigrant from southern Europe. The machine gunners served only a short time under an Italian American officer and none of them obtained a rank above sergeant. To a marked degree their experiences in the army replicated the segregated culture and society they had known in New Haven. If not for the action of the federal government, the Italian machine gun company would never have been created in the first place, nor would it have been merged with non-Italian soldiers. Its frontline training would have been even more negligible, and its contact with a larger sense of nation would have been limited to the localism of the regiment's New England roots.

The Seventy-seventh Division from New York City, in contrast, was a federal creation from the beginning and had no history. Its symbol was the cosmopolitan Statue of Liberty, and its character was of necessity responsive to diversity and innovation. There was nothing in American history that resembled a combat division comprised of more than twenty-seven thousand conscripts. Every draftee entering Camp Upton was a buck private, and most of the officers were fresh from training school. Most important, the heterogeneity of the ranks was lauded even before the men donned uniforms, and the moniker "Melting Pot Division" was proudly embraced by New York's civilians, the division's commanders, and the soldiers themselves.

Since no prior knowledge of military life could be assumed, the instruction given the Jewish members of the Seventy-seventh was more explicitly integrative, more geared toward complete indoctrination, than what their Italian counterparts experienced in France. Education and skill for the most part determined the organization of men at Camp Upton, rather than hometown origins or the desire to serve alongside friends and relatives. Many Jewish draftees were promoted to leadership positions, not only in command of other Jews but also of Gentiles of recent and deep-rooted American origins. Similarly, the design of the camp's barracks, the training program, and even the recreational activities were not left to chance, but directed by the War Department and a number of private national agencies. And even with all this emphasis on planning and efficiency, such a huge enterprise required the active participation of nearby New York and the soldiers themselves. The success of Camp Upton depended on the ranks of its new army and the city they called home as much as on the "army" of progressive-minded officers and welfare workers involved in the massive project.

To a great extent, the differences between National Guard organizations like the Yankee Division and a National Army outfit like the Seventy-seventh reflected the central political tensions of the period. The debates over how America should deal with major domestic problems, over how it should respond to the consequences of dramatic industrial, urban, and population growth, applied directly to the war effort. Were local, tried-and-true institutions capable of doing the job? Or was a sprawling federal bureaucracy the best means of achieving victory? Essential issues of the Progressive Era directly affected the preparation of ethnic soldiers for service in the Great War.

Ultimately, the draft army proved itself to be more inclusive, participatory, and respectful in the way it handled immigrant soldiers than its community-based counterpart. The new National Army did not challenge racial segregation. But among the white conscripts it trained, the War Department placed greater value on individual skill and performance than a man's immigrant or class background. A comparison of how the Italian volunteers and the Jewish draftees were trained illustrates how the "war to make the world safe for democracy" had unforeseen consequences. Ironically, the wartime state, long understood as an engine driving political repression and xenophobic hysteria, also acted in ways that made America a much more democratic country for new immigrants to live in.

★ ★ ★ ★ ★ ★ ★ ★ ★ ★ ★ ★ ★ ★ ★ ★ ★ ★

4 Being Italian in the Yankee Division

⭐ ⭐ ⭐ ⭐ ⭐ ⭐ ⭐ ⭐ ⭐ ⭐ ⭐ ⭐ ⭐ ⭐ ⭐ ⭐ ⭐ ⭐

On September 9, 1917, the Italian members of the 102nd's machine gun company sailed out of Hoboken, New Jersey. Like most soldiers of the American Expeditionary Force, which had no American fleet at its disposal, they made the crossing in a British vessel. Their transport was the *S.S. Adriatic*, a converted ocean liner that impressed the men with its deck guns and bizarre wartime camouflage. Reaching Halifax, Nova Scotia, on the second day of the voyage, they joined a convoy and headed out for Liverpool.[1]

"A cold, ugly, wind-tossed sea" marked most of the passage, one of the machine gunners recalled, and most of the men were seasick during the first days of the crossing. The company ate English rations, which they thought were "very poor," and stayed in shape by doing calisthenic exercises and making frequent equipment inspections. They also spent many hours conducting lifeboat drills and serving as lookouts for enemy submarines. Rumors were rife that German U-boats prowled the area, but the men spotted only sharks, dolphins, and a lonesome whale in the frigid Atlantic. Though the trip passed without incident, the gunners breathed a sigh of relief when an escort of British destroyers arrived to guide their ship through the North Sea and past the coast of Ireland.[2]

The voyage marked a new phase of their military service, providing them with their first real sensation of the dangers that awaited them in France. For the pride of the New Haven *colonia*, both immigrant and American-born, the crossing had additional meanings. Among the company's forty-eight Italian immigrants, the fortnight at sea no doubt brought back memories of coming to America. Nearly all of these men had emigrated as adolescents, and the sights, sounds, and emotions of traveling in steerage were still vivid in their minds. Cussonbrato native Francesco Martinetti, who arrived at Ellis Island in 1911, could compare experiences with Aniello Aiello from Scafati, who landed in New York a year later. Albert Litro, who left

Naples in June 1913 aboard the ocean liner *Berlin*, might have discovered that Amorosi's Gennaro Vivenzio had traveled in the same ship just three months before him.[3]

The present crossing might also have led the men to reflect on their years in America—the little if any schooling they had received, the clubs and societies they had helped form, the jobs they had found, and the difficulties that came with adjusting to life in a new country. These experiences separated them from their friends and relatives in Italy, their *paesani* who had already suffered the war's ravages for two years and whose struggle the gunners were now about to experience firsthand.

Second-generation sons like Ralph Bove and Joseph Cosenzo, meanwhile, could view the voyage from a different perspective. Traveling to the continent their parents had left behind, they were finally going to see a part of the world they had heard about since birth. Many also shared the enthusiasm that caused their non-Italian shipmates to enlist. As factory worker Louis Popolizio recalled, "I was going to travel the world at the government's expense." These men felt the same excitement over leaving the routine of life and work in New Haven and participating in what they called the "Great Adventure."[4] With this jumble of shared and distinctive expectations, the New Haveners finally landed at Liverpool on September 23, 1917.

Being "over there" had yet another meaning for the Italian members of the company, one that aided the consolidation of their newly merged unit. This was experienced as soon as the soldiers boarded trains and made their way to a rest camp in Southampton, where a transport waited to take them to France. During the long trip through the English countryside, they met railroad workers calling them "Yankees," crowds waving American flags, and children asking them for American coins as souvenirs.[5] Regardless of their Italian descent, the gunners were recognized on the basis of their national uniform. The "foreigners" that the men encountered—civilian or soldier, friend or foe—did not call them Italians, dagoes, or wops, but Americans, Yanks, and Sammies. They met the same reception in France. Private Connell Albertine, a YD infantryman, recalled: "We passed several railroad stations and there again the platforms were crowded with people and children waving and yelling, 'Vive les Americains!' " Equally significant is the way in which the soldiers interpreted these scenes. "There was no question," Albertine writes, "but that the morale of the entire French nation was boosted to a new high by the knowledge that the Americans had come to their rescue." Landing in the port of Le Havre, the guardsmen made the same distinction when they spotted troops from other countries. As Ratcliffe Hills, one of the non-Italian members of the unit recalls, it was there that the men encountered "a number of German prisoners, some French 'poilus,' English 'Tommies,' and veterans from the West Indies." The pride of the *colonia* represented a national army fighting an international war on foreign soil.[6]

In this setting, the gunners' ethnicity was not so decisive as in New Haven or at Camp Yale. The seventy-five Italian and one hundred non-

Italian members of the recently merged company found a new source of unity overseas. The ability of the company's members to communicate in the same language (however broken an immigrant's English might be); their common knowledge of company practices and equipment; and their unfamiliarity with the people and ways of France helped to diminish, though certainly not erase, the cultural divide that previously separated Italian from non-Italian, immigrant from native-born Yankee. In terms of experiences, immigrant Frank Giordano now had more in common with an eleventh-generation New Englander like Ratcliffe Hills than either man would have believed possible in America.[7]

The shared sense of being "innocents abroad" was one of a number of factors that helped unify the company. Their assignment after they arrived also brought the men closer together. After landing in Le Havre on September 24, they spent a day and a half traveling by rail to the 102nd regiment's training quarters in Landaville. This small village, located near the city of Neufchâteau and just forty miles from the front, would be their home for the next four months. They now served as the advance party for the regiment and their immediate task was to construct housing and provide a basic infrastructure for the thirty-two hundred other soldiers about to arrive from Camp Yale. "Our duties at Landaville were manifold," remembered Ratcliffe Hills. "We served as firemen, built barracks, made bunks, repaired roads, dug practice trenches, prepared the target range, excavated the sanitary receptacles and drainage systems, and served as mechanics, kitchen police, and guardsmen."[8]

The machine gun company may have been chosen for the assignment because its Italian members had the building and mechanical skills to handle such a big task. In any case, being on their own in a tiny village, with no pay and no place to spend it, the men had little choice but to become more acquainted with their non-Italian comrades. Working together during these first few weeks, they got to know each other's skills and personalities. Outside of work, they shared the same feelings of wonder, anxiety, and homesickness. They ate and billeted together, and for relaxation played cards and held group sing-alongs. When the other regimental companies poured into the area from mid-October through early December, the men were not only veteran *habitiens* of Landaville, but also a much more cohesive unit.[9]

The thousands of New England soldiers who followed the machine gun company into the Neufchâteau area impressed on all of the men the fact that they belonged to a much larger organization. The 175 machine gunners constituted only one company of the thirty-six-hundred-man "Nutmeg" regiment from Connecticut, only a tiny portion of the twenty-seven-thousand-member Yankee Division. They represented a minute fraction of the 2 million soldiers who would ultimately make up the American Expeditionary Force. Set within this mammoth framework, the Italian guardsmen were directly affected by the relationships among the various levels of command. A key influence would be the antagonism between an independent-minded

National Guard organization and the imperatives of the federal government and regular army.

Two events that occurred during the arrival period reveal this tension. The very fact that the troops landed in France in September and October, making them the first guardsmen to arrive overseas, was a dramatic assertion of the Yankee Division's desire for autonomy. Its officers had pushed hard for the early crossing. Military and civilian officials connected with the Twenty-sixth wanted to see the men arrive first in Europe, ahead of any other National Guard organization. The Yankees located transportation on their own and avoided being sent to a camp in the American South for the winter, as was the case for nearly all the other state militias.[10] "In convoys, or by steamers," a captain later wrote, "in ships of all sorts from first-class Atlantic liners . . . down to hastily impressed coastwise fruit boats, the troops made the journey." Describing the move as "winning the final lap of the race" against the rival Forty-second Division, he, like most "YD" men, proudly pointed to the fact that they were the first complete American division to set foot in France.[11]

The rushed crossing displayed precisely the kind of "Rough Rider" spirit the War Department wanted to eliminate. At a time when shipping and supply lines were only just beginning to take shape, the New Englanders moved twenty-seven thousand men into France. The soldiers would feel the inadequacies of the army's fledgling procurement system through the winter. But by avoiding a several-month stint at Camp Greene, North Carolina, the Twenty-sixth was able to control its training more than the other state militias who remained at home. The Yankee Division, not unlike the machine gun company, was to some degree able to become a functioning organization on its own terms during its first months in France.

Also like the machine gun company, the division was soon made aware that it was part of a far larger organizational structure. The first instance of federal interference occurred while the troops were still arriving and involved the 102nd's own commander, Colonel Ernest L. Isbell. Isbell sent a telegram to Connecticut governor Marcus Holcomb on landing in France in mid-October. "All safe and well publish," his wire innocuously read. But when the note appeared on the front pages of several Connecticut newspapers, it set off a storm of protest. The Committee on Public Information (CPI) and the War and Navy departments charged that Isbell had violated their unofficial ban on the publication of troop arrivals in Europe. A CPI spokesman called it "the most flagrant case" the agency had yet encountered and insisted that "instant and drastic action must be taken." On October 14 the *New York Times* claimed that Isbell faced a court-martial.[12]

These initial reports were greatly exaggerated, and no charges were ever pressed. Still, Connecticut papers opposed any punishment, claiming that Isbell's telegram was not only reasonable but comforted a state deeply concerned about the welfare of its sons.[13] Whether the federal government backed off in the face of this outcry is unclear. In any case, the affair resulted in still another statement of Washington's authority over state militias. On October 20, the War Department issued a "sharp reminder" to National Guard officers, declaring that they were no longer "in the service of the states and owe no reports of their movements to their governors."[14] Clearly the federalization and merger of the New England guardsmen had not settled the question of their subservience. Relations between the Yankee Division and Pershing's general headquarters would in fact remain contentious for the remainder of the war: the New Englanders continued to think of themselves as guardsmen first, federal soldiers second.

When immigrant Aniello Aiello was asked in a postwar survey to discuss the training he received before going overseas, his reply was brief but instructive. The nineteen-year-old factory worker claimed simply that he "did not have much training in U.S."[15] As one of the last men to join the Italian machine gun company in June, this response is not surprising. The unit spent most of the summer of 1917 caring for the regiment's horses and mules and learning only the most basic elements of soldiering.[16] When the men departed for France, they carried only their packs and side arms. They left their distinctive tents and wide-brimmed hats back at Camp Yale, along with the company's livestock and machine guns. In short, Private Aiello and the rest of his comrades received no frontline training of any value before arriving in Landaville.

It is striking that a military organization with as little real preparation as the Yankee Division could be so jealous of its independence. But even though the soldiers basically knew only how to salute, march, and handle the equipment they left behind, the organizations they belonged to were well developed. Each company had a core of men who were longtime members, veterans of the weekly drills, annual encampments, and months on the Mexican Border that had preceded the wartime call-up. The crash course in trench warfare they were about to undertake was therefore filtered through a set of preexisting institutions, each with its own, well-defined sense of how things were done. The training period in the Neufchâteau area did not completely remake the Yankee Division. For almost every rookie like Aniello Aiello there was a Sergeant Jimmy Ceriani, whose sense of tradition and community roots preceded the new, federally mandated course of instruction.

The prewar history of the Italian machine gun company, though slightly different than most of the Yankee Division's other units, illuminates this fundamental aspect of their training experience. As we have seen, the *compagnia*, unlike New Haven's much older rifle companies, owed its existence to the federal government. In late 1914 the War Department insisted that the Connecticut National Guard create machine gun units in order to be eligible for federal funds. The Italians started out as a provisional unit under the tutelage of a U.S. Army specialist. From the summer of 1915 until well into the following year, a sergeant with thirty years' experience in the federal army taught the men how to become machine gunners.[17]

As professional as this training may sound, the unit in peacetime actually functioned much like the older New Haven companies. The men held regular jobs (many enlisted to make a little extra money) and were learning how to be soldiers in their spare time. Muster rolls from the winter of 1916–17 document the inadequacy of their instruction. The company met roughly one evening a week for an hour and a half. Attendance was erratic, ranging anywhere from fourteen to thirty-six men at a session, and the lessons remained basic even after the departure of the company's army tutor. As late as February 1917, a month before they were called into federal service, the men still were reviewing the nomenclature of their weapons, how to assemble, aim, and fire them, and of course, how to march and stand at attention.[18]

The fact that they met for training on Friday nights suggests that the company served just as much a recreational as a military purpose. In peacetime the unit acted very much like a social club, as had all American militias since colonial days. It was closer in character to one of the Italian colony's many *circoli* than to a crack army outfit. The members, mostly single men in their twenties, no doubt socialized after their far from grueling training sessions. They held dances and banquets during the year, just like their peers in the New Haven "Grays," "Sarsfields," "City Guards," and "National Blues." Even the weeklong encampments they attended with these other companies in 1915 and 1916 were largely recreational. Supposedly periods of intensive training, the late-spring encampments provided the men with an opportunity to leave the grind of dull jobs and spend a few days roughing it—and drinking beer—under an open sky.[19]

Federal service on the Mexican border during the summer and early fall of 1916 accelerated the company's development along similar lines: its training remained rudimentary, but its cohesiveness as an organization increased. Stationed in Nogales, Arizona, with the rest of the Connecticut National Guard, the men saw no action, spending most of their time building and maintaining campsites, drilling, and monotonously patrolling the border. Arriving in time for the rainy season, they had to endure oppressive heat, flash floods, and dangerous electrical storms, and because of a smallpox scare their first base earned the nickname "Camp Disease." But as would be the case during the winter in Landaville, the more miserable the conditions the greater the pride the men felt in overcoming them. By the end of their four-month stay, the machine gunners had built up enough stamina in the desert heat to complete long hikes and perform well in regimental maneuvers. Though delighted to return home in October 1916, the members of the year-old machine gun company were able to claim a solid, if unglamorous, record of achievement.[20]

The border mobilization also introduced the company to the discontents of being under the control of the federal government and its regular army representatives. A definite "us" and "them" psychology pervades the regimental historian's account of their service. Captain Daniel Strickland wrote that on the first night in Nogales, the men went to sleep "with a feeling that Uncle Sam cared little whether or not the 'Mexies' came over and cut their throats." During the entire period from call-up to federal discharge, "little or no information passed down from high authorities to the troops." But what grated even more than these feelings of uncertainty were the "hard-faced, harsh-voiced" inspector-instructors whom the guardsmen had no choice but to obey. "There was no let up on the part of the 'regular army,' " Strickland recorded, "either in its unfriendly attitude toward the officers of the National Guard, or prejudiced opinion of the men in the ranks." This view of their army superiors as outsiders and rivals took firm root during the months on the Mexican border.[21]

In the five months that passed between their return from Nogales and the American declaration of war in April 1917, the machine gun company, like the Connecticut National Guard as a whole, lost many members. After the hardships and disruptiveness of border service, hundreds of guardsmen obtained discharges and the state's various companies fell far below wartime strength. But more than two dozen Italian machine gunners stayed on. And despite the federally imposed changes that occurred just before the company's departure for France, its leadership remained the same. Captain John Shipke of Wallingford and First Lieutenant Howard "Pop" Williams were still the outfit's commanding officers. Retaining their noncommissioned status were Jimmy Ceriani, Alexander Bon Tempo, and six other company sergeants. Together with the corporals, buglers, cooks, and privates who were also veterans of Nogales, this core of committed members served as the backbone of the unit as it prepared for frontline duty.[22]

The company's prewar function as a local institution made up of friends and relatives, its sense of accomplishment and ability, and its antagonism toward the regular army were shared by most of the other units of the "new" Yankee Division. The company also had a strong sense of community roots, one that was unique in its Italian flavor but very similar to that of its peers. The machine gunners did not identify with the spirit of '76 or '61, or the inspiration of Bunker Hill and Gettysburg. For most members the battles raging on Italy's Isonzo River were far more important. But they certainly felt strong ties to their own New England community, the *colonia* that had celebrated every major event in the unit's brief career.

"Three Anthonys" best expressed this bond in a letter to the company's "godmother," Juliette Poli, after they took up positions on the front lines. "Don't worry that we all take a good look now and then at the flag which was presented to us at Yale Field," wrote Privates Denegro, Della Camera, and Maresca in March 1918. "And of course we all have our crosses with us around our necks since the day they were put there by yourself and your sister."[23] The Yankee Division's sense of autonomy sprang from precisely these sources. The institutional culture of the most independent-minded division in the AEF enabled the Italians' community ties to remain strong.

In Neufchâteau, the company once again confronted federal training policy. While the guardsmen wanted to get right into the fight (or so the regimental historian claims), the War Department had different plans. With the endorsement of Secretary Newton Baker, General Pershing's staff insisted on a three-stage course of instruction for most American soldiers. This "ideal" program consisted of six months of basic and intermediary training in the United States, three months of trench preparation in France, and three months of occupying a quiet sector on the western front. Military planners knew on entering the war that it would take at least a year for the AEF to be a substantial presence in the trenches. In the meantime, they set out to organize the troops in a comprehensive manner.

On paper, the Yankee Division and its Italian machine gunners followed this program. In reality, their training from November 1917 to February 1918 was almost as inconsistent as the preparation they received in the States. Transforming a division of part-time soldiers into full-time combatants would have been difficult under the best of circumstances. But a severe French winter, serious supply problems, and the inability of the nascent AEF to direct the Yankees' training put Pershing's ideal out of reach. Ironically, the division's early arrival in France prevented its instruction from being as thorough as possible. At the same time, the privations the men endured became still another source of regimental pride. With characteristic reverence for the past, most Connecticut guardsmen referred to the Landaville winter as their "Valley Forge."[24]

Private Louis Popolizio might not have been familiar with the Continental Army's hardships in Pennsylvania. But he had ample reason to agree with the comparison. "The first few months in France were hard ones," he later recalled: "Cold winter nights we couldn't keep warm. Cold feet lots of hard training. On the go all the time. That's where I learned to swear."[25] Life did not get any easier for the company after the arrival of the rest of the Nutmeg regiment. In late October, Colonel Isbell reported that the 102nd was "entirely without its own transportation," having only a handful of horses and bicycles at its disposal. The men had to carry heavy sacks of flour and drums of tinned beef on their backs well into November and food was always scarce. Lacking a labor battalion during their first months in the Neufchâteau area, they not only had to continue the difficult work of converting their villages into camps, but also cut and haul their own firewood and do their laundry alongside and in the same age-old manner as their peasant neighbors.[26]

Neither could the soldiers find comfort in the basic necessities of shelter and clothing, which were also of poor quality and in short supply. The unceasing rain of autumn and snowfalls of early winter made these inadequacies all the more aggravating.[27] Most of the men slept in the haylofts of cottages whose livestock inhabitants had just recently been removed, with

lice as uncomfortable bedfellows. With only the remote possibility of receiving new uniforms, the men became experts in mending and creating
makeshift substitutes for their clothing. Especially serious was the lack of
proper footwear, as the summer boots of Camp Yale fell apart. Constant
heavy rains turned the area into a quagmire with a harsh effect on the
soldiers' feet. "The ever present damnable mud all about," recalls one officer,
"mud of the consistency of putty or mid-west 'gumbo,' clinging to shoes,
boots, and clothes so that a soldier worked, drilled, or paraded with anywhere
from one to five pounds of mud attached to each foot." Long before the
102nd entered the frontlines, some men suffered from chilbain or "trench
feet," "which in some cases caused the flesh to fall from the heels and toes."[28]
These conditions delayed and marred the regiment's new training. The
"sunny France" all of the men had envisioned became a cruel joke, and
many developed bronchitis and pneumonia. Morale problems would plague
the 102nd during most of its stay in Landaville.[29]

Only in late November 1917, nearly three months after the machine
gun company left Camp Yale, did the unit have the equipment necessary to
begin preparation for the front. The arrival of the new helmets, gas masks,
and machine guns temporarily alleviated the weariness of camp life, focusing
the men's anxious attention on the hard work that lay ahead. These new
pieces of equipment, which became constant companions for each Italian
gunner through to the armistice, symbolized much more than the start of a
new course of instruction. All were manufactured in British and French
factories, reflecting how unprepared America was to fight a modern war. The
AEF was also totally lacking in officers with trench experience and had to
rely heavily on the expertise of Allied instructors. The machine gunners, like
most doughboys in this early stage of U.S. intervention, now had to master
foreign-made equipment under the direction of foreign soldiers. Their success and survival depended on acquiring an entirely new set of skills under
very difficult conditions and in a very short period of time.

With winter fast approaching, the most basic equipment, the British-
made boots and helmets, arrived first and were the most appreciated by the
men of the company. "The big hobnailed shoes wore well," recalls one gunner, "protected the feet somewhat from rain and mud, and afforded a measure of comfort, if they did not look very attractive." Especially cherished
were the "tin derbies" for which the soldiers found numerous uses other
than protecting the head from shrapnel. "The trench helmets were a Godsend," remembers Private Ratcliffe Hills. The gunners used them as wash-
basins, drinking bowls, umbrellas, bookstands, baskets, and even candle-
sticks. In the muck of campsite and trench, they also discovered that the
helmets made good resting places. "The men used to sit in them and ma-
nipulate them with their feet like a revolving chair," writes Hills. Having
accustomed themselves to the regiment's supply problems, the machine gunners knew to make the most of whatever they received.[30]

Learning to use the new gas masks and machine guns was a much more onerous task. Not only did this equipment require considerable instruction and constant care, but it also provided the men with a detailed knowledge of the many ways a machine gunner could be killed in the frontlines. In mid-November, the company received the most effective protection against chemical warfare at that time, the British Small Box Respirator. "The masks were queer-looking," recalls one gunner, "especially when you saw a whole regiment with them on." Made of rubber cloth, the mask was connected to a filtering canister by a short hose, the whole unit kept in a canvas satchel and worn at a man's side at all times. When a gas alarm sounded, a soldier had to quickly secure the mask to his face with leather straps, then pull the satchel around and attach it to his chest. As Private Hills remembers, "it pinched the nose very tightly, and a fellow consequently had to breathe through a rubber tube, held in the mouth. He peered through a sort of glasses, which looked like those the motorcycle 'cops' wear." The machine gunners learned that in combat they would frequently have to wear the hot, sweaty masks for a period of several hours and would not be able to eat or drink during this time. In addition to protecting themselves, they were also taught how to fit respirators on the company's pack animals and build gas-proof shelters in the field.[31]

As tiring and troublesome as the masks were, the men were well aware of the horrors that befell an unprotected soldier. By the time they started training, all of the major chemical compounds in Germany's arsenal were well known. Through lectures and practice sessions, the guardsmen learned of the gases' deadly effects in graphic detail. The chemical weapons that had been used at the front since mid-1915 were the easiest to defend against. These damaged the respiratory system, causing victims to "drown" from excessive fluid in the lungs and die after hours of agonizing convulsions. In practice gas chambers, the men worked with the two most common gases of this type: Chlorine, with its greenish-yellow tint and pungent odor, and Phosgene, a colorless vapor with a scent that resembled freshly cut hay. Both dissipated quickly and were readily detectable, and the guardsmen's masks provided sufficient protection.[32]

Far worse was Germany's latest chemical weapon, mustard gas. The men learned that its vapor could be absorbed through the skin as well by inhalation, and penetrated ordinary clothing, even their heavy trench boots. Often impossible to detect by sight or smell, mustard gas could persist at a high level of toxicity for days and even weeks. Most insidious was its latency period. Not until well after becoming infected would a soldier suffer from the initial symptoms of vomiting, blindness, and severe skin blistering. By this time great internal damage had already been done, and in fatal cases the circulatory and central nervous systems steadily deteriorated until the victim finally succumbed. Chemical warfare was the one element of the training for which the men had no previous experience. Attending these lectures, they must have felt very far from the days of summer encampments and weekly muster rolls.[33]

Machine gun training, in contrast, was nothing new to the company. But the French Hotchkiss guns the men received were very different from the weapons they were accustomed to using. Back home the company only worked with the complicated Benet Mercier machine rifle, a weapon the Allies had long since rejected as too unreliable for trench use. The Hotchkiss, a much bigger and heavier gun, had become the mainstay of the French infantry, and as a YD officer noted, its "simplicity and dependability were at once apparent."[34]

Although benefiting from Allied experience, the men had to learn to use their new weapons from scratch—a plodding, methodical course of instruction that took nearly two months to complete. Before ever pulling a trigger, they had to know the name and function of every part and be able to assemble and repair the guns while blindfolded. In practice sessions, they studied the Hotchkiss's distinctive traits and foibles. Instructors rigged the weapons to jam, and the men became adept at discovering problems and fixing them as quickly as possible. Along with endless loading, aiming, and firing drills, the company also learned to read topographical maps, build camouflaged nests, and move and find cover in open country. They found the fifty-two-pound Hotchkiss, which was twice the weight of their previous weapon, to be a much greater burden. The company had to march several miles to a firing range and to the regiment's practice trenches, making for a day that started well before dawn and lasted well into the evening. Since pack mules could only be used behind the frontlines, much of the exhausting work of hauling the guns and heavy cartridge strips fell literally on the men's shoulders. Already weighed down with the doughboy's standard seventy pounds of equipment and rations, the men had little to celebrate during December and January.[35]

Looming over this training was the grim knowledge of what a gunner faced in the trenches. The awesome killing power of the machine gun during World War I is well known. Less recognized is the extremely high mortality rate among the men who had to operate them. The company soon discovered machine gun units at the front were called "suicide clubs." Opening fire with a Hotchkiss, a three-man team immediately became the target of every enemy soldier in the vicinity. Bullets, grenades, mortar shells, and flamethrowers then pummeled an active nest until the guns were silenced.[36] If captured, the gunners were shown no mercy. "[They] were never taken prisoner by either side," a marine remembered, adding that "a machine gunner's only chance was to be taken while he was away from the gun, and his captors did not know he had any connection with it." "The reason is obvious," explained Sergeant Carl Brannen, "for when a man sat behind a gun and mowed down a bunch of men, his life was automatically forfeited."[37] The men worked very hard through the winter, knowing the guns were key to their survival. By late January 1918 inspectors deemed them ready to occupy a quiet sector of the front.

Only the Allied armies had enough experience to direct this training.

For much of their stay in Landaville, the Connecticut regiment labored under the scrutiny of France's 167th Regiment d'Infanterie. The machine gun company paired up with its French counterpart, a veteran unit of similar size.[38] Initially, the language barrier was a source of confusion. "Hard as it was to master the [Hotchkiss]," an observer comments, "that task couldn't compare in complexity and intricacy with the mastery of the French language."[39] Even with a Frenchman serving as interpreter and language teacher for the company, the lack of direct communication caused frustration on both sides.[40] A YD gunner described his first day of firing practice: "*Poilus* [French soldiers] trying to teach us how to do it. They got excited because we couldn't 'savvy' their lingo and resorted to shouting and a free use of gesture."[41] Despite these difficulties, the two units got along very well together. The guardsmen listened carefully to each piece of advice the French had to offer. And the *poilus* deeply appreciated the company's presence, not only for coming all the way from America to aid their fight, but also, no doubt, for giving them a reason to be away from the frontlines.[42]

Able to stick together during this training, the Italian gunners most likely did not have as much trouble communicating with the Frenchmen as the rest of the company. The differences between the *colonia* men's native tongue and French were not as great, and some of the soldiers might have been able to speak both languages.[43] The divided character of the machine gun company aided their fraternization. The federal consolidation at Camp Yale combined but did not integrate the New Haveners with their Hartford-based colleagues. When the company broke down into three man teams, the Italians most likely worked together just as before the merger. Ethnic clustering was in fact greatest during the first weeks of instruction, when the unit's non-Italian officers were sent to separate training schools and casualties had not yet begun to take their toll on the unit's membership. During the practice sessions, pockets were therefore able to form where only Italian and French were spoken. For the New Haven Italians, the period in Landaville was one of the few times when being an immigrant in the U.S. Army was not a disadvantage.

The novelty of working with trench equipment and the exotic French *poilus* soon wore off, and by mid-December 1917 regimental morale plummeted to one of its lowest levels during the war. A soldier's description of his typical day best captures the toil and boredom. "Up at daylight to roll call, from hard bottomed bunks or seedy hay lofts," remembered Captain Strickland, "then to the chilly horse trough or no wash at all, followed by 'sowbelly' boiled in its own fat with bread and black coffee, this was the introduction to a hard day's work that ended with supper under lantern light."[44] Landaville offered little escape from the drudgery of winter training, and no leaves of absence were granted during the regiment's entire stay. As with food and supplies, pay was meager and long in coming, and mail from home, that most precious of commodities for the homesick soldier, arrived very late and infrequently. For recreation there was just a small, poorly stocked YMCA hut. Because of the harsh weather, the men were unable to burn off steam by playing outdoor sports and spent more time keeping themselves and their campsites clean. To make matters worse, former rivalries between the old First and Second Connecticut regiments resurfaced, and rumors of widespread dissatisfaction began to "reach the ears" of division headquarters. By late December, the 102nd had acquired the reputation of being a "sick" regiment.[45]

It was at this point that the regular army, having been unable to monitor the New Englanders' training closely, once again reasserted its control over the Yankee Division. In early January 1918, the AEF's general headquarters transferred hundreds of officers to noncombatant branches of the service. The Nutmeg Regiment was hard hit by the orders. It lost nearly all of its line officers, including Colonel Ernest Isbell and machine gun company captain John Shipke. Little more than a month before entering the trenches, the guardsmen found themselves with an entirely different leadership.[46]

The removal of Isbell and Shipke is particularly significant, reflecting how domestic concerns influenced military policy abroad. Colonel Isbell made few friends in the AEF after sending his "all safe and well" telegram, but this was probably not the sole reason for his transfer. As the "sick" condition of the 102nd amply demonstrated, the New Haven lawyer did not have the skills necessary for inspiring a frontline regiment. Having proven himself a capable organizer and administrator, however, he was put in charge of a large base hospital for the remainder of the war. Knowing Isbell was popular back home, the War Department presented his reassignment as a promotion, and the press accepted this official line without criticism. "General Pershing considered Colonel Isbell the best man available for this work," the *New Haven Times Leader* reported."[47] Pershing probably had nothing to do with the transfer, but the story was essentially accurate. To lead the 102nd, it replaced the local attorney with a veteran West Pointer, Colonel John Henry Parker.

The only mark machine gun captain John Shipke had against him was the fact that he was born in Germany. A January 1 special order removed several frontline officers who had emigrated from enemy nations. Officially, the army claimed it was acting in the soldiers' best interests, arguing that if captured, German and Austrian Americans might suffer torture or summary execution. Unofficially, the AEF harbored the same fears of espionage as the Wilson administration back home, and no doubt these suspicions influenced the drafting of the order. The 102nd's regimental historian made sure to exonerate Shipke, describing him as "the loyal and competent Commandant of the Machine Gun Company." A naturalized citizen, Shipke had served in the Connecticut National Guard for more than two decades and had been with the machine gun outfit since its formation. But he was removed nonetheless, and completed his tour of duty commanding ambulance and military police units far from the western front. The gunners would now take orders from his chief subordinate, Lieutenant Howard "Pop" Williams, a native of Georgia.[48]

As disruptive as these transfers were for much of the regiment, the change in leadership turned out to be a blessing for the machine gun company. Colonel Parker, a twenty-five-year regular army veteran, had served in Cuba, the Philippines, Panama, and Mexico. Nicknamed "Gatling Gun" or "Machine Gun" Parker, he was a world-renowned strategist of rapid-fire weapons, having written a number of influential books and articles on their use. Organizer of the first machine gun unit in the history of the United States Army, he was serving as a weapons expert on Pershing's staff when transferred to the 102nd.[49] The Italians clearly gained from their new colonel's expertise, and the rest of the regiment also benefited from his boundless enthusiasm and plain-speaking manner. Addressing the men for the first time, he is quoted as shouting: " 'Now I want just one thing—Spirit!"

> I'm the old man,—the boss—see? But I'm going to give you all the grub and shoes and clothes I can beg, buy or steal. . . . But I want spirit! And here's a secret. Gather in close,—right around me. That's it! We're GOING TO FIGHT! (Cheers again)
>
> Now! Right away! (More cheers)

Captain Daniel Strickland described Parker as "the redeeming angel of the regiment," who welded the men together into a "willful machine" and imbued the 102nd with a tenacity it never would have possessed under the regulation-minded Isbell.[50]

No doubt Strickland and many other guardsmen also saw Parker as a modern-day Von Steuben, pulling the regiment out of the doldrums of its French "Valley Forge."[51] But the new colonel shared much more in common with his friend and San Juan Hill colleague, Theodore Roosevelt. Like the Rough Rider, Parker was a maverick of tremendous energy and ambition. His efforts to reform the army, first by demanding full-scale implementation of the machine gun, and later by calling for universal military training, were outspoken and controversial.[52] Parker's modernizing impulses had firm traditionalist roots, reflecting the "rougher and manlier virtues" his famous friend championed as "rugged individualism." Parker never treated the Connecticut soldiers with the contempt of a technocrat or career office, and his speeches were as appropriate for addressing a cavalryman armed with a saber as a doughboy working a Hotchkiss. "I will never send a man to face any danger, however great," he melodramatically promised the regiment, "that I would not willingly face myself."[53] At the front he would often leave the safety of a command post to man a machine gun alongside his troops.[54]

For the anxious and beleaguered guardsmen, Parker's vigor and confidence proved just the right medicine. Also appealing was his frequent identification in opposition to the military establishment. "You're going to get everything that's coming to you," he once told the men, "and there's no damn staff officers are going to say me no." Siding completely with his troops, he bellowed:

> Men of Connecticut!—You blue-bellied, shad eating Nutmeg Yanks, Damn your Yankee hides to hell! . . . Heads up! Stick your chests out! You're from the best fightin' stock in the world. . . . I'm of Connecticut stock too. My grandmother's cousin married a Connecticut Yank so you see I've got the blood in the family.[55]

This appreciation of the regiment's origins was not limited to the native-born. Nearly two decades earlier Parker had proposed to form a machine gun outfit made up entirely of black soldiers. His color-blind enthusiasm for training units was no less true when it came to commanding the pride of the *colonia*. At the front, he recommended the Distinguished Service Cross to two Italian soldiers and requested furloughs for them to visit kin in Italy. "There are many Italians in this regiment," he explained in his request, "and nothing could do the regiment more good than such a recognition of distinguished gallantry of its Italian members, many of whom have performed splendid service."[56]

In Parker, the machine gunners found an inspiring, yet also highly professional leader who recognized and accommodated himself to the localist culture of the regiment. His technical expertise in the handling and placement of machine guns might well have saved many members from injury and death, while his appreciation of the 102nd's hometown bonds allowed the company to maintain much of its ethnic cohesiveness. Encouraging the soldiers' pride in their communities, the new colonel also achieved the AEF's main objective: to turn the guardsmen into an efficient unit ready for combat. During the rest of the 102nd's stay in Landaville, which ended on February 1, 1918, and for the two months of continued training in the quiet sector of Chemin des Dames, the men acquired much of the confidence of their new leader.[57]

The Italian machine gunners' "education" in Landaville was not limited to military training. Serving in the American army exposed the Italians to the cultural practices and perspectives of their native-born peers. While converting their French village into a suitable AEF campsite, attending the regiment's holiday celebrations and motivational lectures, and fulfilling a variety of obligations as federal soldiers, the men received a crash course in American standards and attitudes (however regional the division's bias). These experiences challenged much of the men's Old World and *colonia* mindset; their identities as Italians and as transplanted Americans were being reformulated and expanded. Like the citizens' militia they belonged to, which the federal government insisted become more modern, the Italians found themselves increasingly having to act like their New England comrades. In both cases, these influences had a limited impact, since the traditionalism of the Connecticut National Guard and its former Italian machine gun company remained strong.

Much of this exposure centered on what one private called the "queer and unique" Neufchâteau area. Most American-born soldiers in the 102nd found their French environment to be "backward" and "a thousand years behind the times." "The village we are in is one of the first places God made instead of one of the last," Private Henry Schmitz of Company F wrote: "There are no street lights, can't call them streets here anyway; no trolley cars or anything that makes a real town or city. I thought West Haven was bad, but it's great compared to this." The guardsmen marveled at how the people still wore wooden shoes, cooked over large fireplaces rather than stoves, and received their news from a town crier who beat a drum. Of special interest were the peasants' homes, usually one-story stone buildings housing a family and its livestock under one thatched roof, and the fifteenth-century Catholic church that dominated the small village square. "The French peasant has not many more comforts and conveniences," concluded Private Hills, "and in some respects he has less, than our pioneer ancestors had."[58]

Much the same could have been said of the small southern Italian villages that most of the machine gunners remembered all too well. Unlike their native-born colleagues, the immigrants viewed Landaville in the context of a three-way comparison, blending memory and nostalgia with the knowledge of how far they had traveled since their childhoods. Many of the gunners might have agreed with the doughboy from the Seventy-seventh Division who remarked, "As I was from Europe, England and France held no surprises for me, that's why I came to the U.S." Whatever they felt about America, the telephones, indoor plumbing, and industrial shops of the Elm City had become an inescapable part of their lives. Most of the men could not afford modern-day "comforts and conveniences." But as auto mechanics and factory workers their experiences in America were defined in ways that had little in common with the rural rhythms of a farming community. Immigrant sergeant Anthony Teta reflected this dislocation when he described Landaville in a letter to a non-Italian friend: "It is one of those old-fashioned towns you often see in movies."[59]

But the small village represented much more than a flashback or cultural reference point for the Italian immigrants. It was also a place that had to be transformed to meet U.S. Army standards of cleanliness and hygiene. The Neufchâteau region had been a training area for French soldiers during the previous two years, but this meant little to AEF commanders. A Yankee Division officer commented after the war: "Anyone who has experience in France knows that a town billeted for five hundred French soldiers will hardly ever accommodate five hundred Americans." The primary concern was with what one observer called "sanitary problems" that were five hundred years old: "We were unaccustomed to a country in which . . . the manure heaps were piled along the streets and regarded as an evidence of wealth on the part of the property holder. To make the town sanitary and fairly decent took the combined strength of our entire outfit." Along with a sewage system, the men built bathhouses and a fire station, and installed street signs with new names like "Capitol Avenue" and "Lafayette Street." When the Italian gunners sang "My Landaville," a tune their native-born comrades had adapted from a popular American song, the possessiveness was not purely sentimental. As much as was possible, the Italian soldiers had converted a place that resembled their land of origin into an American setting.[60]

Day-to-day contact with their Yankee colleagues had a greater impact on the Italians than the French landscape. Other than accounts of the men's recreational activities, little has survived to illustrate this process of "cultural exchange." It is unclear, for example, whether Louis Popolizio learned to swear in English or Italian, or both. In late December, Private Anthony Amici wrote home about snow sledding on "rippers" the soldiers made, a pastime clearly not enjoyed in the province of Salerno. Most significant were the two occasions when the regiment got a break from the drudgery of training. For Thanksgiving and Christmas, the War Department and the state of Connecticut provided the men with the traditional fixings. Many of the Italian gunners experienced their first Thanksgiving dinner in France, which Anthony Teta described as "lots of turkey, apple pie, cranberry sauce, mashed potatoes, stuffing, gravy, etc." For Christmas, in addition to what the Lenzi brothers called a "wonderful feast," the regiment placed and decorated a large tree in the center of Landaville, bought gifts for the children and a stained glass window for the church, and provided a Santa Claus—a clerk from Company M in costume.[61]

Dominated by traditionalism and local pride, the Italian soldiers had only a fleeting sense of belonging to a larger, national culture. Every soldier in the AEF, whether a draftee or volunteer, received a heavy dose of patriotic propaganda, most commonly in the form of rousing talks on American ideals and the causes of the war. But for the YD men, these efforts seem to have focused mainly on Teutonic atrocities. When Major General Clarence Edwards, the Twenty-sixth's commanding officer, toured the different regiments, he would lead the soldiers in singing the Civil War standard "Battle Cry of Freedom," which he held to be the anthem of the division. His speeches were of equally violent righteousness:

> I want you to strike for humanity and civilization, for God and country. Strike for devastated France and little Belgium, strike for the outraged honor of womanhood, strike to rid the seas of the submarine assassinators of innocent little children and cause the German beast to come whining and crawling for undeserved mercy.

In their letters home, old stock and immigrant guardsmen alike transmitted these sentiments, made all the more poignant by their firsthand observations of wartime France. "If you could see the results of the German barbarism," a private wrote to his parents, "you would not wonder why the French nation and its allies are persisting in prosecuting this war until a complete victory is gained." Anthony Teta told a friend, "After all the official reports that are read to us of the Boche atrocities, we won't be apt to show mercy when we get into the trenches." Imbued with a moralistic purpose so strong it could motivate the men to want to kill, the sense of nationhood the Italians received had more in common with a Puritan sermon than a lesson in democracy and citizenship.[62]

Yet a letter that immigrant bugler Alfonso Cappuccio sent to his family illustrates very concretely the new relationship the gunners and their kin were developing with their adopted country and its government, in spite of the Yankee Division's parochialism. "Let me know," Cappuccio wrote to his father Angelo, "if you are getting the $15 a month I am sending you. Starting in February you are to get $50 a month because we have all signed a paper stating how much we were taking home when we worked in the shop." Most of the soldiers, having little need for money abroad, had much of their pay sent to their families. The men also designated their kin as co-owners of Liberty bonds and as beneficiaries of government War Risk Insurance if they died in service. Becoming bondholders and recipients of federal pay was totally new to most if not all of the gunners, and the government's insurance policies were a far cry from the meager assistance of a New Haven *societa di mutuo socorrso*. Cappuccio writes, "I have insurance for $10,000 [the standard soldier's policy]. If I get killed you will get that money inside of a month." Cappuccio's letter proved grimly prophetic. A month after the armistice his family received a War Department telegram stating that Alfonso was killed in action near Verdun. The insurance payments the Cappuccios received over the next several years were the last tangible contact the family had with their twenty-five-year-old son.[63]

Though the New Haven gunners experienced far less exposure than what New York's drafted Jews would encounter, the Italians were able to learn something about American culture and institutions while in Landaville. The popular postwar expression, "how're ya gonna keep 'em down on the farm, after they've seen Paree?" would prove, in a certain sense, to be true of the pride of the *colonia*.

Just before they entered the trenches in early February, the members of the 102nd received their last articles of equipment. Along with ammunition and a first aid kit, each man was issued two aluminum disks stamped with his name, rank, and serial number. The guardsmen tied the new "dog tags" on a piece of cotton string and placed it around their necks. For the Italian gunners, the tags were a second piece of identification, worn alongside the engraved crucifixes the *colonia* had given them at the Yale Field ceremony. A few weeks after leaving Landaville on February 1, 1918, the company endured artillery barrages, bombardments of mustard and phosgene gas, and a number of night patrols near enemy lines. Inexperienced and inadequately trained, the gunners faced their dangerous task as members of an immigrant community, a local institution that was trying to keep its independence, and the army of a nation at war.[64]

A significant manifestation of this complex identity was the fact that no Italian member of the company would ever be promoted to a rank above sergeant, and until casualties began to take their toll, those who wore more than a private's stripe exercised authority only over other Italians. This was not simply the result of ethnic discrimination. A major attraction in joining the original company was to serve with *connazionali*, and dividing the merged unit along linguistic lines made sense. Becoming an officer meant not only three months at a special training school, but reassignment to a different division. This was not a desirable alternative for the machine gunners.

Honoring local ties above all, the 102nd permitted this form of self-segregation. Still maintaining much of its original structure and attitudes, the regiment's tradition of making officers of respected community members also helped enforce it. Federal attempts to modernize the National Guard could only go so far. The Yankee Division's conservatism did not challenge the clustering of Italian soldiers. The *colonia* men were able to sustain their military *colonia*, a characteristic of their army careers that was evident long after they returned home as veterans.

5 Being Jewish in the National Army

✯ ✯ ✯ ✯ ✯ ✯ ✯ ✯ ✯ ✯ ✯ ✯ ✯ ✯ ✯ ✯ ✯ ✯

When Sergeant Anthony Teta of the 102nd Infantry wrote home from France in January 1918, he described a double standard in the treatment of American soldiers. "We occasionally get a New Haven paper here," he told a friend, "and from it, I notice that considerable [*sic*] is being done for the drafted men." Teta, having endured three months in Landaville with the Yankee Division, felt that this attention was unfair, since the draftees "are in the States and so near home. . . . It is certainly overlooking us volunteers," he concludes, "who are soon to see the real stuff and give up their lives for the great cause."[1]

These were not idle complaints. The federal government's treatment of the conscript army, as well as newspaper coverage of the new training camps, was indeed extensive, reflecting both the public's curiosity and its apprehensions over having kin and neighbors drafted into military service. More than 600,000 civilians poured out of local communities and into the National Army's training camps during the fall and winter of 1917–18. Most of the cantonments were located a short drive from major cities, making easy access to the troops possible for both families and the press. This high visibility encouraged close scrutiny of what the young men were experiencing. In addition to concern for the soldiers' safety, the public was well aware of the infamous, disease-ridden conditions of the Spanish-American War and expressed a strong desire to rid the camp communities of the vices traditionally associated with soldier life. New York City's eastern European Jewish population, which provided thousands of men for training at Camp Upton, had even greater cause for worry with its enduring memories of czarist conscription.

The War Department had to counteract these fears. Unlike the Yankee Division's experience in France, draftees were pampered by authorities who made sure they were well fed, housed, and clothed, that they led "exemplary" moral lives and were able to observe their religious beliefs as much as possible.[2]

But the stateside training experience of men like Meyer Siegel, Abraham Krotoshinsky, and Irving Goldberg was more than a story of interaction between local communities and the federal government. Before they were sent overseas, soldiers had to tackle many inadequacies that resulted from the pace and scale of so major a project. Captain Julius Ochs Adler, whose Jewish family owned the *New York Times*, recalled the atmosphere that pervaded the training period. "Everything was new. It was a new life and every day so many new problems had to be solved. Everyone felt they had to be solved before the Regiment was declared proficient enough to embark for France, the great objective."[3] Pressed for time, the men of the polyglot Seventy-seventh Division had to overcome language barriers and cultural differences as well as basic problems of infrastructure and training. Learning how to become "good Americans" and good soldiers, they also taught the War Department a great deal about the needs of a modern, urban, and multiethnic army. The New York draftees did not simply comply with federal orders, but exerted their own influence on the making of this new American institution.

As an immigrant, Sergeant Anthony Teta probably would have found remarkable the respect the federal government accorded draftees from the nation's "melting pot," particularly its eastern European Jews. While the Italian machine gunners still enjoyed much of the ethnic cohesiveness they brought from New Haven, the Jewish draftees of the Seventy-seventh could point to the respect accorded them by the United States government as honored citizens, regardless of birthplace.

In the fall of 1917, New York City's quota for the first installment of the draft was thirty-eight thousand residents. The selected men did not leave for training at once, but in small increments. Wave after wave of recruits gathered at the city's 189 local draft boards in groups of thirty to seventy-five men at each call-up. Draft boards and the neighborhoods they represented held "send-off" celebrations, much like the New Haven *colonia's* farewell for the Italian machine gun company. "New York resembled a series of villages, each with its local board as town centre," a reporter commented on September 10, the first day of the draft call. These events were repeated on more than twenty mobilization dates during the fall of 1917. Many of the men were treated to a farewell dinner the night before their departure. They appeared at their draft board with family and friends the following morning and were honored in ceremonies that included speeches and band concerts. Several boards and community groups provided luncheons, gifts, and comfort kits, and the men traveled to their respective train stations in parades of automobiles donated for each occasion. "The local Board did things up mighty well," a draftee noted. "I find myself possessed of a razor, razor strop, wrist watch, two pocket knives, unbreakable mirror, drinking cup and a lot of other things that I never expected to own or need. I haven't the remotest idea where many of them came from." The men often carried signs that proclaimed their community pride: "We're from Hell's Kitchen, We'll Keep the Kaiser Itchen" and "Gas Bombs for the Kaiser from the Boys of the Gas House District." Crowds anywhere from several hundred to five thousand attended these ceremonies.[4]

Anguish and dissent were also apparent amid all this hoopla. Immigrant women and New York's Jewish population were most conspicuous in lamenting and protesting the departures. On September 29, a reporter covering the departure of a group of East Side draftees witnessed a heart-wrenching scene: "The poise of each of the hundreds of mothers, sweethearts and wives seemingly broke at the same moment. They wept. They screamed. They clung tenaciously to their men. Some swooned. The commotion delayed the trains in leaving." The frequency of these disturbances, which included women fighting with police to stay longer with their men, compelled the city to prohibit onlookers from the train platform. By mid-October the departures were running more smoothly, prompting one official to make the dubious claim that "the women folks are beginning to see the bright side of it."[5]

The only antidraft incident occurred in the heavily Jewish neighborhood of Williamsburg in Brooklyn. On the morning of September 21, 1917, a large group of relatives and friends prevented several inducted men from appearing before their local board. The crowd grew to a few thousand as officials attempted to escort the thirty-three other draftees to a fleet of cars parked nearby. "Here several persons rushed forward," the *New York Herald* reported, "they seized the hands of selected men, attempted to drag them from the automobiles, hurled epithets at the leaders and shouted their opposition to the draft." A reserve police unit rushed over to clear the streets, but not before one car was so badly damaged it broke down on the way to the train station. The *Herald* placed the blame on the circulation of radical leaflets in the area, which "influenced the parents and relatives of the selected men, particularly foreigners and socialists." Though the "near riot" was more spontaneous than planned, it illustrates how anxiety about the draft still ran high among eastern European Jews.[6]

More troubling to authorities were the reports coming from Camp Upton and the city's draft headquarters. Doctors at Yaphank physically disqualified 3.5 percent of the men who arrived at camp that fall, men who were supposed to have been carefully examined at their local boards. And Upton officers found that many men should have been exempted from service because they had dependents or were undocumented aliens. Even more disturbing, New York's Selective Service chief announced that of the nearly twenty-seven thousand draftees who had been called up by late October, fifteen hundred failed to report for induction. Authorities soon discovered mistakes in the draft lists; dozens of men had joined other branches of the armed forces or were already training at Upton. When the city press printed the names and addresses of the supposed delinquents, dozens more claimed they had been ill, in jail, out of town, or had never received their induction notices. But this still left several hundred men who were evading the draft altogether, risking two-year prison sentences rather than taking up arms. War boosters like the *New York Times* quickly vented their disgust. "While none of the [draft evaders] is physically a weakling, all must be lacking in moral strength. They are clearly the victims of the evil influence of the pacifists and other disloyal persons who have been, openly sometimes, but generally by underhand means, persistently trying to defeat the Government's military plans."[7] Blaming an ever-diminishing group of draft opponents, the paper's editors could not accept the fact that many young men did not want to go to war.

Meanwhile, the more than 95 percent of the city's selected men who did not resist the draft were arriving at Camp Upton. Many wore their best clothes, a regrettable choice since the division was unable to issue uniforms until at least a week after each group arrived. Directed immediately to dining halls, they received their first article of army equipment, a six-piece mess kit. Next stop was a warehouse, where they were handed blankets and a mattress sack, which they then filled with, as one private remembers, "that nice new, fresh straw, the same kind that is used for the old grey mare." The conscripts finished out their first day in the army by being assigned to iron bunks in a temporary barracks. Sleep did not come easily. "That most of us worried until far into the night is certain," recalls one recruit. "I know I did, and the Italian on my left cried himself to sleep, and didn't try to hide his unhappiness either."[8]

Now on army time, the draftees were hustled out of bed at 5:30 in the morning for breakfast and calisthenics exercises. Camp doctors then examined them, and each conscript received the first of five shots for typhoid and diphtheria. The men were next shuffled through "matriculation," where they were fingerprinted, questioned about their schooling and occupational background, and asked in which branch of the division—infantry, artillery, engineers—they preferred to serve. After being sworn in to federal service, the new soldiers spent the next few days recovering from their inoculations, learning to salute and march, and waiting for assignment to permanent units.[9]

Conditions in Yaphank came as a surprise to the men, who had expected an impressive training facility. Instead, the newcomers compared early Upton to an Old West "boomtown." A chaplain wrote to his wife in late September 1917: "The camp is a howling wilderness of unfinished houses and unpaved streets and piles of lumber and debris. Some day it will be finished and clean and orderly. Now it is chaos." Upton was one of thirty-two cantonments across the country that the War Department rushed to build in the summer of 1917. The government allotted more than $200 million to provide shelter for 1.4 million soldiers, undertaking the largest construction project since the building of the Panama Canal. "In terms of numbers of men to be housed," recorded historian Edward Robb Ellis, "it was like building Philadelphia from scratch. In terms of space, it was like roofing all Manhattan, all Atlantic City and one square mile more." Despite having an army of more than ten thousand workmen at its disposal, a New York contracting firm had to clear an entire forest and fight swarms of mosquitoes in July and August. In addition to constructing more than fifteen hundred buildings, the builder also had to provide utilities and a three-mile railway extension. When the first recruits began to arrive in September, the camp was still only halfway completed.[10]

Until the conscripts departed for France in early April 1918, they spent much of their time finishing construction and, on their own initiative, securing comforts and necessities that the War Department was only beginning to recognize. The men in turn experienced the government's own method of addressing "chaos," as bureaucratic classifications and transfers became a constant headache. The new soldiers soon found themselves wielding picks and shovels, having few uniforms and no equipment to train with at first. Much of their physical conditioning consisted of hard labor on the camp's barracks and drilling fields. "Since I was one of the early arrivals," recalled Jewish draftee Edward Greenbaum, "pulling up stumps was among our jobs, and it is literally true to say that we helped to build the camp." Hauling lumber and firewood, filling mud holes, and helping raise the barracks' walls were activities that lasted well into November. Recruits who were firemen in civilian life inspected the camp for potential hazards, and former policemen served as traffic cops to direct the steady stream of construction vehicles. Once formed, the division's engineering companies built roads, firing ranges, and practice trenches. The cantonment was essentially completed in December 1917.[11]

The soldiers' contributions were not limited to the landscape of Yaphank. Drawing on the variety of skills and talents each unit contained, the men worked in their spare time to improve the quality of barracks life. This activity is best seen in the mimeographed pages of *The Bugle*, the "newspaper" of a rifle company in the 307th Regiment. Private Milton Weill, who in civilian life was an advertising man and officer in the Young Men's Hebrew Association, created and edited the paper, whose stated purpose was "to cement in close bonds of friendship the members of Company D." Visible among the paper's many inside jokes and complaints is an impressive record of cooperative effort. Men with carpentry experience built an incinerator, a shower platform, and a boardwalk to the company's latrine. Former teachers held English classes for thirty immigrant pupils. The men collected books for a library, officers donated a piano and a victrola for the barracks' recreation room, and the company's amateur musicians and entertainers put together skits and talent shows. Weill's *Bugle* encouraged and applauded these activities, while explaining the intricacies of War Risk Insurance, pay allotments, and the bolt-action rifle. The paper also bristled with a growing sense of esprit de corps, referring to the unit as "the best company in the best regiment in the best army in the world."[12]

These voluntary efforts to bring order to the "howling wilderness" that was early Upton highlighted the presence of ethnic soldiers. In his *New York*

Journal American dispatches, a drafted reporter described the work of "Giuseppi," an Italian barber, who set up a makeshift shop on weekends. "I can't guess how many he shaved," writes Irving Crump, "the line stretched the length of the dormitory from breakfast to dinner time." A large number of Italian and Greek draftees who were cooks in civilian life filled the most prized of army occupations, the professional cook. Jewish tailors and garment workers, so often degraded as "button-hole makers" in civilian life, also found their services greatly appreciated. The poor fit of the uniforms the men received was notorious, requiring a skilled hand to make alterations. Samuel Nagel, who ran a textile shop on the East Side, became the costume-maker for his artillery unit's theatrical productions. Improving camp life was a team effort, which in the polyglot setting of Yaphank included members of all ethnic backgrounds.[13]

The two most famous contributors to the health and well-being of Camp Upton were New York Jews. Benny Leonard, the lightweight boxing champion of the world, voluntarily enlisted in the army and served as a boxing instructor at the camp. Born Benjamin Leiner and raised in Greenwich Village by Russian immigrant parents, Leonard's sense of humor and skills in the ring made him extremely popular with the men at Yaphank. Nearly as famous at the time was songwriter Irving Berlin, who was drafted as a common buck private in the spring of 1918. An immigrant from Mohilev, Russia, the twenty-nine-year-old composer (whose birth name was Israel Baline) was a product of the Lower East Side. Berlin was able to convince Major General J. Franklin Bell to sponsor a big-time musical production on Broadway with actual recruits as performers. The show, entitled "Yip Yip Yaphank" helped raise funds for a camp community building, but Berlin's motives were also self-interested. A lifelong insomniac, he wanted to be exempt from the army's early morning schedule. "I really wasn't fitted to be a soldier," he recalled, "I was a songwriter. I knew entertainment." The musical premiered in August 1918 while the Seventy-seventh Division was fighting on the western front and eventually ran for six weeks on Broadway. The show's most popular number, which the songwriter sang on stage, was not surprisingly "Oh, How I Hate to Get up in the Morning." Another tune that Berlin wrote at Upton, which he shelved because he felt it sounded "just a little too sticky," would not seem at all sentimental during the next world war. It was the pop anthem "God Bless America."[14]

Whether their contributions to camp life were big or small, the soldiers collectively had a great impact on what the army considered a well-rounded training program. In fact, the first waves of conscripts anticipated the many new services that became available toward the end of the war. Auditoriums, libraries, chapels, and *Trench and Camp*, a newspaper published for all of the cantonments, quickly followed the men's arrival at the camps. But services for immigrant soldiers, which included an English language curriculum and special ethnic training battalions, were not created until after the

Seventy-seventh Division left for France. The army observed the behavior and needs of men at such polyglot camps as Upton, Dix, Grant, and Gordon, and developed programs that have been the basis of managing ethnic troops to the present day.[15]

In sharp contrast, the men had little or no control when it came to their unit assignments. Unlike Sergeant Jimmy Ceriani's simple and highly personal style of recruiting, which targeted men of Italian descent for a single company, the Seventy-seventh Division had to slot a wide variety of draftees into its many distinctive arms of service. A new arrival at Upton could end up in one of the division's four infantry regiments (the 305th to the 308th), in one of its three field artillery regiments (the 304th to 306th), in the 302nd Engineers, or in such support departments as the Quartermaster's, Field Signal, and Medical Corps. To complicate matters, Camp Upton housed a Depot Battalion, composed of men with very specialized talents who could be transferred to any part of the army in need of their skills. Finally, many ordinary soldiers could be reassigned to a different camp altogether. In October 1917, for example, seven thousand men left Yaphank to complete their training in Georgia as members of the Eighty-second Division.[16]

Only a large-scale bureaucracy could handle the high volume of incoming recruits. The army's classification system, designed in Washington with the aid of a team of employment analysts, demographers, and psychologists, collected detailed information from every man entering a camp. The most important part of a draftee's "matriculation" was the qualification cards that recorded his schooling and employment experiences. Could he type, handle a team of horses, or speak French? Was he a foreman or club officer in civilian life, accustomed to exercising authority over others? Upton officers sent duplicates of the cards to division headquarters and to the Committee of Personnel Classification in Washington. Based on the job categories of the U.S. Census Department, the army's internal census put key information at the fingertips of distant decision-makers. "No organization outside of an insurance company," Upton's chief personnel officer told the *New York Times*, "has so great and detailed an amount of information about its men."[17]

The impact of this bureaucratic effort may be seen in a postwar questionnaire filled out by Private Harry Litowitz. Asked to write down the names and addresses of other Jewish servicemen he had known, the veteran cited relatives and neighborhood friends. Eleven of these men lived on the same Brooklyn street as Litowitz. Yet of the seven obvious draftees from this list, only two served with him in the Seventy-seventh Division. The rest trained in New Jersey, Maryland, and Georgia and served in the Seventy-eighth, Seventy-ninth, and Eighty-second divisions. The drafted men from Brooklyn's Chester Street were scattered to wherever the army needed them, unlike the young men Jimmy Ceriani harvested from the *colonia*, who remained together unless they were wounded or killed. The ties of family,

neighborhood, and ethnicity, which played such a major role in the formation of the Yankee Division, had little influence on the creation of the
National Army.[18]

The efficiency of this process of classification was celebrated in official
statements and the daily press. But for the officers and men at Camp Upton,
who were busy struggling to make their units as cohesive as possible, the
transfer orders of the fall and winter were a constant source of frustration.
Captain Julius Adler remembers cursing "those pestilential qualification
cards, which, in many cases, were worse than Greek puzzles." A compound-
ing problem was the fact that a high percentage of the draftees only spoke
one of more than forty foreign languages. In the early weeks of mobilization,
Seventy-seventh officers were "in a quandary" because of an immigrant recruit whose language no Uptonite could understand. "Finally his English-
speaking brother arrived and all was well." Once completed, the cards often
revealed the location of a prized cook or mechanic, who would quickly be
reassigned to another unit. When the United States finally declared war on
the Austro-Hungarian Empire in December 1917, the division had to discharge hundreds of Austrian immigrants who were now declared enemy
aliens. The 305th Infantry's historian described the overall impact of these
changes: "In November, December, February, and again in March, each
company had been sifted down to a mere hundred or so [a company at full-
strength numbered 250]; all over again, the company commander would
have to organize his unit, re-size and re-distribute his men in order to balance
the platoons; and start in once more upon the rudiments of drill."[19]

Nor was this "scientific" scheme of assignments free of favoritism, prejudice, or grievous errors. Captain W. Kerr Rainsford recalls how a man with
disciplinary problems or "whose name on the roll call consisted only of
consonants" often found himself transferred to a southern camp. Private
Christian Blumenstein remembers skilled blacksmiths who were made cooks,
and dentistry students assigned as stable hands. But on the whole, Blumenstein endorsed the system. "Of course we do not expect Uncle Sam to always
hit the nail on the head," he writes, "but do the best he can, and which I
believe most of the time was well done [sic]." Service records seem to bear
this out. For example, *Bugle* editor Milton Weill was a graduate of Columbia
University. Born in America of German and Alsatian Jewish parents, he was
quickly promoted to sergeant, selected for officers' training in January 1918,
and assigned to an intelligence unit while in France. Eastern European immigrants Oscar Feinstein, a sweatshop worker and Abraham Krotoshinsky,
a barber, meanwhile, remained privates during their entire time in the service.[20]

Vestiges of neighborhood loyalty that might have survived the assignment process were further reduced when the units began full-time training
in mid-November 1917. Company pride superseded the localism that mo-
tivated "Harlem's Hun Hammerers" and the "Boys from the Gas House
District." But more was involved than boosting interunit rivalry and the

men's testosterone levels. Colonel George Vidmer of the 306th Infantry and many other Upton officers took the rhetoric of a truly democratic army to heart. Vidmer promoted a strong sense of citizenship among the thirty-six hundred soldiers under his command. He told his officers that draft board contingents had to be broken up. "All civilian associations were to be severed," recalls the 306th's historian, "and a new comradeship, based on the men's experiences in the Regiment in peace and war, fostered, so that there might be borne into civilian life after the war a greater understanding of democracy."[21] In theory, a man's birthplace or social status were less important than his abilities and contributions to his unit. Like many reformers of the era, officers such as Vidmer sought to replace the barriers of class and ethnicity with a leveling standard of professionalism and common opportunity. Upton's draftees would eventually take great pride in their cultural diversity, and New York City would regard the division as its "own." But these sentiments were not the defining factor in the Seventy-seventh's organization. A far cry from the Compagnia Italiana di New Haven and the "Nutmeg Regiment" to which it belonged, Gotham's portion of the National Army was imbued with a fundamentally modern impulse.

There was of course a great deal of confusion amid this whirlwind of transfers and promotions, of stump-pulling and technical instruction, which the complete lack of a divisional past did not make any less difficult to overcome. Unlike the Connecticut National Guard, the Seventy-seventh had no previous campaigns from which to draw inspiration, no sense of groundedness or direction that came with the knowledge of belonging to a well-established community organization or a celebrated historical tradition. The emotional power of unit loyalty had to develop from scratch.

Significantly, "that spirit first awakened" among the men of the 306th Infantry in early November when the regiment participated in the War Risk Insurance campaign. At first the draftees showed little interest in the federal program, but when the drive "was made a matter of regimental achievement there was a different reaction." Spurred on by the same kind of boosterism that marked the Liberty Loan and Red Cross campaigns, the "Three-Oh-Six" competed against its sister regiments, finally subscribing 100 percent to the government's insurance plan. Officers continued to encourage this rivalry, making competitions out of drills and organizing interunit boxing matches and sports tournaments. Each of the regiments soon created its own songs, emblems, and mottoes. Bonds of personal loyalty and mutual dependence evolved out of this competitive framework. A doughboy compared the close-knit feeling of his unit to the most basic and intimate of institutions: "We always looked upon the barracks as our home, and in addition to all else, our life resembled that of a great family." Despite the impersonality of the national draft process, the first residents of Yaphank quickly developed a level of psychological comfort to complement what the government provided materially.[22]

Central to this burgeoning sense of unit identity was the men's pride in having forged a fighting organization out of diverse components. Much like the volunteers of the Yankee Division, who prided themselves for overcoming physical hardships, Seventy-seventh men found strength in having successfully trained "the lawyer, the clerk, the storekeeper, the tradesman, and the artist, representing not alone the American born, but the citizen representative of nearly every country of the Old World." This array of ethnicities and occupations had to learn to live and work together at close quarters. Brought together for the first time and for such a deadly purpose, New York's "divers types" had no choice but, in the words of the divisional historian, to "bow down before the military God, *Authority*, and emerge from the melting pot of training, an amalgamated mass of clear-thinking, clean-living men of whom America might well be proud."[23]

With the camp and the division's units essentially in working order by mid-November 1917, the draftees now were able to begin their technical training. Unlike the Italian machine gunners' experience in Landaville, the division did not have to travel overseas to work with trench equipment and Allied advisers; these were provided at Yaphank. In the summer of 1917, the War Department developed a sixteen-week training course for all draftees nationwide. From November to early April 1918, the men at Upton followed Washington's orders, as each arm of the Seventy-seventh Division learned its special functions. Though the quality of this preparation was even more dubious than what the "Nutmeg" Regiment received in France, at least the draftees were learning the rudiments of trench warfare.[24] Infantrymen drilled with rifles and grenades, and practiced defending and attacking the camp's network of trenches. Artillery gunners learned to command and care for their teams of draft horses, to position and fire field guns, and to handle and transport heavy shells at the front. Perhaps the hardest labors fell to the 302nd Engineers, who carved trenches out of the rocklike winter soil and constructed barbed wire entanglements and bomb-proof shelters in subzero temperatures. Unlike the Yankee Division, the Seventy-seventh's conscripts did not have to be retrained for trench fighting. This was the only military training most had ever known. One officer could made an apt civilian comparison: "It was very much like going to school again."[25]

For the most part, the officers directing the men were not professional soldiers. When war was declared against Germany, the vast majority of future captains and lieutenants in the Seventy-seventh had as much military experience as the draftees—none. Nicknamed "ninety-day wonders" because of their three months of instruction, they found themselves constantly just a few steps ahead of the men. With the tremendous expansion of the country's armed forces, the War Department could only assign a skeleton crew of professional soldiers to each cantonment. The situation the 308th Infantry faced in the fall was typical. Of its more than three thousand members, the regiment could only count two officers and a handful of regular army drill sergeants who were active veterans.[26]

But what the division lacked in experience it made up for in the relatively up-to-date character of its preparation. The conscripts started working with frontline equipment at the same time as the 102nd's machine gun company, which had already been in federal service for nine months. By the end of January 1918, the draftees were wearing the same apparel as the Yankee Division and receiving instruction from veteran Allied officers. In the unlikely setting of rural Long Island, they experienced the same anxiety of entering practice gas chambers, hearing the roar of the same French artillery guns that guarded the western front, and observing the same model of tank that assaulted enemy lines at Ypres. Unlike the Compagnia Italiana, whose stateside preparation reflected the limited resources of the Connecticut National Guard, the federally directed training the draftees received was considerably more modern.[27]

It was in this fast-paced environment that the democratic aspirations of officers like Colonel Vidmer took most visible form. Before beginning their advanced training, every regimental company needed to be broken down into even smaller units: batteries, platoons, squads. This required the leadership of noncommissioned officers, which meant plucking some men out of the vast sea of buck privates and promoting them to corporal or sergeant. The liberal ethos of choosing an individual purely on the basis of skill and performance had its limits. Noncoms needed to speak, read, and write English reasonably well. Though a tough prerequisite for most immigrants, men of immigrant descent were well represented among the Seventy-seventh's promotions. Of the Jewish conscripts, New York-born brothers Max and Harry Pariser became corporals in the 308th Infantry, immigrant Nathaniel Kramer wore sergeant's stripes in the 305th, and Philip Beckerman, a native of Bessarabia in Russia, advanced to the rank of lieutenant. Even with the system's biases, most Jews could point to one or several coreligionists who exercised authority at Upton.[28]

Nonetheless, the transformation of Gotham's melting pot into soldiers did not come easily. Anecdotes abound, from the very first roll call, of the confusion between immigrants and native-born: of an Italian draftee answering to two completely different names, of three Morris Cohens serving in the same company, of a drill sergeant so exasperated with pronouncing difficult names he finally shouted, "Well, who in hell ever this is, answer here!" Captain Frank Tiebout describes how language problems were a constant obstacle. "Imagine the difficulties of teaching the rudiments of military art to men, however willing, who couldn't understand; officers have had sometimes to get right down on their hands and knees to show by actual physical persuasion how to 'advance and plant the left foot.' "[29]

Maurice Samuel, a Rumanian-born Jew who would later become a noted translator of Yiddish literature and a novelist, was a private at Upton that fall. His captain asked him to teach the basics of close order drill to immigrant recruits. Samuel would give the commands in English and then explain how to perform them in Yiddish. It was a difficult task, as the immigrants did not take the young man and fellow recruit seriously. A Russian Jew argued with him constantly, telling him at one point: " 'Look Samuel, I've been standing and walking on my feet for over twenty years, and I haven't fallen down since I was a baby. I can stand like this, and I stand like this'—he took up the various postures—'and I'm still standing. Give me a gun and I'll shoot all the Germans you want, but for God's sake *fardreh mir nisht a kop*—don't drive me out of my wits with that rubbishy left right, left right! Just tell me where to go and you'll see, I'll get there.' " When Samuel told his uncle about these problems, his relative could understand. "[My uncle] was also puzzled: where did I get the military terminology? He had never heard of such a thing in Yiddish, Jews had never fought in that language."[30]

Samuel's experience shows how the foreign-speaking draftees often responded to the new training on their own terms. Captain Julius Adler, taking command of a "well-drilled" company in early 1918, felt compelled to reorganize his subordinates according to height. But when he barked out the order "Right by Squads!" under this new arrangement, "some of the men did right face and some did left and some just stood still in consternation." Having previously seen the unit perform the same maneuver with ease, the "mystified" captain discovered that the men had grouped themselves along linguistic lines: "when a command was spoken in English each corporal hastily translated it in the language of his particular squad." Adler "immediately discarded his idea of symmetry," accepting what worked best. The immigrants also showed ingenuity when avoiding work that was not directly related to training. A universal complaint among officers was the use of the phrase "no spigh Ingleesh," which the recruits "discovered early in their military careers excused them from unpleasant duties that otherwise might have been thrust upon them." At first the pet phrase of immigrant draftees, this ruse quickly became popular among the native-born. An hour after excusing a private from a work detail because the man could not "spigh Ingleesh," an officer gathered his unit to give out weekend passes. The same recruit who claimed ignorance now said clearly, "Sure, I want a pass tomorrow." The men of the polyglot Seventy-seventh had developed their own ways of worshiping "the military God, *Authority*."[31]

With time, the Tower of Babel problem diminished. As the departure date for France approached, the men chattered in the military lingo of "mess," "kitchen police," and "communicating trenches," and spoke much less Yiddish, Italian, and Chinese. Despite his constant use of ethnic stereotypes in his newspaper dispatches, even drafted reporter Irving Crump was impressed with the immigrants' rapid progress and committed attitude:

> It is interesting to get their slant on the whole affair. Many of them didn't want to come. They had their own ideas of army life, suggested, doubtless, by tales they have heard of service in the European

armies of former days. But when they were called they came; and be-hold, when they arrived and lived through the first days, they were surprised to find that they still were treated like human beings, had certain indisputable rights, were fed well and cared for properly and worked under officers who took a genuine interest in their welfare. This was something most unexpected.

Right off they decided that they were going to get all they could out of this new life and give in return faithful and honest service.[32]

However they felt about their predicament, all of the men regardless of birthplace knew that survival on the front lines required every unit member to do his part. Observers frequently ascribed the immigrants' vigor to a newfound loyalty to America. But the newcomer trained hard for the same reasons as his old-stock comrades—his life and the lives of his "buddies" depended on it.

Certainly the tensions between nationalities and religions that marked life in New York City were also present at Camp Upton. Though difficult to document, it is hard to imagine that ethnic slurs, heated arguments, and even bare-fisted fights were not part of the men's training camp experience. But being in such close contact, and having overcome the same initial fears, the draftees eventually developed enough familiarity to deal openly with their various ethnic backgrounds. This is seen in the Seventy-seventh's unofficial anthem, "The Democratic Army." Mocking the rhetoric of war boosters, the song ends "Oh the army, the army, the democratic army! / All the Jews and Wops, the Dutch and Irish Cops, / They're all in the army now!" Two doughboys recalled how, when their company sang the tune, the men were "assisted in the grand finale by [unit members] Goldberg, Ginsberg, and Perlberg, holding up the Jewish end, Del Duca, Patrissi, and Carucci as Italian tenors, with Schmidt and Leumann carrying the air for the land of Dikes and Canals, supported by the heavy bassos Curley, Fallace, and Sar-gent, Erin's representatives of 'New York's Best.' "[33]

The draftees' song, however, did not include two other important pop-ulations laboring at Yaphank. A great class divide separated most of the draftees from the Seventy-seventh's officers. And the camp's nearly six thou-sand African Americans were completely excluded from the division because of their skin color. To attend the voluntary officer's training school in Platts-burgh in the spring of 1917, a college education, respected position, and enough personal wealth to leave one's work were necessary. Nearly all of the division's company commanders, men like Captains Tiebout, Adler, and Rainsford, received their commissions in this manner, resulting in a staff of inexperienced officers who had little in common with the ordinary conscript. In the 305th Infantry, nearly a quarter of the regiment's ninety-eight original officers were listed in the New York *Social Register*. In a letter home a lieu-tenant thanked his mother for having the family chauffeur bring a car down for use during weekend leaves, and when Lieutenant James Howard departed with his regiment for France in April, he was happy to find other Ivy Leaguers on board the same ship—all fellow officers.[34]

Little has survived that could document how these officers interacted with the men. Having been raised and educated to be leaders in their professions and communities, they had no doubts as to the legitimacy of their authority. Their attitudes toward their ethnic, working-class subordinates could have ranged anywhere from genuine sympathy to patrician aloofness to fears for the survival of the Anglo-Saxon race. In his regimental history, Captain Frank Tiebout relies constantly on ethnic stereotypes, describing one soldier as a "swarthy little Italian," and how a Jewish recruit, when asked to define a military picket, replied "Oh, yess, vat iss a picket? A picket iss a board mit sticks tacked on it." Another officer posted a sign early in the training that read, "This is an American army, and only English must be spoken."[35]

But there is also evidence of mutual respect between officers and men. After a hard day of training, Captain George Harvey would hold discussions where his draftees could air their concerns. "Dropping all formality," writes a corporal, "he drew the men out, by questions and answers, thus developing a foundation of sympathy and understanding that was the keystone of the company's morale." Private Christian Blumenstein described his "wealthy and proud" unit commander Captain John Prentice, who was listed in the *Social Register*, in similar terms. "Captain Prentice was leaving his beautiful home," writes Blumenstein, "his wife and two fine daughters, everything which he might otherwise enjoy, if he so desired. I used to enjoy to listen to him talk to our company, every word came straight from his heart, a square and fair deal to every soldier in his outfit." Blumenstein concludes that the company "felt quite proud in having a man of this type as their commanding officer." As the officers promoted men on the basis of performance, so did the soldiers judge their superiors on the quality of their leadership skills and character. These bonds would intensify in France.[36]

While many officers were able to negotiate this class and ethnic divide, the line that separated black soldiers from whites at Camp Upton could not be crossed. From the day they signed Selective Service registration cards to the day they were discharged, African-American conscripts found themselves completely segregated. The federal government delayed their mobilization until well into the fall of 1917, then dispersed them across the country so they would not form a majority of the soldiers in any cantonment. Most received only the most rudimentary military training and served as laborers far away from the fighting.[37]

Racism was readily visible at Upton. Black members of the Fifteenth New York National Guard, assigned to patrol the camp during the construction period, were removed soon after the first white draftees arrived. Tensions with construction workers and a fight between the guardsmen and white civilian waiters (which the *New York Times* described as nearly becoming a "serious race war") compelled officials to make the change. Local papers, for the most part ignoring the black draftees' presence, reduced their speech to the vulgar patter of "Mr. Bones" and "Mr. Interlocutor." The record among white conscripts was no better. Along with creating the *Bugle*, Milton Weill organized company minstrel shows filled with "Sambo"-like caricatures. It is unclear how the division's Jewish immigrants felt about this situation. But if racial mores in America were unknown to them before they became soldiers, the six months at Upton gave them an ample education.[38]

An "outside" population of 6 million New Yorkers also helped to frame the men's training experience. Even before Upton officially opened, Seventy-seventh commander General J. Franklin Bell strongly encouraged public accessibility. "There will be no fences around the camp," he proclaimed. "I want these men to feel that they are near home and that their own people are not forgetting, but are looking to them proudly and confidently." The recruits could obtain weekend passes to bring home details of their new lives on a regular basis. Since Yaphank was just sixty miles from New York, friends and family were also able to see for themselves what conditions were like. Nearly every Sunday through the fall and winter, cars, trains, and buses brought thousands of visitors to Yaphank. For those who couldn't make the trip, telephones were available, while the city papers provided regular, if totally uncritical, coverage.[39]

The War Department and camp officials were well aware that the folks back home would have to like what they saw and heard. Under the direction of Secretary Newton Baker, the camp resembled a laboratory for testing the Progressive Era's faith in social planning and middle-class morals. Living conditions at Upton were a step down from what many draftees enjoyed in civilian life, but for the camp's immigrant residents the federal government's first major housing project was in many respects a decided improvement. Each barrack had electricity, showers, and modern plumbing and sanitation, and the men ate three hot meals a day. With an ample supply of fuel, the buildings were kept warm through what was a harsh winter. The soldiers "policed" their area regularly, keeping it scrupulously clean, and medical personnel made frequent barracks inspections.[40]

The prohibition of vice was also strictly enforced. In August 1917, Baker vowed that the army would eliminate the sale of alcohol within range of all camps, and that mothers would not have to worry about their sons frequenting houses of ill repute. Along with the ban on saloons and prostitution, the draftees attended frequent lectures and were bombarded with slogans warning of the ravages (and shame) of venereal disease. In place of these traditional soldier pastimes, the newly created Commission on Training Camp Activities organized "wholesome" entertainments. Coordinating the work of a variety of private associations, the CTCA depended heavily on public fund drives, to which New Yorkers donated hundreds of thousands of dollars. At Upton the YMCA and Knights of Columbus built ten recreation huts, where the men could write letters home, attend lectures, movies, and religious services, and relax from the rigors of training. The American Library Association constructed a library with thousands of donated books, while the YWCA established Hostess Houses where soldiers could spend time with their girlfriends and wives. In addition to a full athletic program, the CTCA also organized a pet interest of General Bell's—chorus singing. "I am anxious to have this camp become well known as one of the singing camps of the army," claimed the general. "We must let these men get the inspiration which comes from doing things together in large units. We want them to grasp and visualize what 10,000, 20,000, and 40,000 soldiers really means. This will give them courage and the true spirit for the work that lies ahead." Whether they liked it or not, the men of the Seventy-seventh sang their way through training.[41]

There were also numerous instances of Gotham's direct involvement in making camp life less monotonous. The New York Hotel Men's Association recruited chefs from some of the city's best restaurants to teach Upton cooks how to prepare meals in mammoth quantities. The New York Athletic Club held an all-day track meet at the camp, where two thousand conscripts participated in traditional competitions and such new challenges as "grenade throwing" and "rescue" races. The New York Federation of Women's Clubs raised fifty thousand dollars for a camp community hall, and the *Herald* posted play-by-play reports of the World Series. The men were treated to visits by a host of luminaries, including the New York Philharmonic, Harry Houdini, and former presidents Roosevelt and Taft. The city also supported the soldiers when they took their own show on the road. The 305th Infantry's performance of "A Day at Camp Upton," a theatrical rendition of daily life in Yaphank, raised money for a regimental auditorium. In early 1918, huge crowds cheered parades of the 308th Infantry and the entire division down Fifth Avenue.[42]

The best examples of local support, however, were the auxiliary associations each regiment formed just before departing for France. Led and staffed mainly by the commanding officers' wives, these groups resembled other charitable women's organizations of the period. But with access to money and political connections, they could aid the men and their families better than any other welfare organization. The record of the 308th Regimental Association, with its rooms on 40th Street, was especially impressive. Along with providing the soldiers "over there" with knitted garments, comfort packages, and a tobacco fund, the group's Welfare Committee offered extensive services to family members. It paid the rent and purchased food, clothing, and coal for destitute families, and by pulling strings in the Council of National Defense sped up the mailing of pay allotment checks. In addition to hiring a visiting nurse, the association made use of contacts at hospitals to care for sick members, especially mothers who were giving birth. Most importantly, the group served as a communication center for loved ones, sending a bulletin to all kin and posting the latest soldiers' letters at its offices. The association was of course busiest when the regiment saw its most intense fighting. "An unending stream of visitors came to our rooms in search of information, encouragement and cheer," writes the group's president. "How often needless anxiety was relieved, and misinformation corrected, no one could well remember."[43] In activities like these, Gotham stamped a firm local imprint on its portion of the National Army.

Inevitably, a World War I division composed of mainly working-class New Yorkers was bound to include a large number of Jews. The prowar Jewish press even boasted that the Seventy-seventh was a "Jewish" organization, wildly estimating that they made up as much as 40 percent of the camp's residents. By early 1918, the real figure was closer to seven thousand, or roughly a quarter of the division. It was still substantially higher than the 20 percent of New York City's population that was Jewish.[44]

This group was as rich and diverse in its ethnic, religious, and political makeup as the Jewish communities from which it was drawn. Men who had emigrated or were descended from the Russian Pale, Germany, and the Austro-Hungarian and Ottoman empires, men who worshipped in Orthodox, Conservative, and Reform synagogues, and those who had abandoned Judaism altogether, were now training in Yaphank. Not surprisingly, sweatshop workers, clerks, and small businessmen predominated. But the camp also housed members of elite German Jewish families, like Captain Adler of the *New York Times* and Lieutenant Harold Bache of the prominent Bache financial firm, and such unconventional workers as former actor Jacob Sarnov, "trick cyclist" Abraham Silverman, and pop songwriter Harry Edelheit. Their political views ran the gamut as well, from dyed-in-the-wool Republicans and socialists to men whose experiences in eastern Europe taught them to shun politics completely.[45]

Upton officials were committed to providing resources for each religious group in the draft pool. They were also deeply concerned about keeping prowar sentiments at a high level.[46] Major challenges to these concerns came soon after the camp opened, involving the Jewish rookies. Among the difficulties that plagued the camp were the celebration of the Jewish High Holidays and the New York mayoralty campaign of socialist Morris Hillquit.

The Ten Days of Penitence that begin with Rosh Hashanah and end on Yom Kippur are the most important holidays of the Hebrew calendar. In 1917 they took place on September 17–27th, just a week after the first draftees arrived in Yaphank. A period of profound self-examination, the Jewish New Year requires Jews to atone for their sins and pray for God's forgiveness. With the sounding of the *shofar*, the ram's horn that symbolizes Abraham's willing sacrifice of Isaac, prayers and rituals are performed daily in preparation for the Lord's judgment. On that day, Yom Kippur, the most stringent rules of abstinence, including fasting, apply. Though the form and degree of observance varied greatly within New York Jewry, the High Holidays were a time for practicing Jews to put work aside and contemplate their lives and relationships to God in the past, present, and future.

For the heterogeneous group of Jews at Upton, celebrating these holidays while training to kill people must have seemed an utter contradiction. For the draftees' superiors, however, the Jewish New Year posed a major logistical and public relations dilemma. Just beginning to fill up with men, Yaphank had a conscript population of around ten thousand on the eve of Rosh Hashanah, roughly twenty-five hundred of whom were Jewish and overwhelmingly Orthodox in background. At this time there was not a single Jewish chaplain in the entire United States Army. The fledging Jewish Welfare Board, despite its vaunted aim of caring for all Jews in the military, still did not have a representative at the camp. With anxiety over conscription and antiwar sentiment running high among Gotham Jews, General J. Franklin Bell faced a sticky situation. He needed to demonstrate toleration and respect for Jewish soldiers, but did not want to appear to be giving them special privileges.[47]

As would be true for the Seventy-seventh's entire stay on Long Island, cooperation between the city and the federal government provided a sufficient, though by no means perfect, answer to Upton's "Jewish Question." Fortunately, General Bell was sincere in his advocacy of religious freedom at the camp. Although the War Department gave him permission to furlough the men for both Rosh Hashanah and Yom Kippur, Bell consulted with city officials and Jewish religious leaders and decided to hold an on-site service for the first holiday (which he attended and addressed), and allowed men to return home for the fast day. Disruption to training and friction among non-Jewish soldiers was minimized, and the furloughed men had nine more days to adapt to their new lives as soldiers before leaving camp. On September 17, 1917, a prominent rabbi conducted New Year's services at Yaphank. For Yom Kippur, the Mayor's Committee on National Defense arranged for special trains to take the draftees home and bought round-trip tickets for poor men who could not afford the expense. A variety of synagogues and Jewish organizations provided lodging and religious services for soldiers who had no homes in the city. Some Gentile privates, like one named Patrick Shea, tried to persuade officers that they too needed a furlough to commemorate the holiday.[48]

This brokered form of cooperation characterized all of the religious care Jewish soldiers received while at Yaphank. Unlike Christian draftees, Jews did not enjoy the spiritual services the YMCA and Knights of Columbus abundantly provided. The Jewish Welfare Board never established a solid presence at Upton during the division's six months of training. Accused of deliberately keeping a low profile so as not to antagonize non-Jews, the organization also suffered from financial and administrative obstacles. Having only twelve thousand dollars at its disposal in November 1917, the board launched a $1 million fund drive in December. By the time money was allocated for recreation huts and representatives, the men of the Seventy-seventh were overseas.[49]

The experiences of Joseph Hyman, the first JWB worker at Upton, best illustrate the limited resources available to observant Jewish soldiers. Arriving just two days before Yom Kippur, the young lawyer and educator depended heavily on outside assistance well into the following spring. Until the completion of a Jewish center in mid-April 1918, he worked and lived in a YMCA building, and initially had to wear a "Y" armband to distinguish himself from incoming recruits because the Jewish Welfare Board did not yet have any insignia. Religious services were conducted in a YMCA hut, and Hyman had a great deal of trouble procuring Orthodox rabbis, who could not travel during the Sabbath, until the camp built a boarding house for visitors. Meanwhile, he found himself deluged with the concerns of thousands of soldiers. "When the boys learned, and the news spread rapidly," Hyman recalls, "that there was a Jewish worker in camp, they flocked into my cubby hole. They brought all sorts of requests—for Kosher kitchens, for separate Jewish barracks, for orthodox and reform services. One group, socialistically inclined, wanted an auditorium for discussion of social and military problems in Yiddish." In February 1918, after acquiring two assistants, Hyman showed a reporter a card index of his numerous "clients." It contained requests to find a recruit's family in Russia, for help with a man's citizenship papers, and to obtain permission for a soldier to say *Kaddish* in his father's memory every morning in the barracks. Along with writing letters for illiterate men, Hyman's office set up English classes. "Space does not allow to enumerate," noted the reporter, "all the activities of the Jewish welfare workers."[50]

In addition to reassuring folks back home that their sons were all right, the office received thousands of gifts from individuals, family members, and Jewish organizations. The city's synagogue sisterhoods proved the most industrious suppliers. The flow of comfort kits, knitted goods, books, and games in fact became so great the JWB men had to channel a good portion of it to non-Jewish soldiers. Though the War Department did not provide special kitchens, this did not dissuade some families from attempting to keep their sons' diets kosher. "One good woman, proprietor of a delicatessen shop," recalls Hyman, "desired to send in daily a quantity of bologna and other delicatessen and was greatly incensed because I declined her offer. But I had to refuse; I had no place to handle the bolognas." Herman Levine, an immigrant private at Camp Dix, received enough kosher food from his father to observe the *kashruth* during his entire stateside training. It is not unlikely that similar efforts were made at Upton.[51]

New York's first wave of Jewish draftees had to make the best of piecemeal services. But their successors at Yaphank and in the army as a whole benefited greatly from their path-breaking presence. After the division left for France in April 1918, the Jewish Welfare Board completed a large community center, assigned rabbis to the camp, and organized community support chapters in the New York and Yaphank area. That summer Upton witnessed the installment of a set of *Sefer Torah* scrolls in its Interdenominational Chapel—"the only Jewish Ark to be found in a training camp in

MUSTERING RECRUITS, CAMP UPTON, L. I. N. Y.

Camp Upton, located on Long Island, was still unfinished when the draftees from New York City began to arrive in September 1917. Approximately seven thousand Jews trained here with the Seventy-seventh Division before departing for France. The camp had no special resources for Jewish troops at first, but by the end of the war Upton boasted an impressive Jewish Welfare Board community building and several Jewish chaplains and social workers. Photo from the author's collection.

this country." General Bell led the dedication ceremony, proclaiming: "If I mistake not, we are making history today, when Jew and Gentile have met in mutual respect to assist in a religious ceremony which is of great importance to worshippers of the Hebrew faith." But the Seventy-seventh did not leave all of these new provisions behind. In October 1917, Congress passed a bill introduced by Harlem Republican Isaac Siegel to commission twenty "at large" military chaplains, seven of whom would be rabbis. Most prominent among them was Elkan Voorsanger, who became the first Jewish senior chaplain of a division in U.S. military history when he was assigned to the Seventy-seventh in June 1918. When the Statue of Liberty men went into battle, the spiritual leader of their outfit was a Jew.[52]

The strong support that much of New York Jewry was giving to the Socialist party that fall was also a delicate issue for camp officers to handle. In October 1917, just weeks after the first men poured into camp, Secretary of War Baker heard rumors that Yaphank was becoming a breeding ground of "disloyal sentiment." The soldiers were not turning into Hun saboteurs. They, like the rest of New York City, were showing great interest in the November 6 mayoralty election, in which socialist candidate Morris Hillquit was a leading contender. The New York Socialist party was energized by its opposition to the war and benefited from having an immigrant Jew and East

Jewish soldiers attend services in the camp's Interdenominational Chapel. Photo from the author's collection.

Side hero as its standard bearer. In an especially weak field of candidates, Hillquit's crystal clear message, conveyed by dozens of speakers, hundreds of party workers, and a socialist press that reached 400,000 people daily, caused great concern among prowar political leaders.[53]

With votes at a premium, all eyes turned to Yaphank with its pool of voting-age men, and in particular its large Jewish population. There was no doubt that the East Side, Brownsville, and Williamsburg were socialist strongholds, an obvious fact during the campaign that was proven decisively in the election results. Would Yaphank vote along similar lines? Especially galling to war boosters was the left's confidence. Hillquit's campaign manager boasted to the press that 50 percent of the men at Upton were "either socialists or socialistically inclined." Many prowar newspapers began to agree with him as the campaign entered its final month.[54]

Again General Bell was put in a difficult spot. He announced that all mayoralty candidates could speak there, keeping true to his commitment that Upton would remain an open camp not isolated from the concerns of the metropolis. A key stipulation in his October 8 offer, however, was that visitors could not utter doctrines "subversive of military discipline." When Socialist party representatives met with him a week later, he requested a signed statement that their candidate would limit his speech to the municipal campaign and refrain from making comments about the war and conscription. The representatives agreed, and *The Call* announced the next day "the

General's permission is considered sure." But the final written request for a visit did not include such a guarantee. Bell then consulted the Socialists' platform, and asked if Hillquit would address all of its stated positions, including the denunciation of war. When the representatives replied yes, Bell denied Hillquit permission to speak at the camp. In an exchange of open letters between the general and the candidate, Bell expressed great respect for Hillquit, adding "I have absolutely no political bias and have never voted in my life." He allowed the circulation of party literature and *The Call* at Upton, but no speech-making. Hillquit and the party received a good deal of publicity from the affair and did not press the point.[55]

A large socialist vote never materialized at Yaphank. One reason was the party's traditional dilemma of relying on an immigrant population that contained so few citizens. The *New York Times* commented on election day, "While there has been a noticeable socialistic sympathy among some of the soldiers . . . it is held that few of these men are voters." But two informal polls of Yaphank men found that support for the socialists was weak. After interviewing a hundred Jewish conscripts chosen at random, the prowar Fusion Committee declared that the soldiers were against Hillquit's pacifism. The *World* published some of their comments. Doughboy Herman Bernstein stated point blank: "Anybody who says we are sorry we are here is a liar." Morris Galtrof of the 308th added, "This is a war a Jew should be in favor of, if ever there was one. What should a Jew fight for at any time if not for this Government at this time? We are treated fine. We have no regrets for being here." In the mock election that Milton Weill's company held, presumably not limited to registered voters, Hillquit came in second with thirty ballots. But the soldiers endorsed John Hylan, the Tammany candidate who also won the city election overwhelmingly, with seventy-nine votes.[56]

What may have played an even larger role in putting a damper on pacifist sentiment was the steady stream of prowar educational work the men encountered all through their months in Yaphank. These efforts were minimal before the election, when the necessity of building the camp took precedence. But the Second Liberty Loan drive swept through Yaphank like a tornado, becoming a vigorous competition between companies. Upton purchased more bonds than any other camp in the country. Immigrant doughboys got caught up in the enthusiasm, volunteering to speak at loan rallies in their neighborhoods. Eighty of the first hundred volunteers were Yiddish-speaking, and they took the assignment of describing their training experiences seriously. "[The folks back home] have heard a lot of stuff from soapbox orators that's all wrong," explained one man. "Those knockers are the wrong kind of soapboxers; we'll be the right kind." Jewish soldiers spread propaganda that directly countered the Hillquit campaign.[57]

After the election, these activities gradually evolved into what amounted to a quasi-curriculum of lectures and classes. Writing to his father in early December 1917, Chaplain James Howard described the educational work that he developed for the immigrants in his regiment. "These classes give an opportunity to teach a good deal besides English":

> The lessons have to do with different phases of drilling and military life, with United States history and customs, with civics, and various things which will be new to these men, and will make better citizens of them as well as better soldiers.
>
> They are very eager to learn and often seem like children in the lower grades of school.

This was a far cry from the atrocity-filled lectures given to the men of the Yankee Division. By the early spring of 1918, Upton was home to a school with eleven hundred students in its English classes. Though it might have encountered more yawns from its "pupils" than cheers, the central message the men received was a good one, one that they rarely, if ever, heard: that they lived in a country that honored their presence and accorded them all the rights and privileges of democracy.[58]

In late March 1918, the Seventy-seventh Division began the time-consuming process of packing and marking all of its equipment for the overseas voyage, and by April 5 its twenty-seven thousand members were crossing on troop transports and converted ocean liners. The trip ended the close contact the draftees enjoyed with their hometown. A captain recalls that while at Yaphank "the men, except those from up-State, never quite cut loose from the city nor gave themselves unreservedly to the military life." So close to home and benefiting from the support of relatives and friends, the draftees did not fully commit to soldiering until they landed in France and underwent training similar to that of the New Haven Italians.[59]

But in several ways the division's Jewish members had come a long way from their neighborhood send-offs and first sight of Yaphank. The most obvious change was in their physical appearance. During the draft board examinations of the previous summer, a noticeably high percentage of Jews were exempted for medical reasons. Generations of poverty and czarist restrictions in eastern Europe had prevented immigrants from obtaining outdoor employment in Gotham, and the cramped working and housing conditions most endured in America took an added heavy toll. For those who were inducted, the exercise, regular meals and showers, and health and dental care provided at Upton were just what the doctor ordered. Unit histories of the division repeatedly describe the great improvement in the physical condition of the soldiers while at Yaphank. Emma Goldman's nephew David Hochstein, though by no means a veteran of the sweatshops, told a reporter how beneficial the regimen had been to his health. "It has done me good," the violinist claimed, "physically—well, I feel like a different person. It is partly the outdoor life and the exercise . . . but it has been even more, I think, the regular hours for sleep and the fact that it has been possible, really, to sleep in these hours." Many men must have realized the grim irony that the government, which had largely ignored immigrant living conditions before the war, was now making them strong enough to go into combat. But the camp also gave many a glimpse of better living conditions, which they would pursue with full force when the fighting was over.[60]

It is difficult to determine how the Jewish conscripts really felt about what they encountered at Yaphank. But it is not too much of a stretch to conclude that the months of training had transformed their initial fears into a hardened (though still very anxious) determination. War boosters frequently ascribed a fervor to Upton's Jews. Damon Runyon, writing in the *Journal American*, answered what had become a "stock interrogation" among camp observers—"how do the Jews take it?" His reply is celebratory to the point of being absurd:

> The spirit of the Hebrew soldiers at Camp Upton has amazed all beholders, not because it was unexpected, but because of the way it has stood out in contrast from the very beginning. The Hebrew soldiers are among the best soldiers in the camp . . .
>
> Of the courage of the Hebrew there is, of course, no question. He has settled that matter on many battlefields, not only in the present war but in the past. However, it is interesting to note the statement of an officer that few expressed a preference for any branch of the service that might take them out of the fighting line.
>
> So that's how 'the Jew takes it.'

More plausible are the comments of Elbert Aidline, who regularly translated Yiddish poetry for the socialist *Call* and wrote several descriptions of life among drafted Jews. "There is no enthusiasm, as the term is commonly understood," he observed in the *American Hebrew*, "no bragging, no boasting, but an earnest, one may say, solemn resolve to do the work they are called upon to do and to do it well." Perhaps the memories of Rumanian-born Jack Herschkowitz offer the best insight. "I didn't feel like going," the decorated veteran recalls, "who wants to get killed?—so I first tried to get out of it—but vonce I was in there, I did it right." Neither superpatriots nor pacifists by the time they left for France, most of the Seventy-seventh's Jews accepted their situation with quiet commitment.[61]

It is significant that the worst case of anti-Semitism in the military during the war occurred in the Seventy-seventh's sister organization, the Twenty-seventh Division. Originally a National Guard organization composed entirely of New York volunteers, the Twenty-seventh moved to a camp in North Carolina just as Yaphank began to fill up with conscripts. Late on the night of October 13, 1917, a Jewish private named Otto Gottschalk was dragged from his bed under a captain's orders, stripped naked, and thrown into a muddy trench. Four soldiers then took him behind a building and beat him with clubs. After the private reported the incident, it was discovered that the officer, Captain Howard Sullivan, had several months before been accused of arbitrarily rejecting twelve Jewish recruits for placement in his artillery unit. Anti-Semitism had defined the captain's personal selection of "the right man for the right job." A man's ethnicity and religion, rather than his talents and eagerness to serve, were the defining criteria, and any Jew who managed his way past this barrier paid a heavy price. Despite the indignation the beating provoked, Sullivan was tried twice by a division tribunal and received only thirty days' suspension from active duty.[62]

The Italian machine gunners of the Yankee Division and the Jewish draftees of the Seventy-seventh never experienced incidents of bigotry equivalent to what Captain Sullivan did in an organization less than 8 percent Jewish. Composing so large a proportion of their respective units, they found security in numbers. Yet there were clear differences between the treatment of the New Haveners and the men from New York as ethnic soldiers in Uncle Sam's vast army. The Italians would have remained segregated from the rest of the Connecticut guardsmen if not for the intervention of the federal government. The volunteers belonged to an organization that cherished its militia roots and was especially jealous of its autonomy. They encountered a more limited sense of inclusion in the country they were fighting to defend. The character of the Yankee Division both permitted and compelled the continued isolationism of the New Haven *colonia*.

But as a Jewish Welfare Board representative observed, the conditions and goals were very different at Camp Upton. Dr. Leon Goldrich identified "the problem" of the drafted soldier after visiting Yaphank in December 1917.[63] "Home ties are severed," he reported, "and the constructive civilizing influences of the social club, the school and the synagogue have been withdrawn . . . the young man feels that he has lost his individuality and social relations, and must now become a unit in a large military machine." Unlike the National Guard (and nearly all of the other armies fighting the war), National Army planners saw the need for reproducing these "civilizing influences" as much as possible. Just as modern warfare dictated a new form of raising an army, so did a new relationship between the state and society define a more responsive federal government. "Society in a democracy," claimed Goldrich, "demands that the soldier shall have opportunities for religious, educational, and social development, even though he spends a greater part of his time in military training." This massive undertaking was a dramatic departure from previous military practice and required the initiative and cooperation of local governments, ethnic groups, and the soldiers themselves. Within three decades, African Americans would benefit from the path-breaking presence of immigrants in the armed forces. The federal government in both cases helped to integrate, not oppress, the ethnically marginalized.

III The Home Front

☆ ☆ ☆ ☆ ☆ ☆ ☆ ☆ ☆ ☆ ☆ ☆ ☆ ☆ ☆ ☆ ☆

Unlike America's Germans and Austrians, New Haven Italians and New York Jews were not considered enemy aliens by the United States government, and repression figured minimally if at all in their lives during the war. Yet both populations were also subject to significant pressures. The nation's New Immigrants faced urgent appeals to their national and group identity on three distinct levels: as Americans, as persons still deeply attached to their European homelands, and as immigrants. The war brought out in bold relief the major contradictions of ethnic life, as the newcomers encountered demands for American unity and cultural separatism, and found themselves at different times celebrated, patronized, and excluded.

Almost every American experienced much of what these two ethnic groups encountered during the war. Signing a food pledge card or buying Liberty Bonds were activities that cut across class, ethnic, and geographical lines. Since so much of the domestic effort depended on voluntary participation, calls to "do your bit" were more urgent and ubiquitous, pervading the school, workplace, church, and social club. This common national effort deepened the claims of Italians and Jews to their adopted country. As important, it expanded their contact with local and federal institutions, and encouraged many to assert themselves outside of their ethnic communities.

At the same time, events overseas appeared to renew immigrant bonds to Europe. The Italian Army's defeat at Caporetto in the fall of 1917 transformed the New Haven *colonia* into the most active and visibly prowar population in the city. That winter New York Jewry's attitude toward the conflict changed even more dramatically. The Balfour Declaration added the promise of a Jewish homeland to the Allied cause, and the German domination of much of the former Russian Pale in early 1918 transformed New York Jewish ambivalence into solid support for the American war effort. War work flourished in the Lower East Side, led by the same unions that opposed it just months before. The antagonisms that separated Neapolitans from Abruzzi and uptown from downtown converged respectively into the campaigns to defend Italy and liberate Europe's Jews. But even though their hearts and minds were so sharply affected by events in their homelands, both groups fell in step with the war aims of the United States. They soon viewed American agencies such as the Red Cross, YMCA, and Jewish Welfare Board as the most effective means of helping kin abroad.

Italians and Jews also continued to be identified and appealed to as immigrants and ethnics. Ethnicity remained a cornerstone of political discourse, despite the demands "to heat up the melting pot" and "erase the hyphenate." Federal, state, and local leaders carefully cultivated the participation of ethnic groups by praising their history and culture, even their stereotypical traits. The city of New Haven sponsored several events honoring Italy, while Gotham newspapers lauded Jewish relief work and the "Maccabaean spirit" of Jews in the armed forces. Though almost always kept separate in the various domestic campaigns and treated more often with condescension than respect, both enclaves moved to a new stage in their development. For the first time their activities in America, both as groups and as individuals, received sustained recognition and praise.[1]

The next two chapters describe how New Haven Italians and New York Jews came to actively support the American war effort, not as a result of government repression or manipulation, but because of each community's continuing ties to Europe and their own aspirations and claims to settlement in the United States. Their participation in local events and their perceptions of major changes taking place worldwide produced a new attitude toward the country that was now their permanent home.

★ ★ ★ ★ ★ ★ ★ ★ ★ ★ ★ ★ ★ ★ ★ ★ ★

6 "More than Ever, We Feel Proud to Be Italians"

✲ ✲ ✲ ✲ ✲ ✲ ✲ ✲ ✲ ✲ ✲ ✲ ✲ ✲ ✲ ✲ ✲ ✲

The event that proved most decisive in pulling the New Haven *colonia* into the war effort took place three thousand miles away, near the small town of Caporetto. There, in the early hours of October 24, 1917, a combined Austrian and German force smashed the Italian Army's lines. By mid-afternoon Italy had lost all of the ground it had gained in the previous two-and-a-half years of fighting, and by nightfall the front had collapsed seventeen miles in what had been one of the most immobile theaters of the war. The Italians did not halt the enemy advance until November 10. By that time their losses were staggering. Forty thousand men were killed or wounded; roughly 300,000 were taken prisoner and nearly as many stragglers deserted their units and fled to safety.[1]

Caporetto was also a catastrophe for the civilian population. Close to half a million refugees were caught in the crossfire. Inevitably their escape clogged the roads the army needed for its retreat, producing a human quagmire of soldiers who had thrown down their weapons and peasants who had gathered whatever belongings and livestock they could save. Venice, only fifteen miles from the Austro-German advance, evacuated in desperation. The city's population of 160,000 fell to 20,000 almost overnight.

Except for a brief period in the spring of 1916, Italy had always been on the offensive and fighting on enemy soil. Thus the disaster at Caporetto left New Haven's Italians stunned. A clergyman encountered a group of immigrants weeping openly in the street over the news that their native village had been captured. "This brings the dark side of the war close to us," he commented. A reporter covering the reaction in Wooster Square agreed: "Interest in the war is at fever intensity . . . The great reverses reported in the press are the topic of conversation wherever Italians meet."[2]

The immigrant population manifested this "fever intensity" in either the most personalized or the most patriotic terms. Consul Nicola Mariani, the Italian government's spokesman in the area, flatly denied all reports of cowardice. He told the city's American press that "large delegations" of local immigrants were "begging" to be sent overseas in order to enlist in the army. Under the banner headline "Invading Barbarians Have Profaned the Soil of Italy," *Il Corriere del Connecticut* agreed. "Italy will fight like a lioness defending her children. The blows of the enemy's sledgehammer will multiply her energy a hundred times over."[3]

It is doubtful that the working-class majority of the enclave adopted the same nationalistic idiom. Few were natives of the northern region under attack; the city's immigrants might well have considered distant Veneto much like a foreign country. Their anxiety surrounding the defeat had a much more personal basis, as a *New Haven Register* article noted. "Hundreds of the local Italian families have relatives in the Italian army, and many fear that some of their own kin are prisoners of the hated Germans." Most frontline troops in the Alps—men who were poor, unskilled, and uneducated—came from the Mezzogiorno and Sicily. The same type of young man who dominated the immigrant tide to America before the war was the mainstay of the Italian infantry. The fact that Italy's limited, offensive struggle for territorial gain—*la piccola guerra*—produced only heavy casualties did not give the colony a burning sense of national pride. Despite the war, the immigrants' traditional concerns for family and region continued to matter most.[4]

Caporetto changed much of this, transforming the war for *sacro egoismo* into a struggle for Italy's independence and survival. The personal and the patriotic quickly combined as New Haven's immigrants threw their energy into a major campaign for refugee relief. Infused with the spirit of national salvation, their new activism persisted through the rest of the war. For the first time the regional prejudices that fragmented the colony now coalesced into a common purpose and helped draw the immigrants into the American war effort. As Allies, New Haven's Italians and their neighbors found themselves working together as never before.

Practically overnight, Italian colonies across America became centers of feverish activity to save the *Madre Patria*. In New York City, the newspaper *Il Progresso Italo-Americano* led a refugee relief fund drive that made full use of its national readership. For two months the paper printed the names of literally thousands of men and women, transplanted Italians from as far away as Appalachia and the Mesabi mining range, who had collected money from their neighbors, clubs, workplaces, and even army units to send to the Italian government. San Francisco's Italian papers raised money for the Italian Red Cross and an Italian soldiers' fund, while *colonie* throughout California held an array of benefit concerts, dances, and film screenings. Italian immigrants in Chicago, Boston, Milwaukee, and Philadelphia condemned the "barbaric" invasion of the Austrian and German armies and scrambled to do what they could to help their families and regions—and *connazionali*—back home.[5]

The New Haven colony was well within the mainstream of this movement, and in both word and deed a new awareness of Italian national identity became visible. *Il Corriere del Connecticut* provides the best documentation of this dramatic shift. Reading the weekly in the final months of 1917, one might think it was printed in the Eternal City rather than the City of Elms. Like Rome, *Il Corriere* avoided criticism of the Italian leadership. It blamed spies who informed the enemy of "the weaker sections" in the Italian lines, and war opponents who deserved to be "shot in the back" by firing squads. Most of all, it placed responsibility on the Allies, who failed to furnish Italy with supplies and refused to form a war council. The weekly also assured readers that "the honor of the Italian Army is intact," and "the morale of the people is not shaken."[6]

But its immigrant publisher Giuseppe Santella did much more than repeat the lies and platitudes of official propaganda. Santella projected a sense of immediacy to his readers, linking them directly to Italy's cultural heritage and present crisis. He punctuated his front-page editorials with bits of *Italianità*—of Italy's epic history and its legacy to the civilized world. Claiming that the "names of the Italian patriots of the last century were on the lips of every man and every woman who loved liberty," he presented Caporetto as a supreme test of democracy worldwide. Though a strong advocate of assimilation, Santella described the situation in Italy as the life struggle of "our fatherland," "our army," and "our King." His prescription for victory thus spoke to local immigrants just as much as to the Italian public: "If the Italian people pull together; if the Italian people respond like the French did three years ago, the disaster of the Isonzo could represent the cornerstone of a united Italy in the future."

On November 3, 1917, *Il Corriere* called for the formation of a relief committee. The proposed group would be formed "without distinction of class, party, religion, or region." No one would receive a special invitation; the paper's goal was to draw a crowd that was "spontaneous, numerous, and voluntary." The provisional committee that Santella chaired, consisting of *prominenti* and the publishers of the city's two other popular Italian weeklies, organized a mass meeting for November 11. Advertising the event on the front page of *Il Corriere*, the committee reasserted its inclusiveness and single-minded purpose: "On the nation's altar we sacrifice whatever dissensions, whatever differences of political or religious opinion we may have."[7]

For the first time since Italy entered the war, this appeal found an extremely receptive audience. Hundreds packed into S. Z. Poli's Bijou Theater to witness the spectacle and participate in the activities. The newly christened Comitato Pro Patria announced its ambitious goal: to raise $100,000 for refugee relief. Targeting a day in late November as "Italy Day," the organization planned to gather the money in a unique manner. "It is the Committee's desire that every *connazionali* who feels Italian blood running in his veins, give, if he is a worker, one day's pay, and if he is a professional, shopkeeper, banker, or businessman, a day's worth of earnings." The funds were to come from within the enclave; all of the solicitors and contributors were to be of Italian descent. A laborer at the Winchester Arms plant launched the effort by giving five dollars. By the end of the meeting, more than five hundred dollars in cash had been collected.[8]

Perhaps the most crucial question facing the campaign concerned the participation of the mutual aid societies. Collectively they represented thousands of members and controlled the largest treasuries of any local Italian institution. One of the purest expressions of homeland provincialism in New Haven, it was quite possible that the members would want to act independently of the committee's campaign. But all of the society presidents attended the November 11 rally and pledged their support. Over the next two weeks their members collected funds and passed fervent resolutions in support of Italy. Four societies gave a thousand dollars apiece, while smaller organizations donated from twenty-five to five hundred dollars. On November 18 the *New Haven Register* reported that the societies had "left no stone unturned to exhaust every resource in aiding the fund." Far from being an obstacle to the Pro Patria drive, these groups were the basis of its success.[9]

The campaign soon permeated the economic and institutional life of the colony. The payday appeal was especially effective, confronting every Italian working in the area. Members of the baker and barber trades contributed collectively, while businessmen and professionals made individual donations of fifty to one hundred dollars apiece. The largest portion of the fund came from the industrial workforce. Shop hands solicited contributions at the Winchester and L. Candee Rubber factories; more than fifty men pleaded the cause in the Sargent hardware company works alone. Wherever Italians labored, at least one co-worker was asking them to donate their earnings. In addition the recreational and political *circoli* [clubs] gave to the fund, the Nutmeg Athletic Club being by far the most ingenious. Its members sponsored a "Boxing Night" that included a parade of Italian sports teams, a vaudeville show, and an impressive fight card featuring Italian-American boxers.[10]

The drive concluded with a mass meeting on December 23, two months after the start of the Caporetto offensive. The committee's relief fund check, made out to Prime Minister Vittorio Orlando himself, came to only a third of the original goal of $100,000. It is unclear whether the organizers overestimated the size of the working population and its resources, or if the *connazionali* sent much of their aid independently. In any case, the sum was one of the largest communitywide offerings made by an Italian colony in the United States.[11]

For needy Italy, the sum was a drop in the ocean. But it was significant to the colony for several reasons. The campaign offered friends and family members a constructive means of channeling their fears and feelings of helplessness. It energized the community with a powerful moral purpose, distinguishing Italians in the most positive manner from the city's other ethnic groups. For a population that for so long had felt the sting of prejudice and the hardships of living near the bottom of the city's social ladder, the campaign to save Italy served an important psychological function. Giuseppe

Santella proclaimed: "More than ever, we feel proud to be Italians," a sentiment that grew throughout the remainder of the war.[12]

One did not have to be Italian in New Haven to feel the shock of Caporetto. The city's English-speaking press carried front-page stories, maps, and editorials describing the Italian retreat. On October 29, 1917, the *New Haven Register* summarized the local as well as global response to the losses: "In a day the attention of the world is shifted from Ypres to the Isonzo." Across the country, the American press agreed, discovering a new sympathy with its forgotten Italian ally.[13]

Until then, the non-Italian population of New Haven and the nation as a whole had paid little attention to the Alpine front. According to Yale professor Charles Bakewell, American perceptions of the Italian war effort were so romanticized as to prevent any emotional bond developing between the two countries. Unlike the outcry over the plight of Belgium and France, Bakewell remembers only "picturesque" images of the struggle in pre-Caporetto Italy. "It was all somehow operatic, a story later to be put on the stage and sung. . . . One did not seem to realize . . . that in Italy too, war meant the grim realism of life in the trenches—dirty, uninspiring, hideously ugly and savage and bloody."[14] Prejudice and the calculating manner in which Italy entered the war probably also fostered New Haven's preference for news from northern Europe. To the broader public, Italy was the least conspicuous of the allies, even in a city with a population more than one-fifth of Italian descent.

But in the last months of 1917 Italy appeared not just as an ally but as an underdog—wounded, desperate, with its back to the wall. The city's American newspapers did their utmost to promote this image. They offered the same excuses that filled *Il Corriere*. "No men in arms ever fought more bravely than have the soldiers of the Italian Army," claimed one paper, "and it is believed that they would have overcome and defeated the Austro-German force of four times their own numbers had the allies furnished the arms and ammunition they needed." Local editors also used Caporetto to reaffirm America's commitment abroad and to promote the new food and fuel conservation measures then sweeping the city. With an internationalist fervor unthinkable a few years before, the *Register* urged: "They must have our men, but they must also have our munitions, our food, our coal, and they must have them immediately."[15]

Awareness of Italy's suffering cast local Italians in a new light, as the wartime concerns of city and *colonia* now converged. The dailies applauded the colony's refugee relief drive and acted as its biggest outside boosters. The *New Haven Times Leader* hailed the new united front. "Italians of New Haven, Connecticut and this country have reason to be proud of their brave brothers in arms, and they, and the American people, will stand by them to the end." Caporetto was the first in a string of events that combined the energies of the city and its Italian enclave.[16]

At the height of the Pro Patria drive, many Italians were beginning to regard the American agencies as an equal or even better means of assisting their families and regions in the mother country. The colony's "intense interest" in the national fund drive of the YMCA, for example, which began in late November, was heightened by the Caporetto crisis. The Y was the only body authorized to provide aid to Italian prisoners of war. After having had little if any contact with the Protestant organization before, Italians became a committed source of support.[17]

The most cloistered segment of the colony, the Italian women of New Haven, in fact ventured furthest from the enclave's confines in gathering funds. At first it seemed that the women's contribution to relief might go untapped or unrecognized, that the masculine bluster of the Comitato Pro Patria would overwhelm all other work. As was typical of most community institutions, the committee's officers and one hundred founding members were men. It was the men who decided to create a women's auxiliary, determining not only what the group would do but also who would lead it.[18]

Once organized, the women adopted a distinctive voice and strategy for themselves. The Comitato feminile never issued statements in the belligerent tones of nationalism. While the men's group revived slogans from Italian history and fulminated over loyalty and treason, the women made more universal appeals, emphasizing above all compassion for the victims. While the men insisted on collecting money only from within the colony, the women did not make such a distinction, and even enlisted the help of non-Italian volunteers. Without a Pro Patria impulse, the auxiliary proved more durable and had a wider impact than the men's group.

Much of this independence was due to Rosa Poli, the auxiliary's leader. A native of Genoa, Poli was by far the best-known Italian woman in the city, whose husband, S. Z. Poli, built a string of movie theaters throughout the Northeast. Her relation to the *colonia* was that of a benefactress rather than a resident, and over the years she gained a considerable reputation as a charity worker for disaster victims and the city's poor. The contrast with Giuseppe Santella could not have been greater. While *Il Corriere*'s publisher advocated assimilation with both feet planted in the enclave, Poli addressed the Italian colony already enjoying the acceptance and admiration of all of New Haven. Rosa Poli was never boasting or parochial, but understated, steady, and well connected. She claimed at a rally that "she was of the silent working class and not accustomed to speaking in public," the kind of remark not heard very often in the *colonia*.[19]

Poli's humility and contacts with the larger New Haven community were put to good use in the auxiliary's main event, a Tag Day fundraiser, on November 24, 1917. Early that morning, six hundred "Italian and American" women took up positions in every ward of the city. Mrs. Poli's *reggimento di ragazze* accepted donations for Italian relief from people of all backgrounds, in amounts ranging from a penny to five dollars. In exchange the women gave each donor a clip-on tag. By the end of the day the group had sold thirty-five thousand of the markers. "It seemed as though every person on the streets Saturday," observed a reporter, "was wearing one of the little tags, men, women, and children alike." But the day's biggest publicity coup was a collection Rosa Poli engineered at the Yale Bowl. At the intermission of the Thanksgiving weekend football game, "the members of the Yale ROTC leaped to their feet . . . each man removed his service cap and passed it among the rows for which he was responsible." The cadets harvested more than four hundred dollars. *Il Corriere* was delighted by the medium as well as the message. "Today, for the first time in the history of New Haven, the students of Yale University, with true fraternal love, are helping to collect IN THEIR HATS for our dear refugees in Italy." All told, the women collected six thousand dollars that day. By overriding the ethnic boundaries of the *colonia* and the separatism of the men's committee, the auxiliary provided nearly a fifth of the relief fund total.[20]

Unlike the Comitato Pro Patria, the women continued their relief efforts well after the fund drive ended. Although the Italian front had restabilized by January 1918, hundreds of thousands of refugees were still struggling with the loss of home and livelihood. *Colonia* women responded by organizing a clothing and blanket drive. Contributions were dropped off at the two Italian nuns' residences in the city or collected by members of several lay societies. Acting now on their own, the women made their compassionate appeal much more explicit, and Rosa Poli handled the press with exceptional skill. In front-page stories such as "Help Save the Italian Baby," the dailies dutifully printed the heart-rending releases she provided. Almost as evocative was the humility of Poli's own appeal. "O, I hope everybody will give us something," she told a reporter, "and give it at once." She also noted the thriftiness of the drive, qualities that met with strong Yankee approval. "These remnants, as for instance of old woolen blankets, will be remade into little blankets for babies; in fact use can be made of every stitch of clothing and wearing apparel of all kinds." Under Poli's guidance the women kept the refugee problem from being solely a concern of the *colonia*.[21]

Indeed, their work soon caught the attention of the Connecticut State Council of Defense. In January 1918 the Council's Committee on Woman's Activities held a meeting to sound out the cooperation of foreign-born women. The agency wanted "not so much [the women's] working cooperation, though this is something we would like, but rather their moral backing." Whatever the committee's intentions might have been, the results of the meeting showed how persuasive an advocate Poli could be. The state authorized a special Italian Women's Subcommittee of the American Red Cross in Connecticut, appointing her as chair. With an office in the state capitol building, Poli set out to form chapters of the new body "in every city and town of the state which has a large Italian population." On February 28 she received permission to ship all of the subcommittee's relief packages directly to Italy. No other ethnic population in Connecticut enjoyed such privileges, let alone its own agency. Though Poli organized chapters in

Bridgeport, Waterbury, Hartford, New London, and Meriden, the strongest support came from her original network in New Haven.[22]

In May the *New Haven Times Leader* reported that one thousand Italian women were knitting garments and making bandages in the city. The four Italian units of the Red Cross in New Haven, including a junior auxiliary, were repeatedly recognized as the city's most productive by state authorities and the press. While Rosa Poli became the most prominent Italian American figure in the state, the women she led received the "highest encomiums" from the local and national Red Cross. For the first time in the colony's history, women were seen as individuals contributing to the welfare of the city and nation. "Here are examples," wrote the *Union*: "Mrs. Mary Conti, widow of the late Louis Conti, knit eight sweaters in seven days, Mrs. J. Celenlano completed five sweaters in one week, Mrs. Theresa Sebastianelli, who has six children, knit six sweaters in one week." For many of the women the attention was ironic. These labors must have seemed quite easy in comparison to what they were accustomed to as workers and mothers in rural Italy and industrial New Haven. Yet knitting socks was what made them worthy of praise after so many years of invisibility. "Of course no human beings could keep up the physical tension at which they have been working," one paper noted, a description that was more apt for what the women did at home and in factories on a regular basis.[23]

With each piece of clothing they sent to Italy, the women inserted a note identifying themselves and expressing moral support. *Il Corriere*'s editor delighted in the possibility that the garment might comfort a person of the same town in Italy, going so far as to imagine "the joy which the poor soldier [might feel] when he discovers that the article is the work of a friend or relative!" The connection with the Old World seemed as strong as ever, but when the women raised funds in May 1918 their appeal was made on the basis of a dual loyalty. "By Helping the American Red Cross You are Helping Italy" read their half-page advertisement in Santella's paper: "Now it's our turn, Italians in America! Do your part!" To be a good Italian in New Haven in the last year of the Great War, one also had to be a good American.[24]

On the first day of 1918, David FitzGerald, the newly elected mayor of New Haven, echoed the exhortations of the Red Cross volunteers. In his inaugural address, FitzGerald spoke of the world situation and the demands it would continue to make on the area. "Every person in the city will have his part to play, men and women, boys and girls," he urged, noting that "the call will perchance be more exacting than in the past." He expressed no doubt that the city's 160,000 residents would comply to the fullest. As Americans, they were "for a unity, a loyalty and a patriotic devotion to those ideals of our country's welfare for which the best blood in every village, hamlet, city and state of the Union is pledged today to uphold." The mayor did not differentiate between the ethnicities and classes that made up this "best blood." New Haven was a prowar hothouse, and he could speak confidently in the first person plural: "We must not, we cannot, we will not fail to respond in doing our part for city, state and nation, yea for the world at large."[25]

The new mayor and his New Year's Day message had serious implications for the *colonia*. Despite his ethnically neutral rhetoric, FitzGerald was more eager than any of his predecessors to cultivate a close relationship with the Italian population. Taking office after eight years of Republican rule, the new mayor was committed to shaping the more recent immigrant groups into a Democratic power base. His efforts to secure the Italians' participation in the war effort and win their electoral loyalty were especially aggressive.[26]

FitzGerald's claim that the demands of war "will perchance be more exacting," meanwhile, was a remarkable understatement. Federal and state agencies, much like his own office, confronted the public with ever greater intensity in 1918. When the new year began, the wartime economy was at its most chaotic. Federal administrators had grossly underestimated what it would take to supply food and fuel not only to the Allies but also to the hundreds of thousands of Americans now in uniform. As a result, the nation witnessed the most drastic examples of state intervention in the economy since Emancipation. Government agencies took control of the country's railroads in December and ordered all nonessential industries to observe heatless "holidays" in January and February. The most significant innovations in economic planning, the War Industries and National War Labor Boards, began to exercise their full powers that spring. Conservation policies went into overdrive when the "Yanks" went into battle in the summer and fall. Since New Haven was home to two of the nation's largest arms-makers, the city felt the impact of these demands and their connection to the war effort keenly. Combined with the strain of having sons, husbands, fathers, and friends overseas, city residents found the new year's call for sacrifice to be ubiquitous.[27]

New Haven's Italians faced a bewildering variety of appeals, as the government urged them to produce more and consume less. In the factories, where forty thousand residents labored, an endless stream of posters, speeches, and rallies dwelt on the patriotic role of the war worker. The impact on the local economy was tremendous. Since 80 percent of New Haven's plants produced goods for the military, demand for labor was very high, boosting wages to their highest levels ever and forcing manufacturers to advertise positions in the English and Italian-language press. The city experienced no significant strikes during the nineteen months of American belligerency. Understaffing was the major problem, not unrest. The hiring of women was also unprecedented, with the number of women factory workers statewide doubling between 1913 and the end of the war. At New Haven's Winchester works, Connecticut's largest employer, the number of women employees doubled (from 2,717 to 5,549) in the two years preceding the armistice. It is unclear how many of the new workers were of Italian descent. But in at least one plant, the city's largest rubber manufacturer, Italian women formed an overwhelming majority.[28]

Meanwhile, a variety of measures confronted New Haven consumers of all ethnic backgrounds. The crusade to "Hooverize"—to comply with the guidelines of U.S. Food Administration chief Herbert Hoover—was the most dogged. In the fall of 1917, the new agency conducted a nationwide campaign to get housewives to sign cards pledging their commitment to food conservation. A large portion of the forty-five thousand New Haveners who agreed to obey the pledge were *colonia* women. The oath they signed, which included such precepts as "watch out for the waste in the community," was printed in Italian. At a rally, Rosa Poli praised "the practical economy of the Italian women who had never been wasteful, therefore to whom Hooverizing was easy." Nevertheless, during the last year of the war the Italian weeklies carried numerous advertisements calling on readers to save on staples like butter and sugar and explained the need to reinforce the government's pleas for wheatless, meatless, porkless, heatless, lightless, and gasless days. On March 31, 1918, all city dwellers obeyed the government's new control over the passage of time itself. On that date New Haven and the rest of the nation got its first taste of Daylight Savings—a fuel conservation measure already observed in Europe.[29]

The city's twenty-seven thousand school children, a third of whom were of Italian descent, also had a substantial role to play in the war effort. In 1918, they purchased $200,000 worth of War Savings Stamps, the highest total of any school district in the state. Schools served as Junior Red Cross Units, in which girls stayed after classes to make bandages and knit sweaters for the soldiers overseas. Students marched in Liberty Bond parades, collected scrap tinfoil and rubber, and participated in patriotic speech contests. Four thousand planted War Gardens in the summer of 1918. Perhaps the best assessment of the students' home front work came from Carmela Anastasio, the valedictorian of Hillhouse High School's class of 1919. "Our class is the war class," she claimed. "The four years of our course have been overshadowed by thoughts of carnage. . . . We have truly witnessed history in the making. Service, sacrifice, victory—this is what has been burned into our very souls."[30]

As students, consumers, and workers living in the state of Connecticut, Elm City Italians found these demands all the more pervasive. The Connecticut State Council of Defense, described by Washington officials as "one of the most if not *the* most vigorous and best organized State Council in the United States," sought to fill whatever gaps in the home front effort the national agencies did not cover. By early 1918, New Haven was home to Connecticut's most active branch, enlisting hundreds of volunteers and taking up a large portion of City Hall. Its Committee on Foreign-Born compiled lists of ethnic leaders throughout the state, people like Father Leonardo Quaglia and Sheriff Frank Palmieri who could speak at rallies and circulate council notices. The Woman's Committee not only helped organize the Italian Subcommittee of the Red Cross, but also conducted a war work registration drive, which recorded the skills of nineteen thousand women. The council's Publicity Committee, of which S. Z. Poli was a member, developed a "Liberty Chorus" program, which became popular nationwide. Locally, an all-Italian chorus of more than one hundred young women learned patriotic songs and performed at numerous events. When combined, the State Council, federal agencies, the mayor's office, and the schools confronted the city and its Italian population with quite a wallop.[31]

The diplomatic moves of the Wilson administration also added to the pressures weighing on the colony. In December 1917, America declared war on the Austro-Hungarian Empire, Italy's most direct rival in the war. The two Allies were now committed to defeating a common enemy. Even more significant was Wilson's statement of war aims in early January, which Italians in New Haven and Rome embraced with equal fervor. The colony hailed the ninth of the President's famous Fourteen Points, which pledged to redraw Italy's boundaries "along clearly recognizable lines of nationality," as the pronouncement of a modern-day Moses. For the members of St. Anthony's Parish, where the emblems of the Austrian territories of Trento and Trieste flanked the church altar, the dreams of the Risorgimento seemed to have full American approval.[32]

B etween the insistent support of their adopted country and the drive for salvation that characterized the struggle in Italy, *colonia* residents became the most outspokenly prowar population in the city. Among the mass of war activities that pervaded their homes, schools, clubs, shops, and workplaces, three events particularly helped to develop their consciousness of being Americans: the nationwide celebration of Italy-America Day, the visits of a dignitary of the Italian government, and two service star flag ceremonies.

Of all the events that proclaimed allied unity in New Haven, none matched Italy-America Day on May 24, 1918, which marked the third anniversary of Italy's entrance into the war. President Wilson called on every American to recognize the courage of the Italian people and asked that all public buildings fly the Italian flag.[33] *Colonie* across the country rose enthusiastically to the occasion. In New York, four hundred Italian societies marched in a "flower-auto" parade, and a crowd of 100,000 gathered to hear Italy's virtues extolled by Theodore Roosevelt. That night at the Metropolitan Opera, an audience of twelve thousand, mainly Italians, heard the great Enrico Caruso sing and Secretary of War Newton D. Baker pledge U.S. troops for the Italian front. In Chicago, Clarence Darrow and other dignitaries praised the courage of Italians at a mass meeting. The *Chicago Tribune* editorialized: "We in America, to which so many of Italy's sons and daughters have come, honor the Italian people and cherish them as brave and faithful allies in war and as good friends in peace." St. Louis and Brooklyn Italians held large parades and rallies, while in Boston and San Francisco flags, flowers, and effusive praise from mayors and state governors were the order of the day.[34]

In New Haven, Mayor FitzGerald and the daily press also made the most of the event. The mayor issued a proclamation instructing residents to wear a flower "in honor of our gallant ally" and "do all in their power to make it a day of deep significance." He helped organize a parade and concert in the city center and enlisted the participation of such decidedly non-Italian groups as the Hibernians and Knights of Columbus. FitzGerald declared, "The cause of democracy will never die in America as long as there is this union of the red, white and blue and the red, white and green."[35]

The *colonia*, meanwhile, jumped at the opportunity to show its appreciation and patriotism. Giuseppe Santella, thrilled by what he saw as "the apotheosis of Italy in America," vowed that "New Haven will be second to no other city in the Union" in showing its support. On the "day of satisfaction and honor," S. Z. Poli presented the Yale ROTC with the national colors of Italy. That night all of the societies marched along a two-mile parade route decorated with hundreds of Italian flags. Floats, bands, and a squad of elderly men who had fought with Garibaldi passed from Wooster Square to the city green. The evening closed with the burning of an effigy of the kaiser on a funeral pyre.[36]

While the event stressed the wartime union of America and Italy, for the New Haven colony it was probably the strongest assertion of *Italian* unity by local immigrants. Regional societies provided two thousand marchers for the parade. The Amalfi-based St. Andrea society offered the most poignant spectacle, when fifty of its youngest members carried an enormous Italian flag like a blanket, the national tricolor covered with carnations. Community leaders urged *connazionali* to hang Italian flags in their windows and write letters of support to relatives in the Old Country. The speeches on the city green drove home any patriotic points somehow left unmade. If the immigrants in the crowd could not understand Yale professor Charles Bakewell, who spoke on the legacy of "Mazzini, Cavour and Garibaldi," they could certainly appreciate Father Leonardo Quaglia's address in Italian, which brought tears to the eyes of many listeners.[37]

As important, the event highlighted the peculiar wartime status of local Italians, who found themselves separated from older stock Americans at the same time they were given center stage. The rally cry of 100-percent Americanism did not mean the disappearance of ethnic and cultural difference from public life. It judged individuals and groups on the basis of whether they were 100-percent prowar and pro-Ally. From this principle the aggressive enlistment and recognition of immigrant support followed, of which Italy-America Day was the most dramatic but not the only example in New Haven. Less than a week before the Italian celebration, three thousand women paraded for the Red Cross, with fifteen nationalities (the Italians the largest) having separate contingents in the line of march. For the fourth of

July, President Wilson and the Committee on National Defense instructed every city to celebrate the cultures and races that made up their communities. Once again the New Haven parade consisted of a series of ethnic delegations. And of course there were the Italian teams and subunits, of which the Dante School Liberty Chorus was the most recent and the Italian machine gun company the best-known examples. Lauded as loyal Americans, they were also perceived as "hyphenates," as people still not completely assimilated and accepted.[38]

That separatism revealed not only the weak position of the Italians, but also the temporary character of the treatment they were receiving. It was fortunate that the *colonia* could count on Mayor FitzGerald to "give the Italians in this city the respect and honor due them," for that was not the primary intention of the people who proposed the Italy-America Day event. The idea for the celebration did not emanate from an immigrant organiza-tion but from the Italy-America Society, a lobbying group of prominent Americans chaired by Charles Evans Hughes. Its purpose was to foster good relations with Italy, not to honor the country's Italian immigrants. The power to accept an ethnic group remained in the same hands during the war as before. War rhetoric accepted that American society was multiethnic, but for new immigrants American democracy still far from recognized that fact.[39]

The treatment of the kaiser's effigy showed what it meant to be on the right side of 100-percent Americanism during the war—and an omen of what was to follow. When the mock funeral pyre was lit police had to restrain a crowd of Italian youths from causing even more damage. The boys had a clear local precedent for behaving so raucously. Five months earlier a gang of thirty "prominent" American men abducted a German-American attorney from his home at gunpoint, forced him to kiss an American flag, and beat him severely. The local Italian press did not protest the violence. Indeed, S. Z. Poli displayed the flag in his theaters with an arrow pointing to the spot where it had been kissed.[40] For now, the colony and the native-born population were united in fighting Hun autocracy. But what would happen when the common enemy was vanquished, the same power structure re-mained, and the aspirations of the newer immigrants and the native-born collided? The answer would emerge soon after the armistice.

The visits of an Italian dignitary in April and October 1918, meanwhile, were very similar in form to Italy-America Day, but had a more specific purpose. General Emilio Guglielmotti was military attaché to the Italian embassy in Washington and traveled the country to promote the sale of Liberty Bonds. The *colonia* and the mayor's office honored him with parades and banquets. While boosting the Third Liberty Loan during his appearance in April, the general made a tour of the Italian enclave, visiting a school, St. Michael's church, and the city's largest Italian-owned company. In October for the Fourth Liberty Loan, he accompanied a squad of Alpini soldiers, veterans of the front, whose dashing appearance produced an outpouring of emotion. "Throngs of people crowded the streets," noted a reporter, "and swarmed about the men shaking hands with them, cheering them and even, in many cases kissing them." Like the Italy-America Day, these visits by representatives of the Italian government focused the attention of the colony on its national rather than regional origins and heritage.[41]

In his first speech at Yale's Woolsey Hall, Guglielmotti spoke in Italian to the audience of five thousand, but offered a quotation from Napoleon: "L'argent fait la guerre." Since the federal government planned to finance two-thirds of the war effort through its heavily publicized bond campaigns, no New Havener needed a translation. But the appeal had never before been made so directly to the city's Italians. The Treasury Department targeted immigrant groups for the Third Loan, and ethnic leaders and institutions led the way at the grass-roots level. To explain the bonds, *prominenti* held mass meetings, and the Italian press printed question-and-answer columns. Once again the societies served as the effort's backbone. Given the heated drives taking place in the city as a whole—contests inside the factories, War Saving Stamps sales in the schools, rousing speeches in theaters—there was no way to avoid the call for war funds. On the two occasions the general came to the city, Italians bought more than $200,000 worth of bonds.[42]

All over the United States, Italian communities distinguished themselves in their support for the Liberty Loan and War Savings Stamps campaigns. Soon after visiting New Haven in April, General Guglielmotti "invaded the Loop" as the guest of honor in a Loan parade of more than thirty thousand Chicago Italians. The parade was larger than "any foreign language demonstration that has ever taken place in the city," and prompted the governor of Illinois to hit a high note of praise: "I have never doubted since the war arose . . . where our Americans of Italian birth would be, for their race has been engaged in fighting for liberty for centuries." In Philadelphia, an Italian committee collected a stunning $5.6 million for the Fourth Liberty Loan, while Boston Italians purchased $300,000 worth of War Savings Stamps. In New York, Italians purchased an estimated $20 million worth of bonds in a single drive, and even in the former Industrial Workers of the World stronghold of Lawrence, Massachusetts, Italians stood out as major contributors to the war finance campaigns.[43]

While General Guglielmotti and other Italian dignitaries played an important role in this response, Liberty Loan officials approached the immigrants from a different angle. Prior to the general's first visit to New Haven, full-page advertisements appeared in the English-speaking and Italian press, cultivating the newcomers' sense of obligation to the United States.[44] "Men of Foreign Birth, you left your native land because you wanted to make your home here. You left because you wanted the freedom, progress and *opportunity* which America offers, and which no other country in the whole world offers in such full measure." Illustrating these words is a drawing of immigrants gazing at the Statue of Liberty from the deck of a ship. The ad reminds foreign-born readers of the rights they share with the native population, speaking as if they had already found success and acceptance in America. The enemy threat to the United States was therefore a direct threat to their own well-being. "For this is your country now. Your homes are here. You have raised your children here." The ad concludes by imploring immigrants to buy bonds "for the sake of the country where your children's children will be born." The experience of most Italians of course fell far short of prosperity and tolerance. But the Liberty Loan drives, by according equal status to people, if only rhetorically, and encouraging their participation in the country's present and future welfare offered the *connazionali* a new role on a very different playing field. City institutions like the major banks, municipal departments, and state agencies the Italians had previously avoided or been excluded from, and the political life the newcomers normally shunned, were no longer so distant, abstract, and intimidating.[45]

The Liberty Loan in particular offered the *colonia* an education in the benefits of American banking. Guglielmotti's first visit coincided with a period of financial distress for the colony. During the fall and winter of 1917–18 three private Italian banks in the city collapsed, obliterating the savings of hundreds of depositors. The bankruptcies revealed gross mismanagement, speculation, and high living. The worst failure occurred in February, when a bank run uncovered a discrepancy of nearly $120,000 in one firm's accounts. The response was not limited to the *famiglia*. During the initial hearings large crowds, primarily of women who controlled their households' purse strings, went to the courthouse. Though their pleas were in vain and their money lost, the women's outbursts did not go unnoticed. *Il Corriere* called for new banking laws and the formation of a fully regulated Italian-American savings bank. As important, the paper urged immigrants to think twice about trusting their money to someone purely on the basis of nationality. Meanwhile, the non-Italian banking community was quick to identify a market for its services, and many firms advertised in the Italian press. "Deposit Your Money in a Strong and Secure Bank," the First National Bank advised in Italian, "we have protected our depositors for more than 54 years." Indeed, Liberty Bonds, offering an attractive interest rate and the guarantees of the federal government, could not have come at a better time. "Invest in your country!" the billboards cried, and thousands of immigrants did.[46]

Where one deposited one's savings might not be considered a form of political expression, but protests over the price of bread have long been. The price in question bore the mark of Herbert Hoover, whose agency's push for a standard eight-cent loaf was going unheeded. In March, twenty-five Italian bakers agreed to raise their price to ten cents, which set off a week of protests within the colony, since they sold nearly thirty thousand loaves to the Italian population each day. While many customers vowed to go without bread rather than patronize the bakeries, others took their grievance to the local food administration office, demanding the Hoover price be enforced. Giuseppe Santella offered to lead a mass meeting on the issue, and Alderman

Leopoldo Cobianchi began an investigation. The outcome is unclear, but it appears that the bakers withdrew the increase. Though hardly an echo of the more famous food riots in Petrograd, Turin, and New York of the previous year, these events in New Haven made the visits of Guglielmotti all the more meaningful. While the immigrants hosted a representative of the government that was their past, they also were developing a new relationship with the government that was their future.[47]

Whatever the activity, whether it was baking bread with flour substitutes, donating books to the training camp library fund, or saving peach pits for the manufacture of gas mask filters, nearly all of the war work in New Haven was framed in terms of helping "the boys over there." "We are facing drive after drive for money, but what of it?" argued a daily paper: "Many of our boys are facing the great German drive on the western front that means not money but life itself." Through the last year of the war, city residents heard this plea at every turn. Rosa Poli spoke in the same idiom. "When peace comes, the Italians here can greet with a clear conscience the returning soldiers because they have done their duty here at home to care for those who were fighting abroad." When casualty lists began to appear in April 1918, the demand became more emotional. "NEW HAVEN BLOOD HAS DYED THE FIELDS OF FRANCE," one notice bellowed, urging everyone to buy Liberty Bonds.[48]

Under these circumstances it is not surprising that city residents, like people all across the country, embraced a new means of demonstrating their commitment to the soldiers. The service star flag, created soon after America entered the war, quickly assumed the sanctity of a time-honored ritual. Made of white cloth with a red trim border, the flag displayed a blue star for each man in the armed forces, and a gold star for each man who died in uniform. New Haveners posted thousands of the emblems in their windows, while local factories, schools, clubs, and churches dedicated giant versions of the flag to recognize employees and members in the service. In September 1918 the St. Michael's and St. Anthony's parishes held elaborate ceremonies to bless two of the largest service star banners in the city. Each congregation held a parade of its parish societies, then conducted a High Mass, where a female member presented the flag to the clergy for dedication and blessing. An outdoor celebration followed, with musical performances, speeches, and the raising of the special banner. The St. Michael's flag contained 717 stars and was unique because two hundred of its stars represented parishioners serving in the *Italian* Army. The parish saw no conflict in using this American invention to honor all of its soldiers. Over in the city's Hill district, Rosa Poli presented a flag with 308 stars to St. Anthony's church. In the spirit and manner of the times, she asked God for their return "where they will live with us a credit to their race." Like other ceremonies the colony held during the war, the flag raisings addressed the desire for respect from outside the enclave.[49]

Even though Poli did not have a son in the service, the *Union* noted

"To Persons of Foreign Birth–Write a Letter to your Soldier Boy in the Language of the United States." This poster describes the predicament of Italian immigrant parents who wanted to communicate with their American-born sons overseas. "They can understand your language when spoken," the poster sympathizes, "but don't know how to read or write it." The solution: attend free English classes sponsored by the Connecticut State Council of Defense. Courtesy of the New Haven Colony Historical Society.

she was "almost overcome with emotion." The flag raisings must have been powerful and moving occasions. In New Haven the wait for any kind of news was particularly excruciating. The city had one of the longest casualty rolls of any medium-sized city in the country, and due to the restraints of official secrecy, the daily casualty list was the only sure way to figure out where a man was on the front. The mail took at least a month to arrive from France, and the men who saw action did not discuss or were deliberately vague about what they encountered, so as not to exacerbate the fears of friends and family. This is apparent in the letters that Corporal Louis

Popolizio, a member of the all-Italian machine gun company, sent home after being wounded. "I have been doing wonderful work, dear mother, with the boys in the line," he wrote reluctantly, "and by the way I stopped one of their bullets. But I am not much hurt, so do not worry."[50]

While news from abroad was meager, New Haven's coverage and recognition of local Italian men in uniform was remarkably abundant. Nearly forty of the members of the all-Italian machine gun company appeared in soldier profiles columns, complete with photos and biographical sketches. "Italian Gun Co. Work Interests All the City," claimed a headline, a true statement judging from the many articles and letters published. In September, one of the company's non-Italian officers returned to New Haven from the frontlines. He described the gunners' courage not only to Italian clubs but also to gatherings of American reporters and Masons.[51] Syndicated poet Edmund Vance Cooke also presented an explicit (and absurd) paean to the Italian fighting man, asking Americans to discard their ethnic prejudices:

> Do you see that brisk chap going over the top?
> You call him a "guinea," a "dago," a "wop."
> Well, names are but names and our words are but wordy,
> But he might be a Rafael, Dante or Verdi,
> Galileo or Angelo! Where would I stop
> If I opened the scroll
> Of that marvelous roll
> Whom you might have called "guinea," or "dago," or "wop"?[52]

Prowar sentiment could be this generous, praising people who were previously objects of indifference or scorn. An estimated 300,000 men of Italian descent served in the United States armed forces, and accounted for perhaps as much as 10 percent of American casualties in the war.[53] All across the country the names of Italian dead were engraved on plaques, monuments, and federal grave markers, while their families grieved along with thousands of other non-Italian families. For the generation of Italian Americans who lived through the war, these sacrifices for the United States would not be quickly forgotten.

On September 15, 1918, New Haven held its last great war parade before the armistice. "Commemoration Day" marked the anniversary of a local regiment's departure for France and included the largest march ever held in the city. Thirty thousand people paraded, many honoring their sons in the special "Mothers" and "Fathers" contingents. City Hall raised a service flag with more than eight thousand stars and the mayor and governor unveiled an honor roll on the New Haven Green.[54]

Il Corriere called the event a "fiasco," however. For the standard "Italian division" of the parade, only seventy people showed up. The *connazionali* preferred to march with co-workers in the factory delegations, with organizations like the Red Cross, and with the parents' contingents. But local

Italians showed that new forms of association were being kindled, competing with the ties that had bound the enclave since the 1880s.[55]

While colony residents "did their bit" over here, their former *Patria*, the Republic of Italy, remained on the defensive. Not until October 24, 1918, a year after Caporetto, did the Italian Army flex its muscle again on a major scale. Within ten days Italy crushed the disintegrating Austro-Hungarian forces. Its infantry marched into Trento and the navy landed in Trieste, the principal cities of *Italia Irredenta* that had tempted the Republic of Italy ever since unification. On November 4, Austria-Hungary capitulated, ending the war that had cost more than 500,000 Italian lives.

In the homeland and in immigrant enclaves around the world, *connazionali* rejoiced. New Haven's Italian churches held solemn High Masses to commemorate the dead and to pray that the men overseas were safe and would return home soon. Community leaders, in predictable fashion, planned their biggest celebration ever for Monday, November 11. A parade, band concert, and special banquet would precede the pièce de résistance—a fireworks display on the city green.[56]

The colony would not be alone in celebrating the end of hostilities on that date. News of the great armistice that quieted the entire western front reached the city shortly after 4:00 A.M. The train yard received the message first and let loose with horns and steam whistles. Soon the factory gongs of the Winchester Arms plant joined in, followed by the bells of the City Hall tower and every fire station and church in the area. Crowds surged toward the city green with whatever instruments, pots, pans, and cowbells they had. Until well into the night they "took possession of the streets and made them their own." The only thing Mayor FitzGerald could do under the circumstances was declare a holiday and close all the saloons.[57]

Local Italians were not lost in the chaos. The colony had the only festivities planned and ready for that evening. "There are a lot of people right here in New Haven who haven't stopped celebrating since the news came that Italy had whipped Austria to a fare-thee-well." At 5:00 A.M., "a delegation of at least 6,000 Italians" marched to the mayor's home and serenaded him until he appeared and gave a speech. The crowd then lifted FitzGerald on their shoulders and later held a banquet in his honor. But the main event was the fireworks display, which the entire city came out to watch. Paid for by the Italian-owned G & O Company, the show drew "a crowd which, in numbers and *unity of purpose*, has probably never been equaled in the history of New Haven." Purely by coincidence, the Elm City depended on its Italian immigrants to conclude "one of the greatest days in American history."[58]

This "unity of purpose" would be short-lived. In the weeks following the armistice, dozens of Italians appeared daily at City Hall to request papers enabling them to return to Italy. One immigrant, asked why there was such a rush to go back, bluntly told a reporter, "Our country needs re-construction, yours don't." In reply the *Register* commented that all of the applicants "had good rolls of Uncle Samuel's yellowbacks," implying that they had made their pile of money and were now through with America. These sentiments had been absent from public discourse in New Haven for more than a year. They gave voice to the disillusionment of the native-born population, in whom the war had developed a false sense of security and accomplishment in handling ethnic relations. Glorifying the strength of American ideals and institutions, the older stock viewed immigrant contri-butions to the war effort as proof of the melting pot's greatness. Instead, the unity of the "Great Crusade" proved as elusive after the armistice as it did before 1917. During the next five years, these feelings of frustration combined with a fear of the new bogeyman of bolshevism to reverse the immigration policies of the United States.[59]

The vast majority of Italians in New Haven did not go back to Europe. Many waited for sons and husbands to return from France. Many more decided to settle permanently, having obtained a stable life in America in contrast to the turmoil in Italy. With children in city schools, an array of colony institutions, and a taste of steady, well-paid employment, Italians solidified their local position during the four years the war had cut off immigration. The advances made in status and political clout in the larger city were meager in comparison. But the home front campaigns that max-imized public participation and hailed all contributors regardless of ethnicity pointed to something far better in the future. Indeed, what is most striking about wartime *colonia* life is how the population made the most of every opportunity, not only to demonstrate their commitment to the war effort but also show their sheer physical presence in the city. The colony had come of age. Marching to the mayor's house and forcing him out of bed—this was not the kind of thing Italians would have dreamed of doing just a few years before.

7 "New York Jewry Must Do Its Duty"

✶ ✶ ✶ ✶ ✶ ✶ ✶ ✶ ✶ ✶ ✶ ✶ ✶ ✶ ✶ ✶ ✶ ✶

New York Jewry's response to the home front effort was a good deal more complicated than the Italian experience in New Haven. For the overwhelmingly Orthodox Jewish immigrant population, the government's secular demands inevitably created a number of cultural and religious problems. The *Yiddishes Tageblatt*, one of the Orthodox newspapers, found itself acting as a mediator on repeated occasions. In May 1918 the paper had to clear up confusion about the International Red Cross. Many immigrant Jews thought the Red Cross was a Christian organization because of its emblem and ignored its pleas for contributions. The *Tageblatt*'s editors had to insist that all donations would go to help needy Jews and Gentiles alike. "And let it be said right here that no contributor to the Red Cross need wear the button," the paper urged, "or place in the window of his home the little poster with the Red Cross on it. Let no Jew or Jewess be deterred from giving to the Red Cross because of that symbol." A few months later it was not the immigrant Jew who needed to be educated, but the leaders of the city's Fourth Liberty Loan campaign. When organizers held a parade on the Lower East Side on a Saturday, the Sabbath day when much of the area's population did not carry money, bond sales were disappointing. The *Tageblatt* publicly scolded the campaign managers: "Let whoever is in charge, profit by this lesson and in future pay regard to the religious convictions of the people of the neighborhood. Tactlessness always recoils upon the heads of those guilty of such errors."[1]

Cultural misunderstandings like these mirrored a deeper discrepancy between downtown Jewry and the federal government. Not only did cultural and religious differences set many of New York's eastern European Jews apart from the rest of the nation but so did their attitudes on the war. While most of the country was supporting the war effort or at least acquiescing to it, the city's new immigrant Jews were vocal about their pacifism and had political strength. As we have seen, they provided the People's Council for Democracy and Peace with much of its support in the summer of 1917.

Simply put, it would take much more than a single event like Caporetto to mobilize the Jewish population behind the Allied cause, as had been the case in the New Haven *colonia*. Several key differences between New York Jewry and the Italian population complicated matters greatly. Jews of eastern European descent had little if any of the patriotic attachment to their homelands that inspired the Italian communities of America. Not surprisingly, most had no sympathy for the empires that had denied Jews basic rights for centuries. The leaders of uptown Jewry, meanwhile, were also very different from the Italian *prominenti*. War advocates such as Louis Marshall and Jacob Schiff called for undivided loyalty to the United States and were ever fearful that Jewish dissent might provoke an outbreak of anti-Semitism. They would have choked on the ethnic boosterism that the Comitato Pro Patria made its stock in trade. The crucial difference between these two ethnic populations, however, was the well-organized and very popular antiwar movement led by the Jewish left. During the summer and fall of 1917 the city's garment unions, the *Jewish Daily Forward*, and the Socialist party commanded the greatest attention from downtown Jewry. The feeling among local eastern European Jews toward the war was marked more by resignation and resentment than by open advocacy.

But within less than a year this divisiveness evaporated, and New York Jewry became active and outspoken in its support for the American war effort. The Socialist party's dramatic campaign in the city elections of 1917 marked the apex of Jewish opposition to the war, as thousands of Jewish trade unionists, women, and students helped to make American political history. But from that point on, the departure of New York men for the western front, a major city drive for Jewish refugee relief, and a series of earth-shaking events overseas, including the Bolshevik Revolution and Britain's Balfour Declaration on Palestine, helped to transform downtown Jewry's pacifism into a strong commitment to Allied victory.

As the scale and significance of these events suggest, the home front experience was an important moment for New York's eastern European Jews.[2] The war pulled the city's most recent Jewish residents into public life more than ever before and redefined the world map, providing new and reinvigorated sources of cultural pride. Given the Jewish population's varying national origins, religious attitudes, and political ideologies, its transformation into a prowar bulwark inevitably took time and was contingent on a series of dramatic events and pressures. Out of this turbulent experience emerged a new voice in politics, one that combined an innovative and articulate desire for social justice with an activist role in foreign affairs. Participation in the American war effort provided the sense of security and entitlement necessary to make these demands in the electoral arena. Whatever their initial positions on the war, their permanent home was now in

America. For the vast majority of New York Jews, the last year of the conflict made that relationship all the more important.

War or no war, 1917 was still an election year for Gotham. Every two years the people of New York chose their state and municipal representatives and voted on a variety of ballot measures. But in this particular election season, the political landscape was strikingly different. For the first time in the city's history, the local Socialist party, running on an antiwar platform, appeared to have a very good chance of winning the mayoralty race and a host of other offices. The bulk of this support came from New York's eastern European Jews, a population that had never made its presence so visible in local politics, but now, through their unions and socialist press, seemed poised to make an extremely powerful statement on American participation in the Great War.

Although Louis Marshall feared that the city's downtown Jews were seen as "creating for themselves in the United States a ghetto of separatism, of taking themselves out of American life, and of nullifying all that has been done through these many years to prove that the Jew is a faithful, patriotic American citizen," no anti-Semitic backlash materialized.[3] The impressive mayoralty bid of Morris Hillquit, a Latvian-born Jew, and the promising candidacies of more than twenty Socialists from largely Jewish city wards was certainly proof of ethnic difference.[4] But Jewish support for the Socialist party also illustrated how actions could speak louder than political platforms. Participating in the campaign, downtown Jewry behaved no differently than any native-born community on an important election day. War opponents in the spring and summer of 1917 stayed within the law when protesting intervention and the draft. By attempting to reverse those policies in the voting booth that fall they went the extra mile, demonstrating a clear and forceful commitment to the American political system (or at least its New York variant). The enthusiasm that greeted victorious Socialist candidates in Jewish Harlem, the Bronx, Brownsville, Williamsburg, and the East Side represented a declaration of ethnic political independence that could no longer be ignored.[5]

Ironically, this declaration took place in the midst of one of the most destructive periods of political repression in American history. During the three months leading up to the November election, mobs lynched an Industrial Workers of the World organizer in Montana and horsewhipped a People's Council activist in Ohio. In the late summer, Justice Department officers in Chicago raided the national headquarters of the IWW and the Socialist party, and state and local authorities prohibited the People's Council from convening in one Midwestern city after another. In New York the Postmaster General's office threatened to withdraw the mailing privileges of the Socialist *Call* and the *Jewish Daily Forward*, and two Columbia University professors were fired for their pacifist activities. Across the country, dissent had become an offense punishable by federal mandate and brute force.

Nevertheless, New York's immigrant and second-generation eastern European Jews strongly supported a party that ran on a pacifist platform. "We are the party of peace," a Socialist candidate proclaimed at an East Side rally, "and we are the party that will work for peace, and there is no crime in saying that." Though hardly seeking to usher in a socialist millennium, a large body of Gotham voters (most notably elements within the Irish, German, and African-American populations who were disgusted with the American war effort and its alliances) lent their support. This third party protest vote gave Hillquit a chance in the mayoralty race. But the Jewish neighborhoods alone provided the Socialist majorities needed to elect the party's candidates to office. Energized by the Russian Revolution and the Kerensky government's peace proposals, much of downtown Jewry had the feeling that anything was possible. With strong institutions to back up their convictions—the unions, radical Jewish press, Workmen's Circle branches, and Rand School among them—they had the ability to put up a good fight. Unlike the rest of the country, New York City had a remarkably open discussion of the war in English and many other languages, though dissent was most often articulated in Yiddish.[6]

Opposition to the war provided the unifying theme for the Socialists' campaign, but so did concerns about the troubled economy. Economic conditions in the city were reaching a crisis point for working-class immigrants in late 1917. Gotham did not have the munitions industries that fueled New Haven's early wartime prosperity, nor did it enjoy the kind of home front boom associated with World War II. Earlier in the year there had been widespread rioting, when primarily Jewish immigrant women protested exorbitant food costs by overturning pushcarts, dousing goods with kerosene, and forming the Mothers' Anti-High Price and Socialist Consumers Leagues.[7] On the eve of the election, prices remained at the same high levels that had ignited the riots, and most workers' wages did not increase until the following spring. An investigator for the Food Administration at the time discounted the possibility of more rioting on the Lower East Side, but reported that:

> The people look pasty, white and hollow eyed. Most of the foods on the stands and push carts are starchy foods—potatoes, cereals, etc. Very little meat is bought and eggs are beyond the price of an ordinary tailor's wage. . . .
>
> Suggest to the Federal Food Administrator in New York not to send Food Posters such as the beautiful basket of vegetables—or the dish of fruit to the East Side. Those people never see such things. It makes them indignant when asked not to waste them.[8]

More than a fifth of the city's half million public school children were found to be suffering from malnutrition, and about fifty thousand workers were without jobs in the garment district. Rumors of an approaching "coal famine" appeared even in the prowar press. The disruptions that came with sending tens of thousands of young breadwinners into the armed forces only increased the burden on working-class families. "The revolutionary spirit is in the air everywhere," the same Food Administration investigator wrote, "and there is nothing to prevent it blowing this way."[9]

The occupants of City Hall were ill-suited to handle an economic crisis, especially one that landed so squarely on the backs of the working poor. The reform administration of Mayor John Purroy Mitchel, who was running for reelection, opposed the kind of patronage that Tammany Hall traditionally offered immigrants, let alone a comprehensive program of emergency relief.[10] In these circumstances, the Socialists provided the sharpest critique and the most concrete proposals to address the city's unrest. Unlike their opponents, who were bound to the war effort, the party freely attacked military mobilization as the cause of working-class misery and offered well-crafted measures that cut to the quick of popular need. Along with demands for an immediate, general peace, the party called for lunch programs at all public schools, municipal ownership of utilities and railways, and city-operated markets that would sell food, coal, and ice at wholesale prices. The socialists also addressed the immigrants' future opportunities as well as their current problems, advocating a free city university system and social insurance. The socialist *New York Call* vividly portrayed the economic crisis in an illustration dominating its front page in mid-September.[11] Clinging desperately to a rock labeled "wages," a worker and his wife and children are about to be engulfed by waves, whose crests are named "increased cost of coal," "rent," "flour," and other necessities. The *Call*, however, does not leave the reader in complete despair. Beneath the drawing it gives instructions on how to vote Socialist in the city primary. Tens of thousands of Jewish voters would follow the paper's advice.

The fact that the party's standard-bearer shared the same ethnic background as the majority of these voters was as crucial as the poor economy to the Socialists' success. With Morris Hillquit, downtown Jews could truly claim that the head of the Socialist ticket was "one of our own." Born Morris Hillkowitz in Riga, Latvia, the party's national secretary emigrated in his teens to the Lower East Side and made his way out of the sweatshops by attending night school and becoming a journalist and labor lawyer. A hero among immigrants for his role in organizing the garment unions, Hillquit possessed the idealism, intellectual toughness, and moral integrity that had inspired immigrant Jews to support such local and national candidates as Henry George, Theodore Roosevelt, and Woodrow Wilson in the past. Though he would finish third in the race, Hillquit polled five to fifteen times the number of votes that non-Jewish Socialist candidates had received in previous mayoralty elections. Most of the eighteen Socialists who were elected to lesser offices that fall had essentially the same life path. Sixteen were Jews of eastern European descent who began in the ghetto, and all were political veterans with close ties to either the *Jewish Daily Forward* or one of the Jewish-led unions.[12] These shared backgrounds and aspirations were in sharp contrast to the main message of incumbent Mayor Mitchel. A reformer whom New York Jewry overwhelmingly supported in the 1915 election, Mitchel made loyalty and patriotism his chief concerns, waging a campaign of thinly veiled nativism that was anathema to most immigrant and second-generation ethnic voters.

Not surprisingly, Mitchel's highly polarizing message did not go over well with a vast population struggling to create a home in the United States. But for Socialist candidates like Louis Waldman, who emigrated from the Ukraine, and Baruch Vladeck, who left Russian Poland, the mayor's gross miscalculation was a godsend.[13] After years of defeat, success was within reach. "There is at this time a sentiment in favor of us as has never existed before," noted a party leader in early September. "If we grasp the opportunity we can make the East Side red this year." The possibility of "making New York safe for socialism" fueled activity in neighborhoods that the party had always written off, demanding a much larger supply of campaign materials and a far greater number of volunteers. With little money at their disposal, the Socialists' effort was highly labor-intensive. Union members, women, and even school children contributed to the most participatory electoral season in the history of Jewish immigration to Gotham. "These were indeed exciting times, unforgettable and delirious nights," recalls one candidate, whose Harlem district during the campaign "was ablaze with hope of victory and great enthusiasm."[14]

With many union officers running on the Socialist slate, Jewish organized labor provided the party with most of its muscle. Announcing their endorsements of the party early on, the garment unions and a variety of locals affiliated with the AFL and United Hebrew Trades formed their own election and "educational campaign" committees. The most impressive of these was the Amalgamated Socialist Campaign League, created by the Amalgamated Clothing Workers, which launched a $10,000 election fund drive in late September. Collecting money in the shops through subscription lists and the purchase of special stamps, the union utilized the techniques of both the Comitato Pro Patria and the federal government. The Amalgamated allowed its offices to be used as party headquarters, sponsored rallies, led torchlight parades, and provided campaign volunteers. Union leaders stumped openly for the socialist ticket. Committee chairman Louis Hollander held that the older political parties had made themselves irrelevant that year: "They have permitted the workers and their families to starve. . . . It is time for the organized workers of the city to awaken and turn these rascals out." Together with the aid of the predominantly Jewish locals of the Ladies Garment Workers, Cap Makers, Fur Workers, Neckwear Makers, Bakers, and Painters, organized labor abandoned the independent, apolitical stance that had been a cornerstone of Gompers's "bread and butter" unionism. For Sidney Hillman and the two-year-old Amalgamated Clothing Workers, the election of 1917 foreshadowed the direct campaigning the CIO would later bring to electoral politics in the 1930s.[15]

Though ineligible to vote, Jewish immigrant women played a significant role in the election. A critical issue of the 1917 election was women's suffrage, which the state of New York faced in a referendum ballot for the second time in three years. Since there was not a single state east of the Mississippi that offered women full voting rights, the referendum's passage in New York was by no means a foregone conclusion in 1917.[16] Many female activists in the party and unions now made the need for equality in the political realm their top priority and worked hard for the power of the ballot. Angered by the harsh treatment of suffragist pickets in Washington, D.C., that fall, many Jewish women joined the Socialist Suffrage Campaign Committee. In late October, sixteen women's organizations met at the *Daily Forward* building and passed resolutions in complete support of the socialist campaign. "Resolved," one of them read, "that from tomorrow on our work be commenced with a city-wide distribution of suitable literature, holding of meetings and the organization of working-class house-wives, tenement by tenement." In the last month of the campaign, volunteers distributed thousands of leaflets, cards, and posters with titles such as "Woman Suffrage, Democracy and Justice." Canvassing the men of their unions, they held rallies outside factories every day during lunch hour and between the day and evening work shifts.[17]

Refusing to participate in the city's largest suffrage demonstration, the committee sponsored its own "Woman's Pageant." In New York's most compelling example of political theater during the war, more than three hundred different women "from all walks of life" appeared in Union Square, demonstrating the work they performed on a daily basis. Wearing placards that described conditions for women in their respective occupations, squads of needle trades workers, domestics, office employees, teachers, actresses, and housewives appeared onstage with the tools and props of their trades. "The deductions to be drawn from such a demonstration are legion," the *Call* announced. "If women are entrusted with the performance of rearing, teaching and nursing the future citizens of the country, they are surely entitled to voice their opinions in the politics of the nation." Labor activist Pauline Newman, herself a candidate for county clerk, put in more concrete terms the hardships of being excluded from the electoral process. "Without a vote," she argued, "these women have had to strike every time they wanted a raise in their wages and better conditions." Within ten days of the pageant, disfranchisement was no longer an issue. Even more than the men of the party, women were able to celebrate a major victory, as suffrage won in New York State by more than 100,000 votes. Morris Hillquit's claim that the Socialist surge made the difference was no exaggeration. Outside of the city, the measure passed by only a thin margin of one thousand ballots; Gotham provided nearly all of the plurality. Within a generation the food rioters and their descendants would become committed New Deal voters.[18]

By far the most unconventional group contributing to that autumn's "uprising of democracy" were Jewish school children. Beginning in mid-October, elementary students in the city's Jewish neighborhoods led a full-scale revolt against reform measures in their schools. Mayor Mitchel's attempt to revise the school system according to the Gary Plan, a popular Progressive era scheme with a focus on Americanization, provoked widespread fears among the city's new immigrants. Downtown Jewry viewed the program as a form of industrial education, one that would permanently subjugate working-class families to poverty, and took the lead in fighting the reforms. For ten days thousands of students, with their parents' backing, participated in riots and demonstrations. Nearly all of the children who were arrested for vandalism and clashes with police were Jewish. High school students joined them in late October, calling a general strike to protest the recent extension of their school day by one hour and the introduction of military training courses. Again, class conflict framed the issue: many high schoolers needed to work in the afternoons to support their families and fund their continuing education. The fact that the longer day was made in the name of military preparedness only further inflamed the ire of immigrant Jews.[19]

The students eventually won most of their demands, and though they were years from voting eligibility, their protests articulated the same aspirations as the women's suffrage and labor movements. Though street orators and campaign rhetoric might have helped to exacerbate tensions, the youngsters acted on their own initiative and for very pragmatic reasons. At an early age, they imbibed downtown Jewry's abiding faith in education as the best pathway out of the ghetto.[20]

In the pro-Socialist atmosphere of the city's Jewish neighborhoods that fall, the transition from student protester to party advocate was easy for many young Jews. At the height of the school controversy, two hundred children held an impromptu parade through East Harlem, "led by a lad in his early teens carrying a banner with a picture of Hillquit and underneath the inscription 'Votes for Socialism.' " That same night three thousand children between the ages of seven and fourteen made a similar march on the East Side. This involvement was not limited to street demonstrations, as students also participated in traditional campaign activities. Twenty-year-old Joseph Freeman and his brother became soap box orators for the party, along with many others who "trained" as public speakers at the Rand School. Leonora Fishbine offered her help after reading a *Forward* appeal for tenant fundraisers. "With this subscription list in hand," she wrote to a party leader when enclosing her collection, "I went from door to door in our building and asked for a contribution. To tell the truth, when I first started out with this noble message I felt a little discouraged on account of my personality (I am only 13 years of age)." Like Leonora, most of Gotham's eastern European Jews were slightly hesitant about asserting themselves in politics "on account of" their ethnic background, class, or sex. The Socialist campaign was pervasive enough to erase this uncertainty, and then some.[21]

With this solid level of support, downtown Jewry was able to overcome both the obstacles that had kept the Socialist vote so low in the past and the repressive atmosphere that was smothering the antiwar movement nationwide. In the weeks leading up to November 6, teams of volunteers wearing red armbands distributed an estimated 5 million pieces of party literature and 200,000 campaign buttons. With rallies in dozens of public schools, posters in shop windows and subway platforms, and red banners stretched across busy intersections, it was obvious the party was not working in a vigilante-ruled nightmare.

Three activities in particular show how the campaign brought downtown Jewry into the rough-and-tumble world of New York politics.[22] The first, street speaking, was the mainstay of any Socialist campaign. With the added participation of trade unionists, women, and students, it was ubiquitous in Jewish neighborhoods that fall. The party sponsored literally hundreds of open-air meetings, including a "Red Night" in Brownsville that presented more than eighty speakers. Though participants' accounts glow with nostalgia, the fundamentally democratic quality of their work is evident. Socialist candidate Louis Waldman recalls the immediacy that existed between speaker and audience in an age before microphones and sterile auditoriums: "There was something intimate and inspiring about those street corner meetings. . . . We had the sky above us, and on clear nights the moon and stars." As idyllic as this sounds, plainclothes policemen were frequently present; at one gathering, a reporter estimated eight hundred people and two detectives in attendance. But there were no arrests of party speakers during the campaign. In fact the surveillance boosted the candidates' reputation, their courage in defending free speech elevating them in downtown's esteem. More troublesome were off-duty soldiers, Knights of Columbus members, and prowar socialists, who at random tried to drown out speeches or provoke fights, and the virtual state of war between the party and the Tammany Hall men whose livelihoods depended on an election day triumph. But by mid-October, the *Call* was no longer reporting losses in the fight for pavement space. As a Tammany veteran recalls, "By no stretch of the imagination were all Socialist campaigners either scholars or gentlemen."[23]

A second set of campaign activities, more critical to the party's success, was the effort to make the election as clean as possible. The existence of an entrenched system of corruption made Socialist vote counting difficult and often dangerous work. The varieties of fraud taking place before, during, and after the balloting were not only numerous, but also frequently aided and abetted by the police. Louis Waldman remembers, "It was a commonplace occurrence for toughs and gangsters to lounge about the polls, intimidating and browbeating voters." Only on those rare occasions when an outside party was able to mount a strong challenge to Tammany did New York's immigrants really experience something resembling an honest election.[24]

The election held in 1917 was definitely one of those occasions, and the sense of moral authority that came with fighting corruption clearly contributed to the campaign's enthusiasm and crusadelike appeal. In the weeks leading up to the election, the party organized "an army of honest ballot soldiers" who went from tenement to tenement to validate persons registered to vote. It was the canvassers' job to mark off the "cemetery" and "mattress" (deceased and bed-ridden) voters, and disqualify "residents" whom Tammany moved into assembly districts the night before the election. At each of the city's more than two thousand polling places, election observers were needed to watch the voting process and count the ballots. The party held preparatory classes on the finer points of machine rule. Advertising the work as an "opportunity of gaining some legal knowledge," the watchers' committee built a mock election site and practiced role-playing. Volunteers were also taught the enemy's various tricks. Many had to fight just to get into their designated polling places when the votes were being counted, and it was not uncommon to see watchers return to party headquarters with black eyes and bruises. But on election day, the Socialist surge was too large for Tammany Hall boss Charles Murphy to undermine, and most of the training went to good use.[25]

The last experience drawing downtown Jewry into the political system that fall was the thrill of winning an electoral victory. "The East Side didn't sleep election night," the *Call* reported, as residents either waited for the results of close races or reveled in their triumphs. In a spontaneous act of celebration, thousands of men and women marched from the party's campaign headquarters to Cahan's *Daily Forward* building, where they listened to bands and their victorious candidates giving speeches from the building's balcony.[26]

In the end, Mayor Mitchel and Morris Hillquit finished very close together in the running. Tammany Hall's nondescript candidate, Judge "Red Mike" Hylan, who talked about the war the least, won more ballots than the reformist hawk and the Socialist dove combined. Yet the election foreshadowed how downtown Jewry would continue to play a major role in city politics. New York's Democratic machine co-opted various elements of the Socialist platform during the campaign, calling for school lunches and municipal ownership of the street railway system. More direct evidence of the Jewish voters' power was found in the election results. Jewish enclaves sent an unprecedented ten Socialists to the New York State Assembly and seven to Gotham's Board of Aldermen, and elected the first (and only) Socialist judge in city history. Hillquit called the campaign "an uprising of democracy, for human happiness, and for lasting peace." Within a decade the Socialist victories would be little more than a fond memory, but the commitment of downtown Jews to electoral politics established firm roots in the election of 1917.[27]

In the months following the election the Socialists, far from provoking the anti-Semitism that Louis Marshall and other uptown leaders feared, continued to divert Jewish unrest into established political channels. At the height of the coal crisis in late December, the party and its Consumers' League organized mass meetings and pressed for immediate fuel relief for the city's poor.[28] But like so much of downtown Jewry's high hopes that fall, the Socialist agenda would not hit pay dirt for another generation. Vastly outnumbered in both the state assembly (10 party members in a body of 150) and the Board of Aldermen (7 votes out of 70), the Socialists' proposals for municipal ownership and social insurance languished. "Our work was therefore mainly confined to voting against obnoxious bills and criticizing them," remembers Benjamin Gitlow, who represented a Bronx district in the state assembly. "We were tolerated but not liked." And though they tried to maximize public participation, holding open meetings with constituents and publishing reports of their work, most of the Socialists could not win reelection a year later.[29]

By that time, however, downtown Jewry, while maintaining its solid commitment to social democracy, had abandoned pacifism and vigorously supported the American war effort. The local scene had not produced this change of heart. The catalyst was a series of events taking place far away, in Petrograd and London, in Palestine and the Ukraine, in the trenches along the Vesle River and deep in the Argonne Forest. In the last year of the Great War, from the end of the 1917 New York election season through the signing of the armistice, the world map changed dramatically, and Gotham's Jews felt this transformation very deeply. The Bolshevik Revolution, the collapse of the German, Austro-Hungarian, and Ottoman empires, and the real possibility of a Jewish homeland in Palestine created new relationships between Jews of eastern European descent and their adopted country. While the election campaign signified a new stage of settlement for downtown Jews in New York City, the transformation of Europe signaled an equally important cutting of ties to the past.

A fund drive for refugee aid and welfare work set the tone for Jewish perceptions of the dramatic events of late 1917. Even before the United States entered the conflict, the major Jewish relief agencies had agreed to raise $10 million nationwide during the course of the year. As December approached, the various divisions of the Joint Distribution Committee were still $4 million short of their goal. With financier Jacob Schiff as its chairman, a drive to raise all of the remaining amount in New York City alone was set for December 3 to 16. Though only a month had passed since the municipal elections, organizer Rabbi Nathan Krass was optimistic that the city's diverse Jewish population would work together to save 3 million Jews living in desperate conditions. "We are no longer orthodox and reformed, conservative and radical," he urged on December 2, 1917, "but we find all Jews dropping their distinctions in the face of the common suffering, united by that ancient formula, I am a Jew."[30]

New York Jews had been raising money for war sufferers in Europe and Palestine since the autumn of 1914. What made this new campaign special was not only the huge sum involved, but also the fact that it was being collected simultaneously with a $1 million appeal for the Jewish Welfare Board to provide religious and recreational services for the tens of thousands of Jews serving in the armed forces. Leaders of the Joint Distribution Committee and the JWB shared essentially the same prowar attitude and decided that money for the two causes would be collected in common. Though both drives sought to assist fellow Jews, it was clear that the welfare drive benefited tremendously from its link to refugee work. It is hard to imagine that the Lower East Side, so soon after the Socialists' electoral triumph, would have thrilled to a campaign that would support the war effort, however indirectly.[31]

Yet the pairing of the two drives provoked very little opposition. The *American Jewish Chronicle* briefly attacked the move, claiming that the JWB would take funds away from the far more needy war sufferers. "Have we a right to do this? Is it dignified? Is it just? We say no."[32] But when the campaign was kicked off, the *Chronicle* quietly withdrew its protest, agreeing that both needs could be met by giving just a few dollars extra for the boys in uniform. Most important, the Jewish trade unions supported both causes. Downtown labor drew a line between opposition to the war and helping soldiers and sailors who came from its working-class ranks. The Jewish National Workers' Alliance, a labor Zionist organization, had already launched its own welfare effort, the People's League for Jewish Soldiers. "It is high time to stop debating about militarism and pacifism," an alliance leader claimed in mid-November, "when the community is faced by the fact that thousands of Jewish boys in the camps have to resort to the YMCA for their spiritual comfort." Though dwarfed by the Welfare Board, the People's League demonstrated how concern for hometown servicemen was not a class or partisan issue.[33]

With this universal support, the two-week effort was a smashing success. Fund-raisers repeatedly invoked the fact that the city now had the world's largest Jewish population, and wealthy Zionist Nathan Straus voiced what became an unofficial slogan for the campaign, "New York Jewry must do its duty." At the Astor Hotel banquet kicking off the drive, Jacob Schiff donated $200,000 and goaded his rich dining companions into contributing a one-night total of more than a million. A few days later the *New York Herald* reported from the other side of the giving spectrum. "One woman yesterday brought an ordinary bed pillow—all she had to offer. This represented her sacrifice she said, and might bring a few cents for the cause." Children from the city's Talmud Torah schools donated their Hanukkah gift money, the stars of the Yiddish stage held benefit performances, and Kosher butchers donated a percentage of their earnings. Meanwhile, future entertainment moguls William Fox, Adolph Zukor, and Marcus Loew formed a committee to solicit funds from the theater industry. Al Jolson told a mass meeting that "he remembered enough of his early life in Shrednik, near Kovno, to realize how much the money was needed" when he gave two thousand dollars.

Pharmacists gave a large portion of a day's receipts, and aspiring professionals at City College formed a group to solicit funds campuswide. These activities did not go unrecognized. President Wilson, the secretary of war, and the mayor and mayor-elect sent letters of praise, while the city papers provided daily coverage of the campaign, complete with lists of the major contributors.[34]

Though familiar "our crowd" names such as Morgenthau, Lehman, and Sachs dominated the donor lists, Jewish labor provided the most audacious contribution. As the campaign drew to a close, Jacob Schiff hinted publicly that an unnamed source planned to give more than a million dollars to put the effort "over the top." On the last day of the drive, volunteers were surprised to learn that it was not a Warburg or Guggenheim "who stepped into the breach" with the money, but the sixty thousand local members of the Ladies' Garment Workers Union. The union targeted Washington's Birthday (February 22) for a general collection, when production for the spring season was booming and union workers earned double-time or time-and-a-half for working on the holiday. "We hardly doubt whether the manufacturers will grudge the extra pay in view of the noble purpose for which the money will be devoted," commented the union newspaper. Combined with efforts made by the United Hebrew Trades, Amalgamated Clothing Workers, and other downtown unions, Jewish labor pledged $1.25 million, by far the largest single donation to the cause. A YMCA executive who advised the citywide drive went so far as to pronounce it the "greatest act on the part of organized labor since the world began."[35]

In appealing to their members, the unions spoke virtually the same language as the uptown millionaires who led the general campaign. Stressing the ability and "sacred duty" of the Jewish working class to provide refugee aid, Joseph Schlossberg of the Amalgamated claimed that "no one can bring them help except we here, in this country. . . . It is now our turn to do our share." Though Schlossberg could speak to union members as one eastern European immigrant to another, his conception of Jewish prosperity in America and tragedy abroad was remarkably similar to that offered by Schiff or Marshall. "Most of us come from those very countries where this terrible conflagration is now raging," Schlossberg wrote in the *Advance*. "We have found a home of refuge in this country. . . . Let us show that we are worthy of the advantages we enjoy in this country by responding to the cry of despair coming from our fellow human beings on the other side of the globe."[36] Bombarded simultaneously by reports of starvation in Europe and pleas to comfort "the soul of the Jewish immigrant" in uniform, downtown labor's opposition to the war effort rapidly weakened. Raising $5 million in a fortnight, the drive was also dramatic proof to the immigrant population of its success in the New World. Gotham Jewry had great resources at its disposal and knew how to use them.

Events in Petrograd did much to make this rapprochement on the war issue possible. Within days of the November 1917 election, news of Russia's second great revolution commanded the headlines of every New York Yiddish daily. The Bolsheviks took power on November 8 and immediately called for peace talks between the belligerent nations. Ignored by the Allies, the new government agreed with Germany to cease hostilities and begin negotiations to end the war on the eastern Front. Eight months after the fall of the czar, the Bolsheviks were satisfying their country's greatest desire— to get out of a war that had already cost more than 1.5 million Russian lives.

The response of New York Jewry was naturally as diverse as the population itself, ranging from outright condemnation to fervent support. The conservative Yiddish and Anglo-Jewish newspapers and most uptown spokesmen attacked the "Maximalists" for smothering democracy, accusing them of being paid German agents. But the majority of downtown Jews knew little about the new regime.[37] A Food Administration investigator studying pro-Bolshevik sentiment on the East Side was able to dissuade his superiors' fears. Though a portion of the garment workers were supportive, the man or woman on the street seemed complacent about affairs in Russia rather than committed to the revolutionary banner. "The term 'Bolsheviki' is tossed about loosely," the observer reported in early February 1918, "and used to describe or cover any form of insurgency":

> For instance, a push cart man had his cart on the wrong side of the street; the policeman told him to move it; his neighbors laughed, shrugged their shoulders, and called "Bolshevik." A youngster played truant from school; his mother told the teacher at the settlement house that she did not know what to do with Aaron, he was a "Bolshevik." A grocer was found hoarding sugar; the people said he was a "Bolshevik."[38]

Though the label quickly became part of the local lexicon, it was hardly embraced in the manner envisioned by Lenin or Trotsky.

More than any other single factor, the October Revolution stilled the downtown left's opposition to the war. Preserving the new revolutionary government in Russia from destruction became the main priority of many Jewish socialists, and overnight Germany became the chief threat and needed to be stopped. This change in policy was most visible among the radical wing of the socialist movement, which quickly abandoned its former pacifism. Benjamin Gitlow, recently elected to the state assembly, was very active in the People's Council for Democracy and Peace, and campaigned hardest on his antiwar beliefs. But the revolution completely transformed his thinking. Rejecting the idea that "socialism could be attained peacefully through a gradual accommodation of reforms," he now viewed this approach as a betrayal of working-class interests. "I deduced from the war that brutal force and violence were the final arbitrators, and concluded that Socialism would come as the result of revolution in which the masses would use force and violence in overthrowing their oppressors." Gitlow left the state assembly after one term, the Socialists soon after, and together with John Reed helped form the Communist Labor party.[39]

Less colorful but more complicated was the response of the majority of Jews in the Socialist party and the downtown unions. The *Forward* and other radical Yiddish papers had been staunch critics of the Bolsheviki before the revolution, favoring Kerensky's Provisional Government during the fall of 1917. The moderate Jewish left not only opposed the new regime on theoretical grounds (for moving too fast for underdeveloped Russia) but also feared its autocratic tendencies. Despite these concerns, downtown could not resist admiring the first workers' state in world history, or the Bolsheviks' principled demands for open diplomacy and a democratic peace. "When the Bolsheviki first took hold of the government," admitted the *Advance*, "we were all startled and feared the worst for Russia." But in mid-January 1918, the paper's editors praised the new government for its "directness, frankness, and firmness" in working to bring an end to the war.[40]

While a range of opinions greeted the "ten days that shook the world," immigrant Jewry's response to the Treaty of Brest-Litovsk was unanimous. For most Brownsville and Williamsburg residents, the earth trembled far more during February and early March of 1918, when Bolshevik foreign minister Leon Trotsky broke off negotiations with the Central Powers and adopted a policy of "no war, no peace." The decision to demobilize the Russian Army proved disastrous, as German troops immediately swept into the Baltic provinces, Russian Poland, and the Ukraine. Now compelled to sign an even more drastic treaty, the Bolsheviks ceded roughly 60 million Russians and one-third of the country's factories and arable land to foreign rule. Most important for downtown Jews, the occupied territory contained nearly all of the former Jewish Pale of Settlement. While most Americans understood the treaty in terms of a "Bolshevik betrayal," immigrant Jewry saw only the naked aggression of the Central Powers. So recently liberated from czarist tyranny, their kindred back home once again fell under the domain of an autocratic power. Attitudes now came full circle. A year before, downtown Jews supported Germany because of their hatred of the czar. Now they vigorously supported the United States out of hatred for the kaiser.

For the second time in less than a year, immigrant Jewish concerns coincided with the initiatives of the Wilson administration. Wilson's Fourteen Points peace proposal of January 8, a calculated attempt to satisfy much of the democratic program of liberals and the left, finally provided Jewish leaders of the unions and Socialist party with a statement of principles they could endorse. The Third Liberty Loan offered an ideal opportunity to demonstrate this support in action as well as words. On March 11, 1918, Secretary Max Pine of the United Hebrew Trades, once a strong advocate of the People's Council for Democracy and Peace, announced his organization's commitment to the loan. The UHT bought $1 million worth of bonds in the April-May campaign, followed by the Amalgamated Clothing Workers' purchase of half a million. "The United States of America, of which we all are good and loyal citizens," declared the press organ of the Ladies Garment Workers Union in May, "is waging a life-and-death struggle with a militarist power that tramples upon and outrages every free country upon which it can manage to lay its blood-and-iron claws." For this reason the ILGWU's leadership argued that its loan subscription of $100,000 expressed "the wish and desire of the entire membership." The prowar tide rolled through the rest of the Jewish left's organizations and presses during the spring and summer, as the Jewish Socialist Federation, Workmen's Circle, and People's Relief Committee joined the downtown unions in declaring their support at conventions and May Day celebrations. "It is no longer a capitalist war," Cahan's *Daily Forward* exclaimed as early as April, "neither is it imperialistic or nationalistic. It is a war for humanity."[41]

This reversal in attitudes was the subject of a *New York Times Magazine* article in early August 1918. Now that dissent in the city had practically disappeared, the paper admitted the pacifists' strength during the previous year. To discover what caused this transformation, and to see if it was genuine, a reporter interviewed Bernard Marcus, chairman of both the East Side Liberty Loan and East Side Red Cross Committees. Marcus credited the kaiser for the tremendous jump in bond subscriptions in his district, from $500,000 in the first Liberty Loan drive to over $15,000,000 in the third. "No sooner was the ink dry on the treaty of Brest-Litovsk," he claimed, "than the east side began to turn all allegiance, not only of the lip but of the heart, to the United States. It was then that they saw the foul methods and the malignant purpose of Germany in all its hideous intent, and then realized the true reason why this country had to be at war with the world's chief enemy." Typical of war advocates concerned with the loyalty of the foreign-born, Marcus was quick to present this sea change as proof of assimilation and correctly sensed that more was going on in the ghetto than met the eye. The immigrants' primary concern may have been with conditions in the Old World, but they were also making a statement about their relationship to their new home.[42]

This was especially so in the case of downtown's working-class leaders and institutions. Committing themselves to the American war effort, they abandoned a heritage of revolutionary mass movement politics made increasingly irrelevant by two decades of development in the United States. The success the immigrant left enjoyed in Gotham clearly distanced them from their radical Bundist past in Russia. No longer harassed or outlawed, the trade unions and radical Yiddish press flourished in New York, and despite the government's repressive tactics during the war, the Socialists reached their greatest strength, and the membership and influence of the downtown unions expanded dramatically.[43]

The Jewish left was ultimately exempt from what labor journalist Melech Epstein called "by far the greatest single factor" compelling many socialists in America to take such a strong stand against the war. "Unfortunately for the American party," Epstein argued, "it was not burdened with the heavy responsibility of the European Socialists . . . It was in no way accountable for the bread and butter of masses of people." But this was not true for Gotham's Jewish left in the winter of 1917–18. With constituencies that were several hundred thousands strong, local Socialist office holders and the Jewish-led unions shared more in common with the British Labour party than with the rest of the American Socialist party. With representatives in the state and municipal legislatures and a voice in the various federal labor boards, leaders like Abraham Cahan, Benjamin Schlesinger, and Pauline Newman saw no need to take to the barricades. Newman, an ILGWU organizer, socialist candidate, and pacifist, recalled years later how the decision to support the war was difficult but ultimately pragmatic. "It wasn't just a feeling that you had against war—you had to think of the consequences if you stayed out. To say that we liked it, or were terribly enthusiastic about it, I would say no. . . . We wanted Germany not to win, and if we didn't want Germany to win, we had to do our share." During the war downtown's moderate left did not lose faith in gradualism and the power of the ballot. Leon Trotsky best expressed the differences between the moderate Jewish left of New York and their revolutionary comrades in Russia. Having lived briefly in New York, Trotsky claimed that Morris Hillquit's brand of socialism was most popular among "successful dentists."[44]

A veteran social worker on the East Side pointed out the full political meaning of these developments. Writing less than a week before Brest-Litovsk, Dr. Henry Moskowitz viewed the East Side as a "political barometer" for New York rather than a radical aberration. He claimed that the ghetto thus far had experienced three different and coexisting stages of political development: the power and patronage of Tammany Hall, the idealism of the progressives, and the welfare program of the Socialist party. The future lay in the weaving together of these strands. "We are on the eve of a fundamental change in our municipal policies," Moskowitz wrote, pointing to the immigrant Jews' independence and keen sense of social justice as a crucial factor. More concretely, he saw the benefits of a healthy rivalry between the socialists and the Tammany machine that co-opted their program, and identified Al Smith and Robert Wagner as important leaders of a new urban politics. After the Red Scare and the left's struggle with Bolshevism in the immediate postwar years, progressives like Moskowitz and Wagner and Jewish socialists like Louis Waldman and Sidney Hillman would be working for a middle way, somewhere between laissez-faire and the Comintern. Within a generation these hopes would culminate in the CIO and the New Deal.[45]

Events in the Middle East coincided with the Bolsheviks' seizure of power in Russia, giving New York Jews still another major connection with the war. In a carefully worded letter, the foreign minister of Great Britain, J. Arthur Balfour, appeared to usher in a new epoch in Jewish history: "His Majesty's Government view with favor the establishment in Palestine of a national home for the Jewish people and will use their best efforts to facilitate the achievement of this object." The statement captured the imagination of Jews worldwide. In New York, the Orthodox and center-left Yiddish press hailed the note's intentions, while the *Forward* stood alone in opposition, calling the pledge a capitalist ploy. But when British troops captured Jerusalem on December 11, 1917, a sense of its tremendous historical significance pervaded all of the Yiddish papers. Coinciding with Hanukkah and New York Jewry's $5 million fund drive, the victory demonstrated how Allied power could make the British declaration a reality.[46]

The issue of Palestine never generated the same level of anxiety or activity among Gotham's Jews as the horrors confronting Jews still living in the former Russian Pale. But the profound cultural resonance of Zionism helped swing support to the Allied cause.[47] Regardless of how small the Zionist societies' memberships were, or how meager the circulation of their journals, Jewish nationalism served as an important lens for interpreting current concerns. The war, by exposing the vulnerability of eastern European Jewry more than ever, bridged the gap between culture and action, as relief efforts and hopes for security in the postwar future pointed increasingly to Palestine. With at most 15,000 adherents nationwide in 1914, American Zionist groups approached the 200,000 mark by the armistice. Most of these new members were of eastern European origin, and their support for the war and the Allies was never stronger.[48]

The dramatic growth in Zionism's popularity might seem surprising in the hyperpatriotic atmosphere of wartime America. But the movement in the United States brought into play contradictory impulses, enabling it not only to coexist with 100-percent Americanism but also to overcome two major opponents within the Jewish population, uptown Jewry and the left. During the war, assimilated leaders such as Louis Brandeis, Stephen S. Wise, Horace Kallen, and Henrietta Szold advocated the homeland idea in terms of universal benefit rather than narrow political or religious self-interest, proposing a democratic and progressive society that would serve as a model for the entire world. This appeal, identified by historian Allon Gal as the movement's "mission motif," was fully compatible with the crusading spirit of the United States' war aims. As important, American Zionists accepted their status as a diasporic population and did not insist on the *Aliyah*, the return migration to Palestine. Jewish statehood was conceived first and foremost as a refuge for persecuted Jews from Europe, not the United States. With their European coreligionists living in ruins or on rations, American Jewry accepted fund-raising and advocacy as its main contribution to the Zionist cause. This combination of universalist principles and limited participation set a precedent for American Jewish involvement in Palestine that would persist for the rest of the twentieth century.[49]

With Wilson's tacit approval of the Balfour Declaration, the American Jewish Committee's traditional anxiety over the charge of "dual loyalty" further diminished. On April 28, 1918, the organization cautiously endorsed the British pledge, stressing once again its conviction that the primary allegiance of American Jewry would be to the United States.[50] The left, in contrast, responded more to grass-roots sentiment than high-level diplomacy. For decades, downtown Socialists had condemned Zionism as a bourgeois diversion and a veil for British imperial interests. But conditions in Russia and the pressing need for protection of Jewish rights worldwide changed the minds of many union leaders and rank and file members. In late April, delegates from more than two hundred organizations met at the *Forward* building to form the Jewish Labor Conference for Palestine. "We are convinced," one of their resolutions proclaimed, "that Palestine can become a Jewish land only when Jewish labor will devote its strength and energy for Palestine and in Palestine." The ILGWU and Amalgamated Clothing Workers eventually passed statements of sympathy for a homeland at their 1918 conventions, while the *Forward* and other radical publications discontinued their attacks.[51]

With these opponents either quieted or converted, the Zionist presence in New York was able to blossom. Membership swelled in local branches of the Federation of American Zionists and its successor, the Zionist Organization of America. Smaller organizations of women (Hadassah), youth (Young Judea and the Intercollegiate Zionist Association), and workers (the Poale Zion) launched campaigns to raise medicine, food, and money for Palestine. Public display of the Zionist flag was one of the clearest manifestations of the movement's growth in confidence as well as numbers, and the symbol of the future state of Israel became a standard feature at meetings and rallies.[52]

The boldest example of local Zionist support was the campaign to recruit men for the Jewish Legion then preparing to fight in Palestine. Less than a year earlier, conservative leaders in both the pro- and anti-Zionist camps attacked the legion and its separatist message. But by the spring of 1918 former critics like the *American Jewish Chronicle* aggressively supported the idea. "The very fact that Jews as Jews are participating in the struggle for Palestine," the paper urged, "will not fail to impress the nations and will strengthen our position considerably in every respect." This rhetoric mirrored the legion's own exaggerated sense of its importance. Since the United States was not at war with Turkey, only men who were exempt from the American draft could join, and then could only serve as British soldiers. Though of meager military value, the roughly five hundred volunteers from New York were a public relations triumph. Imitating the previous year's draft calls, Zionist clubs held send-off celebrations on the Lower East Side, drawing huge crowds. One member described the legionnaires' loyalties in the most acceptable manner possible. "These men prefer service in the ranks of the Jewish Regiment not because they love America less," explained Gershon Agronsky, "but because they love Palestine too, they do not cherish American culture less, but they cherish Hebrew culture too, they do not glory in America's past less, but they glory in their own history too. No true American requires a fuller explanation." In April the legion received the approval of Mayor Hylan, who reviewed a contingent of volunteers at City Hall and presented them with "the flag of David." With Tammany Hall's endorsement, the men began their long journey to the Palestinian front.[53]

It was not until August 31, 1918, the eve of the Jewish New Year, that Woodrow Wilson publicly endorsed the Balfour Declaration and the Zionist cause for the first time. The president followed the lead of Mayor "Red Mike" Hylan, as well as the governments of Britain, France, and Italy, both of the wartime popes, and such diverse American groups as Protestant clergymen, the AFL, Irish and Polish Catholic nationalists, and the prowar Jewish Socialist League. Whether truly sympathetic to a Jewish homeland or based purely on self-interest, these declarations of support boosted the movement's respectability and the optimism of Zionist supporters to unprecedented heights. Despite the failure of Versailles and the schism that divided the Zionists after the war, the goal of restoration was never again so strongly attacked as a hopeless dream or so vilified as a dangerous call for self-segregation as it had been before 1918. American Zionism was able to move out of the ethnic enclave and into the mainstream, working effectively within the cultural and political institutions of the United States.

At about the same time Wilson finally gave his approval, Rabbi Leon Spitz witnessed a curious melding of these two forms of national identification. A Jewish Welfare Board representative at Camp Upton, Spitz assisted new recruits as they stepped off the New York trains and marched past the camp's athletic field. One day at a baseball game, a band played "Hatikvah," the Zionist hymn that later became the anthem of the state of Israel. "Can you imagine," the rabbi comments, "how those hundreds of Jewish rookies hailing from Pitkin Avenue and Herzl Street in good old Brownsville on their first day in camp felt?" Spitz appreciated the psychological comfort of the moment, if not the cross-cultural irony: "The strains of 'Hatikvah' on the baseball diamond of Yaphank dissipated much of that void and heartache and loneliness that every new recruit experiences." Baseball and the diaspora, *shtetl* migrants and the United States Army, John Phillip Souza and Theodor Herzl, the war brought these disparate elements together, and for the time being they were able to work together toward a common goal.[54]

When the armistice was declared, New York responded much like New Haven, with a daylong party in the streets. Serenaded by sirens and church bells, New Yorkers built bonfires, blanketed the streets with confetti, and danced and marched in hundreds of spontaneous parades. Lewis Feuer, then a young boy living on the East Side, remembers how his heavily Jewish neighborhood did its full share of celebrating. "When the War ended, it evoked such a display of American patriotism as I have not since witnessed," he wrote six decades later. "Our street, like many others, had a great block party. The Kaiser in effigy was berated, while American flags and banners waved from lines strung from houses across the street. The children sang

'Over There' and 'My country, 'tis of thee'; the men in uniform were heroes."[55]

Feuer's recollection illustrates how the war at home for New York Jewry both resembled and contrasted sharply with the experience of the New Haven *colonia*. Gotham's Jews had proved to be just as receptive to the government's call to arms. Though the reversal of the left certainly accelerated this process, booming demand in the garment industry also made Jewish sections hum with prowar activity in the spring of 1918. Schoolchildren selling War Savings Stamps, neighborhoods raising service star flags, and women marching in Red Cross uniforms became familiar activities in Williamsburg or Jewish Harlem as they were in any other large city district. Residents also encountered the federal government in a variety of new ways, from regulation of the needle trades to the setting of a fair price for matzoh for Passover.[56]

Perhaps most important was the deepened sense of commitment, and the mounting peer pressure within the community, that came with having local men overseas. Service flags flew from tenements as well as shops, schools, and synagogues. "I have a boy at Yaphank," was the reason a Kiev-born pushcart vendor gave for aiding a Thrift drive. "He is helping the government and I would be ashamed of myself, if for one day I could not give up socks and suspenders for War Stamps." During the armistice celebration, garment workers paraded behind a banner marked "We made the clothes worn by the boys who canned the Kaiser." So strongly opposed to conscription a year earlier, the Jewish-led unions now boasted of its members in the service and vowed to protect their "returning heroes" from postwar unemployment and exploitation. By late summer opposition to the war was a vague memory. "Today one may travel the length and breadth of the east side and see not a red button," gloated the *New York Times* in August. "All Socialist propaganda is useless." The same could be said of the New Haven *colonia*, which never had a significant socialist movement.[57]

Yet Lewis Feuer's recollections also reveal the singular meaning of the armistice for New York Jewry. In contrast to the dual celebration of Italian and Allied victory that took place in New Haven, the songs the East Side children sang, the flags the people waved, and the soldiers that everyone cheered were American. Downtown Jews brandished no evidence of their Russian or Romanian pasts, nor did they display symbols of future nations or homelands, of Poland or Palestine, the Baltics or the Balkans. However deeply New York Jewry might have felt about the suffering in eastern Europe or the prospect of creating a Jewish state in the Middle East, there was very little sentiment for their own return migration. The political and cultural aspirations downtown articulated during the Socialist campaign of 1917 and the final year of the war had become linked to life in the United States. New York's immigrant Jews proved their ability to assimilate on their own terms. Committing themselves to a role in the political arena and establishing a new cultural reference point in Palestine, Gotham Jewry thought and acted within a very different framework after 1918. Events of local, national, and worldwide significance made this possible. Acting on humanitarian, ideological, and ethnocultural impulses, New York Jews discovered enduring sources of unity in the maelstrom of the last year of the war.

8 "They Were Good Americans"

Survival and Victory on the Western Front

★ ★ ★ ★ ★ ★ ★ ★ ★ ★ ★ ★ ★ ★ ★ ★ ★ ★ ★ ★

Private Harold Kalloch, an American-born member of the Yankee Division, received an unusual assignment as his unit took up combat positions for the first time. "We had Polish Americans, German and Italian Americans, about 40 in the battery," Kalloch explained in a postwar questionnaire. "Just before we went to the front in April the Captain called me to his office. He told me to watch the Germans etc. and report to a major at the front." Kalloch encountered nothing that was suspicious in the immigrants' behavior. "I never found anything," he concludes, "they were good Americans."[1]

If being a "good American" in the trenches meant being a reliable soldier, then Kalloch's comments were also valid for describing his division's Italian machine gunners and the Jewish draftees of the Seventy-seventh. These men did not distinguish themselves as members of different ethnic groups, but as American soldiers who helped bring an end to a war that had wiped out approximately 10 million lives. Despite the many cultural, religious, and linguistic differences that pervaded the American Expeditionary Force, doughboys of all backgrounds learned quickly that they had to work together and rely on and trust each other if they were to survive. Lacking in training and combat experience, they showed tremendous courage and commitment in a series of major offensives in the last months of the war.

A number of historians have observed that the AEF never experienced the depths of disillusionment and despair that pervaded the European armies.[2] But though they fought in France for a comparatively brief period, the Italian machine gunners from New Haven and the Jews of the Seventy-seventh Division were well acquainted with the war's carnage. Most fought in the infantry, the branch of the American armed forces that suffered by far the highest number of casualties. The Yankee Division suffered nearly fifteen thousand killed, wounded, and missing, while more than twelve thousand losses were inflicted on the Seventy-seventh. These men were no strangers to modern warfare. They learned as much about shell shock and self-inflicted wounds, of no man's land and aerial bombing, as any other soldier on the western front. They also participated in two of the most famous incidents of the American war effort: the Italian gunners helped drive back the German surprise attack at Seicheprey, and many of the Seventy-seventh's New York Jews survived the ordeal of the "Lost Battalion" in the Argonne Forest.[3]

To describe how the AEF's ethnic soldiers felt about these experiences is a difficult task, because like most of their comrades in the Great War they usually concealed from family and friends the destruction they had seen and endured in France. This chapter will examine the limited "literature" the doughboys themselves produced to communicate what the war was like: the letters and diary entries they wrote in the field, the unit histories they produced shortly after the war, and the questionnaires and memoirs they completed many years later. What emerges is a much more complicated picture than the story of tragedy and loss of innocence that has so strongly colored the modern imagination. The ethnic soldiers of the AEF suffered and sacrificed on the western front, but they did not become a "Lost Generation" who rejected and turned their backs on American institutions and politics when they returned to the United States. Service overseas was a point of honor for most and bound them closer to their homes in America than ever before.

Many officers and enlisted men of the Yankee and Seventy-seventh divisions published histories of their units after the war, which were distributed by the organizations' veteran clubs at reunions and Armistice Day ceremonies. A genre of American war writing that the works of Hemingway, Dos Passos, and Fitzgerald completely overshadowed, these amateur histories nevertheless describe the engagements and conditions that the Italians from New Haven and the Jews of New York encountered from a soldier's perspective. The bonds of friendship that had developed between the men inspired them to preserve this past. After helping each other through the intense fears and hardships of being combat soldiers, most veterans wanted to possess something that would recall and honor their fellows. Many of the unit histories resemble school yearbooks, a souvenir of the war filled with soldier songs, drawings, and verse. The most important feature of each volume is its honor roll, listing all of a unit's casualties. Citing the date, location, and often the circumstances of each man's death, the histories also provide the address of his next of kin in case a surviving "buddy" wished to contact the family. The books reflected the durability of these ties. Well into the 1960s, groups like the 304th Field Artillery Association continued to publish newsletters, hold reunions, attend funerals, and place flowers on their members' graves.

The soldiers' pride in their accomplishments in France is a major theme of the narratives. Chroniclers of the Yankee Twenty-sixth Division, which served on the western front longer than any other American division, describe eight months of heroic endurance, of flash points of terrible fighting separated by periods of holding turbulent sections of the line. After training with a French unit in March 1918, the division and its Italian machine gunners moved to the Toul and Chateau Thierry sectors, fought in the Champagne Marne defensive in late July and the St. Mihiel campaign in September. The Yankees served out the rest of the war near Troyon and north of Verdun. True to form, the organization's historians emphasize how the division was able to do the job despite the meddling of its regular army superiors.[4]

The career of the Seventy-seventh Division and its Jewish draftees was even more dramatic. Training with the French in the Baccarat sector in late June and July 1918, the New Yorkers moved to active fighting near the Vesle and Aisne rivers. From late September to the armistice, they advanced the greatest distance under enemy fire of any U.S. division and played a critical role in the Meuse-Argonne offensive that ended the war. The story line of the division's histories is theatrical, complete with character development, thrilling climax, and inspiring denouement. Repeatedly we are told about the "hardy back woodsmen from the Bowery, Fifth Avenue and Hester Street," green rookies who became the heroes of the AEF.[5]

Clearly, the veterans who kept these books on their shelves for decades to come felt very strongly about their role in the Allied victory. But what the soldier-historians chose to commemorate excluded much of the reality of the AEF in France. The war that the Italian guardsmen and the Jewish draftees fought was not nearly so heroic and sanitized. By the time the American presence in the trenches began to be felt, the enemy's war machine was essentially beaten. As the AEF approached the 2-million-soldier mark in the fall of 1918, the Allies were simply choosing weak sections of the western front and obliterating them with superior force and firepower. In the two major American offensives, the St. Mihiel and Meuse-Argonne campaigns, the Germans were actually in the process of bringing their forces closer to home for the inevitable peace negotiations. Captain W. Kerr Rainsford of the 307th Infantry was one of the few unit historians to acknowledge the true nature of the fighting. "The war, as it was found by American troops, seems very seldom to have involved a fight to the finish on any one bit of ground; and the most that was usually accomplished was to hurry a withdrawal, for which the enemy were prepared at a later date." For all the talk of the Americans' martial qualities, it was really the ability to put millions of fresh soldiers in the line that caused the Kaiser to capitulate.[6]

The AEF did not benefit as much from the enemy's weakened condition—or the four long years of Allied experience—as one might expect. The Italian and Jewish doughboys in fact fought very much like their doomed predecessors in the naive and horrific days of Verdun, the Isonzo, and the Somme. With over 200,000 killed and wounded in a few months of combat, the American army suffered casualties at a rate comparable to the major belligerents. Much of the blame for the excessive losses can be attributed directly to the leadership of General John J. Pershing. In addition to his famous refusal to integrate Americans into the Allied armies, Pershing insisted on a nebulous doctrine of what he called "open warfare," a strategy of movement and concentrated rifle fire that was only slightly more enlightened than the disastrous thinking that had reigned in the early years of the war.[7] Fortunately, the war ended before the American command's faith in military élan and moral courage could exterminate its own generation of young men. A French soldier provided perhaps the best commentary on the AEF's method of fighting. "I don't know if I will live to see the end of this," the veteran *poilu* told a private in the Seventy-seventh Division, "but the way you Americans fight this cannot last long. Why you don't stop, you go right on, you don't care about the loss of life, you go, go, go, and go."[8] The AEF memorial at Montfaucon backs up his claim. With the remains of more than fourteen thousand men killed in the Meuse-Argonne offensive, it is the largest American cemetery in Europe.

Sadly, the courage and accomplishments of the divisions in which the Italian and Jewish soldiers served were the product of what amounted to a wasteful strategy of attrition. The fact that so many of the doughboys were grossly unprepared for the tasks assigned to them further muddies the AEF's reputation. When asked in a postwar survey about the quality of their training, weapons, and supplies, veterans of the Meuse-Argonne drive were overwhelmingly negative in their responses. The more candid American memoirs tell of men sent into combat who barely knew how to fire their weapons, and officers who could not read maps or navigate with a compass. Then there were the thousands of soldiers who avoided the fighting whenever possible, either collapsing under the strain or deliberately slipping away to escape what seemed to be suicide. As was true of the home front experience, a rhetoric and presentation of facts that routinely outstripped reality defined the Great Adventure in Europe.[9]

Two incidents during the war, the battle for Seicheprey and the struggle of the so-called "Lost Battalion," best illustrate the tragic nature of the doughboys' sacrifices and the common experiences they shared regardless of their ethnic backgrounds. The Italian machine gunners from New Haven participated in the Seicheprey fight, the first major action involving U.S. ground troops. New York Jews played important roles in the story of the Lost Battalion, which took place during the last offensive of the war. Two of the most heavily publicized events of the American war effort, these actions demonstrated the AEF's capacity for both inspiring commitment and inexcusable waste.

The Connecticut men of the Yankee Division occupied a two-mile stretch of trenches near the village of Seicheprey in April 1918. It was their first stint in the lines without French supervision, and the sector had been mildly active. But late on the night of April 20, "all hell was let loose," when gas and high explosive shells raked the Yankee lines with devastating accuracy, isolating the five hundred men in the frontlines from the rest of the regiment. As the first streaks of daylight appeared, so did the enemy: three thousand German soldiers, led by a crack storm trooper battalion. The *Stosstruppen* employed the same techniques that nearly crushed the Allies earlier that spring and overran the Yankee defenses. They quickly advanced a mile into the American lines.[10]

Desperate hand-to-hand fighting took place throughout the day, as the confused and battered Connecticut soldiers tried to hold their ground wherever possible. The Italian members of the 102nd's machine gun company, meanwhile, hurried in to force the enemy back. Their regimental commander, the flamboyant Colonel John "Machine Gun" Parker, later gave a great deal of credit to the company (and himself) for stifling the drive. Corporal Louis Popolizio's recollections were less self-congratulatory. "Some of my guns was firing over the left of the town during the conflict. Lots of the Germans were hanging on the barbed wire in the morning." When the smoke settled the next morning, the attackers had withdrawn to their original lines. It was a raid; they had no intention of staying. Yankee casualties totaled more than six hundred killed, wounded, and missing; the enemy suffered at least that number. The bodies of 129 Germans littered the area. Colonel Parker defined the battle as nothing less than "a turning point in the 'World War,' " and a clear demonstration to the Central Powers (and the Allies) that the American soldier could beat the best the enemy had to offer.[11]

The American press, having waited more than a year for a combat story, feasted on the Seicheprey fight and endorsed Parker's version of events. Yet the heroic spin they pushed on the public glossed over what was hardly a victory. At least 130 Yankees were taken prisoner, an unusually high proportion of the casualties, and the German government immediately used the captives for propaganda purposes. Privately, General Pershing and his staff viewed the action as further proof of the incompetence of the National Guard. They had good reason to feel that way. Chaos had ruled in the Yankee lines throughout the daylong battle: communication was nonexistent, friendly artillery bombarded its own men, and a counterattack was botched, resulting in an officer's court-martial.[12]

The proud comments of the regimental historian celebrate what was probably the New Englanders' gravest error. "The front line trench was to be held at all costs,—" wrote Captain Daniel Strickland, "there was to be no falling back. And there had been no falling back. The men of Connecticut had held the line until annihilated! There they were, dead,—in windrows almost, out in front of the fire trenches which by reason of the mud made poor places from which to fight."[13]

To an even greater degree than Pershing, Yankee Division commanders viewed the Allies' trench mentality as defeatist. They ignored the reigning defense-in-depth system, which assigned only a token force to the frontline, allowing it to be pulled back quickly to the support lines in the event of an attack. The New Haven–based C and D companies of the 102nd Regiment paid the price for their leaders' obstinacy. A day after the fighting only ninety-five of their five hundred original members were still fit for duty. Seicheprey, the event that served as a lesson in courage and patriotism for a generation of Connecticut schoolchildren, was a deadly and perhaps avoidable mess.[14]

Six months after Seicheprey, the Seventy-seventh Division and its Jewish draftees provided the country with a far more dramatic but no less equivocal story of sacrifice. In late September 1918 the division was assigned to push through the most difficult section of land in the Meuse-Argonne offensive. While most of the 900,000 Americans who went "over the top" faced open country, the Liberty men had to fight within the confines of the Argonne Forest. The area resembled a wild jungle, with thick undergrowth that covered a maze of deep ravines. On October 2, after struggling and suffering for a week, the remnants of several rifle companies and a contingent of machine gunners were able to break out in front of the main attacking force. The next morning, however, they found that the enemy had moved in behind them, enveloping their position in what was roughly the size of three football fields placed end to end. This plot of ground became known as the "Pocket," where 554 doughboys spent the next four and a half days completely surrounded.[15]

The soldiers were woefully unprepared for a siege. They carried a short supply of ammunition and barely a day's worth of food and water. They left behind their blankets, tents, overcoats, and rain slickers, bulky items that tangled in the thorny underbrush. Worst of all, the group lacked a doctor and adequate medical supplies. Under continuous mortar, machine gun, and sniper fire, the men had no choice but to remove the bandages from their dead comrades to use on the wounded. It eventually became too dangerous and exhausting to bury the dead. All attempts to escape the trap failed— only the outfit's carrier pigeons made it to the American lines safely. The force was not really "lost." Its position was well known to the divisional headquarters, but nothing could get through. Several units were nearly decimated trying to reach the surrounded men, while two planes were lost in an unsuccessful effort to airdrop supplies.[16]

The fifth day of the ordeal provided one of the most romanticized events of the American war effort. On the afternoon of October 7 a wounded doughboy limped toward the encircled position carrying a white flag. Taken prisoner the day before, he was sent back with a typed message asking the Americans to surrender. "The sufferings of your wounded can be heard in the German lines," an enemy officer wrote, "and we are appealing to your humane sentiments." The press later claimed that the American commander, Major Charles W. Whittlesey, yelled a defiant "Go to Hell!" in reply. In reality, Whittlesey and his officers simply looked at each other, smiled quietly, and gave no response. The doughboys never capitulated. Within a few hours the 307th Infantry broke through to their position and ended what had become a killing field. Of the 554 soldiers who went into the "Pocket," fewer than 200 were able to walk out on their own.[17]

Jewish soldiers played important roles in every aspect of the Lost Battalion ordeal. Two of the unit's runners, Privates Joseph Friel and Abraham Krotoshinsky, received the Distinguished Service Cross. Private Friel "tirelessly and cheerfully ran messages to all parts of the position," his citation reads, "showing an utter disregard for his own personal safety." He was killed trying to find a way through the German lines. Krotoshinsky, an immigrant barber from the Bronx, was the only runner who succeeded. He led a rescue party back to the battalion on the night of October 7, earning him the unofficial title "New York's Greatest Hero of the War." But the individual commitment and performance of most of the soldiers went unnoticed. In a postwar survey, Corporal Irving Goldberg describes how he spent "three days looking after my 1st Sergeant and a medical man both of whom were seriously wounded." The men were isolated from the rest of the group and Goldberg "could not get any word back to tell where we were." Though he could have returned to the unit on his own, he stayed with the injured men until they were all taken prisoner. In a letter home, Sergeant Major Irving Liner tried to put a humorous spin on his ordeal. "Do you remember how hard it used to be for me to go without food for twenty-four hours on Yom Kippur? Well, I had to go without food for five days, and it didn't affect me in the least."[18]

Corporal Meyer Siegel, the immigrant law student who was arrested before his draft board physical, was with the rescuing force that broke through after several costly attempts. "At that time," he recalls in his memoirs, "we felt that we wouldn't let them down; we must save the trapped men." He also remembers how their rescue was no cause for celebration. "It was one of the saddest moments of the entire war."[19]

While American propagandists succeeded in characterizing the event as one of the most heroic moments of the First World War, Meyer Siegel's comment hits closer to the mark.[20] The plight of the unit was in fact emblematic of the grave communication and supply problems that affected the AEF throughout the Argonne campaign. The Americans' progress was much slower and more costly than that of their Allies, a fact that prompted French premier Georges Clemenceau to call for Pershing's dismissal. The gross inexperience of the vast majority of the troops and their officers resulted in the same frontal assaults that the Allies had learned at such great cost to abandon. As historian David Kennedy has observed, the AEF in this last offensive "made most of its advances simply by smothering the enemy with flesh." Criticism of the American leadership did not surface until well after the war. In the meantime, it was the Lost Battalion's commander, Major Charles Whittlesey, who provided the most damning indictment of the myths that arose about the Argonne. He committed suicide in 1921, still bearing an overwhelming sense of responsibility for what had happened to his troops.[21]

Nearly everyone living in the United States knew of the struggles at Seicheprey and in the Argonne Forest. As combatants, immigrant and second-generation Italian and Jewish Americans made history in a way the nation recognized and applauded. While ethnic differences certainly helped to frame the time the Italian and Jewish veterans spent overseas, they endured these hardships in common with all frontline troops. The tragic scope of their months on the western front is succinctly expressed by a doughboy in the Seventy-seventh Division. "There are days in there that wreaked torture to body and minds beyond the power of man to describe," wrote Private Ruby Hughes in his diary, "and the memories of these terrible days are seared on our brains until we will go to our graves remembering it as vividly as if it were yesterday."[22] The new perspective the soldiers brought home was not only based on the victory they had won, but also on the dangers they were able to survive together.

A grim combination of expectancy, chaos, and ignorance shaped what was for the men of the Yankee and the Seventy-seventh divisions essentially a two-part story. It began with weeks of occupying the line in the same manner as their French and British predecessors. For the remainder of the war, the doughboys chased the enemy eastward—a mobility unknown to the Allies up to that time.

The Seventy-seventh Division, with more than twenty unit histories and published memoirs, provides us with the most voluminous doughboy literature of any American division on the western front. The New York Jewish draftees spent the end of June and July 1918 in an area known as the Baccarat sector. At night the lines were a beehive of activity, while the daylight hours saw hardly any movement. The men worked in patrols to study the Germans' defenses and to repair their own. Each side routinely sent out raiding parties to capture prisoners for information and occasionally tested its opponent with a small-scale assault. But the soldiers passed most of their time peering into the darkness, hiding from flares, and listening for the sound of an approaching enemy. During the day they had little to do other than keep well hidden. With snipers waiting to pick them off, planes ready to strafe and bomb, and observation balloons capable of directing artillery fire at a moment's notice, daytime was far too deadly for movement. This inactivity produced a strange sensation among the Americans. As Sergeant Morton Greenwald, a second-generation Jew from Brooklyn, described it after the war: "[I] stayed in the lines about twenty-two days and found this spot a recreation area as to what came later."[23]

In this largely static setting, the doughboys' earliest taste of the fighting came in the form of artillery fire. More than any other aspect of the front, the millions of shells expended by each side embodied the insidious nature of modern warfare. In their letters and diaries the men describe in detail the pulverized towns they passed through and the guns' deafening noise and destructive force. "It began all at once," a captain in the Seventy-seventh Division recalled of his first barrage, "as if at one moment an organist had pulled out all the stops, pressed down all the keys, and stepped hard on all the pedals." Corporal Meyer Siegel could still feel a "suffocating recollection" of his first experience under fire when writing his memoirs sixty years later.[24] No matter how they responded to the shelling, the soldiers got an education in what one unit history calls "the ethics of high explosive society." Initially dropping to the ground at the sound of every shell, the men were soon able to distinguish between the different types of ordnance hurled at them. They learned to call the massive high explosive bombs "ash cans," "trolley cars," and "Jack Johnsons," and to fear the gurgle and hiss of the gas shells, which spewed out their vapors after crashing with a dull explosion. The attention the soldiers devoted to all of these weapons was understandable. About 70 percent of the war's casualties were the result of artillery fire.[25]

Huddling in the trenches as shells screamed, exploded, and threw up earth and rubble all around them, the soldiers quickly developed a mode of thinking and talking about their chances of survival. As one officer described it, they were "suffering casualties cruelly and being cruelly punished by an unseen enemy five miles away." Most of the men learned to abandon the idea that they could do anything to change their fate. They combined a faith in predestination with a gambler's odds and dispensed with traditional beliefs in piety, hard work, and character. As Siegel, an Orthodox Jew, later claimed: "I don't think I survived because of talent or know-how, that I avoided being killed. It was a matter of luck, I think I can safely say this, if not for the forces that guided me." In his homely way, Siegel expressed the logic of the common soldier. "So you watch and you know you live by luck alone. If you are lucky and get away with it, you're okay; and you can write home that you're okay and still alive." Others, like Sergeant Harry Weisburg, a second-generation Jew from Brooklyn, still tried to assert some control over their situation. "They claim that a man's shell has his name on it, if it's for him," Weisburg wrote home, "but it is the part of a wise man to keep his nose out of the way of another man's shell."[26]

Trench life did not last very long for Weisburg, Siegel, or any other soldier in the AEF. By mid-July 1918 the Central Powers' advance was exhausted and the Allies began to hit back. Its stint in a quiet sector now over, the Seventy-seventh moved near the Vesle River to take and hold positions recently vacated by the German Army. However difficult the trenches might have been, conditions for advancing troops were far worse. The basic necessities of shelter, food, and clothing became the focus of their concern.

During the final months of the war, the soldiers of both the Yankee and the Seventy-seventh divisions for the most part had to construct their own shelter in areas of heavy fighting. "Some shallow funk holes, dug hastily under fire," an infantryman explains, "or some shell holes scooped out with a mess-kit cover or bayonet—that was all." Time did not permit the construction of more permanent defenses. "Besides," the soldier adds, "we did not intend to stay long enough to use them." Mobility and heavy fighting produced an additional menace that had been absent from the trenches. Dead men and horses littered the battlefield, attracting tremendous swarms of flies, not only annoying pests, but also carriers of disease. "There was considerable dysentery," a captain recalled. "The water was doubtless accountable for this, and the flies helped to spread it."[27]

Most of the time the men were too exhausted to complain about their lodgings. It was food, or really the lack of it, that caused the most constant concern. On paper the AEF was the best-fed army in the war. But this would have come as a great surprise to the combat troops. Even before the Seventy-seventh drove into the Argonne, the men were well acquainted with the army's supply problems. Nearly all of the unit histories record some instance of foraging, of soldiers feasting on German black bread, coffee, mineral water, or apple butter. When the 306th Infantry crossed a vegetable field on the eve of the armistice, "it was rare to see a man who was not supplied with at least two heads of cabbage," Captain Julius Adler recalled. Enjoyment of this find was short-lived, for on November 11 "almost the entire Regiment was disabled by dysentery and diarrhoea."[28]

Lack of clothing and far greater physical demands on the soldiers rounded out an almost animallike existence. The Seventy-seventh's effectiveness in battle kept it on the move through most of September and October, eliminating the regular rest periods the men would have enjoyed had they still been in the trenches. Their mobility largely denied them such comforts as new clothes, baths, and trips to the delousing stations, which provided at least temporary respite from the dreaded lice or "cooties." As Sergeant Harry Weisburg explained in a letter home: 'You see a man may be very well equipped, and a day later have lost everything, like hat, overcoat, equipment, and of course, all extras." Despite the astonishment of foreigners over the AEF's wealth of supplies, the men in the field knew better.[29]

They also found their assignments far more exhausting than anything they encountered in the trenches. A private's perception of geography speaks volumes. "I would say [France] was the largest country in the world," wrote Private Christian Blumenstein, "due to the fact that it seemed so, in all of the hiking that we did when I was there." The Seventy-seventh's travails in France would have been hard even if there had been no shellfire, no mustard gas, and no machine guns.[30]

While physical hardships exhausted the body, an array of psychological pressures confronted the mind and spirit. The enemy contributed to this anxiety. So did the doughboys' own personalities and the tasks that were assigned to them. But the most serious emotional strain had no single, identifiable cause. It was the product of an industrial form of warfare that had taken on a life of its own.

Many of the soldiers convey this tension with images rather than commentary. Most frequent and shocking was their contact with dead soldiers. In August, Corporal Charles Minder and his unit found the bodies of two Americans. "There wasn't anything left of those poor devils but large pieces of their torsos and a couple of legs," he writes in his diary. "There were no heads around at all. Thousands of flies were all over them and the stench was something terrible." He wonders how the bodies could ever be identified. Contact was far more frequent with the many enemy corpses strewn in the division's path. Private Louis Zirinsky, a Brooklyn native whose parents were Russian Jews, wrote home that "on several occasions" he awoke to find himself "lying beside dead Germans."[31]

Surrounded by death, the thoughts and activities of the living took on a surreal quality. The soldiers found themselves and the French civilians they encountered doing things that had no place or meaning in the peacetime world. The civilians were long accustomed to the fighting and provided the war zone with some of its most bizarre imagery. When Lieutenant Robert Haas, a Jewish officer, helped to liberate a town in November, he discovered more than a hundred and fifty people living in a church. They had been there "for some time, and clothes, food, etc. are all over the altar and every other imaginable place." The soldiers were often able to buy eggs and milk from nearby farmers, and "it was no strange sight" to see peasants wearing gas masks when they worked in fields very close to the lines. Captain Arthur Wolff, another Jewish officer in the Seventy-seventh, described how refugees would typically "crawl along" behind the soldiers' advance. "Every so often they are told that a certain town or village can be reoccupied," he wrote to his family. "They drift back then in one and two, or whole families. Of course their houses are shot to pieces, and they are grateful to find just the walls standing. . . . Inside of a week a change is very noticeable. Sometimes little stores, or stands are opened up, where they sell fruit, or vegetables; and especially cheese." Life went on, even amid "battered buildings," "shell-marked roads," and the "hundred and one odors of the battlefields." The makeup of this population made the front seem all the more unreal. "You see it's so long since I've seen any women," Lieutenant Haas explains, unable to describe the women of France to relatives back home. "Think of seeing thousands and thousands of people everyday, but not any women or children!"[32]

How the men perceived an enemy they seldom if ever saw was another source of tension. Based on rumors as much as actual experience, their knowledge reveals how unconventional methods were integral to the fighting, particularly the methods of psychological warfare. When the New York draftees went to the front for the first time, a German observation balloon carried a banner with the chilling greeting "Goodbye 42nd [Division], Hello Seventy-seventh." Enemy leaflets, which preyed on the men's fears and resentments, inundated the AEF lines, as did tales of spies wearing Allied uniforms and gathering information at will. The enemy's tactics—laying traps, shouting orders in English, poisoning water supplies—clashed with the high moral purpose the Americans were supposed to uphold. In the most widely repeated tale of treachery, German soldiers would pretend to surrender, calling out "Kamerad!," then pull grenades or guns on their unsuspecting captors. For the most part apocryphal, these stories nevertheless showed how cunning the doughboys perceived their rivals to be. This perception was acute in the Argonne, where machine gun fire suddenly opened up and disappeared just as quickly, with devastating results. For the most part unseen, the enemy much of the time seemed all seeing.[33]

To be responsible for others in this deadly setting also gnawed at the soldiers' nerves. An officer recalled what it was like to have human lives depending on one's own "often faulty" judgment. According to Captain L. Wardlaw Miles, "even if you went back wounded to safer regions, this heavy sense of responsibility was not left behind; for in your dreams it was still with you—only more confused, importunate, and unappeased than when you had felt it in waking hours." All soldiers regardless of rank shouldered this burden and the deep sense of guilt it often generated. Late in his life, Corporal Meyer Siegel still felt regret over a patrol he sent out the morning of the armistice. By not going himself he probably saved his life, for none of the men in the party returned. "So sixty years later I salute those comrades," he wrote in his memoirs, "and today they are remembered by one of their old comrades." He then added, as if to console himself: "The cause was good. The world is growing up."[34]

It was when friends like these were killed and wounded, and when the men had to kill others like themselves in the enemy lines, that the war took its greatest toll on their emotions and consciences. Artillery fire was the cause of death most commonly described by the frontline soldiers. Suddenly, from some unknown origin, a shell would obliterate a "buddy" with whom one had been talking to, sharing food with, or running alongside a few moments before. These were people the survivor had come to know in some ways better than anyone else in the world, who were "snuffed out" in a manner that denied any time to offer comfort or aid. Seventy-seventh members describe many deaths but expressed very little of their feelings about them. A doughboy of the 305th Infantry admitted the difficulty of describing an assault on a machine gun emplacement, the image of the Great War that has been impressed so deeply on the modern mind:

> A man standing upright would have been riddled from head to foot.
> ... It was awful. The poor boys were getting slaughtered as fast as
> sheep could go up a plank. No one could ever describe the horror of
> it. The screams of the wounded were terrible, but we stuck to it.

Even in instances of close personal contact with the killing, its emotional impact could be just as perplexing—and far more traumatic. Captain W. Kerr Rainsford described how enemy soldiers who were plainly visible shot one of his men, who then died in his arms. "I went over to the sergeant," he writes, "who was bleeding, but not very fast, from a wound in the thigh. He asked for a drink of water and died as I gave it to him; I never knew why." Often it was not until the men came out of the line, gathered for roll call, and saw the full extent of the casualties that their sense of personal loss was greatest. A private and his brother were a bittersweet exception to this rule. Even though they served in the same company, they did not see each other for several weeks before the armistice. "Out of the remains [of the company] were my brother and I," Private Christian Blumenstein wrote. "The only set of brothers that came back alive."[35]

A Russian immigrant, Simon Maslan owned a small "Candy and Cigars business" in Manhattan when he was drafted. Serving as a stretcher-bearer in the Seventy-seventh Division, he was severely wounded, probably by shrapnel, which in his words "Fractured Spine and both sides near Kidney." These photos, taken after the armistice and submitted by Maslan to the American Jewish Committee, capture both the pride and sacrifices of a generation of new immigrant veterans. Courtesy of the American Jewish Historical Society.

Given these conditions, it is not surprising that the war introduced shell shock and self-inflicted wounds into the modern soldier's vocabulary. Many of the memoirs and unit histories describe men suffering from shell shock: physical and nervous exhaustion turning a soldier into a staring catatonic or a "mad, jabbering idiot" when under fire. Self-inflicted wounds on the scale seen in the Great War were also a new development. Medical science now made it almost certain that a man could recover from a minor gunshot wound, and thousands of soldiers on both sides of the conflict chose to shoot themselves rather than stay in the fighting. Corporal Herman Kleinfeld, a Polish Jew who accidentally shot himself "after ten days and nights of hard going in the Argonne woods" could understand why many men did it on purpose. Explaining the circumstances of his wound in a postwar questionnaire, "That night I fell asleep from sheer exhaustion with my automatic pistol in my hand, and was awakened by rustling in the bushes. In waking up with a sudden start, the gun went off in my hand and it was some time before I even knew I was hit." Hunger, weariness, and individual experiences like these were what pulled the soldiers closer together—and set them apart from their peers back home.[36]

Corporal Charles Minder, whose published diary is the most complete and evocative account of the war by any member of the Seventy-seventh or Yankee divisions, commended only one aspect of his military experience. "The last six months of my life in the army, living and suffering with these fellows, has done more for me to get rid of race-prejudice than anything else could have done." A German American, he wrote this after giving a haircut to a Jewish soldier named Selig. Apparently for Minder nothing could have better illustrated what it was like to get "mixed up in an outfit like this" than close contact with an immigrant Jew. Minder embraced this sense of comradeship, describing his contact with the polyglot members of his company as "the finest thing in the world for anyone, who like myself, has always suffered with race-prejudice." Lieutenant Samuel Nash, a North Carolina native who served in the Seventy-seventh, also praised this camaraderie in a letter home to his family: "The real man of the whole crowd is the ordinary garden variety of enlisted man, sgt., cpl. or private, the fellow who really does the work and the suffering. And in the American Army it didn't seem to make any difference whether he spoke Polish, Italian, Yiddish, Irish or plain American, he was a wonderful soldier."[37]

Minder and Nash understood ethnicity and race in the broader terms prevalent in early-twentieth-century America, when not only skin color but also language, religion, and national origin determined the "strain" of humanity a person represented. The Hebrew race, the Slavic race—these are the peoples they felt they had come to appreciate as friends and comrades. Though the two men mentioned only white descendants from Europe, the Seventy-seventh Division also had small numbers of Asian, Hispanic, and Native American men in its ranks.

African Americans were completely excluded, and no doubt the immigrant and second-generation ethnic soldier benefited from this drawing of the race line in simpler terms. The barrier that separated white from black in the army determined that the newer white ethnics be accepted as fellow soldiers. Desegregation was not an issue for the young Italians and Jews of the AEF. The rights and recognition they would press for after the war were their own.[38]

There was little to distinguish the ethnic soldiers' experiences overseas from that of all other combat soldiers, regardless of their roots in America. While serving in the trenches and especially when the AEF was on the move, the soldiers had no choice but to rely on each other. Ultimately, the Italian guardsmen from New Haven and the Jewish draftees from New York felt pride and profound loyalty rather than any kind of resentment toward the government that sent them to France. Their differences with the native born-population would emerge with the claims they made of the nation after the war, not during the time spent overseas.

There is very little to suggest that the New Haven Italians fought a "different" war than their Yankee peers. Letters home reflect the same mix of self-censorship, nostalgia, and concern for family and friends common of nearly every soldier in the AEF. Sergeant Andrew Anastasio described his injuries from mustard gas in a typically nonchalant manner. Praising his doctors and nurses, he tells a friend: "I got it in the eyes and burned between my legs, also under my arms and have a little cough. . . . It won't leave any scars, so I should [sic] worry." Corporal Louis Popolizio, who spent four months in the hospital for a gunshot wound, daydreamed about the future in a letter to his brother. "When I get home I will find a nice girl and get married. You know I am getting old now. I will be 24 on April 3d and we will have a swell time." There is nothing particularly "ethnic" about these thoughts. The anxiety of being in a dangerous place far from home and the desire to conceal it from loved ones appear to have been universal.[39]

One of the few documentable differences lay in the realm of religious practice. Though Italian Catholics were a tiny minority in the Yankee Division, they enjoyed some advantages in France. During rest periods they could attend Mass in the local churches, and the French environment resonated strongly with their own religious backgrounds. Writing to a friend, Corporal Joseph Currano described how belief in the miraculous power of saints, so vivid a feature of *colonia* life, was also part of the French countryside. On his first day near the lines he walked through the ruins of a church. "How many Saints do you think was not spoiled?" he asks. Only the Virgin Mary stood untouched. For many the fighting revitalized traditional beliefs. In a letter home Sergeant Ralph Bove told how the men revered the golden crucifixes given to them by the colony before their departure. "I think the little crucifix is doing miracles," Bove writes in April 1918, as if describing the amulets of his southern Italian past. "Some of the boys lost theirs through no carelessness but in action and feel very badly over it as everyone of us thinks the world of it especially after all we've been through untouched or slightly wounded." The gunners' folkways did not pose the dilemma that immigrant Jewish soldiers faced. As Christians in a predominantly Protestant division, the Italians did not have to request dietary restrictions or special holidays.[40]

From the soldiers' letters it is clear that their closest contact continued to be with other Italian-Americans in the company. But heavy casualties made these friendships difficult if not impossible to maintain. The Yankee Division served at the front nearly twice as long as Charles Minder's Seventy-seventh, and by August the Nutmeg regiment had lost so many of its original members that it ceased to be a truly Connecticut organization. By late October the machine gun company lacked officers and consisted almost entirely of replacement troops. Not all of the losses were due to casualties. Some of the noncommissioned officers were sent back home to train new soldiers. Café Mellone owner Jimmy Ceriani, the chief recruiter for the original *compagnia*, was one of the fortunate few. On the night of the armistice, he attended the New York Metropolitan Opera premiere of his friend, soprano Rosa Ponselle, while the unit he had brought together was scattered all over the world. The majority were recovering in hospitals at home and abroad; some were still occupying the lines. Four were buried in shallow graves near Chateau Thierry and Verdun.[41]

Though evidence is circumstantial, it seems unlikely that the Italian soldiers experienced severe prejudice and discrimination. In postwar questionnaires, they spoke very positively of the impact the service had on their lives. "The little fighting that I experienced," Corporal Popolizio observed, "was sufficient proof to let anybody know when I got home there would never be any job too big for me to tackle." Private Carmen Miranda, who was gassed three different times, described his experience as "excellent." Even those who were critical of the war and army conditions agreed. Private Aniello Aiello, also a gas victim, felt that "too much was lost for the gain." But his personal comments are similar: "I became strong and grew taller, and have more confidence in myself." Immigrant Private Noe Spinaci, who was "scared to death" through much of his time in service, commented simply: "It made me a better man." Perhaps the most telling sign of this attitude is the men's extensive participation in veterans' groups long after the war. The gunners formed their own club in 1922, were very active in the Yankee Division Association, and belonged to national groups such as the Italian American War Veterans, American Legion, Veterans of Foreign Wars, and Disabled American Veterans. Cited in their obituaries, these ties to their service were expressions of comradeship and pride, not disillusionment.[42]

In a rare account of the machine gun company in action, Private Anthony Amici described the sense of responsibility the men felt toward one another. The twenty-one-year-old Amici was wounded in the Chateau

Thierry counteroffensive, which began on July 18, 1918 and accounted for most of the unit's casualties. He recalled the commotion as the men readied themselves for the assault. "There was hurrying here and hurrying there. Everyone busy packing up his belongings and seeing that their rifles, pistols and machine guns were in nick-nack shape to do their worst." They left the lines in the mid-afternoon. "As we were going out of the woods you could hear our boys hollering to each other: 'Good luck, Buddy' and 'Give 'em hell.'" The first two waves of attackers were able to advance unseen. But when more troops came out, "holy smoke, they were bursting all around!" Now marked by enemy artillery, the men had no choice but to keep moving.[43]

A hundred yards into the advance, shell fragments hit Amici. "The concussion threw me into a small dugout in a three foot trench," he writes, "and all at once I heard someone calling me." It was Lieutenant Howard "Pop" Williams, the Georgia native, who had taken charge of the company in January. He helped Amici into a bombed-out building, and almost as soon as they made the move explosions obliterated the area where the private had first fallen. "If it wasn't for Lt. Williams I might have been there yet," Amici claims. He declared that "all the boys that know [Williams] will back these words up." It appears that a sense of mutual dependency pervaded the company regardless of ethnic background. The punishment the Connecticut volunteers took from March 1918 until the very last day of the war made the segregation of the *colonia* impossible to sustain. For that eight-month period at least, their lives were inextricably bound together with everyone in the unit.[44]

In terms of cultural folkways and ethnic prejudice, the New York Jewish members of the Seventy-seventh Division faced a much more challenging situation than their New Haven Italian peers. Most were Orthodox Jews, with religious needs that set them well apart from the Christian majority of their unit. The prejudice they faced in civilian life followed them overseas.

Yet in some ways they were in a stronger position to deal with issues of ethnic difference than New Haven's Italians. Jews constituted a far greater portion of their division, numbering perhaps as many as seven thousand officers and men, close to 25 percent of the total. Army officials were responsive to their religious needs from the beginning, making provisions at Camp Upton for the High Holidays of 1917. This sensitivity was true as well at the federal level. For the first time in American history, Congress commissioned rabbis for service, granted them at-large status and special insignia, and designated the Star of David for marking Jewish graves. Elkan Voorsanger of the Seventy-seventh was the first rabbi to receive a captain's commission, and the first to be made senior chaplain of a division in the United States Army. Jews in all branches of the service also had a major welfare work agency, the Jewish Welfare Board, devoted to their care.[45]

But like so many other aspects of the AEF, what sounded good on paper was practically unknown to the men at the front. Even for "New York City's Own" the resources available for religious observance were inadequate at best. Of the more than thirty clergy who served under Voorsanger, only one other chaplain was Jewish, Lieutenant Benjamin Friedman, a Reform rabbi, who did not reach the division until September 1918. "Why are you so late getting here?" was one of the first things Voorsanger said to him. According to Friedman, the senior chaplain was "a nervous wreck from carrying on all alone" and "madder than hell" at Jewish leaders for not making welfare work in France a greater priority. The two men did their best under the circumstances, holding services, listening to the soldiers' personal concerns, and caring for the wounded and dying. As a rabbi in another division remarked, a chaplain "could only work day by day, clearing a little pathway ahead of him but never making an impression on the great jungle about." Still, conditions for Jews in the Seventy-seventh were better than in other organizations of the AEF. On the day the war ended there were only six Jewish chaplains serving in an overseas army 2 million men strong. Jews accounted for perhaps as many as 100,000 of these soldiers.[46]

The "fighting rabbis" did find one critical source of assistance: their non-Jewish fellow chaplains. In the Seventy-seventh, Voorsanger enjoyed the "enthusiastic support" of his divisional commander and his subordinate clergy. "There were no distinctions," he told a reporter after the war: "a Chaplain was a Chaplain, not a Jewish Chaplain, a Catholic Chaplain, or a Protestant. . . . Each chaplain was responsible for the religion of every man." A Jewish doughboy in the 308th Infantry agreed, claiming that his unit's Catholic priest "was a good Rabbi to us," while the two men who *were* rabbis found Gentile soldiers to be respectful and attentive. In a sermon long after the war, Voorsanger recalled how this cooperative spirit was greatest during the High Holidays of September 1918. Though the War Department authorized furloughs to all Jews in the service, the Seventy-seventh was at the front and could not afford the loss of manpower. The men spent Rosh Hashanah in the trenches and the Day of Atonement marching to get into position for the Meuse-Argonne offensive. But Voorsanger's fellow clergy made arrangements along the line of march on Yom Kippur, and the senior chaplain was able to hold six different services. It was probably the most memorable day of Voorsanger's long rabbinical career.[47]

The Presbyterian chaplain of one of the Seventy-seventh's artillery units kept a wartime diary that best documents this need for cooperative effort. On the voyage over, Lieutenant James M. Howard expressed mild prejudice toward an Orthodox rabbi.[48] But he never made comments like these again in his diary, as the chaos, close contact, and heavy casualties of the front demanded all of his time, leaving little room for discrimination. Like Voorsanger, he did his best to care for every soldier in his charge. Near the Aisne River he performed a funeral service for three men who died together: "a Roman Catholic, a Protestant, and a Jew all killed in a foxhole by a single shell on August 20th." The very next day, when flying shrapnel took the life of Private Nathan Moserowitz, Howard read the Jewish burial service. "Not all of it," he noted, "for it is very long, but some of the most beautiful parts of it." Less than a week before the armistice, the young chaplain attended to still another shell blast victim. "He was badly hurt and in great pain, but responded when I spoke to him." Howard slowly recited a prayer, allowing the wounded man to repeat each phrase. "But when I said, 'O Christ who died for me,' he interrupted. 'I'm of Jewish faith, sir.' " Howard paused. " 'All right boy,' I said, 'we won't put it just that way,' and I substituted a different phrase." They continued until the chaplain had to leave to see the other wounded. Later he heard the man died before an ambulance could arrive. Chaplain Howard, a Yale-trained divinity student, was the Jewish soldier's last human contact.[49]

While the chaplaincy's manpower inadequacies seemed to bring out the best in the troops, the absence of the Jewish Welfare Board overseas drew heavy criticism. The board did not commit itself to relief work in France until well into 1918. Only in the summer of that year was it able to send a commission to investigate conditions, and its presence by the time of the armistice was limited to a Paris office and four relief workers. Lieutenant Louis Egelson, a Conservative rabbi serving as a chaplain in the Ninety-first Division, was one of the agency's most caustic critics. "For Goodness' sake, wake up!" he wrote to the board in December 1918. Like many soldiers in France, Egelson believed the agency was more concerned with public relations at home, concentrating its efforts on the American training camps. He also thought it too restrained by the need to satisfy the different ethnic and religious constituencies of American Jewry. The Jewish members of the Seventy-seventh Division probably would have agreed, having had very little contact with the board during the war. Not until early 1919, as U.S. soldiers waited to return home, was the agency finally able to put together a substantial array of social services.[50]

Some critics feared the JWB's failure would leave a permanent scar on American Jewry. Lieutenant Jacob Rader Marcus, who interrupted his rabbinic studies at Hebrew Union College to enlist, published a devastating article in the *American Hebrew*. He viewed welfare work overseas as a lost and "irretrievable opportunity" to make the "broad principles of Judaism" a part of the soldiers' lives. Marcus was convinced that Jewish veterans would be indifferent to religion when they returned home, having been abandoned by their faith when its comfort and direction were needed most.[51]

Despite these attacks, Chaplain Lee J. Levinger, the author of the most extensive study of the Jewish soldier's "religion," sounded an optimistic note. He was much more concerned with the impact the fighting had on the men than the inadequacy of welfare work.[52] According to Levinger, Jews entering the service knew that it would be difficult if not impossible to observe the Sabbath and dietary laws, but also that the Talmud allowed them dispensation as soldiers. The more devout brought their own scriptures, prayer shawls, and phylacteries into the lines, having no expectations that a welfare agency or chaplains would minister to their every spiritual need. In Levinger's view the vast majority of Jewish doughboys only differed with their non-Jewish comrades in the particulars of their faiths. At the front, Jew and Gentile alike were devout adherents of fatalism, and both craved in worship a nostalgic connection to their communities and childhoods. Most who experienced combat developed what Levinger calls "a personal religion," universal in character. "The men *prayed* at the front. They wanted safety and they felt the need of God. After a battle they were eager to offer thanks for their own safety and to say the memorial prayers for their friends who had just laid down their lives." What intrigued the chaplain most was the new attitude the men brought to traditional religious practice. In the services Levinger conducted, which he soon learned to hold as "open forums," the congregants were inquisitive and demanding. They had no time for preaching, "sham," or condescension. Religion had to have immediate applicability; whether ancient or modern, theology had to satisfy the needs of human beings who faced death on a daily basis. "The war did not shatter all ideals," he observed. "But it did shift emphases, exposed the hollowness of many easy beliefs, and implanted new ideas in minds which otherwise might not have been ready for them." Thus he did not think of the war years as a lost opportunity. To incorporate the new perspectives that came out of the war—which the veteran sensed more keenly than any civilian—proved to be a much greater challenge. Writing in 1921, Levinger concluded: "Judaism is on trial today."[53]

Burial of the dead, however, was a critical distinction between Jew and Gentile that demonstrated the limits of their shared experience under fire. In the rush and confusion of the front, Jewish soldiers killed in action were often not buried as Jews. Private Samuel Kaplan, a Russian immigrant, was appalled by what happened to a buddy. "I met the 1st platoon and they told me that they made a nice wooden cross and put it on his grave. They meant well for they did not know." The dead man was one of only three Jews in his company. "Ben Margolis was a dear friend and a good fellow," writes Kaplan, "and I suffered much at the loss and on account of the cross." Something similar happened in the Seventy-seventh Division. A soldier asked Chaplain Benjamin Friedman to remove a cross from a Jewish friend's grave. Friedman had officiated at the funeral, but the burial detail forgot the deceased was a Jew.[54] The Red Cross unintentionally exacerbated this problem after the war when it offered to take photographs of individual graves and send them to grieving kin. Several Jewish families were shocked to find crucifixes standing over their loved one's remains.[55]

Anti-Semitism, the ugly, "living" manifestation of these differences, was by no means absent from the American Expeditionary Force. But it does not appear that prejudice played a major role in relations among the men of the Seventy-seventh Division. The wartime comments of Lieutenant Jacob Rader Marcus are instructive on this point. A rabbinic student who later became one of American Jewry's leading historians, Marcus kept an extensive diary. As a volunteer in the Ohio National Guard, he witnessed all kinds of discrimination. Jewish enlisted men were removed from desirable units and prevented from entering others. Some officers punished Jews arbitrarily, denying them promotions and permission to observe religious holidays. Ethnic slurs and fights came with the abuse. For Marcus, the situation was so discouraging that while training in Alabama he compared the Jews' predicament to that of southern blacks. "I am forcibly impressed everyday by the fact that a negro is not considered as being human in the South. He is like the Jew, extra human." Acting as an unofficial chaplain in France, he met men from other units and asked them about the anti-Semitism they had encountered. The response was grim. "Even in the fighting divisions right on the lines the Jewish boys had trouble," he writes. "It exists at all times and under all circumstances."[56]

The Seventy-seventh Division provided the one exception. Marcus came across the division in late August 1918 and spent time with some of its Jewish soldiers. By his estimate "they were 40% Jews, all New Yorkers." The young officer was impressed by what he saw. "Jews got along well in the whole Division for there were so many of them." For Marcus it was not only the principle of "security in numbers" that made the difference, but the constant interaction with Gentiles and the confidence to fight bigotry that a large Jewish presence generated. He observed at various times that contact usually broke down prejudice and that soldiers who were open about their ethnic identity were less subject to abuse. "I find that the boys who stick up for their rights have little trouble tho' they meet the A. S. [anti-Semitism] invariably. Others, weaker members, suffer a great deal." Some Jews tried to pass as Gentiles, but according to Marcus the ruse rarely worked.[57]

The numerous cases of discrimination that attorney Louis Marshall dealt with during the war confirm much of Marcus's assessment. All of the incidents Marshall reviewed as head of the American Jewish Committee involved isolated Jews in units, training camps, and government agencies that were practically all-Gentile in composition. The fact that the men of the Seventy-seventh came from the largest Jewish community in America clearly mattered. It is hard to imagine that the drive and assertiveness of downtown Jewry would disappear when seven thousand of its young men became members of the same military organization.[58]

This is not to say that the New York division was free of anti-Semitism. After the war several officers used crude stereotypes when praising the Jewish soldier. The Seventy-seventh's commander, Major General Robert Alexander, was consistently supportive of Jews in the ranks. But by claiming "the Hebrew boy paid his full share of the price of Victory," he demonstrated an awkwardness and distance toward them that the war had left unchanged. Captain William Hardigan claimed "there is no better soldier anywhere than the Jewish boy," explaining, "They used their keen Jewish intelligence in the business of fighting just as they would use it in any other business. They would go after a concealed German battery just as they would go after the conquest of some business difficulty—and they'd get it!" Major Charles Whittlesey, the leader of the Lost Battalion, pushed the line between praise and prejudice even further when describing a man in his unit who won the Distinguished Service Cross. "There was one chap for example (Herschkowitz was his name) who seemed the worst possible material from which to make soldier stuff. He was thick-set, stupid looking, extremely foreign, thoroughly East Side." Though they might have respected Jews as soldiers, these officers hardly considered them close friends or social equals.[59]

Their comments in fact are very similar to the awkward praise heaped on Jewish soldiers by writers who never fought overseas. A member of the National Security League concluded "To Hester Street," a poem published in the *New York Herald* and widely reprinted, with the same self-distancing, even absurd, applause:

Hirsch and Pollack and Feingold, Radski, Finkel and Pelz,
Epstein, Jacobs and Mandel, Weinstein, Baruch and Seltz,
Feiner, Horowitz, Isaacs, Bashwitz, Levy and Franks,
Sachs and Mirsky and Lehner—all of them in the ranks!
Then honor to Joseph Schnitzer and honor to Heyman Behr,
And all the Hebrew brethren in khaki over there.
Put prejudice in your pocket. They fought in the days of yore,
And now when the world is threatened, they are fighting,
Men can no more.[60]

The war did not transform relations between native-born and immigrant groups for all time and for the better. The satisfaction that the ethnic veterans and their communities back home derived from the Great Crusade existed first and foremost in their own knowledge of what they had done to win the war, and only secondarily in the recognition they received from their older stock peers.

When the war ended "on the eleventh hour, of the eleventh day, of the eleventh month," the Yankee and Seventy-seventh divisions were mere skeletons of their former selves. The New Haveners held the line near Verdun, where in 1916 the French and Germans had lost more than 700,000 men. An officer found the Yankees in a battered condition. "The Division, especially the infantry," he reported, "is now in such a state of exhaustion that it is unfit for even defensive operations." The Italian members of the 102nd Regiment's machine gun company fought up to the very end of the war. Sergeant Alexander Bon Tempo and his brother James were wounded on November 10, and the company participated in an advance less than two hours before the cease-fire. "New York City's Own," meanwhile, were huddled in funk holes near Sedan, the site of Napoleon III's surrender to German forces in 1870. Though victorious, the Seventy-seventh was also exhausted, having lost more than five thousand men in the Meuse-Argonne offensive alone. Many of its units were also gearing up for another assault in the final hours of the war.[61]

When word of the armistice finally filtered through the lines that cold November morning, the doughboys did not celebrate. Those who experienced the cease-fire describe an initial feeling of numbness, almost shock, an inability to accept what had happened. "A man almost had to pinch himself to realize that the war was over and he was still in one piece," commented a doughboy in the Seventy-seventh. "It was more like the lifting of a load from our souls," noted another: "Everybody felt it—not one of us could express it." The men responded with none of the revelry that took place back home. "There was very little noise," wrote Captain Frank Tiebout of the 305th Infantry. "There were no horns to blow, no cow-bells to ring, no jobs to quit, no holiday. All such nonsense is for silly, civilized people who live in houses and work when not celebrating." The men of the 102nd's machine gun company also sensed the great divide between the front and peacetime life. "The troops gathered in little groups, expressing the opinion that the event was incredible," recalled Private Ratcliffe Hills. "It seemed too good to be true. To many, it had seemed that the war was the natural and normal state and that this would never end." The long months of fighting and hardships cultivated a mood of reflection and thanksgiving rather than joy. As Private Christian Blumenstein remembered: "We looked upon one another, tired and worn. Every boy seemed to have a prayer on his lips and was thanking God for giving us the success which he did and bringing at last to an end the world's greatest conflict."[62]

It actually took a day or two before the doughboys showed any signs of exuberance. After the cease-fire they simply built bonfires, smoked, and sang songs—activities that were forbidden during the fighting. Members of the Seventy-seventh Division did not feel a rush of excitement until a French regiment relieved them on November 13. The stirring music of the French unit's band and the Americans' subsequent march to a reserve area marked for many the real end of the war. The soldiers then focused their attention on the most elemental comforts in life: the sleep, food, and shelter of which they had been deprived for so long. "After a steaming hot bath and new underwear issued," one man recalled, "we commenced to get something of the feel of being men again instead of animals." It was at this point that the desire to return home overtook all other thoughts. "The future seemed a rosy vision," a captain remembered, "with warm billets, plenty of food and rest at the front of the stage, and at the back an inclined gang plank mounting straight to Hoboken and Home,—the equivalents of heaven."[63]

The soldiers' dreams of returning would not be realized for another six months. The Yankee and Seventy-seventh divisions did not become part of the army of occupation in Germany. But they still had to wait their turn for troop ships along with 2 million other men. Scholars have recently focused on the ability of some soldiers to attend the AEF's makeshift "university" in Beaune, France, and to travel as tourists during this waiting period. But the average doughboy knew little or nothing of these opportunities. For the overwhelming majority the winter of 1918–19 was long and boring, filled with drills and sports and the straight-laced activities of the YMCA, JWB, and other agencies to keep them out of trouble. Some immigrant soldiers, like Frank Antonio of the 102nd's machine gun company, hoped in vain for a furlough to visit relatives in Italy or eastern Europe.[64] Steamship passage back to America was the most coveted commodity. In a letter home, Lieutenant Robert Haas referred to a song that captured the mood: "We're going to be home by Christmas, but nobody knows what year!"[65]

In the early spring of 1919 both the Yankee and Seventy-seventh divisions moved to the debarkation port of Brest, and then to Liverpool to board ships for the homeward voyage. Unlike their departures for France, which were made under cover of night and in great secrecy, the two divisions arrived in their respective homeports to public fanfare. The Italian machine gunners pulled into Boston on April 9. There they were greeted by the original leader of their division, General Clarence Edwards, whom Pershing had relieved of command in the last weeks of the war. Edwards's removal was a highly controversial act that the men of the division forever resented. In Boston harbor they honored him with a long ovation, demonstrating their enduring pride for the National Guard. The draftees of the Seventy-seventh Division, meanwhile, arrived in Hoboken at the end of April, after completing a full year in France. An infantry captain remembered how anxious the men were to be returning home. Passing the Statue of Liberty, one soldier shouted "Old Girl, if you ever look me in the face again, you'll have to turn 'round on your pedestal!"[66]

The cheering continued at special events during the weeks after the voyage home. Across the nation, cities, among them New Haven and New York, celebrated the return of their "hometown" units. The Italian machine gunners participated in no less than four parades, each reflecting a source of regional and personal identification. In Boston they marched with the entire Yankee Division of New England. As members of Connecticut's 102nd Regiment, they marched past the state capitol in Hartford and New Haven's City Hall. And finally, on June 22, 1919, they faced a welcome home celebration sponsored by their very own *colonia*. With more than four hundred other local Italian-American servicemen, the machine gun company paraded through New Haven and its Italian neighborhoods. Joined by twenty-six immigrant societies and four bands, they were then treated to a banquet and concert ball. In a series of speeches, company officers told of the gunners' courage and hardships; Father Quaglia spoke of the bravery (and territorial demands) of the Italian people; and Sheriff Frank Palmieri presented new crucifixes to the men who had lost them in action. Though Rosa Poli was unable to attend, her Red Cross lieutenant, Mary Popolizio, the city's only Italian-American schoolteacher and a sister of Corporal Louis Popolizio of the Italian Machine Gun Company, chaired the banquet. Mayor David Fitz-Gerald, by now a fixture at all major *colonia* functions, declared the men to be "no longer sons of Italians, but sons of New Haven."[67]

In contrast, the men of the Seventy-seventh Division participated in only one parade. On May 6, 1919, 2 million New Yorkers watched the division march for the last time. The *New York Herald* reported that the men's relatives, "who crowded the line of march despite their many races, had been waiting along the route since early dawn." They witnessed a spectacular display of sentimentalism, whose flashy manner was pure Gotham. Marching up Fifth Avenue, the soldiers crossed an area covered with "Virgin Sand, upon which no other feet than those of the victorious troops are permitted." They filed through the city's "Arch of Victory," which honored their struggles for "the free peoples of the world and for the promise of an enduring peace." On the steps of the Public Library stood the Court of the Heroic Dead, containing hundreds of funeral wreaths. Secretary of War Newton D. Baker, the man who two years before selected the first draft number, was the honored guest. He, Mayor Hylan, and the new governor, Al Smith, reviewed the march of more than twenty-four thousand soldiers. A fleet of cars carried the division's wounded, and a funeral cortege symbolized the nearly three thousand members killed. An inscription on one of the many decorations proclaimed: "God give us the privilege of knowing that we did it without counting the cost."[68]

For the division's Jews, the welcome home was also a time of ethnic celebration, as a variety of Jewish clubs and neighborhood groups held banquets, block parties, and dances. Unlike the *colonia*, Jewish organizations devoted a great deal of attention to the problems of reconstruction. An editorial in the *Hebrew Standard* referred to the task ahead as "the Communal Duty" of all Jews. The garment unions, the Yiddish press, the *landsmanshaftn*, and a number of downtown manufacturers pledged their aid and resources to help the men make a smooth transition to civilian life. The most prominent groups, not surprisingly, were the wealthier uptown institutions. By the spring of 1919 the Jewish Welfare Board operated a major office in Manhattan and a servicemen's canteen on the Lower East Side, helping soldiers to get jobs and job training, reach families in eastern Europe, and straighten out problems with pay, Liberty Bonds, and War Risk Insurance. At a meeting of the Jewish Welfare Board's employment service, Jacob Schiff urged leading Jewish manufacturers and merchants: "We must tide the men over the present era of unemployment by giving them jobs." The Young Men's Hebrew Association, which had five hundred members in the service, focused on the needs of jobless and wounded veterans, while the American Jewish Committee created a special department to collect information on Jewish participation in the war. The AJC wanted to provide indisputable proof that the nation's Jews were loyal. Their estimate of at least 200,000 Jewish men and women in uniform would be cited to counteract anti-Semitism during the 1920s and 1930s. Sensitive to the high stakes of the war, New York Jewry was also well focused on the dangers that lurked in peacetime.[69]

The last official act the men experienced as soldiers was their discharge from federal service. Waiting at Camp Devens and Camp Upton, the members of the Yankee and Seventy-seventh divisions received their final physical examinations. They turned in their rifles and other equipment, keeping their uniforms, helmets, and gas masks. Congress had recently granted each of them a meager bonus of sixty dollars, which they collected along with a discharge certificate and train tickets to get home. For the men of the Seventy-seventh Division, most of whom were mustered out by May 10, 1919, there was very little sentimentality during these last few hours in uniform. A captain recalled how his "well-organized and functioning unit" disappeared in the blink of an eye: "Those who wanted to say 'Farewell,' forgot to. . . . About all they really cared for was getting back to the home they had left—as they had left it—and back to the old job—or a better one, which they deserved." As historian Dixon Wecter observed, "The age of fond recollection had not yet begun."[70]

But for many foreign-born soldiers, these last days in the service were indeed momentous. A May 1918 Act of Congress had waived all naturalization requirements for soldiers who served in the wartime army and received honorable discharges. The Italian men of the 102nd's machine gun company took full advantage of the opportunity. Seventeen became citizens before being mustered out, and eight got their papers soon after returning to New Haven. Vincenzo Darrico, Domenico Faiella, and Peter Tinelli easily showed how deserving they were of special consideration. Each man left the service with a facial scar, a fact noted on their naturalization papers. The desire for citizenship was also very strong in the Seventy-seventh Division. About four thousand became American citizens, or roughly one out of every seven doughboys in the organization. They were among more than 280,000 alien soldiers nationwide who became citizens as a result of their wartime service.[71]

Few of the returning soldiers fulfilled their aspirations for a new and better life in the immediate postwar years. Most went back to the same jobs and ethnic neighborhoods they had known before going into the service. The wave of reaction that hounded new immigrants during the early 1920s helped to keep them in their place. But the divisiveness of peacetime did not erase their memories of the war. For many of the original members of the Yankee and Seventy-seventh divisions, the words sacrifice and service would never ring completely hollow. "War is the loss of reason among people," Meyer Siegel wrote sixty years after the fighting. But his disgust with the Great Adventure did not make him a pacifist. "If you are satisfied with a country which looks out for your existence, you should show your appreciation by even giving your life. It's a must, and I do hope my offspring will do the same." The new immigrant soldiers, in other words, did not become a disillusioned "Lost Generation." America was a contested landscape, not a war zone, and the ethnic veterans' appreciation of this difference could be felt by both their families and their communities. Behind the fireworks of the drive for 100 percent Americanism was this sense of entitlement, a significant legacy of the Great War that has for the most part gone unrecognized. The bonds of loyalty the immigrant doughboy forged when he returned to Europe as an American soldier would remain strong through the turmoil and prosperity of the next half century.[72]

Epilogue

A New Voice in Politics

★ ★ ★ ★ ★ ★ ★ ★ ★ ★ ★ ★ ★ ★ ★ ★ ★ ★

Observers frequently commented on the confidence and high expectations of the returning soldiers. Immigrant and second-generation Italian and Jewish veterans were no exception to this rule. The young men soon
discovered, however, that the situation at home was far from rosy. One of
the first things they encountered was the severity of the great influenza
epidemic, which took far more American lives than the war in France. Between September 1918 and the soldiers' return, more than a thousand people
died of the disease in New Haven, and more than thirty-three thousand died
in New York. In addition, millions of workers nationwide had begun to feel
the rapid dismantling of the wartime economy. An estimated 4,000 men
and women were unemployed in New Haven; in New York, well over
100,000. And while the soldiers were welcomed home, garment workers
were on strike in both cities and a tenant strike raged in Brownsville. Militancy was not yet unthinkable—the Red Scare and the movements for
Americanization and the open shop were still several months from hitting
full stride. It was during these months, from May to December 1919, that
workers and immigrants pressed for a larger piece of the American pie,
provoking a wave of reaction that affected national politics for the next
decade.[1]

New immigrant soldiers played a significant role in this agitation, a fact
of the postwar period that has been neglected. Important events in New
Haven and New York illustrate how ethnic veterans served both as a symbol
of immigrant aspirations and as agents in their own right. In New Haven,
a town-gown riot erupted when Yale students insulted the 102nd Regiment.
In New York, Jewish veterans led two "monster demonstrations" to protest
a new wave of eastern European pogroms. In each case, immigrants and
their children gave voice to a new sense of legitimacy and entitlement, an
assertion of rights and achievement that foreshadowed their ascending role
in the political landscape of the United States.[2]

These sentiments would continue into the 1920s, even as a wave of nativism and antiradicalism swept the country. New immigrant communities were not steam-rolled out of existence by a "racially exclusive, culturally conformist, militaristic patriotism."[3] On the contrary, the debate over national identity that continued after the war encouraged them to take an even greater role in politics. Losing in the "culture wars" of the early 1920s, Italians, Jews, and other ethnic groups by the end of the decade were well aware of the need for political involvement. The decline of native-born domination of public life and the unraveling of the tight-knit new immigrant enclave went hand-in-hand.[4]

In New Haven, the Italian population gave expression to these developments in two nights of rioting that took place less than a month after the 102nd Infantry returned from France. On May 24, 1919, the regiment and its Italian machine gunners marched in the city's welcome home celebration. But when they passed the Yale campus, students insulted them. Later that night veterans went to the college and "invited the students out" for a fight. Only words, rocks, and some old shoes were exchanged. But three days later students booed the regimental band at a concert, and Yale authorities and the police still took no steps to defuse the tension, which proved to be a bad miscalculation. In the early evening of Wednesday, May 28, an angry crowd of more than two thousand gathered on the New Haven Green. When some students passed by, the mob gave chase and beat them severely, then surged over to the main campus. For the next several hours, Yale was the target of some of the worst rioting in the city's history.[5]

The raw violence of the evening came as a complete shock. "The crowds paraded about the college buildings," reported the *New Haven Union*, "broke thousands of windows, battered hundreds of doors, and ripped down scores of picket fences which they used to arm themselves in their drive upon everything in the city which was 'Yale' as they called it." The "townies" attacked anyone who appeared to be a student, pulling people out of cars and restaurants and leaving them bloody and often unconscious. At one point only a police squad "with revolvers drawn" prevented a wide-open battle between several hundred students and the crowd. Students, meanwhile, fired on the mob from dormitory windows, slightly wounding two city youths. Not until well after midnight did the violence simmer down. Fearing a sequel the following evening, Mayor FitzGerald assembled police, soldiers, and the security forces of the larger factories. The second night of unrest produced only minor skirmishes.[6]

Though insults to the 102nd provoked the violence, there were in fact very few soldiers involved. Captain Daniel Strickland, who rushed over to act as a peacemaker, recognized almost none of the rioters, while the few YD men he found were also trying to bring an end to the fighting. City leaders were quick to exonerate the regiment and Yale, pointing to a few students and a horde of city youths as responsible. According to Mayor FitzGerald, it was the Red Menace that really drove the violence. "I blame the seriousness of the demonstration," he claimed, "upon the bolshevik element, which apparently awaited a time like this to make use of their poisonous fangs." Yale and the daily press agreed, quoting the inflammatory remarks of one of the mob leaders. As throughout the country in the coming months, the radical left provided an easy scapegoat for civil strife.[7]

It is significant that only the editor of *Il Corriere del Connecticut* suggested otherwise. Though a staunch Republican, Giuseppe Santella believed that the influence of the "bolshevik or anarchist movement" was exaggerated. "We have no affection for those fellows," he argued, "but we do not believe they played a prominent part in the affair."[8] Santella knew something the city's fathers failed to recognize: much of the mob was composed of local Italian-American teenagers. The young men who suffered gunshot wounds were two seventeen-year-olds from Wooster Square. Gennaro Giangrande, the speaker the press labeled a Bolshevik, and Albert Macri, the only youth arrested during the first night of the affray, were also Italian, as were the six "ringleaders" held for blocking trolleys on the second night of rioting. One of these young men was the brother of Private Anthony Amici, the soldier who described being carried to safety at Chateau Thierry.[9]

Though press accounts were vague on the subject of motivation, it seems clear that the riots were not simply acts of juvenile delinquency. Gennaro Giangrande's remarks give some idea of the crowd's concerns. At first he spoke as if the group were 102nd veterans like himself: "Are you fellows going to stand for this, you fellows who wouldn't take half as much from the German Army?" These words appealed to the Italian youths in the audience, boys who never went overseas but who had brothers, friends, and fathers who did. Giangrande also addressed the young men in very direct terms. "These [Yale] students are being educated to keep the poor man down!" he shouted. "Now is the chance to get them before that education is completed." To what extent the crowd accepted the radical implications of these charges is unclear. More important is the fact that so many Italian-Americans felt capable of acting on their hatred of Yale's privileged: they were secure enough in their own aspirations and strength in the community to challenge, and vandalize, its most prized institution. It was this younger generation of New Haven Italians who would play a major role in transforming the cultural and political life of the city, building on the foundation of sacrifice that veterans like the machine gunners rendered during the war.[10]

These sentiments of pride and assertiveness deepened in the 1920s. World War I did not transform American society or the city of New Haven: there was no G.I. Bill, Baby Boom, or rapid migration to the suburbs as would follow the next world war. Nevertheless, during the 1920s the New Haven *colonia* experienced steady expansion and a good degree of social and economic mobility. The Italians' four-decade presence in the city finally bore fruit. The immigrant generation no longer predominated, and many if not most of their American-born children had several years of education in the public school system. Able to read and write English, they were able to enter the workforce at a higher level than their parents, far more often as semi-skilled and skilled workers and clerks than as day laborers. Helping them in their pursuit of a good livelihood was the city's booming economy, which after the disruption of the immediate postwar years prompted a New Haven historian to label the decade "the Fabulous Twenties." Yale sociologist Jerome Myers, who conducted an extensive analysis of the *colonia*'s employment and residential patterns, found that the gains the Italians made in the 1920s were greater than in any decade since they began to arrive in the state. Their presence in the city's better occupations and housing by 1930 doubled the figures based on the 1920 census.[11]

These aspects of the era were more salient to local Italian Americans than the nativism and antiradicalism that took center stage in other parts of the country. The Ku Klux Klan was nonexistent in New Haven, while the infamous Red Scare raids of 1920 netted a grand total of three leafleteers, none of whom were Italian. The drive for Americanization seems to have had a very shallow and fleeting impact on the colony, as evidence of cultural persistence and ethnic pride is abundant throughout the decade. Postwar prosperity fueled an increase in the number of local Italian institutions. A WPA researcher reported over sixty mutual aid societies in the city (a third more than existed in 1918) and eight Italian-language periodicals (double the wartime number). A 1935 study of the diet of several New Haven households discovered that Italian families were buying, preparing, and eating foods much like their immigrant parents at the turn of the century. While support for the left was moribund through the 1920s, the popularity of right-wing Italian nationalism reached an all-time high. When Woodrow Wilson objected to Italy's territorial demands at Versailles, *Il Corriere* condemned the man it previously hailed as a savior, and local *Italia Irredenta* clubs formed overnight. Of the thousands of immigrant mutual aid societies in the state, the Sons of Italy, which grew dramatically in the 1920s, was the strongest promoter of cultural self-esteem, while local support for Mussolini was significant right up to the bombing of Pearl Harbor. It seems that colony residents became more "Italian" in the interwar period than ever before, as the process of moving beyond Old World regional and hometown loyalties, which the Caporetto disaster helped initiate, gained greater momentum.[12]

But as the comments of a St. Anthony's parishioner suggest, these features of *colonia* life did not represent a circling of the wagons against outsiders or a complete return to the "tribal" insularity of the prewar enclave. In his brief history of St. Anthony's church, George DiCenzo remembered a blend of impulses at work, a simultaneous desire to preserve the past as well as assimilate in the present and future.[13] Describing why the parish decided to build a parochial school in the 1920s, he cited a new attitude among the congregants. "The American citizen of Italian extraction of 1925 was a somewhat different person than the Italian immigrant of 1900":

He had become a citizen of the United States, he had adopted American customs, he had learned to appreciate the greatness of his 'new country,' and his children had been attending American schools, high schools and colleges. This American lived in a better home, amid better surroundings and the rough edges were being polished. He recognized the great importance of learning and was desirous of giving his children the very best in education. The most humble worker dreamt of sending his son to college, some to become doctors, others to become technical experts; many of these immigrants accomplished their objectives.

To *continue* to succeed in America, the Italian immigrants of the Hill neighborhood felt it necessary to build a Catholic school staffed by Italian nuns as teachers. The parishioners' devotion to this paradoxical goal was evident in the hard times that followed. They purchased a plot of land in 1926 and spent the next nine years paying off the debt. Their new school was not completed until midway through the Great Depression, and it was not until well after World War II that all of its construction costs were covered. There is little sense of coercion in this story, and DiCenzo makes no mention of the Red Scare or an invasive drive for Americanization in his narrative. More accurately, the church community had become financially secure enough to undertake such a major project and of sufficient *cultural* strength to structure the pace of its assimilation. According to DiCenzo, the immigrant generation wanted a school to limit the influence of 1920s popular culture, which seemed to them a distraction from the hard work needed to secure a comfortable life in America.

Amid these signs of durability and expansion, political representation was the one facet of colony life that lagged behind. The city elected an Italian-American state senator for the first time in 1920, and the number of Italians holding elective offices and city jobs increased during the decade. But Italian membership on municipal boards declined, and the community still fell far short of wielding the power its proportion of the city population should have commanded. Not until after World War II, when the first Italian-American mayor took office, did the situation dramatically change.[14]

This did not mean that Italians had no interest or pull in politics during the 1920s. A local Italian correspondent claimed in a 1922 series of special articles in the *New Haven Register*: "We feel now that there is not a single office in the Elm City to which the Italo-American may not aspire." The most significant example of this attitude was the Italo-American Civic League, an umbrella organization created after the Columbus Day celebration of 1919. Similar to the wartime Comitato Pro Patria, the league consisted of forty of the colony's largest societies. Representing a variety of political party affiliations and regional origins, it worked to educate immigrants in the naturalization process, helped pass a state bill allowing workmen's compensation benefits to be paid to relatives living abroad, and secured the observance of Columbus Day by the city's school district. The league was especially proud of its success in creating a series of nighttime civics classes "to impart into the young generation that which was denied their fathers and forefathers, namely an elementary education of the Italian and American languages, histories, etc."[15]

On the two most ethnically charged issues of the era, prohibition and immigrant exclusion, the colony received solid support from its non-Italian representatives. Connecticut did not ratify the Eighteenth Amendment, and New Haven's representatives in Congress consistently voted against immigration limits. Longtime congressman John Q. Tilson even secured the passage of a bill allowing Italians who had served in the U.S. armed forces to return to America and become citizens. "Those fanatics who look upon Italian immigration as a menace to this Republic," Tilson declared at the time, "should ponder well the statistics of [Italian compliance with] the World War draft." Locally, Mayor David FitzGerald reaped the benefits of working closely with the Italian community. After suffering the new immigrants' anti-Democratic fury in 1919, FitzGerald enjoyed great majorities from the city's Italian sections in 1921 and 1923. The colony's increasing awareness that not "all politics is local" was obvious even before the Great Depression. In the presidential election of 1928, the city and state got a good glimpse of the shape of things to come. In New Haven's three main Italian wards, the vote for Al Smith ranged from 18 percent to 25 percent higher than in the city as a whole. The *colonia* was now helping to propel the Democratic party into a new era of politics, one meeting their concerns as urban workers and status-conscious ethnic Americans.[16]

In New York City, the returning Jewish members of the Seventy-seventh Division also inspired their ethnic community to assert its concerns in the public arena on a scale never seen before. On May 21 and November 24, 1919, New York veterans led two of the largest marches of American Jews in U.S. history. To a greater extent than in New Haven, these events signaled the emergence of an important new player in the American political process.

The purpose of their demonstrations was not to protest inequality, but to raise public awareness of the pogroms raging in eastern Europe. After the end of the war, a wave of anti-Semitic violence swept through Poland, Galicia, and Rumania. Jews in more than 120 towns fell victim to rape, looting, and arson. Hundreds were brutally murdered. Even worse was the news that came out of the Ukraine in mid-1919. Peasant bands and White Army units unleashed by the Russian civil war targeted the region's Jewry for extermination and slaughter on a scale never before seen. "It is heartrendingly certain," commented the *Maccabaean* in December, "that the number of Ukrainian Jews slain mounts up to forty thousand."[17]

Though the massacres were well documented, the Allied governments did not take any action. When the doughboys returned home in May, the Allies were still preoccupied with carving out their new spheres of influence.

The New York daily press also kept silent, as did many assimilated Jewish leaders who were weary of disturbing the negotiations at Versailles. But downtown Jewry forced the issue into the open on May 21 by staging a massive "Mourners' Parade" of between 200,000 and half a million marchers. *The New York Times*, conspicuously timid in covering the pogroms, marveled at the spontaneity of the event. "The big human protest on the east side occurred without an advance plan or program, parades forming everywhere." The procession, taking place on a rain-soaked "black and dreary" day, was a street protest pure and simple; a great, surging human tide. "Most of the men and women working in factories quit work at noon to start the demonstrations. Thousands of school children left their classrooms. Hundreds of small shops closed." The *Forward* captured the mood with an illustration on its editorial page. It pictured a giant workman in midstride towering over the city, with the caption "Rise Up in Your Might!"[18]

Jewish veterans played a crucial role in the march. Wearing their uniforms, ten thousand servicemen got it rolling, gathering up crowds from random street meetings and collecting tens of thousands of onlookers as they wound their way through the East Side. For once their endless drilling in the army was put to good use, as they took control of the march and kept it orderly. "Poland stop killing," one of their banners demanded; "We who fought for your freedom are given pogroms in return." The *Yiddishes Tageblatt* made much of the presence of wounded men in the line of march. Riding in automobiles "were Jewish soldiers with both legs shot off, with missing arms and carrying other scars of battle." Speakers at the Madison Square Garden rally that evening repeatedly invoked the Jewish soldier when urging the American government to take action. "They stand for what America stands," Jacob Schiff declared. "They stand for the self-determination of the Polish people and Russia." When Chaplain Benjamin Friedman of the Seventy-seventh Division addressed the audience, he offered a simple explanation for the Jewish doughboy's perseverance. "America to us held the promise of a just life for the world." Hadn't Jews won the right, he asked, to live in the countries inhabited by her allies?[19]

The march and rally were dramatic successes. The city's dailies applauded the event and denounced the killing, while New York politicians sent resolutions calling for diplomatic action. "The American people," claimed the *New York Mail*, "join as a whole in the demand thus formulated that a stop be put to the pogroms."[20]

But as the attacks in Poland and Rumania began to subside, the terror in the Ukraine heightened. Downtown Jewry wanted to stage another massive protest in November, but this time met resistance. Antiradical and anti-immigrant hysteria in the country was reaching its peak in late 1919, and City Hall was reluctant to allow a parade of tens of thousands of foreign-born Jews. Only through the efforts of a Jewish city commissioner was permission finally granted. On November 24 perhaps as many as 100,000 Jews participated in a "Day of Sorrow" march for the dead, which made its way from the East Side to a mass rally at Carnegie Hall. Unlike the earlier demonstration, this protest involved more than a thousand Jewish organizations and was well planned and executed. An estimated twenty-five thousand Jewish soldiers paraded. Leading the way were the Great War veterans, carrying service star banners noting Jewish participation in the AEF. The veterans' presence made the event possible, calming city leaders and checking the fears of uptown Jewry. "It was dignified and impressive," Louis Marshall admitted to a friend. "Yet I can assure you that I am breathing easier now that it is all over."[21]

A new generation of American Jews did not share Marshall's apprehension. They did not need the *shtadlonim* to intervene in private. Corporal Meyer Siegel exemplified this new attitude. Moving to upstate New York after the war, he found himself leading a community effort to drive out the recruiting efforts of the Ku Klux Klan. "This was the first time that events interested me in trying out my experiences as an ex-soldier." He viewed the Klan in terms of his comrades' sacrifices—"For this my buddies died in France?"—and formed a branch of the Jewish War Veterans of America. His motivations echoed a JWV flier of the 1920s, which declared: "As American defenders, we feel we are privileged and can demand that the Jew be not discriminated against, and shall have his rightful place in the sun." In the interwar period Jewish veterans became an important voice in the fight against anti-Semitism both in America and abroad.[22]

This level of self-confidence was true for many New York Jews during the 1920s, who would have direct experience with the bigotry and repression of the immediate postwar years. Unlike the Italians of New Haven, Gotham Jews encountered the fanaticism of the Red Scare firsthand. They also served as unwilling symbols in the nativist drive for Americanization, exclusion, and even deportation. New York State's own Lusk Committee raided the offices of several left-wing organizations, and the state assembly drew national headlines for prohibiting five Jewish Socialists from taking office. While no wave of anti-Semitism rolled through Gotham, negative depictions of Jews figured prominently in the debate over immigrant restriction and helped fuel the stunning rebirth of the Ku Klux Klan.[23]

But to claim that these events and trends had a long-lasting impact on New York Jewry is a difficult point to argue. Ironically, it was the strength of the Jewish left, not its weakness, that caused the disintegration of the local Socialist movement. Jewish support for the Socialists was rock solid at the height of the Red Scare. In the 1919 and 1920 elections, downtown Jewry voted its disgust with the intolerant policies of the Democratic party by pulling the Socialist lever. The garment unions, meanwhile, celebrated the armistice with membership levels at an all-time high and scored the biggest union organizing victories of the early 1920s. But these successes represented the swan song of the moderate socialist left. Local machine politics, not the iron heel of the federal government, quickly eliminated the conditions that produced the "uprising of democracy" in 1917. As political veterans of the era recall, there was nothing personal (or ideological) about gerrymandering districts or running a fusion candidate to beat a Socialist rival. For city bosses like Charles Murphy, quashing a popular third-party movement was politics as usual. More damaging was the emergence of the communist left. Not surprisingly, the most revolutionary elements in the labor movement, almost nonexistent in the rest of the country in the mid-1920s, were very active in the garment shops of New York. Radicals of various stripes did more to divide and weaken the party and the International Ladies Garment Workers Union than any office raid or deportation. However ugly the postwar suppression of radicals was on the national level, in Gotham the most devastating enemies came from within.[24]

It is also difficult to judge the impact anti-Semitism had on New York Jewry in the 1920s when one considers the population's tremendous economic and social mobility. The movement of Jews out of the poor and densely populated Lower East Side, well under way by 1917, exploded after the armistice. Composing 40 percent of the city's Jewish population in 1920, Manhattan was home to only 16 percent a decade later. Secondary enclaves like Brownsville and newer, more affluent neighborhoods such as Flatbush attracted hundreds of thousands of second-generation eastern European Jews. The ranks of the Jewish working class also declined sharply. A study at the height of the Great Depression placed 47 percent of local Jewish families in the white-collar category, while the Jewish portion of the ILGWU's membership declined from 80 percent in 1920 to less than half in 1935. By 1930 Jews made up the majority of students attending Gotham's high schools, and more than half of the city's doctors, lawyers, and other professionals were Jewish.[25]

Studies of New York Jewry during the interwar period have characterized the 1920s as a time of optimism and cultural regeneration. Deborah Dash Moore has interpreted the population as essentially middle-class in outlook as well as income level, able to build synagogues at an unprecedented pace and create a wide array of new Jewish social and recreational institutions. Coming of age in the Jazz Age, second-generation eastern European Jews felt "at home" in the multicultural milieu of New York. In an interesting contrast to the New Haven *colonia*, they did not feel a need to build separate elementary schools for their children. Under the Americanizing gaze of Gentile teachers before the war, Jews by the end of the 1920s had enough teachers and clout in the public school system to tailor it to their needs and concerns. Most important, there is little sense of sadness overshadowing these gains, few signs of the mourning over a lost past that Abraham Cahan ascribed to his immigrant protagonist David Levinsky. Feeling secure in the United States, Gotham Jewry established a new, prideful attitude toward their religious and cultural heritage, blending elements of modernity and tradition into an American model of Judaism that has endured through the twentieth century. The decade's anti-Semitism might have accelerated this development, but it certainly did not prevent New York Jews from contributing to the dynamic culture of their hometown. As Beth Wenger has argued, the bigotry that emerged during the hard times of the Depression shook Jewish aspirations far more profoundly.[26]

This increasing confidence and cohesiveness had clear manifestations in the realm of electoral politics. Moving into better neighborhoods and jobs and making the most of New York's schools and its tolerance of different religions and peoples, postwar Jewry wasted little time in transferring its loyalties from the divided and disintegrating left to the increasingly reform-minded Democratic party. With tremendous Jewish support, the key liberals of the interwar period rose to national prominence. Franklin D. Roosevelt, Al Smith, Fiorello LaGuardia, Robert Wagner, Sr., and Herbert Lehman championed the platform of social legislation, civil rights, and internationalism that New York's Jews brought aggressively to the political landscape. The continuity between the World War I years and the New Deal was obvious. It was no coincidence that the leading lights of the wartime Jewish left were staunch supporters of the New Deal. Many of them helped found the American Labor party, New York's means of delivering worker votes for the Roosevelt administration. Like the population they inspired in 1917–18, leaders such as Abraham Cahan, Jacob Panken, and Sidney Hillman were committed to the brand of liberalism the Democratic party had come to embrace.[27]

This brief overview of the 1920s in New Haven and New York suggests an important continuity in new immigrant attitudes. The enthusiastic participation of Italians and Jews in the American war effort was not fundamentally coerced or manipulated, nor was it an anomaly in their immigrant experiences. Their behavior during the war represented a genuine, inspired articulation of achievements and rights, one that linked the difficult, early decades of settlement to the relatively prosperous 1920s and the political triumphs of the New Deal liberal coalition. Carving livelihoods and communities out of the urban industrial landscape of the United States, immigrant Italians and Jews wanted recognition of their presence and contributions. The fact that their support of the "Great Crusade" helped not only the American Expeditionary Force but also kin who were suffering in the Old World reinforced this desire. Regardless of how Americans of older stock thought of them after the war, southern and eastern European immigrants and their children knew they had "done their bit" at home and overseas, and most knew there was no returning to their European pasts. With a much more defined sense of who they were, where they had been, and where they were going, Italian and Jewish Americans made the most of the postwar era's good times and could articulate their concerns and aspirations when times went bad. When viewed from their perspective, the 1920s were not a dark age of fear and self-effacement, but a period of deepening settlement and growing assertiveness.

This story adds a new dimension to the many case studies on southern and eastern European immigrants that have been written over the last thirty years. A generation of social and labor historians has provided a great deal of evidence to refute the idea of a political consensus in American life, proposing instead a model of cultural difference and struggle.[28] But as I have attempted to chronicle here, events that have been traditionally considered to have nationwide significance—wars, elections, and federal legislation— are tremendously useful for understanding immigrant agency and a specific population's status and aspirations. After more than three years of neutrality, old stock and new immigrant Americans reached a consensus (or at least a critical mass) on the European War issue: the devastating conflict had to end, the German, Austro-Hungarian, and Ottoman empires had to fall, and the United States could no longer remain a spectator if these ends were to be achieved. Coming to this conclusion for very different reasons, the myriad ethnic groups in America also derived a variety of meanings from their participation in the war. Rather than focusing on the wave of reaction that followed, this book attempts to describe what was going on beneath this turbulent surface, what I feel is the more significant story of growth, enti- tlement, and politicization that brought Italians and Jews to a position of power in the Depression decade. The Great Crusade, rather than crushing new immigrant aspirations in America, provided a firm foundation for their achievement in the years to come.

Notes

Introduction

1. Private Abraham Krotoshinsky, American Jewish Committee War Records Questionnaire, American Jewish Historical Society (hereafter AJC War Records, AJHS); "Krotoshinsky's Own Story," in *Jewish Welfare Board Sentinel*, Aug. 1919; Thomas M. Johnson and Fletcher Pratt, *The Lost Battalion* (Indianapolis: Bobbs-Merrill), 223, 250–251, 255; and *Jewish Forum*, Oct. 1941.

2. Surprisingly, this subject has attracted very little attention from historians. There are no full-length studies of Italian immigrants during the war. And despite a good deal of research on the Italian community of New Haven, the years 1917–1919 have been virtually ignored. Only two older works have dealt with wartime Jewry, and the numerous social histories written on New York's Jews have given the war only minimal, if any attention.

For the war and Italian immigrants, see Gary Mormino, "Over Here: St. Louis Italo–Americans and the First World War," *Missouri Historical Society Bulletin* 30 (October 1973), 44–53; and Humbert Nelli, "Chicago's Italian Language Press and World War I," in Francesco Cordasco, ed., *Studies in Italian American Social History* (Totowa, N.J.: Rowman and Littlefield, 1975). The numerous community studies that appeared on Italian Americans in the 1970s and 1980s pay almost no attention to the impact of the war. See Humbert Nelli, *Italians in Chicago, 1880–1930: A Study in Ethnic Mobility* (New York: Oxford University Press, 1970); Virginia Yans-McLaughlin, *Family and Community: Italian Immigrants in Buffalo, 1880–1920* (Ithaca, N.Y.: Cornell University Press, 1978); Donna Gabaccia, *From Sicily to Elizabeth Street: Housing and Social Change Among Italian Immigrants, 1880–1930* (Albany: State University of New York Press, 1984); Judith E. Smith, *Family Connections: A History of Italian and Jewish Immigrant Lives in Providence, Rhode Island, 1900–1940* (Albany: State University of New York Press, 1985); and Gary Mormino, *Immigrants on the Hill: Italian Americans in St. Louis, 1882–1982* (Urbana: Illinois University Press, 1986).

Studies of New Haven's Italian population include Phyllis Williams, *South Italian Folkways in Europe and America* (New Haven, Conn.: Yale University Press, 1938); Irvin Child, *Italian or American? The Second Generation in Conflict* (New Haven, Conn.: Yale University Press, 1943); Jerome K. Myers, "Time Differential Factor in Assimilation: A

Study of the Aspects and Processes of Assimilation among the Italians of New Haven" (Ph.D. diss., Yale University, 1949); William Johnston, "On the Outside Looking In: Irish, Italian, and Black Ethnic Politics in an American City" (Ph.D. diss., Yale University, 1978); and Steve Lassonde, "Learning to Forget: Schooling and Family Life in New Haven's Working Class, 1870–1940" (Ph.D. diss., Yale University, 1994).

Most significant among the scholarly works on New York Jewry during the period are Joseph Rappaport, "Jewish Immigrants and World War I: A Study of Yiddish Press Attitudes" (Ph.D. diss., Columbia University, 1951); Zosa Szajkowski, *Jews, Wars, and Communism* (New York: KTAV, 1972); Moses Rischin, *The Promised City: New York's Jews, 1870–1914* (Cambridge, Mass.: Harvard University Press, 1962); Deborah Dash Moore, *At Home in America: Second Generation New York Jews* (New York: Columbia University Press, 1981); Arthur Goren, *New York's Jews and the Quest for Community: The Kehillah Experiment, 1908–1922* (New York: Columbia University Press, 1970); Irving Howe, *World of Our Fathers: The Journey of the East European Jews to America and the Life They Found and Made* (New York: Simon and Schuster, 1976); Jeffrey Gurock, *When Harlem Was Jewish, 1870–1930* (New York: Columbia University Press, 1979); Elizabeth Ewen, *Immigrant Women in the Land of Dollars: Life and Culture on the Lower East Side, 1890–1925* (New York: Monthly Review Press, 1985); and Beth Wenger, *New York Jews and the Great Depression: Uncertain Promise* (New Haven, Conn.: Yale University Press, 1996).

3. Of this vast literature, see especially Cecilia O'Leary, *To Die For: The Paradox of American Patriotism* (Princeton, N.J.: Princeton University Press, 1999); Ronald Takaki, *A Different Mirror: A History of Multicultural America* (Boston, Mass.: Little, Brown, 1993); and John Bodnar, *The Transplanted: A History of Immigrants in Urban America* (Bloomington: Indiana University Press, 1986).

4. Three notable exceptions to this characterization that employ very different approaches are: Matthew Jacobson, *Special Sorrows: The Diasporic Imagination of Irish, Polish, and Jewish Immigrants in the United States* (Cambridge, Mass.: Harvard University Press, 1995); Lizabeth Cohen, *Making a New Deal: Industrial Workers in Chicago, 1919–1939* (New York: Cambridge University Press, 1990); and David H. Fischer, *Albion's Seed: Four British Folkways in America* (New York: Oxford University Press, 1989).

5. *New York Times*, 19 Dec. 1918; *Jewish Tribune*, 1 Feb. 1929.

6. *New York Times*, 3 Dec. 1921; 10, 18 Dec. 1927; 2 Feb. 1940; 5 Nov. 1953.

Chapter 1

1. Antonio Cannelli, *La Colonia Italiana di New Haven* (New Haven: Privately printed, 1921).

2. Ibid.; and A. Frangini, *Italiani nel Connecticut* (New Haven, Conn.: De Lucia Jorio, 1908).

3. Robert Foerster, *Italian Emigration of Our Times* (Cambridge, Mass.: Harvard University Press, 1919), 47–126; Virginia Yans-McLaughlin, *Family and Community* (Ithaca, N.Y.: Cornell University Press, 1978), 25–35; and Humbert Nelli, *From Immigrants to Ethnics* (New York: Oxford University Press, 1983), 19–34.

4. Everett Hill, *A Modern History of New Haven and Eastern New Haven County* (New York: S.J. Clarke, 1918), 1:216–225; and Rollin Osterweis, *Three Centuries of New Haven, 1638–1938* (New Haven, Conn: Yale University Press, 1975), 367–375.

5. Osterweis, *Three Centuries of New Haven*, 351–366; Hill, *Modern History of New Haven*, 1:174–193; Carleton Beals, *Our Yankee Heritage: The Making of Greater*

New Haven (New Haven, Conn.: Bradley, 1951), 104–117, 170, 241–5, 255–258, 341–342; and Industry Clippings Collection, New Haven Free Public Library (hereafter NHFPL).

6. Morty Miller, "New Haven: The Italian Community" (Undergraduate thesis, Yale University, 1969), 6–11; and Samuel Koenig, *Immigrant Settlements in Connecticut: Their Growth and Characteristics* (Hartford: Connecticut WPA Federal Writers' Project, 1938), 25.

7. Commissariato dell'Emigrazione, *Bolletino Dell'Emigrazione*, no. 5 (Rome: 1902), 11; Mark Wright, "Factory, Neighborhood, and Workers: Sargent and Company, Wooster Square, and Italian Immigrants in 1890" (seminar paper, Yale University, 1981); NHCHS, 5; Jerome K. Myers, "Time Differential Factor in Assimilation," (Ph.D. diss., Yale University, 1949) 39, 99; and Miller, "New Haven, The Italian Community," 23, 61–62.

8. Myers, "Time Differential Factor," 100–101, 111–112; Foerster, *Italian Emigration*, 338; and *New Haven Directory* (New Haven, Conn.: Price and Lee, 1905, 1917).

9. Selective Service registration cards for the city illustrate this dispersal of employment. In a random sample of four hundred Italian men twenty-one years or older, over sixty manufacturers were listed as employers. Selective Service Registration Records for New Haven, Boxes 120–122, RG–12, Connecticut State Library (hereafter CSL); Beals, *Our Yankee Heritage*, 252–253, 261–262; and Myers, "Time Differential Factor," 91–108.

10. Betty Boyd Caroli, ed., *The Italian Immigrant Woman in North America* (Toronto: Multicultural History Society of Ontario, 1978), 3–12, 206–221, 234–244, 273–287; and Yans-McLaughlin, *Family and Community*, 69–71, 50–54, 164–173. "Report of the Superintendent of Schools," in *New Haven City Year Book—1917* (New Haven, Conn.: S. Z. Field, 1917), 261–266; George DiCenzo, "The History of The Church of St. Anthony from 1904 to 1954," in "Fiftieth Anniversary of St. Anthony Parish" (New Haven, Conn.: n.p. 1954); Myers, "Time Differential Factor," 26–27; and New Haven Civic Federation, "An Industrial Survey of a New Haven District," document 11 (New Haven, Conn: 1913), 5.

11. Miller, "New Haven, The Italian Community," 23; St. Michael's Parish, "100th Anniversary: Church of Saint Michael," (New Haven, Conn.: n.p., 1989); and Cannelli, *La Colonia Italiana*, 92–94, 125–126, 221–222.

12. DiCenzo, "History of the Church of St. Anthony"; and Records of St. Michael's and St. Anthony's Roman Catholic Parishes, Center for Migration Studies, Staten Island, New York. Cannelli, *La Colonia Italiana*, 221–225; and *New Haven Register*, 30 May 1915.

13. "A Very Unique Celebration of Southern Italy Religious Societies" (New Haven, Conn.: n.p., 1987); and Cannelli, *La Colonia Italiana*, 131–155.

14. By 1900, New Haven was home to the tenth largest Italian population in the country. Eliot Lord et al., *The Italian in America* (New York: Buck, 1905), 8; and *New Haven Register*, 30 May 1915.

15. See also Robert Orsi, *The Madonna of 115th Street* (New Haven, Conn.: Yale University Press, 1985); Silvano Tomasi, *Piety and Power: The Role of the Italian Parishes in the New York Metropolitan Area, 1880–1930* (New York: Center for Migration Studies, 1975); and Rudolph Vecoli, "Cult and Occult in Italian–American Culture," in Miller and Marzik, eds., *Immigrants and Religion in Urban America* (Philadelphia, Pa.: Temple University Press, 1977): 45–57.

16. Phyllis Williams, *South Italian Folkways* (New Haven, Conn.: Yale University Press, 1938), 10–11, 13–14; and William Johnston, "Building an Ethnic Identity," *Journal of the New Haven Colony Historical Society* 26 (summer 1979), 25–26.

17. John Briggs, *Italian Passage* (New Haven, Conn.: Yale University Press, 1978), 126; and Myers, "Time Differential Factor," 100–101, 122–123.

18. Myers, "Time Differential Factor," 100, 121–125; Kathryn J. Oberdeck, "Labor's Vicar and the Variety Show: Popular Religion, Popular Theatre, and Cultural Class Conflict in Turn-of-the-Century America" (Ph.D diss., Yale University, 1991); Joseph Carlevale, *Who's Who Among Americans of Italian Descent in Connecticut* (New Haven, Conn.: Carlevale, 1942), 343; and New Haven Civic Federation, "Information for Voters at the City Election of October 2, 1917," 3–4.

19. Jonathan H. Gillette, "Inside Contracting at the Sargent Hardware Company: A Case Study of a Factory in Transition at the Turn of the Century," *Theory and Society* 17 (Mar. 1988), 159–178; Wright, "Factory, Neighborhood, and Workers," 10; Frank Annunziato, ed. *Labor Almanac: New Haven's Unions in the 1990's* (New Haven, Conn.: Greater New Haven Labor History Association, 1995), 47; and Cannelli, *La Colonia Italiana*, 223; Box 1, New Haven Socialist Party Records, Yale University Manuscripts and Archives (hereafter YMA); and *New Haven Register*, 18 May 1919.

20. Cannelli, *La Colonia Italiana*, 90–91, 94–95.

21. Ibid., 95–96; Myers, "Time Differential Factor," 41, 49, 103; and Johnston, "Building an Ethnic Identity," 28.

22. Raymond E. Wolfinger, "The Development and Persistence of Ethnic Voting," *American Political Science Review* 59 (Dec. 1965), 900–901; *New Haven City Year Book— 1917*, 142–146, 219–228; and Myers, "Time Differential Factor," 134–170.

23. *New Haven Register*, 27–29 Mar. 1917.

24. *New Haven Journal-Courier*, 28 Mar. 1917; and *New Haven Evening Union*, 11 Apr. 1917.

25. *New Haven Register*, 29 Mar. 1917; and *New Haven Journal-Courier*, 28 Mar. 1917.

26. Cannelli, *La Colonia Italiana*, 95; and *New Haven Journal-Courier*, 28 Mar. 1917.

27. Kehillah (Jewish Community) of New York City, *Jewish Communal Register of New York City, 1917–1918* (New York: Kehillah [Jewish Community] of New York, 1918).

28. *Jewish Communal Register*, 111–116, 349–357, 637–640, 865–869; and Goren, *New York Jews*.

29. Moses Rischin, *Promised City* (Cambridge, Mass.: Harvard University Press, 1962), 4–9, 61–74; Elizabeth Ewen, *Immigrant Women* (New York: Monthly Review Press, 1985), 2–13; Egal Feldman, "Jews in the Early Growth of New York City's Men's Clothing Trade," *American Jewish Archives* 12 (April 1960), 3–14; and Melvyn Dubofsky, *When Workers Organize: New York City Trade Unions and the Progressive Era* (Amherst: University of Massachusetts Press, 1968).

30. Judith Greenfield, "The Role of the Jews in the Development of the Clothing Industry," *YIVO Annual* 2–3 (1947–48): 180–204; Isaac M. Rubinow, "Economic and Industrial Condition: New York," in Charles Bernheimer, ed., *The Russian Jew in the United States* (Philadelphia, Pa.: J. C. Winston, 1905); Ezra Mendelsohn, "The Russian Roots of the American Jewish Labor Movement," *YIVO Annual* 16 (1976), 160–185; and Irving Howe, *World of Our Fathers* (New York: Simon and Schuster, 1976), 287–324.

31. Allan M. Kraut, "The Butcher, the Baker, the Pushcart Peddler: Jewish Foodways and Entrepreneurial Opportunity in the East European Immigrant Community, 1880–1940," *Journal of American Culture* 6 (winter 1983), 68–90.

32. Thomas Kessner, "Jobs, Ghettoes, and the Urban Economy, 1880–1935," *American Jewish History* 71 (Dec. 1981), 229–255.

33. Deborah Dvorak, "Health Conditions of Immigrant Jews on the Lower East Side of New York: 1880–1914," *Medical History* 25 (Jan. 1981), 1–40; and Jacob Jay Lindenthal, "Abi Gezunt: Health and the Eastern European Jewish Immigrant," *American Jewish History* 70 (June 1981), 417–435.

34. Gerald Sorin, *Time for Building* (Baltimore, Md: Johns Hopkins University Press, 1992), 69–108.

35. Jonathan Sarna, ed., *The People Walk on their Heads* (New York: Holmes and Meier, 1982); Hutchins Hapgood, *The Spirit of the Ghetto: Studies of the Jewish Quarter in New York* (Cambridge, Mass.: Harvard University Press, 1967), 44–70; and Goren, *New York Jews,* 12.

36. Rischin, *Promised City,* 118–127; Ronald Sanders, *The Downtown Jews: Portraits of the Immigrant Generation* (New York: Harper and Row, 1967), 97–125, 148–180; and Howe, *World of Our Fathers,* 518–551.

37. Charles Jaret, "The Greek, Italian, and Jewish American Ethnic Press," *Journal of Ethnic Studies* (summer 1979): 47–70; and Mordechai Soltes, *The Yiddish Press: An Americanizing Agency* (New York: New York Teachers College, Columbia University, 1950).

38. Hasia Diner, *A Time for Gathering: The Second Migration* (Baltimore, Md.: Johns Hopkins University Press, 1989); Naomi Cohen, *Encounter With Emancipation: The German Jews in the United States* (Philadelphia, Pa.: Jewish Publication Society, 1984); Avraham Barkai, *Branching Out: German Jewish Immigration to the United States: 1820–1914* (New York: Holmes and Meier, 1994); Hyman Grinstein, *The Rise of the Jewish Community of New York, 1654–1860* (Philadelphia, Pa.: Jewish Publication Society, 1946); Gershon Greenberg, "A German Jewish Immigrant's Perception of America, 1853–54," *American Jewish Historical Quarterly* 67 (1978), 307–341; Stephen Birmingham, *"Our Crowd": The Great Jewish Families of New York* (New York: Harper and Row, 1967); Rudolf Glanz, "German Jews in New York City in the Nineteenth Century," *YIVO Annual* 11 (1956–57), 9–28; and Glanz, "The Immigration of German Jews up to 1880," *YIVO Annual* 2–3 (1947), 81–99; Michael Meyer, "German Jewish Identity in Nineteenth-Century America," in Jacob Katz, ed. *Toward Modernity: The European Jewish Model* (New Brunswick, N.J.: Rutgers University Press, 1987); Meyer, *Response to Modernity: A History of the Reform Movement in Judaism* (New York: 1988); and Stanley Nadel, "Jewish Race and German Soul in Nineteenth Century America," *American Jewish History* 67 (1987), 6–26.

39. Rischin, *Promised City,* 19–33; Sorin, *Time for Building,* 12–37; and Bernard K. Johnpoll, "Why They Left: Russian-Jewish Migration and Repressive Laws, 1881–1917," *American Jewish Archives* 47 (spring–summer 1995), 17–54.

40. Rischin, *Promised City,* 95–111; Zosa Szajkowski, "The Yahudi and the Immigrant: A Reappraisal," *American Jewish Historical Quarterly* 63 (1973), 13–44; Gerald Sorin, "Mutual Contempt, Mutual Benefit: The Strained Encounter Between German and Eastern European Jews in America, 1880–1920," *American Jewish History* 81 (autumn 1993), 34–59; and Selma Berrol, "Germans Versus Russians: An Update," *American Jewish History* 73 (Dec. 1983), 142–156.

41. Hyman Grinstein, "The Efforts of East European Jewry to Organize Its Own

Community in the United States," *Publications of the American Jewish Historical Society* 49 (Dec. 1959), 73–89; and Sheldon M. Neuringer, *American Jewry and United States Immigration Policy, 1881–1953* (New York: Arno Press, 1980).

42. Oscar Handlin, *A Continuing Task: The American Jewish Joint Distribution Committee, 1914–1964* (New York: Random House, 1964); Zosa Szajkowski, "Private and Organized American Jewish Overseas Relief (1914–1938)," *American Jewish Historical Quarterly* 57 (Sept. 1967), 28–56; Jonathan Frankel, "The Jewish Socialists and the American Jewish Congress Movement," *YIVO Annual* 16 (1976), 202–341; and Melvyn Urofsky, *American Zionism, from Herzl to the Holocaust* (New York: Anchor Press, 1975), 117–163.

43. *American Hebrew*, 1 Nov. 1912.

44. Lawrence Fuchs, *The Political Behavior of American Jews* (Glencoe, Ill.: Free Press, 1956), 49–69; Rischin, *Promised City*, 221–235; and Sorin, *Time for Building*, 191–218.

45. Howe, *World of Our Fathers*, 287–324; Gerald Sorin, *Prophetic Minority: American Jewish Immigrant Radicals, 1880–1920* (Bloomington: Indiana University Press, 1985); and Bernard H. Bloom, "Yiddish-Speaking Socialists in America, 1892–1905," *American Jewish Archives* 12 (Apr. 1960), 34–70.

46. Dubofsky, *When Workers Organize*, 7; Lucy Dawidowicz, "The Jewishness of the Jewish Labor Movement in the United States," in Jonathan Sarna, ed., *The American Jewish Experience* (New York: Holmes and Meier, 1986); Paula Hyman, "Immigrant Women and Consumer Protest: The New York City Kosher Meat Boycott of 1902," *American Jewish History* 70 (Sept. 1980), 91–105; Diane Ravitch, *The Great School Wars, New York City, 1805–1973* (New York: Basic Books, 1974); Szajkowski, "Yahudi and the Immigrant," 13–44; and Gary Dean Best, *To Free a People: American Jewish Leaders and the Jewish Problem in Eastern Europe, 1880–1914* (Westport, Conn.: Greenwood Press, 1982).

47. Oscar Handlin, "American Views of the Jew at the Opening of the 20th Century," *Publications of the American Jewish Historical Society* 40 (1950), 323–344.

48. Richard Hofstadter, *The Age of Reform* (New York: Knopf, 1955); John Higham, *Send These To Me: Jews and Other Immigrants in Urban America* (New York: Atheneum, 1975), 138–173; Leonard Dinnerstein, *Uneasy at Home: Anti-Semitism and the American Jewish Experience* (New York: Columbia University Press, 1987), 15–59; David Gerber, "Cutting Out Shylock: Elite Anti-Semitism and the Quest for Moral Order in the Mid-Nineteenth Century American Market Place," *Journal of American History* 69 (Dec. 1982), 615–637; and Naomi W. Cohen, "Anti-Semitism in the Gilded Age: The Jewish View," *Jewish Social Studies* 41 (summer–fall 1979), 187–210.

49. Leonard Dinnerstein, *The Leo Frank Case* (New York: Columbia University Press, 1968); Jonathan Sarna, "Anti-Semitism in American History," *Commentary* 71 (Mar. 1981), 42–47; and Rischin, *Promised City*, 258–267.

50. Michael E. Lipset to Felix Warburg, 8 June 1917, Folder 7, Box 172, Warburg Papers, American Jewish Archives (hereafter AJA); *American Jewish Chronicle*, 31 Aug., 14, 28 Sept. 1917; *New York Times*, 29 Aug. 1917; *New York World*, 26, 29 Aug. 1917; *New York Tribune*, 26 Aug. 1917; and *New York Herald*, 26, 29 Aug. 1917; *New York Journal*, 29 Aug. 1917.

51. *American Jewish Chronicle*, 31 Aug., 5 Oct., 1917; *New York World*, 29 Aug. 1917; Louis Marshall to Arthur Woods, 27 Aug. 1917; to Louis Friedman, 27 Aug. 1917, Marshall Papers, AJA; and *New York Times*, 29 Aug. 1917.

52. *New York World*, 26 Aug. 1917; and *New York Times*, 29 Aug. 1917.

53. *American Jewish Chronicle*, 31 Aug. and 19 Oct. 1917; 12 Jan. 1918; and *New York World*, 26 Aug. 1917.

Chapter 2

1. A local favorite, the dailies carried occasional stories on "Jimmy" during the war. But his greatest claim to fame did not become apparent until well into the 1920s. Ceriani was the man who discovered the singing talents of Rosa Ponzillo, a local Italian girl who later became known to the world as opera superstar Rosa Ponselle. *New Haven Evening Register*, 18 Mar. 1917; New Haven Pleas Court, *Naturalization Petitions*, vol. 3 under 18, 461, 23 Oct. 1900, National Archives and Records Administration, Waltham, MA. Branch (hereafter NARA—Waltham); *New Haven City Directory*, 1908–1917; Joseph L. Carlevale, *Who's Who Among Americans of Italian Descent* (New Haven, Conn.: Carlevale, 1942), 85; and Mary Jane Phillips-Matz, *Rosa Ponselle: American Diva* (Boston, Mass.: Northeastern University Press, 1997), 36–39.

2. *New Haven Register*, 14 Apr. and 10 June, 1917; *New Haven Union*, 15 Apr. 1917; *State of Connecticut: Report of the Adjutant General, 1918* (Hartford: 1918), 208–9; and *Service Records: Connecticut Men and Women in the Armed Forces of the United States During the World War 1917–1920* (Hartford, Conn.: Office of the Adjutant General, 1941), 3:1713.

3. These older companies included the "Grays" of Co. F, formed in 1816, the "National Blues" of Co. D (1828), and "Light Guards" of Co. E (1862). *New Haven Journal-Courier*, 17 Apr. 1919.

4. William Burton, *Melting Pot Soldiers: The Union's Ethnic Regiments* (Ames: Iowa State University Press, 1988), 56, 44–71.

5. *Corriere del Connecticut*, 30 Jan. and 15 May, 1915; 21 Apr. and 17 Jul. 1917; *Forche Caudine*, 17 Jul. 1917; *New Haven Register*, 23 July 1917; and *New Haven Journal-Courier*, 20 Aug. 1917.

6. *New York Times*, 26, 27, 28, 31 Mar. 1917; 2 Apr. 1917; and Edward Coffman, *The War To End All Wars: The American Military Experience in World War I* (New York: Oxford University Press, 1968), 59–61.

7. For descriptions of this struggle to create a "new army," see: Russell Weigley, *History of the United States Army* (New York: Macmillan, 1967), 313–354; John Patrick Finnegan, *Against the Specter of a Dragon: The Campaign for American Military Preparedness, 1914–1917* (Westport, Conn.: Greenwood Press, 1974); and Stephen Skowronek, *Building a New American State: The Expansion of National Administrative Capacities, 1877–1920* (Cambridge, Mass.: Harvard University Press, 1982).

8. *New Haven Register*, 28 Mar. 1917; *New Haven Journal-Courier* 29 Mar. 1917; and *Report of the Adjutant General, 1918*, 7.

9. *New Haven Register*, 28 Mar. 1917; *New Haven Times Leader*, 28 Mar. 1917; and Strickland, *Connecticut Fights*, 56.

10. See also Philip H. English, *Diary* 1, New Haven Colony Historical Society (hereafter NHCHS); Cosenzo, Military Service Questionnaire—New Haven, CSL; *Service Records*, 2:1713, 1733; *New Haven Union*, 28 and 29 Mar. 1917; and Daniel Strickland, *Connecticut Fights* (New Haven, Conn.: Quinnipiack Press, 1930), 56.

11. *New Haven Times Leader*, 22, 29, 30, and 31 Mar. 1917; Strickland, *Connecticut Fights*, 56; English, *Diary*, 1; *New Haven Journal-Courier*, 29 Mar. 1917; and *New Haven Register*, 30 Mar. 1917.

12. *New Haven Times Leader*, 29 Mar. 1917; Strickland, *Connecticut Fights*, 56, 57; and *New Haven Register*, 2, 10, Apr. 1917.

13. *New Haven Journal-Courier*, 30 Mar. 1917 and 2 Apr. 1917; *New Haven Union*, 6 Apr. 1917; and Strickland, *Connecticut Fights*, 3–34.

14. *New Haven Times Leader*, 29 Mar. 1917.

15. *New Haven Times Leader*, 29, 30 Mar. 1917; *New Haven Journal-Courier*, 29, 30, 31 Mar., 4 April 1917; *New Haven Union*, 28, 29, 30 Mar. 1917; *New Haven Register*, 2, 4 Apr. 1917.

16. *New Haven Register*, 12 Apr. 1917; *New Haven Union*, 5, 11 Apr. 1917; and Connecticut Adjutant General's Office, General Orders #18 and 20, dated 13 Apr. 1917, 20 Apr. 1917, CSL.

17. Letters dated 14 and 16 Oct. 1914, Endorsements for formation of Connecticut National Guard machine gun companies, Box E–32, "Petitions and Hearings to Board of Location," RG–13, CSL; and *Corriere del Connecticut*, 15 Dec. 1914.

18. None of the other companies had men of Italian descent in their recruiting parties in 1917, and the members of the machine gun company accounted for more than half of the total number of Italian-American New Haveners in the regiment as a whole. The other units in the Second were just as discriminatory in their recruiting work, with the exception of infantry Co. B, which took on thirty Italians. CNG Enlistment Papers—2nd Regiment, 1917 CSL; and *Service Records*, vol. 2 (New Haven, Conn.: Office of the Adjutant General, 1941).

19. *Report of the Adjutant General, 1918*, 208–9.

20. *New Haven Register*, 12 Apr. 1917.

21. *New Haven Union*, 8 Apr. 1917.

22. *New Haven Journal-Courier*, 10 Mar. 1917; *New Haven Register*, 13 Feb., 9, 13, 24, 27 Mar., 3, 7, 11 Apr., 20, 25 May, and 1–10, 17–22 June 1917; and clippings in Boxes 1, 2, 4, European War Collection, NHFPL.

23. *New Haven Register* 5, 30 April 1917; 15, 20, 31 May 1917; 1, 3, 5, 6, 12 June 1917; and clippings in Boxes 1, 2, 4, European War Collection, NHFPL.

24. The evening *Register* and morning *Journal-Courier* were owned by the same publisher and supported the GOP. The *Times Leader* and *Union* favored the Democratic party.

25. *New Haven Register*, 4 June 1917; and *New Haven Times-Leader*, strips running from April through June 1917.

26. *New Haven Register*, 23 Apr. 1967. English, *Diary*, 1–2; *New Haven Times Leader*, 16, 18, 23 Apr. 1917; and *New Haven Journal-Courier*, 13, 16, 17, 18, 20 Apr. 1917; and *New Haven Union*, 15 Apr. 1917.

27. *New Haven Union*, 15, 23, 24 Apr. 1917; *New Haven Register*, 18, 24, 25 Apr. 1917; and *New Haven Times Leader*, 23, 24 Apr. 1917.

28. Connecticut and the Northeast's voluntary enlistment totals were among the highest in the nation, and the Second Regiment raised three hundred more men than its twin, the First Conn. Infantry based in Hartford. Strickland, *Connecticut Fights*, 61; and Marvin A. Kriedberg and Merton G. Henry, *History of Military Mobilization* (Washington, D.C.: GPO, 1955), 248–252. *New Haven Register* 25, 28, 29 Apr. 1917; and *New Haven Journal Courier* 25, 28, 29 Apr. 1917.

29. *New Haven Times Leader*, 28, 29 Apr. 1917; *New Haven Register*, 21, 24 Apr. 1917; *New Haven Journal Courier*, 30 Apr. 1917; and *New Haven Union*, 10 June 1917.

30. *New Haven Times Leader* 4 June 1917; *New Haven Register*, 25, 27, 30 Apr. 1917; and *New Haven Evening Union*, 6 May 1917.

31. On the openness of American coverage of the war before intervention, see

Kevin J. O'Keefe, *A Thousand Deadlines: The New York City Press and American Neutrality* (The Hague: Martinus Nijhoff, 1972).

32. English, *Diary*, 3–5; *New Haven Times Leader*, 4, 5, 9, 18 Apr. 1917; *New Haven Union*, 19 Apr. 1917; *New Haven Register*, 5, 10, 14 Apr., 22 May, and 20 June 1917; and *New Haven Journal-Courier*, 17, 18 Apr. 1917.

33. *New Haven Journal-Courier*, 16 May 1917; *New Haven Times Leader*, 4–14, 17 Apr. 1917; *New Haven Union*, 6 May 1917; and Ratcliffe M. Hills, *War History of the 102d Regiment United States Infantry* (Hartford, Conn.: privately printed, 1924), 4.

34. Hills, *War History*, 3; *New Haven Times Leader*, 6, 17, 18 Apr. and 2 May 1917; and *New Haven Register*, 19, 29 Apr. and 23 May 1917.

35. Several guards with dependents opted to stay in service even after the War Department's seemingly airtight prohibition. *New Haven Register*, 17, 20 Apr. 1917; and *New Haven Union*, 27, 28 Apr. 1917.

36. *New Haven Union*, 13, 17, 19 Apr. and 1 May 1917; *New Haven Times Leader*, 19 Apr. 1917; *New Haven Register*, 14, 19 Apr. 1917; and Connecticut Adjutant General's Office, General Order #15, dated 26 March 1917, CSL. Government interference did not always have a negative impact on recruiting. Washington eventually granted federal soldier's pay to the guardsmen (thirty dollars per month for privates), and demanded their services only for the duration of the wartime emergency, lifting temporarily the prewar obligation of six years' duty.

37. *New Haven Register*, 30 Apr., 1 June 1917; and *New Haven Times Leader* 30 Apr., 9, 11 May 1917.

38. *New Haven Times Leader*, 30 Apr. and 9, 11 May 1917; *New Haven Journal-Courier*, 27 Apr. 1917; *New Haven Register*, 30 Apr. and 18 May 1917; and Connecticut National Guard Enlistment Papers—Second Regiment, 1915–1917, Boxes 140, 143, RG–13, CSL.

39. This type of response was prevalent nationwide during the 1917 Selective Service draft calls. Kriedberg and Henry, *History of Military Mobilization*, 248–252; and CNG Enlistment Papers—2nd Regiment, 1917.

40. A *Journal-Courier* editorial was most explicit. "We want the gratification, the immense neighborhood satisfaction, of knowing that, when the Second regiment is ordered into action on the plains of sunny France in support of principles of life we hold dear, the men themselves elected to go that their nation and their state might be made secure against the invasion of a foreign foe." *New Haven Journal-Courier*, 11 July 1917.

41. *New Haven Register*, 1, 2, 5, 7, 8 June 1917; and *New Haven Times Leader*, 7 June 1917.

42. *New Haven Register*, 1, 5, 7 June 1917; *New Haven Times Leader*, 1 June 1917; and *New Haven Union*, 10 June 1917.

43. *New Haven Times Leader*, 18 Apr. 1917; and *New Haven Register*, 21 Mar., 8 Apr. and 10, 17, 19, 20 June 1917.

44. CNG Enlistment Papers—Second Regiment, 1917; and *New Haven Register* 16 June and 19, 20 July 1917.

45. *New Haven Register*, 10, 15 June 1917; and *New Haven Times Leader* 15 June 1917.

46. *Corriere del Connecticut*, 21, 28 Apr. 1917.

47. Local Italian boosters could also put plenty of heat on the city's young men. While others were volunteering for the machine gun company, *Il Corriere* exclaimed: "thousands of young men are living like parasites in the bars, pool rooms and dance

halls . . . remaining indifferent to the call of honor and duty." *Corriere del Connecticut*, 28 Apr. 1917.

48. *New Haven Register*, 14 Apr. 1917; CNG Enlistment Papers—Second Regiment, 1915–1917; and Darrico, Morno, and Liguore Military Service Records Questionnaires—New Haven, CSL. See also the strongly patriotic comments of other New Haven Italian veterans—e.g., Anthony Adinolfi, Andrew Bove, Frank Carrano, John Pantalena, Sebastian Pesce, Joseph Sabatini, Joseph Sandacata, and James Torello, Military Service Questionnaires—New Haven, CSL.

49. *New Haven Times Leader*, 16 Apr. 1917; *New Haven Register*, 16 Apr. and 10 June 1917; and Connecticut Adjutant General's Office, General Order #21, dated 28 Apr. 1917.

50. Popolizio, Military Service Records Questionnaire—New Haven, CSL; *New Haven Register*, 10 June 1917; and CNG Enlistment Papers—Second Regiment, 1917.

51. *Corriere del Connecticut*, May 1915–April 1917; and *New Haven Register*, 21–26, 30 May and 3–8, 14 June 1915

52. CNG Enlistment Papers—2nd Regiment, 1917; *Corriere del Connecticut*, 28 Apr.; 26 May; 2, 23, 30 June; and 14 July 1917; and *Service Records*, vol. 2 (New Haven).

53. *New Haven Register*, 22 May 1917; and *Corriere del Connecticut*, May–Dec. 1915.

54. *New Haven Register*, 23 Apr. and 1 June 1917

55. *Corriere del Connecticut*, May–Sept. 1915.

56. *New Haven Register*, 5 Apr., 12, 17 June 1917; *New Haven Times Leader*, 2, 4 June 1917; *New Haven Journal-Courier*, 3 Apr. 1917; and *Corriere del Connecticut*, 14, 21, 28 Apr., 26 May, 30 June 1917.

57. *New Haven Register*, 3 Apr. 1917. Only German immigrants were considered "enemy aliens" at this point in the war. The United States did not declare war against Austria until December 1917 and never applied surveillance measures to the nation's Bulgarian and Turkish immigrants.

58. *Corriere del Connecticut*, 21 Apr., 23 June 1917.

59. *New Haven Register*, 23 June 1919; and *Corriere del Connecticut*, 8 July 1916.

60. *New Haven Union*, 22, 23 July 1917; and *New Haven Register*, 29 July 1917.

61. *New Haven Union*, 23 July 1917.

62. *New Haven Journal-Courier*, 18, 20 Aug. 1917; and *New Haven Register*, 19, 20 Aug. 1917.

63. *New Haven Register*, 23 May 1918.

64. *New Haven Journal-Courier*, 1 July 1917; and *New Haven Register*, 24–29 June, 22–25, 28 Aug. 1917.

65. Strickland, *Connecticut Fights*, 58–60; and Henry S. Johnson, "Camp Yale—1917 at Yale Bowl Area," typescript memoir, in File J, Box 1, Johnson Family Papers, NHCHS.

66. English, *Diary*, 5–6; Strickland, *Connecticut Fights*, 60–64; Hills, *War History*, 5, 6; and Johnson, "Camp Yale."

67. *Report of the Adjutant General, 1918*, 137–138; Hills, *War History*, 7; Strickland, *Connecticut Fights*, 289–320; and *Service Records*, vols. 1–3.

68. The machine gun company and Company D were the first to leave for Europe of the Twenty-sixth "Yankee Division," which was the first National Guard Division to go "over there." Strickland, *Connecticut Fights*, 65–67; and Taylor, *New England in France* (Boston, Mass.: Houghton Mifflin, 1920), 12–24.

69. CNG Enlistment Papers—Second Regiment, 1917; Military Service Question-

naires—New Haven, CSL; New Haven Military Collection, NHCHS; *Service Records*, vol. 2; *New Haven City Directory*, 1916–1920; and Carlevale, *Who's Who Among Americans of Italian Descent*, 85.

70. Files for Bon Tempo, Massaro, Cappuccio, Giordano, and Dellacamera in New Haven Military Collection, NHCHS; Popolizio, Military Service Questionnaire—New Haven, CSL; and Bove file, World War I Survey, United States Military History Institute Archives (hereafter USMHIA).

71. Spinaci, Military Service Questionnaire—New Haven, CSL.

Chapter 3

1. Meyer Siegel, "A Measure of Life: Memoirs of Meyer Siegel, 1894–1980," (unpublished manuscript) AJA, 11–13.

2. Ibid., 16.

3. Ibid., 13–15.

4. Mark Sullivan, *Our Times: The United States, 1900–1925* (New York: Scribner's, 1920–35), 5:312.

5. The authoritative account of Wilson's decision to conduct a draft is John Whiteclay Chambers II, *To Raise An Army: The Draft Comes to Modern America* (New York: Free Press, 1987), 125–151.

6. For more detailed discussions of the World War I draft, see David Kennedy, *Over Here: The First World War and American Society* (New York: Oxford University Press, 1980), 144–167; Chambers, *Raise An Army*, 125–237; *Second Report of the Provost Marshal General*, (Washington, D.C.: Government Printing Office, 1919); Daniel R. Beaver, *Newton D. Baker and the American War Effort, 1917–1919* (Lincoln: University of Nebraska Press, 1966); Seward Livermore, *Politics Is Adjourned: Woodrow Wilson and the War Congress, 1916–1918* (Middletown, Conn.: Wesleyan University Press, 1966), 15–32; and Marvin Kriedberg and Merton Henry, *History of Military Mobilization in the United States Army, 1775–1945* (Washington, D.C.: Government Printing Office, 1955), 241–280.

7. Chambers, *Raise An Army*, 153–177; Kennedy, *Over Here*, 144–149; and Livermore, *Politics Is Adjourned*, 15–32.

8. Kriedberg and Henry, *History of Military Mobilization*, 250; *Second Report*, 277.

9. John Whiteclay Chambers II, "Conscripting for Colossus: The Progressive Era and the Origin of the Military Draft in the United States in World War I," in Peter Karsten, ed., *The Military in America: From the Colonial Era to the Present* (New York: Free Press, 1980), 201.

10. Kennedy, *Over Here*, 163–167; Chambers, *To Raise An Army*, 211–215.

11. Nancy Ford Gentile, "War and Ethnicity: Foreign-born Soldiers and U.S. Military Policy During World War I" (Ph.D. diss., Temple University, 1994), 97–124; James B. Jacobs and Leslie Anne Hays, "Aliens in the U.S. Armed Forces: A Historico-Legal Analysis," *Armed Forces and Society* 7 (winter 1980), 187–208; and Chambers, *To Raise an Army*, 226–231.

12. *Second Report*, 103. The State Department received close to 6,000 diplomatic protests on the behalf of alien draftees who were both properly and improperly drafted. This resulted in the discharge of 1,842 men. In July 1918 the Selective Service exempted immigrants from neutral countries if they renounced all intention of becoming American citizens; 2,035 aliens avoided the draft under this provision. Ford, "War and Ethnicity," 109–111.

13. *New York Tribune*, 3 June 1917.

14. Historical interpretations of the New York riots include: Joel Tyler Headley, *The Great Riots of New York, 1712–1873* (Indianapolis, Ind.: Bobbs-Merrill, 1970); Adrian Cook, *The Armies of the Streets: the New York City Draft Riots of 1863* (Lexington: University of Kentucky Press, 1974); and Iver Bernstein, *The New York City Draft Riots: Their Significance in American Society and Politics in the Age of the Civil War* (New York: Oxford University Press, 1990).

15. Enoch Crowder, *Spirit of Selective Service* (New York: Century, 1920), 125.

16. *New York Times*, 23, 26–30 May 1917; 2–5 June, 1917.

17. Ibid., 3, 4 June.

18. Ibid., 23, 29, 30 May 1917; 1, 3, 5 June 1917.

19. Ibid., 29, 30 May; 2, 3, 5 June 1917.

20. *New York Herald*, 29 May 1917.

21. *New York World*, 29 May 1917.

22. *New York Times*, 3 June 1917.

23. *New York Herald*, 1 June 1917; and Emma Goldman, *Living My Life* (New York: Alfred Knopf, 1931).

24. *New York Herald*, 1 June 1917; Morris Hillquit, *Loose Leaves from a Busy Life* (New York: Da Capo Press, 1940), 170–172; and *The Masses* (July 1917), 18–19, 31, 43 ("Petition to the President and Congress of the United States for the Immediate Repeal of the Present Conscription Law.")

25. *New York Times*, 1 June 1917; and *New York Journal American*, 6 June 1917; and Goldman, *Living My Life*, 2:603.

26. Benjamin Gitlow, *I Confess: The Truth About American Communism* (New York: E. P. Dutton, 1940), 19; *New York Tribune*, 4 June 1917; *American Jewish Chronicle*, 8 June 1917; *Advance*, 1 June 1917; and *New York Herald*, 30 May, 3 June 1917; *New York Times*, 23 May 1917; *New York Tribune*, 28 May 1917; *New York World*, 3 June 1917; and Goldman, *Living My Life*, 2:642.

27. *New York Herald*, 1, 5 June 1917; and *New York Times*, 1 June 1917.

28. *New York Times*, 5 June 1917; *New York World*, 4, 5 1917; and *New York Herald*, 3–5 1917.

29. *New York Herald*, 5 June 1917; and *New York World*, 1, 5 June 1917.

30. At the Garden rally, Jennie Deimer, Louis Sternberg, Morris Becker, Louis Kramer, and Joseph Walden were arrested. The *Tribune* noted that "all are natives of Russia." Arrested at the No Conscription League meeting were: Aaron Cohen, Ernest Greenbaum, Samuel Cohen, Jacob Newman, Leiger Klinetsky, Rose Rolys, Maurice Marks, Jacob Axelrad, and Harry Fritz. *New York Tribune*, 1 June 1917; *New York World*, 5 June 1917; *New York Journal American*, 6 June 1917.

31. *New York Tribune*, 1 June 1917; *New York World*, 4, 5 June 1917; *New York Herald*, 5 June 1917.

32. Joseph Rappaport, "Jewish Immigrants and World War I: A Study of Yiddish Press Attitudes" (Ph.D. diss., Columbia University, 1951), 78.

33. Ibid., 88, 90.

34. Beryl Segal, "A Jew in the Russian Army During the First World War," *Rhode Island Jewish History Notes* 7 (Nov. 1975), 105–139; Salo W. Baron, *The Russian Jew Under Tsars and Soviets* (New York: Shocken Books, 1984), 156–167; Abraham G. Duker, *Jews in the World War: A Brief Historical Sketch* (New York: American Jewish Committee, 1939); American Jewish Committee, *The Jews in the Eastern War Zone* (New

York: American Jewish Committee, 1916); and National Workmen's Committee, *The War and the Jews in Russia* (New York: National Workmen's Committee, 1916).

35. See Michael Stanislawski, *Tsar Nicholas I and the Jews: The Transformation of Jewish Society in Russia, 1825–1855* (Philadelphia, Pa.: Jewish Publication Society of America, 1983), 3–34; S. M. Dubnow, *History of the Jews in Russia and Poland* trans. by I. Friedlaender (Philadelphia, Pa.: Jewish Publication Society of America, 1916–1920), 1:13–30, 145–149, 354–357; John Doyle Klier, *Imperial Russia's Jewish Question, 1855–1881* (Cambridge: Cambridge University Press, 1995), 332–349; W. Bruce Lincoln, *The Great Reforms: Autocracy, Bureaucracy, and the Politics of Change in Imperial Russia* (De-kalb: Northern Illinois University Press, 1990), 143–158; and W. E. Mosse, *Alexander II and the Modernization of Russia* (London: I. B. Tauris, 1990).

36. Mary Antin, *The Promised Land*, 2d ed. (Boston, Mass.: Houghton Mifflin, 1969), 13–14; and Jacob Panken, Autobiographical Questionnaire, AJA.

37. Sociologist Abraham Duker describes the various sources of Russian Jewry's support for the war: "The wave of patriotic emotion which swept across the country could not fail to affect the Jewish community. The fact that Russia was fighting on the side of the democracies was regarded by all the oppressed and underprivileged and by reformers as a harbinger of better treatment. The feeling of national unity in the face of a common danger, too, was considered a guarantee of a better future. The more far-seeing realized that the war was bound to result in the destruction or modification of the Tsarist tyranny." Duker, *Jews in the World War*, 4–5.

38. Norman Stone, *The Eastern Front, 1914–1917* (London: Hodder and Stough-ton, 1975), 212–215; and Samuel Greenberg, *The Jews in Russia* (New Haven, Conn.: Yale University Press, 1951), 2:96–101.

39. *Advance*, 1 June 1917.

40. The *Advance* praised the People's Council: "No other name could so well express its true character. This is a people's movement. And the word Council will always serve as an inspiring reminder of the great leader of democracy today—the Russian Council of Workers and Soldiers." *Advance*, 8 June 1917. See also Christopher Lasch, *The American Liberals and the Russian Revolution* (New York: Columbia University Press, 1962), 40.

41. "If we are to make Germany a democracy," Magnes asked the audience, "is the degree of democracy to be determined by our own standards or by those of the freer democracy of the new Russia?" *New York Times*, 1 June 1917; *New York World*, 1 June 1917. "Address of Morris Hillquit, Madison Square Garden, May 31st, 1917," in Hill-quit Papers (Microfilm edition) State Historical Society of Wisconsin, 1969, Reel 5, Document #86.

42. This contrast between pro- and antiwar Jews was especially visible when the Russian Commission (a group of dignitaries touring the United States to elicit support for the new government) visited New York in early July. *Forward* editor Abraham Cahan repeatedly referred to "our beloved Mother Russia" in his speech at a Madison Square Garden rally for the commission. "Our native country in Russia is a real home to us," he stated, claiming that hundreds of thousands of immigrant Jews still considered Russia as their "Fatherland." The editors of the *American Jewish Chronicle* harshly criticized Cahan for these remarks, calling them "at the same time untrue, misleading and politi-cally unwise. The bulk of American Jewry, which consists of Jews from many countries, came to America not merely as political exiles with the object of returning to their old countries, but to stay and to live here. . . . They are loyal to only one country and that

country is America . . . [Cahan] has no right to ascribe such a conception to the bulk of American Jewry." *American Jewish Chronicle*, 13 July 1917.

43. *New York Journal American*, 4 June 1917; and *New York Times*, 3 June 1917.

44. *New York Times*, 3, 5 June 1917.

45. *New York Herald*, 5, 6 June 1917; *New York Times*, 5, 6 June 1917; and *New York Tribune*, 6 June 1917.

46. *New York Times*, 5, 6 June 1917.

47. Ibid., 5 June 1917.

48. *New York Times*, 5, 6 June 1917; *New York Tribune*, 6 June 1917; and *New York Journal American*, 5, 6 1917.

49. *New York World*, 6 June 1917.

50. Marshall to Albert Lasker, 5 Nov. 1917, Marshall Papers.

51. Local Board 13, Bronx, N.Y. Questionnaire, "Local Board Experience File," RG–163, NARA (copy in author's possession).

52. *American Jewish Chronicle*, 10 Aug. 1917.

53. Siegel, "Measure of Life," 4, 10, 12.

54. Novin Questionnaire, Box 7, Folder 13, AJC War Records Collection, AJHS; Morrison quoted in Berry, *Make the Kaiser Dance*, 322–323. See also the comments of Maurice Samuel and Ralph Henry Lasser in respectively, Samuel, *Little Did I Know: Recollections and Reflections* (New York: Alfred A. Knopf, 1963) 14–15; and M. A. DeWolfe Howe. ed., *Memoirs of the Harvard Dead in the War Against Germany* (Cambridge: Harvard University Press, 1922) 3:248–270.

55. Shalinsky Questionnaire, Box 8, Folder 16c, AJC War Records Collection, AJHS; quoted in Berry, *Make the Kaiser Dance*, 343.

56. Kovar Questionnaire, Box 7, Folder 10b, AJC War Records Collection, AJHS.

57. Crowder, *Spirit of Selective Service*, 123, 131.

58. *New York Times*, 16, 21, 22, June 1917; and Goldman, *Living My Life*, 610–612.

59. "What Happened to the August Masses," *The Masses*, Sept. 1917, 3; and *New York Times*, 25 July 1917. Staff members of the magazine were tried on antidraft conspiracy charges in April 1918. But by that time, three of the four defendants—Max Eastman, Floyd Dell, and Merrill Rogers—supported the war. The government dropped its case after two different juries failed to agree on a conviction. Hillquit, *Loose Leaves from a Busy Life*, 228–229.

60. *New York Times*, 16, 17, 24 June 1917.

61. *New York Times*, 20, 21, 22 June, 29, 31 July 1917; and Goldman, *Living My Life*, 603, 610–623.

62. *New York Times*, 16, 17, 24 June 1917; and *New York World*, 16, 17, June 1917.

63. *New York Times*, 24 June 1917; and *New York World*, 19 Aug. 1917.

64. *Second Report of the Provost Marshal General*, 161.

65. Capt. W. Kerr Rainsford, *From Upton to the Meuse with the 307th Infantry* (New York: Appleton, 1920), 10; Siegel, "Measure of Life," 13–14; *New York Times*, 6 Jan. 1918; and *American Jewish Chronicle*, 31 Aug. 1917.

66. Local Board 13, Bronx, N.Y. Questionnaire.

67. *New York Times*, 11, 12, 14 Aug. 1917; *American Jewish Chronicle*, 17, 24 Aug., 12 Oct. 1917; and Goldman, *Living My Life*, 681.

68. *Warheit*, 12, 22 Aug. 1917; *American Jewish Chronicle*, 17 Aug. 1917.

69. Quoted in Zosa Szajkowski, *Jews, Wars, and Communism* (New York: KTAV, 1972), 344–345.

70. The five papers referred to, during the months of June to December 1917, are: the *New York Times, New York World, New York Herald, New York Tribune,* and *New York Journal American.* See *American Jewish Chronicle,* 8, 10 Aug. and 7 Sept. 1917.

71. In his study of the AALD, Frank L. Grubbs, Jr. comments: "The Alliance's officials were aware that the success of their program depended on gaining the loyalty of the Jewish worker." Grubbs, *The Struggle for Labor Loyalty: Gompers, the A.F. of L., and the Pacifists, 1917–1920* (Durham, N.C.: Duke University Press, 1968), 72, 38–45.

72. *New York Times,* 21 June, 30 July, and 14 Aug. 1917

73. What is significant in this confrontation between the AALD and the Jewish unions is the fact that it was not a battle involving federal or municipal authorities. Washington and City Hall made no attempt to suppress the United Hebrew Trades and the garment unions during the war. The issue of labor disloyalty in Gotham was fought by Gompers and the AF of L, not the Wilson or Mitchel administrations. Committee of Public Information funding was intermittent, as the correspondence between Robert Maisel and CPI director George Creel illustrates. Grubbs, *Struggle for Labor Loyalty,* 71–72; and Szajkowski, *Jews, Wars, and Communism,* 166–172.

74. Postmaster General Albert Burleson threatened to suspend the *Forward'*s mailing privileges in October. But on the intercession of Louis Marshall, and a written pledge by Abraham Cahan not to print objectionable material about the war, the paper never missed a day's edition. See *American Jewish Chronicle,* 12, 19 Oct. 1917; Louis Marshall's letters to Abraham Cahan and Albert Burleson, in Charles Reznikoff, ed., *Louis Marshall: Champion of Liberty, Selected Papers and Addresses* (Philadelphia, Pa.: Jewish Publication Society of America, 1957), 2:974–976; and Lucy S. Davidowicz, "Louis Marshall and the Jewish Daily Forward: An Episode in Wartime Censorship, 1917–1918," in *For Max Weinreich on His 70th Birthday* (The Hague: Mouton, 1964), 31–43.

75. Jonathan Frankel, "The Jewish Socialists and the American Jewish Congress Movement," *YIVO Annual* 16 (1976), 202–341; Frankel, *Prophecy and Politics, Socialism, Nationalism, and the Russian Jews, 1862–1917* (Cambridge: Cambridge University Press, 1981), 509–547; and Moses Rischin, "The American Jewish Committee and Zionism," in *Herzl Year Book* 5 (1963), 65–81.

76. *American Jewish Chronicle,* 1, 8, 15, June and 7 Sept. 1917; and Frankel, "Jewish Socialists."

77. *American Jewish Chronicle,* 28 Sept. 1917; and *American Hebrew,* 17 Aug. 1917.

78. For descriptions of the board's formation and extensive activities, see: *American Hebrew,* 13 Apr. and 17 Sept. 1917; Jewish Welfare Board, *First Annual Report* (New York: Jewish Welfare Board, 1919), 77–117; Chester Teller, "The Jewish Welfare Board," in *American Jewish Yearbook 5679* (1919) 88–102; and Cyrus Adler, *I Have Considered the Days* (Philadelphia, Pa.: Jewish Publication Society, 1941), 300–303.

79. Notices for these activities can be found in the *American Jewish Chronicle'*s "Coast To Coast" section for New York and Brooklyn, June–December 1917; and War Emergency Committee Reports for New York and Brooklyn, Box 73, Women of Reform Judaism Collection, AJA.

80. *New York Times,* 14 Sept. 1917. Conkling wrote *"That Damn Jew"* in 1940.

81. *New York Times,* 1, 5 Sept. 1917; *New York Tribune,* 5 Sept. 1917; and *New York Herald,* 1, 4, 5 Sept. 1917.

82. *New York Times*, 5 Sept. 1917; and *New York Herald*, 4, 5 Sept. 1917.

83. *New York Times*, 5 Sept. 1917; *New York World*, 5 Sept. 1917; and *New York Herald*, 5 Sept. 1917.

84. Fred Baldwin, "The Enlisted Man in World War I" (Ph.D. diss., Princeton University, 1964), 87–91. See also Arthur Barbeau and Henri Florette, *The Unknown Soldiers: Black American Troops in World War I* (Philadelphia, Pa.: Temple University Press, 1974).

85. *New York Times*, 14 Mar. 1918.

86. The estimate of one-third is based on the total number of New York area Jewish drafted men, approximately seven thousand, who served in the Seventy-seventh Division. See also the inflated estimates in *American Jewish Chronicle*, 2 Nov. 1917; and *American Hebrew*, 21 Sept. 1917.

87. For descriptions of the American Jewish Committee's military survey, see Julian Leavitt, "The Collection of Jewish War Statistics," in *American Jewish Year Book, 1919* (Philadelphia, Pa.: American Jewish Committe, 1919), 103–112; and the first report of the AJC's findings, American Jewish Committee, *The War Record of American Jews* (New York: American Jewish Committee, 1919).

88. For complete statistical tables of this information see my dissertation, "Melting Pot Goes to War" (Ph.D diss, Brandeis University, 1999), 175–178.

89. Siegel, "Measure of Life," 15; Goldberg (Box 10), Krotoshinsky (10), and Klausner (7:10b) Questionnaires, AJC War Records, AJHS; and Goldman, *Living My Life*, 674.

90. *New York Times*, 25 Aug. 1917.

Chapter 4

1. Ratcliffe Hills, *War History* (Hartford, Conn.: privately printed, 1924), 7; and Daniel Strickland, *Connecticut Fights* (New Haven, Conn.: Quinnipiack Press, 1930), 65.

2. Hills, *War History*, 7–8; and Strickland, *Connecticut Fights*, 67.

3. Naturalization certificates for Martinetti (#2469), Aiello (#1957), Litro (#1950), and Vivenzio (#2465) in "Camp Devens Naturalizations," NARA—Waltham.

4. Louis Popolizio, Military Service Questionnaire—New Haven, CSL. "We were just kids, anxious to go," recalled James Carton, another member of the 102nd Regiment. "We just wanted to find out what it was all about—and we did." *New Haven Register*, 23 Apr. 1967.

5. Connell Albertine, *Yankee Doughboy* (Boston, Mass.: Branden Press, 1969), 45.

6. Hills, *War History*, 7–8. Louis Ranlett, a member of the Seventy-seventh Division, found Allied soldiers just as curious about the Americans. "They were much interested to learn that a large part of the Seventy-seventh Division men were of foreign birth. Apparently it had never occurred to them there could be an Italian in the American army." Ranlett, *Let's Go! The Story of A.S. No. 2448602* (Boston, Mass.: Houghton Mifflin, 1927), 27.

7. William Sanford Hills, *The Hills Family in America* (New York: Grafton Press, 1906), 252.

8. Strickland, *Connecticut Fights*, 69; and Hills quoted in *War History*, 10.

9. Hills, *War History*, 9–10.

10. Harry Benwell, *History of the Yankee Division* (Boston, Mass.: Cornhill, 1919), 24–31; and Emerson Taylor, *New England in France, 1917–1919: A History of the Twenty-sixth Division USA* (Boston, Mass.: Houghton Mifflin, 1920), 25–30.

11. Taylor, *New England in France*, 28, 29. "Our ships were all European," remembered Lieutenant Philip English of New Haven, "and culled from many seas, as their names clearly indicated: Mongolian, Orita, Orissa, Mokoia, Rualina, Carpathian, Canada, Carmania, Kroonland, Anchises, Miltiades, Themistocles, and Victorian." Philip H. English Diary, 9.

12. The verbatim text of the telegram, which contained typographical errors, was "ALL SAFE AND MILL PUBLISH," sent by "ISABELL." Isbell to Governor Holcomb, 13 Oct. 1917, Box 258, File #124, Holcomb Papers; *New Haven Times Leader*, 13, 15, and 16 Oct. 1917; *New Haven Register*, 15 Oct. 1917; and *New York Times*, 14 Oct. 1917.

13. *New Haven Times Leader*, 16 Oct. 1917; and *New Haven Register*, 16 Oct. 1917.

14. *New Haven Times Leader*, 21 Oct. 1917.

15. Aniello Aiello, Military Service Questionnaire—New Haven, CSL.

16. In a postwar questionnaire, Louis Popolizio described his physical training during this period, but made no comment about the unit's military preparation: "I never felt better in my life physically. I used to suffer constipation a lot before and after regulating my stomach on three meals a day exercise and regular sleep I felt like a giant." Popolizio, Military Service Questionnaire—New Haven, CSL.

17. *New Haven Register*, 26 Mar. 1916.

18. "Record for Attendance at Drills"—Connecticut National Guard, 2nd Regiment machine gun company, Nov. 1916–Feb. 1917, Box D–36, RG–13, CSL.

19. Hills, *War History*, 36; *New Haven Register*, 15 July 1917; and *State of Connecticut: Biennial Report of the Adjutant General* (Hartford, Conn.: Office of the Adjutant General, 1916).

20. Strickland, *Connecticut Fights*, 40, 41; Hills, *War History*, 36–37; and *Report of the Adjutant General, 1918*, 3–9.

21. Strickland, *Connecticut Fights*, 40, 41.

22. "Records for Attendance at Drills," Nov. 1916–Feb. 1917; and *Service Records*, 2:1645–2083.

23. Letter printed in *New Haven Register*, 14 Apr. 1918.

24. Ben B. Fischer, comp., "Hände Hoch! Hands High! An American Hero's Tale of the Great War: The Story of James F. Carty, DSC" (McLean, Va.: privately printed, 1995), 17–19.

25. Louis Popolizio, Military Service Questionnaire—New Haven, CSL; and Fischer, "Hände Hoch!" 18–19.

26. "During predawn roll-calls, cows wandered through our ranks." Philip English, quoted in *New Haven Register*, 23 Apr. 1967; Hills, *War History*, 10; letter of Private Thomas Healy in *New Haven Register*, 25 Feb. 1918; Benwell, *History of the Yankee Division*, 32–38; and Albertine, *Yankee Doughboy*, 61–62.

27. *New Haven Times Leader*, 9 Mar. 1918; and English, *Diary*, 17.

28. Strickland, *Connecticut Fights*, 74; English, *Diary*, 17, 19; William R. J. Carroll, Military Service Questionnaire—Hartford, CSL; and Fischer, "Hände Hoch!" 18–19.

29. Strickland, *Connecticut Fights*, 70. Carmen Miranda and Charles Alfonzio of the machine gun company were hospitalized during the months of winter training. Alfonzio, who suffered from trench foot, received disability benefits after the war. Miranda and Alfonzio, Military Service Questionnaires—New Haven, CSL; and Fischer, "Hände Hoch!" 19.

30. Quotations from Hills, *War History*, 10.

31. Quotations from Hills, *War History*, 10. See also Albertine, *Yankee Doughboy*,

59; and Augustin M. Prentiss, *Chemicals in War: A Treatise on Chemical Warfare* (New York: McGraw-Hill, 1937), 540–543.

32. L. F. Haber, *Poisonous Cloud: Chemical Warfare in the First World War* (Oxford: Clarendon Press, 1986), 80; F. A. Hessel et al., *Chemistry in Warfare: Its Strategic Importance* (New York: Hastings House, 1940), 79–120; Curt Wachtel, *Chemical Warfare* (Brooklyn, N.Y.: Chemical, 1941), 147–169.

33. Haber, *Poisonous Cloud*, 255–256; Hessel, *Chemistry in Warfare*, 89–93; Wachtel, *Chemical Warfare*, 221–239; *Chemicals in War*, 178–189.

34. Lieutenant Harold Amory, in Philip S. Wainwright, ed., *History of the 101st Machine Gun Battalion* (Hartford, Conn.: 101st Machine Gun Battalion Association, 1922), 22; Robert J. McCarthy, *History of Troop A, Cavalry, Connecticut National Guard and its Service in the Great War as Co. D, 102d Machine Gun Battalion* (New Haven, Conn.: Tuttle, Morehouse and Taylor, 1919), 26; W. H. B. Smith, *Basic Manual of Military Small Arms* (Harrisburg, Pa.: Military Service, 1945), 66–67; Sevellon Brown, *The Story of Ordnance in the World War* (Washington, D.C.: Brian Press, 1920), 128; and Fred H. Colvin and Ethan Viall, *United States Rifles and Machine Guns* (New York: McGraw Hill, 1917), 305–314.

35. Hills, *War History*, 15–20; Wainwright, *History of the 101st Machine Gun Battalion*, 18–28; and Colvin, *United States Rifles*, 305–314.

36. Concealment was a large part of this training. Because of what their gunfire attracted, the machine gunners were taught to hold back until crucial moments and learned a variety of camouflage tricks. See Captain Julian S. Hatcher et al., *Machine Guns* (Menasha, Wis.: George Banta, 1917); and Army War College, *Machine Gun Drill Regulations* (Washington, D.C.: Government Printing Office, 1917).

37. Carl Brannen, *Over There: A Marine in the Great War* (College Station, Tex: Texas A&M Press, 1996), 48–49.

38. Strickland, *Connecticut Fights*, 73; General Weygand, *Histoire de L'Armée Française* (Paris: E. Flammarion, 1938), 372; and Gen. René Radiquet, *The Making of a Modern Army* (New York: G. P. Putnam, 1938), 113.

39. Rev. Ernest DeF. Miel, in Wainwright, *History of the 101st Machine Gun Battalion*, 59.

40. Corporal Louis Popolizio wrote home to his brother: "Just think of when I come home there will be a Frenchman in the house, for I am studying the French language every night." Letter in *New Haven Times Leader*, 12 Dec. 1917.

41. Bannister et al., "War Diary of a Machine Gunner," in Wainwright, *101st Machine Gun Battalion*, 87.

42. Ibid., 22; English, *Diary*, 16; Strickland, *Connecticut Fights*, 76; and letter in *New Haven Register*, 24 Dec. 1917.

43. See Ralph Montecalvo's comments in Bernard Edelman, ed., *Centenarians: The Story of the Twentieth Century by the Americans Who Lived It* (New York: Farrar, Straus, and Giroux, 1999), 251.

44. Strickland, *Connecticut Fights*, 75.

45. Ibid., 73–75, 78; and Fischer, "Hände Hoch!" 19.

46. Strickland, *Connecticut Fights*, 78–79.

47. *New Haven Times Leader*, 25 Feb. 1918; Strickland, *Connecticut Fights*, 78–79.

48. Strickland, *Connecticut Fights*, 79; *Service Records*, 3:2692; and *Biennial Report of the Adjutant General—1916*, 101.

49. "The name of Parker remains that of one of the pioneers," noted a British weapons expert after the war, "for until his teaching, military thought, cold indeed as it was, had not considered the machine gun as anything beyond an aid to defense." Lt. Col. G. S. Hutchinson, *Machine Guns: Their History and Tactical Employment* (London: Macmillan, 1938), 73, 74. See also *New Haven Register*, 20 Feb. 1918; and Parker's unpublished autobiography, "Action Front! A Saga of Service," Parker Papers, United States Military Academy Archives.

50. Strickland, *Connecticut Fights*, 80; and Hills, *War History*, 10.

51. *New Haven Times Leader*, 22 Feb. 1918.

52. David A. Armstrong, *Bullets and Bureaucrats: The Machine Gun and the United States Army* (Westport, Conn.: Greenwood Press, 1982), 96–124.

53. Hills, *War History*, 10.

54. Parker, "Action Front!" 218.

55. Strickland, *Connecticut Fights*, 80.

56. Armstrong, *Bullets and Bureaucrats*, 105–106; transcript of request in Strickland, *Connecticut Fights*, 128–129.

57. The devotion the regiment felt toward Parker contrasted strongly with the way men from other units viewed him. A private recalled: "We all thought Parker was a little nuts." Henry Berry, *Make the Kaiser Dance* (New York: Doubleday, 1978), 32–33, 177.

58. Hills, *War History*, 32; English, *Diary*, 14; letters of Foye, Schmitz, and Lt. Albert Johnson in *New Haven Union*, 3 Mar. 1918, *New Haven Times Leader*, 26 Jan. and 5 Feb. 1918; and Albertine, *Yankee Doughboy*, 53–57.

59. Morris J. Gutentag file, World War I Survey, USMHIA; and Teta letter in *New Haven Union*, 3 Mar. 1918.

60. Lieutenant Harold Amory, in Wainwright, *101st Machine Gun Battalion*, 21; Rev. Ernest DeF. Miel in *New Haven Union*, 4 Feb. 1918 and Wainwright, 57–58; soldiers' letters in *New Haven Register*, 24 Dec. 1917 and *New Haven Times Leader*, 26 Jan., 5 Feb. 1918; Hills, *War History*, 9, 32; and Albertine, *Yankee Doughboy*, 54–55.

61. Hills, *War History*, 26, 32; soldiers' letters in *New Haven Union*, 27 Jan. 1918, *New Haven Times Leader*, 23 Jan. 1918, and *New Haven Journal Courier*, 11 Mar. 1918.

62. Edwards quoted in Hills, *War History*, 22; Albertine, *Yankee Doughboy*, 80; and soldiers' letters in *New Haven Union*, 3 Mar. 1918.

63. Letter in *New Haven Times Leader*, 26 Mar. 1918; Hills, *War History*, 25–26; *Service Records*, 2:1705; and *New Haven Register*, 12 Dec. 1918.

64. Albertine, *Yankee Doughboy*, 81.

Chapter 5

1. *New Haven Union*, 3 Mar. 1918. See also the comments of Jacob R. Marcus, 19 June 1918 entry in "Diary for 1917–1918," Marcus Papers, AJA.

2. Even the socialist daily, the *New York Call*, praised conditions at the camp. The paper reprinted an anonymous (and quite possibly fictitious) letter of a draftee to his mother early in the mobilization process: "Now just to set at rest a few worries. The food here is bully, the beds are warm and comfortable and the fellows seem to be a mighty fine lot, especially the officers. I know I could follow any one of them right through any kind of trenches to Berlin easily." *New York Call*, 13 Sep. 1917.

3. Julius O. Adler, *History of the 306th* (New York: 306th Infantry Association, 1935), 18.

4. *New York Times*, 11, 22 Sept., 9 Oct. 1917; *New York Herald*, 10, 11, 21 Sept.

1917; Irving Crump, *Conscript 2989: Experiences of a Drafted Man* (New York: Dodd, Mead, 1918), 6; *American Jewish Chronicle*, 14 Sept. 1917; *New York Tribune*, 19, 20 Sept. 1917; and *New York World*, 11 Sept., 13 Oct. 1917.

5. *New York Herald*, 30 Sept. 1917; *New York World*, 29 Sept. and 13 Oct. 1917; and *New York Call*, 10, 21, 23 Sept., 1, 14 Oct. 1917.

6. *New York Herald*, 22 Sept. 1917; *New York Call*, 22 Sept. 1917; *New York Times*, 22 Sept. 1917; and *New York World*, 29 Sept. 1917.

7. *New York Times*, 12, 13, 20, 25 Sept., 1, 29 Oct., and 4 Nov. 1917.

8. L. Wardlaw Miles, *History of the 308th Infantry* (New York: G. P. Putnam's Sons, 1927), 7; Christian Blumenstein, *Whiz Bang!* (Buffalo, N.Y.: privately printed, 1927), 5; and Crump, *Conscript 2989*, 7.

9. *New York World*, 12 Sept. 1917; Corporal Joseph P. Demaree, *Company A of the Lost Battalion* (New York: George U. Harvey, 1920), 9–11; and Crump, *Conscript 2989*, 6–14.

10. Chaplain James M. Howard to wife dated 27 Sept. 1917, Howard Papers; Julius O. Adler, ed., *History of the Seventy-seventh Division* (New York: W. H. Crawford Printers, 1919), 11–12; Edward Robb Ellis, *Echoes of Distant Thunder: Life in the United States 1914–1918* (New York: Coward, McCann and Geoghegan, 1975), 355–357; *New York Times*, 17, 19, 23 Sept. 1917; and *New York World*, 12 Sept. 1917.

11. *New York World*, 18 Sept. 1918; *New York Times*, 25 Sept. 1917; *New York Herald*, 23 Sept. 1917; Edward S. Greenbaum, *A Lawyer's Job: In Court, In the Army, In the Office* (New York: Harcourt, Brace & World, 1967), 49; Gilbert Crawford, *The 302nd Engineers: A History* (New York: privately printed, 1919), 18–19; and Adler, *History of the Seventy-seventh Division*, 11–14.

12. Copies of *The Bugle* are found in Weill Scrapbook, Milton Weill Papers, AJHS; Anonymous, *Through the War With Company D, 307th Infantry*, Seventy-seventh *Division* (New York: privately printed, 1919), 5.

13. Crump, *Conscript 2989*, 48; *New York Journal American*, 17 Sept. 1917, 6 Jan. 1918; and conversation with Nagel's son David, 4 Jan. 1997.

14. Lawrence Bergreen, *As Thousands Cheer: The Life of Irving Berlin* (New York: Viking, 1990), 160.

15. For more on how the War Department addressed the draftees' cultural and recreational needs, see Nancy K. Bristow, *Making Men Moral: Social Engineering during the Great War* (New York: New York University Press, 1996); Jennifer D. Keene, *Doughboys: The Great War and the Remaking of America* (Baltimore, Md.: Johns Hopkins University Press, 2001); Nancy Gentile Ford, *Americans All: Foreign-Born Soldiers in World War I* (College Station, Tex.: Texas A & M University Press, 2001); and Bruce White, "The Military and the Melting Pot: The American Army and Minority Groups, 1865–1924" (Ph.D. diss., University of Wisconsin–Madison, 1968).

16. *New York Times*, 14 Oct. 1917; and *New York World*, 14 Oct. 1917.

17. *New York Times Magazine*, 2 Dec. 1917.

18. Harry Litowitz, Questionnaire, Box 7, Folder 11d, AJC War Records, AJHS.

19. Adler, *History of the 306th*, 4; Adler, *History of the Seventy-seventh Division*, 13; *New York Times*, 9 Dec. 1917; and Frank Tiebout, *History of the 305th* (New York: 305th Infantry Auxiliary, 1919), 26.

20. W. Kerr Rainsford, *From Upton to the Meuse* (New York: Appleton, 1920), 6–7; Blumenstein, *Whiz Bang!* 6; Weill (Box 16), Krotoshinsky (10), and Arthur Wolf (16: 1), AJC War Records Questionnaires, AJHS.

21. Adler, *History of the 306th*, 5; and Colonel George Vidmer, "Addresses Deliv-

ered Before the Lawyers Club . . . on the Subject of America at War," (New York: pamphlet dated 12 Jan. 1918), copy in author's possession.

22. Adler, *History of the 306th*, 13, 14–15; Crawford, *302nd Engineers*, 20–21; and *New York World*, 13 Oct. 1917.

23. Alexander T. Hussey and R. M. Flynn, *The History of Company E, 308th Infantry, 1917–1919* (New York: Knickerbocker, 1919), 2; and Adler, ed., *History of the Seventy-seventh Division*, 13.

24. Although the infantrymen became proficient with rifle and bayonet work, gas masks, trench building, and basic maneuvers, Captain Rainsford remembers how their training lacked in advanced equipment and tactics. "The throwing of dummy grenades was practiced as taught by a French lieutenant, but live hand-grenades or rifle-grenades were never available. The instruction with automatic rifles did not go beyond that of the mechanism of the Lewis Gun and chauchat for two N.C.O.'s and a lieutenant from each company, with a single day's firing on the range. The guns were never available for the training of squads in the companies." Rainsford, *From Upton to the Meuse*, 11–12.

25. *New York Times*, 23 Oct. 1917, 11, 13 Nov. 1917; Crawford, *302nd Engineers*, 18–19; Tiebout, *History of the 305th*, 19.

26. *New York Times*, 23 Sept. 1917; Miles, *History of the 308th*, 5.

27. *New York Journal American*, 21 Dec. 1917, 15 Jan. 1918; Rainsford, *From Upton to the Meuse*, 13–14; Adler, *History of the Seventy-seventh Division*, 15–18; *New York Times*, 17 Oct., 13 Nov. 1917; and *New York World*, 15 Oct. 1917.

28. Pariser (Box 7, Folder 14), Kramer (7:10c), and Beckerman (11) AJC War Records Questionnaires, AJHS.

29. Rainsford, *From Upton to the Meuse*, 4; *New York Times*, 9 Oct. 1917; Tiebout, *History of the 305th*, 19–20; Adler, *History of the 306th*, 7–9; and Blumenstein, *Whiz Bang!* 6.

30. Maurice Samuel, *Little Did I Know: Recollections and Reflections* (New York: Alfred A. Knopf, 1963) 16–17.

31. Adler, *History of the 306th*, 7–9; and Tiebout, *History of the 305th*, 18.

32. Crump, *Conscript 2989*, 72–73.

33. Hussey and Flynn, *History of Company E*, 5.

34. Tiebout, *History of the 305th*, 312–343; *New York Social Register* (New York: Social Register Association, 1918, 1919); Thomas Johnson and Fletcher Pratt, *Lost Battalion* (Indianapolis, Ind.: Bobbs-Merrill, 1938), 128; Lieutenant Robert Haas to mother, n.d. (early Sept. 1917), Haas Papers; and Howard, *Diary*, iii, Howard Papers.

35. Tiebout, *History of the 305th*, 20, 99; Johnson and Pratt, *Lost Battalion*, 128–132; and *New York Journal American*, 25 Sept. 1917.

36. Demaree, *Company A of the Lost Battalion*, 7, 14; Blumenstein, *Whiz Bang!* 8; and *New York Social Register*, 1918.

37. *New York Times*, 27 Sept. and 10 Oct. 1917; and Arthur E. Barbeau and Henri Florette, *Unknown Soldiers* (Philadelphia, Pa.: Temple University 1974).

38. *New York Times*, 14 Sept. 1917; *New York Herald*, 14 Sept. 1917; *Bugle*, 1 Nov. 1917; and "Buck" McCollum, *History and Rhymes of the Lost Battalion* (New York: Bucklee, 1919).

39. *New York Times*, 2 Sept. 1917; *New York Tribune*, 17 Sept. 1917; *New York Journal American*, 17 Sept., 15 Oct. 1917; and *New York Herald*, Oct.–Dec. 1917.

40. Hussey and Flynn, *History of Co. E*, 3.

41. *New York Journal American*, 28 Nov., 5 Dec. 1917; and *New York Times*, 27 Aug., 23, 30 Sept., 19 Oct. 1917.

42. *New York Journal American*, 27, 28 Dec. 1917, 6, 13, 20, 22 Feb. 1918; *New York Herald*, 15 Sept. 1917; and *New York Times*, 11 Sept., 24, 27 Nov., 3, 5 Dec. 1917.

43. Elizabeth Bertron Fahnestock in Miles, *History of the 308th*, 351–355; and *304th Field Artillery Battalion Association Newsletter* in Howard Papers, Yale University Manuscripts and Archives (hereafter YMA).

44. *American Jewish Chronicle*, 2 Nov. 1917; and *American Hebrew*, 21 Sept. 1917.

45. Adler (Box 16, Folder 1), Bache (Box 11), Sarnov (9:16f), Silverman (8:16d), and Edelheit (6:5) AJC War Records Questionnaires, AJHS.

46. *New York Tribune*, 13 Sept. 1917.

47. *JWB Sentinel*, Nov. 1918, Feb. 1919; *New York Times*, 25 Sept. 1917; and *American Jewish Chronicle*, 14, 28 Sept. 1917.

48. *New York World*, 18, 25 Sept. 1917; *American Hebrew*, 21 Sept. 1917; *American Jewish Chronicle*, 14, 28 Sept. 1917; *JWB Sentinel*, Feb. 1919; and Tiebout, *History of the 305th*, 18.

49. In a highly critical report the JWB reviewed the reasons for its slow start in providing services at the camps, particularly its failure to meet the needs of the "between six and seven thousand Jewish soldiers" at Upton. Organizational problems received the most attention. The study also cited a "strong feeling" early on "against separating the Jewish welfare work too sharply from the general welfare work." The board was slow to realize that "thousands of Yiddish boys" were not going to the YMCA and K. of C. for assistance, and only in early 1918 did the agency commit itself to a highly visible presence in the camps. "Report of the Committee on Investigation—Jewish Welfare Board," Box 1351, Jewish Welfare Board Papers, AJHS; *American Jewish Chronicle*, 5 Oct., 2 Nov., 7 Dec. 1917; and *American Hebrew*, 1 Mar. 1918.

50. *JWB Sentinel*, Dec. 1918; *American Hebrew*, 30 Nov. 1917, 15 Feb. 1918; and Leon W. Goldrich, "Report of the Field Secretary—Camp Upton—4 Dec. 1917, Box 174, Folder 1, Warburg Papers, AJA.

51. *Young Men's Hebrew Association Bulletin*, Nov. 1917, Dec. 1917; *American Jewish Chronicle*, 2 Nov. 1917; *American Hebrew*, 30 Nov. 1917, 15 Feb. 1918; *JWB Sentinel*, Dec. 1918; Goldrich, "Report of the Field Secretary, 4 Dec. 1917;" Henry Berry, *Make the Kaiser Dance* (New York: Doubleday, 1978), 322; and Samuel, *Little Did I Know*, 15–16.

52. Through the course of the war Congress commissioned twenty-three rabbis as military chaplains. *American Hebrew*, 22 Mar. 1918; *JWB Sentinel*, Nov. 1918, Feb. 1919; Leon W. Goldrich, "Report of the Field Secretary—Camp Upton—29 Aug. 1918," Folder 17, Box 178, Warburg Papers, AJA; *American Jewish Weekly News*, 2 Aug. 1918; *American Jewish Chronicle*, 21 Sept., 16 Nov. 1917; *New York Times*, 12 Oct. 1919; and assorted clippings and military orders in Voorsanger Papers, AJA.

53. Frederick Palmer, *Newton D. Baker: America at War* (New York: Dodd Mead, 1931), 2:163.

54. *New York Times*, 13 Oct. 1917; *New York Journal American*, 3 Nov. 1917; and *New York World*, 4 Nov. 1917.

55. *New York Call*, 18, 20 Oct., 2 Nov. 1917; *New York Times*, 26, 31 Oct. 1917; and Hillquit, *Loose Leaves*, 194–197.

56. *New York Times*, 7 Nov. 1917; *New York World*, 18 Nov. 1917; and *The Bugle*, 3 Nov. 1917, Weill Papers, AJHS.

57. *New York Times*, 13, 19, 26 Oct. 1917; and *Camp Upton News*, 13 Oct. 1917.

58. The field secretary of the JWB, after visiting Camp Upton, noted the irony of

lecturing the soldiers on patriotism. "We must not forget that the man who has donned the uniform and who is now ready to fight for the American ideals of democracy, has already done a great deal towards proving his thoroughgoing Americanism. As a matter of fact, all the soldiers in camp—Jew and non–Jew—do not listen enthusiastically to talks on patriotism. The man in uniform needs no enlightenment on his patriotic duties and obligations." Goldrich, "Report of the Field Secretary—29 Aug. 1918;" Howard to Father, 2 Dec. 1917, Howard Papers, YMA; and Baldwin, "American Enlisted Man," 116–119.

59. Rainsford, *From Upton to the Meuse*, 10–11.

60. *American Jewish Chronicle*, 10 Aug. 1917; and *New York Times Magazine*, 10 Mar. 1918.

61. *New York Journal American*, 17 Sept. 1917; *American Jewish Chronicle*, 21 Sep. 1917; *American Hebrew*, 15 Feb. 1918; and Berry, *Make the Kaiser Dance*, 353.

62. Sullivan reportedly told the soldiers: "If I were you, I would go further, I would beat him to a pulp." *New York Times*, 17, 27 Oct., 21 Nov. 1917; Louis Marshall to Newton D. Baker, 17 Oct. 1917; and Marshall to Henry Rosensohn, 17, 21 Nov. 1917, Marshall Papers, AJA.

63. Goldrich, "Report of the Field Secretary, 4 Dec. 1917."

Part III

1. For a very different interpretation of ethnicity and patriotism in the twentieth century, which largely ignores the nationality issues and cross-cultural experiences that are described in the following two chapters, see Cecilia O'Leary, *To Die For: The Paradox of American Patriotism* (Princeton, N.J.: Princeton University Press, 1999); John Bodnar, *Remaking America: Public Memory, Commemoration, and Patriotism in the Twentieth Century* (Princeton, N.J.: Princeton University Press, 1992); and Bodnar, ed., *Bonds of Affection: Americans Define Their Patriotism* (Princeton, N.J.: Princeton University Press, 1996); David Montgomery, "Nationalism, American Patriotism, and Class Consciousness among Immigrant Workers in the United States in the Epoch of World War I," in Dirk Hoerder, ed., *"Struggle a Hard Battle": Essays on Working Class Immigrants* (DeKalb: Northern Illinois University Press, 1986), 327–354; and James H. Barrett, "Americanization from the Bottom Up: Immigration and the Remaking of the Working Class in the United States, 1880–1930," *Journal of American History* 79 (Dec. 1992), 996–1020.

Chapter 6

1. For more on Caporetto, see Cyril Falls, *The Battle of Caporetto* (Philadelphia, Pa.: J. B. Lippincott, 1966); Ronald Seth, *Caporetto: The Scapegoat Battle* (London: MacDonald, 1965), 147–169; H. James Burgwyn, *The Legend of the Mutilated Victory: Italy, the Great War, and the Paris Peace Conference, 1915–1919* (Westport, Conn.: Greenwood Press, 1993); and Christopher Seton-Watson, *Italy From Liberalism to Fascism, 1870–1925* (London: Methuen, 1967), 450–504.

2. *New Haven Register*, 30 Oct. and 18 Nov. 1917.

3. *New Haven Journal-Courier*, 31 Oct. 1917; and *Corriere del Connecticut*, 3 Nov. 1917.

4. *New Haven Register*, 30 Oct. 1917.

5. *Il Progresso Italo-Americano* (New York), 13, 23–26 Nov., 18, 25, 31 Dec. 1917; *L'Italia* (San Francisco), 19 Nov., 1 Dec. 1917; *La Voce del Popolo* (San Francisco), 4, 17, 19 Nov., 1, 15, 22–23 Dec. 1917.

6. *Corriere del Connecticut*, 3, 17 Nov., 1 Dec. 1917. Of the four Italian weekly papers that published in New Haven during the war era, only *Il Corriere* has survived.

7. *Corriere del Connecticut*, 3, 10 Nov. 1917; *New Haven Register*, 10 Nov. 1917.

8. *Corriere del Connecticut*, 10, 17 Nov. 1917.

9. Some of the groups continued to send money directly to their *paesani* in Italy, but gave equal or greater amounts to the committee. The Cerreto Sannita society, composed of Naples area immigrants, donated $150 to both the relief fund and their hometown's board of public assistance. *New Haven Register*, 18 Nov. 1917.

10. *Il Corriere* printed the names and amounts of every contributor to the fund through the months of November and December. *New Haven Register*, 18 Nov., 7 Dec. 1917; and *Corriere del Connecticut*, 1 Dec. 1917.

11. *Corriere del Connecticut*, 29 Dec. 1917, 5 Jan. 1918.

12. *Corriere del Connecticut*, 3 Nov. 1918. The editors of the *Register* made the same observation. "The campaign is unique for the reason that the loyalty of the Italian people of New Haven has never been more in evidence than on this occasion." *New Haven Register*, 2 Dec. 1917.

13. *New Haven Register*, 29 Oct. 1917.

14. Charles Bakewell, *The Story of the American Red Cross in Italy* (New York: Macmillan, 1920), 14.

15. The *Times Leader* agreed completely, calling the defeat "a tremendous and significant lesson for us Americans. . . . There has lurked in the minds of most of us the hope or the belief that some miracle would happen, and that Germany's power in the world at war would suddenly crumble away. . . . The Italian news, bad as it is, gloomy as it is, will in another way prove a fortunate thing. It will open the eyes of the Americans to the task before them." *New Haven Times Leader*, 30 Oct. and 2 Nov. 1917; *New Haven Union*, 30 Oct. 1917; *New Haven Register*, 31 Oct. 1917.

16. An exchange between the *Times Leader* and Santella's weekly was one of the first examples of the common ground created in the wake of the defeat. In an editorial entitled "Cruelly Unjust To Italians," the *Times Leader* condemned a Hartford paper for claiming that cowardice was the main reason for Italy's defeat. *Il Corriere* immediately showed its appreciation, reprinting the entire "just and brilliant" commentary on the front page of its November 3 issue. *New Haven Times Leader*, 30, 31 Oct. 1917; *Corriere del Connecticut*, 3 Nov. 1917.

17. *New Haven Register*, 4, 18 Nov. 1917.

18. *Corriere del Connecticut*, 10, 17 Nov. 1917; *New Haven Register*, 16 Nov. 1917.

19. Joseph Carlevale, *Who's Who Among Americans of Italian Descent*, 414; *New Haven Times Leader*, 4 May 1918; and *New Haven Register*, 15 Feb. 1918.

20. *New Haven Times Leader*, 23, 26, 28 Nov. 1917; *New Haven Register*, 25 Nov. 1917; *Corriere del Connecticut*, 24 Nov. 1917.

21. The men of the *Circolo del Sannio* provided a clear contrast to this sort of work when they put on a theatrical performance to benefit wounded soldiers in Italy. A war melodrama performed in Italian, "*I Due Sargenti*," demonstrated all of the masculine-nationalist traits of the *Comitato Pro Patria*. Playing to an all-Italian audience, the show's martial spirit and intended beneficiaries clearly differed from the women's work. *Corriere del Connecticut*, 4 May 1918. *New Haven Register*, 15–17 Feb. 1918; *New Haven Journal Courier*, 23 Feb. 1918; *New Haven Union*, 2, 14 Feb. 1918.

22. Letter of Chairwoman Caroline Ruutz-Rees to Poli, dated 20 Dec. 1917, Council of Defense—Woman's Division Classified file, 1917–1919, Box 363, Folder T19, RG–30, Connecticut State Library and Archives; *Report of the Connecticut State*

Council of Defense, December 1918 (Hartford: Printed for the Council, 1919), 141–142; *Connecticut Bulletin* (newsletter of the State Council of Defense), 25 Jan. and 22 Feb. 1918; and *Corriere del Connecticut*, 23, 30 Mar. 1918.

23. *New Haven Times Leader*, 4 May 1918; *New Haven Union*, 17, 28 Mar., 26 May, 28 June, 10 Aug., 7 Sept. 1918; *Corriere del Connecticut*, 8 June 1918.

24. *Corriere del Connecticut*, 23 Mar. and 24 May 1918; *New Haven Union*, 28 Mar. 1918.

25. *New Haven Journal Courier*, 2 Jan. 1918.

26. *New Haven Register*, 2 Jan. 1918; Robert Dahl, *Who Governs? Democracy and Power in an American City* (New Haven, Conn.: Yale University Press, 1961), 14; Raymond E. Wolfinger, "Persistence of Ethnic Voting," *American Political Science Review* 59 (Dec. 1965), 900–901; N. G. Osborn, *Men of Mark in Connecticut* (Hartford, Conn.: Goodspeed, 1910), 5:508–511; Mary H. Mitchell, *History of New Haven County, Connecticut* (Chicago, Ill.: Pioneer, 1930), 2:106–111.

27. For more on the crises facing the war effort in the winter of 1917–1918 and the bureaucratic developments that followed, see David Kennedy, *Over Here: The First World War and American Society* (Oxford: Oxford University Press, 1980), 113–144; James Johnson, "The Wilsonians as War Managers: Coal and the 1917–1918 Winter Crisis," *Prologue* 9 (1977), 193–208; Daniel Beaver, *Newton D. Baker and the American War Effort* (Lincoln: University of Nebraska Press, 1966), 50–109; Robert D. Cuff, *The War Industries Board: Business-Government Relations During World War I* (Baltimore, Md.: Johns Hopkins University Press, 1973); and Valerie Jean Conner, *The National War Labor Board: Stability, Social Justice and the Voluntary State* (Chapel Hill: University of North Carolina Press, 1983).

28. State of Connecticut, *Twenty-Eighth Report of the Bureau of Labor for the Two Years Ended November 30 1918* (Hartford: State of Connecticut, 1918), 39–50; *New Haven Journal Courier*, 24 Mar. 1918; *New Haven Register*, 17, 25 Jan. 1918; and Charlotte Holloway, *Report of the Department of Labor on the Conditions of Wage-Earners in the State* (Hartford: State of Connecticut, 1918), 14, 17.

29. *New Haven Union*, 25 Jan., 17 Mar. 1918; *New Haven Register*, 29 Oct. 1917, 31 Mar. 1918; and *Corriere del Connecticut*, 5 Jan., 2 Feb., 7 Sept. 1918.

30. *New Haven Register*, 15 June 1919; *City Yearbook of the City of New Haven for 1918* (New Haven: 1919) 296–302, 318–321; *New Haven Union*, 16, 17 May, 5, 6 Nov. 1918. See also Child, "A Psychological Study of Second Generation Italians" (Ph.D. diss., Yale University, 1939), 115; and Stephen Lassonde, "Learning to Forget," (Ph.D. diss., Yale University, 1994), 220–221.

31. William J. Breen, *Uncle Sam at Home: Civilian Mobilization, Wartime Federalism, and the Council of National Defense* (Westport, Conn.: Greenwood Press, 1984), 53–69; and Breen, "Mobilization and Cooperative Federalism: The Connecticut State Council of Defense, 1917–1919," *The Historian* 42 (Nov. 1994), 58–84; Bruce Fraser, "Yankees at War: Social Mobilization on the Connecticut Home Front, 1917–1918" (Ph.D. diss., Columbia University, 1976); New Haven War Bureau, *A Statement of the Work of the New Haven War Bureau of the Connecticut State Council of Defense* (New Haven: Connecticut State Council of Defense, Aug. 1918); *Connecticut Bulletin*, 21 Sept. 1917, 8 Mar., 19 Apr. 1918; *New Haven Register*, 2 Dec. 1917, 3 Feb., 10 Mar., 1 Sept. 1918; *New Haven Union*, 4 Nov. 1918; and *Corriere del Connecticut*, 24 Nov. 1917, 8, 29 June 1918.

32. The popular response of Italians and Italian Americans to the Fourteen Points contrasted sharply with the negative view of most Italian leaders. The secret Treaty of

London, Italy's compact with France and Britain, which delineated postwar spoils, promised a much larger and clearer expansion of Italian borders. C. J. Lowe and F. Marzari, *Italian Foreign Policy, 1870–1940* (London: Routledge and Kegan Paul, 1975), 133–180. Postcard of the St. Anthony's Church altar, found in the Parish Historical Files, St. Anthony's Parish of New Haven folder, Archives of the Diocese of Hartford; *Corriere del Connecticut*, 12 Jan. 1918.

33. *New York Times*, 24, 25 May 1918.

34. *New York World*, 24, 25 May 1918; *New York Herald*, 25 May 1918; *Chicago Tribune*, 24 May 1918; *St. Louis Post-Dispatch*, 25 May 1918; *L'Italia* (San Francisco), 24, 25 May 1918; and *Boston Evening Transcript*, 23 May 1918.

35. *New Haven Times Leader*, 22, 23 May 1918; *New Haven Union*, 24 May 1918; *Connecticut Bulletin*, 31 May 1918; *Corriere del Connecticut*, 24 May 1918.

36. *New Haven Journal Courier*, 25 May 1918; *New Haven Union*, 25 May 1918; and Cannelli, *Colonia Italiana*, 301.

37. *Corriere del Connecticut*, 24 May, 1 June 1918; *New Haven Journal Courier*, 25 May 1918.

38. *Corriere del Connecticut*, 8, 15 June 1918.

39. *New York Times*, 24, 25 May 1918; *Corriere del Connecticut*, 24 May 1918.

40. Maximilian Von Hoegen, the man attacked on the night of January 5, 1918, was an American citizen. His comments on a draft questionnaire, including the phrase "Deutschland Uber Alles" and the remark that he had "the doubtful honor" of being an American citizen, were reprinted in highly inflammatory articles in the daily press. A day before the beating the *Register* branded him as a "self-styled agent of the Imperial German government" and claimed provocatively that no legal action could be taken against him. Despite Von Hoegen's pleas that he was blind in one eye and a cripple, the vigilantes pulled him from his house right in front of his family and beat him in the middle of the street until police arrived. He reported later "he fully expected to be lynched." *New Haven Union*, 24 May 1918; *Corriere del Connecticut*, 12 Jan., 24 May 1918; and *New Haven Register*, 4, 6, 7 Jan. 1918.

41. *Corriere del Connecticut*, 27 Apr., 4 May 1918; *New Haven Union*, 30 Apr. 1918; *New Haven Register*, 16 Oct. 1918; and Cannelli, *Colonia Italiana*, 302.

42. For the Fourth Liberty Loan, national campaign leaders enlisted between 700,000 and 800,000 women as bond selling agents. Rosa Poli shone in this work as well, directing the campaign for New Haven's Third and Fourth wards. She organized the city's only loan block party, a dance festival in the ethnically mixed Hill neighborhood that netted twenty-five thousand dollars worth of subscriptions. Colony women also staffed loan booths in the heavily Italian Fifth and Sixth wards. *New Haven Union*, 6 Oct. 1918; *New Haven Register*, 10, 13 Oct. 1918; *New Haven Times Leader*, 15, 30 Apr. 1918; *Corriere del Connecticut*, 13, 20, 27 Apr. 1918; and *New Haven Union*, 11, 16, 20 Apr. 1918.

43. *Chicago Tribune*, 21, 22 Apr. 1918; Philadelphia War History Committee, *Philadelphia in the World War, 1914–1919* (New York: Wynkoop, 1922), 489–90; John H. Mariano, *Second-generation Italians in New York City* (Boston, Mass.: Christopher, 1921), 54–55; *St. Louis Post-Dispatch*, 27–28 Apr. 1918; Donald Cole, *Immigrant City: Lawrence, Massachusetts, 1845–1921* (Chapel Hill: University of North Carolina Press, 1963), 198.

44. The *Register* understood the intentions of this new approach. In an editorial entitled "The Liberty Loan a Melting Pot" it described the Third Loan drive as "the greatest of all amalgamating processes with the single exception of the American armed

forces. As men learn to love one another by fighting side by side, so men learn to love their government the more they are brought actively in support of it." *New Haven Register*, 27 Apr. 1918.

45. *New Haven Register*, 27 Apr. 1918; *Corriere del Connecticut*, 6 Apr. 1918.

46. *New Haven Union*, 2, 3 Apr. 1918; *New Haven Register*, 9 Mar. 1918; and *Corriere del Connecticut*, 9, 16, 23 Feb., 9 Mar. 13 Apr. 1918, 24 May 1918. Lizabeth Cohen has described similar issues for ethnic banking in the 1920s. Cohen, *Making a New Deal*, 75–83.

47. *New Haven Times Leader*, 16 Mar. 1918; *Corriere del Connecticut*, 23 Mar. 1918; and *New Haven Union*, 3 Apr. 1918.

48. *New Haven Journal Courier*, 19 February 1918; *New Haven Union*, 17 Mar. 1918; and *New Haven Register*, 21, 30 Apr. 1918.

49. *Corriere del Connecticut*, 17, 31 Aug., 7, 14 Sept. 1918; *New Haven Journal Courier*, 2, 9 Sept. 1918; *New Haven Union*, 31 Aug., 3, 9 Sept. 1918.

50. *New Haven Union*, 9 Sept. 1918; *New Haven Register*, 21 Aug., 19 Sept. 1918; *New Haven Times Leader*, 27 Aug., 17 Oct. 1918.

51. *New Haven Union*, 15 Apr. 1918; *New Haven Register*, 4 Sept. 1918; *New Haven Times Leader*, 7, 10 Sept. 1918; and *Corriere del Connecticut*, 7 Sept. 1918.

52. *New Haven Times Leader*, 3 May 1918.

53. Nelli, *Italians in Chicago*, 202.

54. *New Haven Register*, 15, 16 Sept. 1918.

55. *Corriere del Connecticut*, 21 Sept. 1918.

56. *Corriere del Connecticut*, 9 Nov. 1918; and *New Haven Journal Courier*, 11 Nov. 1918.

57. *New Haven Register*, 11 Nov. 1918; and *New Haven Journal Courier*, 12 Nov. 1918.

58. *New Haven Times Leader*, 11 Nov. 1918; *New Haven Journal Courier*, 12 Nov. 1918; *Corriere del Connecticut*, 9, 16 Nov. 1918; and Cannelli, *Colonia Italiana*, 302.

59. *New Haven Register*, 25 Nov., 9, 16, 23 Dec. 1918.

Chapter 7

1. *Yiddishes Tageblatt*, 19 May, 7 Oct. 1918.

2. Studies of Jewish assimilation in the first half of the twentieth century have largely ignored the war. See in particular Deborah Dash Moore, *At Home in America* (New York: Columbia University Press, 1981); Andrew R. Heinze, *Adapting to Abundance: Jewish Immigrants, Mass Consumption, and the Search for American Identity* (New York: Columbia University Press, 1990); and Jenna Weissman Joselit, *The Wonders of America, Reinventing Jewish Culture, 1880–1950* (New York: Hill and Wang, 1994). Two works on the interwar period also devote very little attention to the Great War's impact: Henry Feingold, *A Time for Searching: Entering the Mainstream, 1920–1945* (Baltimore, Md.: Johns Hopkins University Press, 1992); and Beth Wenger, *New York Jews and the Great Depression* (New Haven, Conn.: Yale University Press, 1996).

3. Marshall to Albert Lasker, 5 Nov. 1917; Marshall to Cahan, 5 Nov. 1917; and Marshall to Sulzberger, 16 Aug. 1917, Marshall Papers, AJA.

4. On the election, see John F. McClymer, "Of 'Mornin' Glories' and 'Fine Old Oaks': John Purroy Mitchel, Al Smith, and Reform as an Expression of Irish American Aspiration," in Ronald H. Bayor and Timothy J. Meagher, eds., *The New York Irish* (Baltimore, Md.: Johns Hopkins University Press, 1996), 374–394; Kenneth S. Chern, "The Politics of Patriotism: War, Ethnicity, and the New York Mayoralty Campaign,

1917," *New York Historical Society Quarterly* 63 (1979), 290–313; Thomas Henderson, *Tammany Hall and the New Immigrants: The Progressive Years* (New York: Arno Press, 1976), 193–219; and Edwin R. Lewinson, *John Purroy Mitchel: The Boy Mayor of New York* (New York: Astra Books, 1965), 206–247.

5. For two studies that deal more specifically with Jewish aspects of the campaign, see Irwin Yellowitz, "Morris Hillquit: American Socialism and Jewish Concerns," *American Jewish History* 68 (Dec. 1978), 163–188; and Zosa Szajkowski, *Jews, Wars, and Communism* (New York: KTAV, 1972), 141–161.

6. *New York Call*, 20 Sept. 1917.

7. William Freiburger, "War Prosperity and Hunger: The New York Food Riots of 1917," *Labor History* 25 (spring 1984), 217–239; and Dana Frank, "Housewives, Socialists, and the Politics of Food: The 1917 New York Cost-of-Living Protests," *Feminist Studies* 11 (summer 1985), 255–286.

8. Unsigned report dated 1 Feb., U.S. Food Administration Records, 6–H, Box 15, New York file, Hoover Institution Archives (hereafter HIA).

9. *New York Herald*, 3 Dec. 1917; and letter included with unsigned report, dated 1 Feb., USFA Records, HIA.

10. Louis Eisenstein, *Stripe of Tammany's Tiger* (New York: R. Speller, 1966), 20–21; John McClymer, "Of 'Mornin' Glories' and 'Fine Old Oaks,'" 374–394; Thomas Henderson, *Tammany Hall and the New Immigrants* (New York: Arno Press, 1976), 193–219; and Diane Ravitch, *Great School Wars* (New York: Basic Books, 1974), 219–227.

11. *New York Call*, 19 Sept. 1917.

12. Bernard K. Johnpoll and Harvery Klehr, *Biographical Dictionary of the American Left* (Westport, Conn.: Greenwood Press, 1986), 69–71, 156–157, 244–246, 308–309, 364–365, 392–397, 400–402.

13. *New York Times*, 3 Nov. 1917.

14. *New York Call*, 8 Sept., 23 Oct. 1917; and August Claessens, *Didn't We Have Fun* (New York: Rand School Press 1953), 89.

15. *Advance*, Sept.–Nov. 1917; *New York Call*, 21, 22, 27 Sept., 7 Oct. 1917; and Melvyn Dubofsky, "The Success and Failure of Socialism in New York City, 1900–1918: A Case Study," *Labor History* 9 (fall 1968), 369–372.

16. *American Labor Year Book, 1918–1919* (New York: Rand School, 1919), 291.

17. Claessens, *Didn't We Have Fun*, 88; Sally M. Miller, "From Sweatshop Worker to Labor Leader: Theresa Malkiel, a Case Study," *American Jewish History* 68 (Dec. 1978), 189–205; and *New York Call*, 2, 4, 6, 13, 23 Oct. 1917.

18. Kathleen Kennedy, "Declaring War on War: Gender and the American Socialist Attack on Militarism, 1914–1918," *Journal of Women's History* 7 (summer 1995), 27–51; *New York Call*, 24, 30 Oct., 4 Nov. 1917; *Ladies Garment Worker*, Nov., Dec. 1917; *Advance*, 26 Oct., 28 Dec. 1917; *New York Times*, 28 Oct., 7 Nov. 1918; *American Labor Year Book, 1918–1919*, 291.

19. *New York Times*, 4, 14–20, Oct. 1917; Ravitch, *Great School Wars*, 195–230; Lewinson, *John Purroy Mitchel*, 150–169; and *New York Call*, 14, 16 Oct. 1917.

20. *New York Call*, 26 Sept. 1917; Ravitch, *Great School Wars*, 224–230; and Louis Waldman, *Labor Lawyer* (New York: E. P. Dutton, 1944), 45.

21. Joseph Freeman, *An American Testament: A Narrative of Rebels and Romantics* (New York: Farrar and Rinehart, 1936), 109–110; and *New York Call*, 18, 26 Oct., 4 Nov. 1917.

22. *New York Call*, 23 Oct. 1917.

23. Waldman, *Labor Lawyer*, 44; Baruch C. Vladeck, Memoirs, Vladeck Papers

(on microfilm) Section 2, General Material, c. 1907–1938, Box 7, Tamiment Library; Charles Leinenweber, "Socialists in the Streets: The New York City Socialist Party in Working-Class Neighborhoods, 1908–1918," *Science and Society* 41 (summer 1977), 152–171; *New York Call*, 17, 18 Sept., 3 Oct. 1917; and Eisenstein, *Stripe of Tammany's Tiger*, 27.

24. Claessens, *Didn't We Have Fun*, 101; and Waldman, *Labor Lawyer*, 79.

25. *New York Call*, 26 Sept., 22, 23 Oct., 5, 6 Nov. 1917; and Waldman, *Labor Lawyer*, 79–81.

26. *New York Call*, 7, 8 Nov. 1917; and Vladeck, Memoirs, 98.

27. *New York Times*, 6, 7 Nov. 1917.

28. *New York Call*, 5, 6, 9, 12–14 Jan., 3 Mar. 1918; *Advance*, 9, 16 Nov., 7 Dec. 1917.

29. Benjamin Gitlow, *I Confess: The Truth About American Communism* (New York: E. P. Dutton, 1940), 19, 20; August Claessens and William Feigenbaum, *The Socialists in the New York Assembly* (New York: Rand School, 1918); and Vladeck, Memoirs, 99–100, 109–110.

30. *New York Times*, 3 Dec. 1917; New York Kehillah, *Jewish Communal Register*, 1917–1918, 1462–1478; and *American Hebrew*, 30 Nov., 7 Dec. 1917.

31. *New York Times*, 4, 12, 21 Nov., 3 Dec. 1917.

32. *American Jewish Chronicle*, 2 Nov. 1917. There was also debate over the wisdom of the campaign among members of the Joint Distribution Committee. Albert Lasker, a JDC officer from Chicago, argued that "by dividing the moneys collected with the Welfare Board, I am afraid the showing will be so small for War Relief work as to spell the death of the movement." Lasker to Jacob Billikopf, 26 Oct. 1917, Folder 1, Box 452, Schiff Papers; and Jacob Schiff to Lasker, 29 Oct. 1917, Folder 6, Box 453, Schiff Papers, AJA.

33. *American Jewish Chronicle*, 9, 16 Nov., 7 Dec. 1917; *Advance*, 28 Dec. 1917. See also correspondence of Jacob Schiff to Dr. William Sirovich, 25 Sept. 1917; and Sirovich to Schiff, 19 Sept., 2 Oct. 1917, Folder 2, Box 452, Schiff Papers.

34. *New York Herald*, 5, 8, 9 Dec. 1917; *New York Call*, 17 Feb. 1917; and *New York Times*, 3, 5, 10, 11 Dec. 1917.

35. *Ladies' Garment Worker*, Jan., Feb. 1918; *New York Call*, 4, 5, 10, 15 Dec. 1917, 13 Feb. 1918; *New York Herald*, 14 Dec. 1917; *New York Times*, 14, 30 Dec. 1917: Letters of Louis Marshall to Schiff, 9 Jan. 1918; to Garfield, 24 Jan. 1918; and to Schlesinger, 18 May 1918, Marshall Papers, AJA.

36. *Advance*, 7–28 Dec. 1917; 4 Jan., 1 Mar. 1918; and *Ladies' Garment Worker*, Jan., Feb. 1918.

37. Joseph Rappaport, "Jewish Immigrants and World War I," (Ph.D. diss., Columbia University, 1951), 324; and Harry Roskolenko, *The Time That Was Then: The Lower East Side, 1900–1914, An Intimate Chronicle* (New York: Dial Press, 1971) 30.

38. Unsigned report dated 1 Feb. 1918, U.S. Food Administration Records, 6–H, Box #15, New York file, HIA.

39. Gitlow, *I Confess*, 18, 20–21; *Advance*, 26 Oct. 1917; *New York Journal American*, 1 Mar. 1918; and *New York Call*, 2, 27 Mar. 1918.

40. Rappaport, "Jewish Immigrants and World War I," 302–303, 323–324, 354–355; Roskolenko, *Time That Was Then*, 85; and *Advance*, 30 Nov. 1917, 18 Jan. 1918.

41. See Marshall to Al Smith, 10 Apr. 1918, and to James Marshall, 9 May 1918, Marshall Papers; *American Hebrew*, 19 Apr., 3 May 1918; *Ladies Garment Worker*, Apr., May 1918; *Advance*, 15 Mar., 26 Apr., 3 May 1918; *New York Call*, 11, 14 Apr., 11

May 1918; *American Jewish Chronicle*, 29 Mar., 5, 12 Apr. 1918; Rappaport, "Jewish Immigrants and World War I," 346–351

42. *New York Times*, 4 Aug. 1918; and *American Jewish Chronicle*, 19 Oct. 1917.

43. Eisenstein, *Stripe of Tammany's Tiger*, 26; Steve Fraser, *Labor Will Rule: Sidney Hillman and the Rise of American Labor* (New York: Free Press, 1991), 114–178; and Melvyn Dubofsky, "Organized Labor in New York City and the First World War, 1914–1918," *New York History* (October 1961), 380–401.

44. Melech Epstein, *Jewish Labor in U.S.A.* (N.Y.: Trade Union Sponsoring Committee, 1953), 2:71; *Advance*, 30 Nov. 1917, 22 Feb. 1918; *New York Call*, 14, 29 Mar. 1918; and transcript of Newman interview by Barbara Wertheimer, "The Twentieth Century Trade Union Woman: Vehicle for Social Change Oral History Project" (Ann Arbor: University of Michigan, 1978) 51–52.

45. *The Outlook*, 27 Feb. 1918, 327.

46. Charles Goldblatt, "The Impact of the Balfour Declaration in America," *American Jewish Historical Quarterly* 58 (June 1968), 480–483; Rappaport, "Jewish Immigrants and World War I," 326–334; *New York Times*, 13 Dec. 1917; *New York Herald*, 11 Dec. 1917; and *Maccabaean*, Jan. 1918.

47. Matthew Jacobson, *Special Sorrows: The Diasporic Imagination of Irish, Polish, and Jewish Immigrants in the United States* (Cambridge, Mass.: Harvard University Press, 1995), 72.

48. Melvin Urofsky, *American Zionism, From Herzl to the Holocaust* (New York: Anchor Press, 1975), 195–245.

49. Allon Gal, "The Mission Motif in American Zionism," *American Jewish History*, 76 (June 1986), 363–385; and "Independence and Universal Mission in Modern Jewish Nationalism: Comparative Analysis of European and American Zionism (1898–1948)," *Studies in Contemporary Jewry* 5 (1989), 242–274 (especially useful are the comments of Arthur Goren and Ezra Mendelsohn). See also Michael Berkowitz, *Western Jewry and the Zionist Project, 1914–1933* (Cambridge: Cambridge University Press, 1997); Urofsky, *American Zionism*, 195–245; and Yonathan Shapiro, *Leadership of the American Zionist Organization, 1897–1930* (Urbana: University of Illinois Press, 1971), 99–134.

50. Moses Rischin, "The American Jewish Committee and Zionism, 1906–1922," *Herzl Year Book* 5 (1963), 65–81.

51. *American Jewish Chronicle*, 7 Dec. 1917, 26 Apr., 3 May 1918; *New York Call*, 19 May 1918; and Joseph Rappaport, "Zionism as a Factor in Allied–Central Power Controversy (1914–1918)," in Isidore S. Meyer, *Early History of Zionism in America* (New York: Arno Press, 1977), 311–325.

52. New York Kehillah, *Jewish Communal Register*, 1340–1409; Selig Adler, "The Palestine Question in the Wilson Era," *Jewish Social Studies* 10 (1948), 315; *New York Times*, 31 Oct., 6 Dec. 1918; *New York Herald*, 31 Oct. 1918; *American Jewish Weekly News*, 25 Oct., 1, 8 Nov. 1918; and *Maccabaean*, July to Dec., 1918.

53. *American Jewish Chronicle*, 8, 29 Mar., 5, 12 Apr. 1918; *American Hebrew*, 6 Apr. 1917; 1, 8 Mar. 1918; William Braiterman, "Memories of the Palestine Jewish Legion of 1917," typescript, in Small Collections, SC–1303, AJA; and Joshua H. Neumann, "The Jewish Battalions and the Palestine Campaign," in *American Jewish Year Book, 1919–1920* (Philadelphia, Pa.: American Jewish Committee, 1920), 120–140.

54. Leon Spitz, *The Memoirs of a Camp Rabbi* (New York: Bloch, 1927), 7.

55. *New York Times*, 12, 13 Nov. 1918; Lewis S. Feuer, "The Legend of the Socialist East Side," *Midstream* (Feb. 1978), 25; and Marie Jastrow, *Looking Back: The*

American Dream Through Immigrant Eyes (New York: W. W. Norton, 1986), 165–166; *American Hebrew*, 15 Nov. 1918.

56. Abraham Okun to Louis Marshall, 7 Oct. 1918, Marshall Papers; B. Hoffman to Cyrus Miller, 25 Nov. 1918, 178:6, Warburg Papers; *Yiddishes Tageblatt*, 12 Sept. 1918; *American Hebrew*, 15 Feb., 15 Mar., 3 May, 18 Oct. 1918; and *American Jewish Weekly News*, 17 May, 5, 12 July 1918.

57. *Advance*, 12 Oct. 1917; *Ladies Garment Worker*, Apr., May, June 1918; *New York Times*, 18, 27 Feb., 4 Aug., 12 Nov. 1918; and *New York Call*, 1 Mar. 1918.

Chapter 8

1. Harold Kalloch questionnaire, World War I Survey, USMHIA.

2. Mark Meigs, *Optimism at Armageddon: Voices of American Participants in the First World War* (New York: New York University Press, 1997); Ronald Schaffer, *America in the Great War: The Rise of the War Welfare State* (New York: Oxford University Press, 1991), 194–198; and David Kennedy, *Over Here* (New York: Oxford University Press, 1980), 205–230.

3. American Battlefield Monuments Commission, *Twenty-sixth Division: Summary of Operations in the World War* (Washington, D.C.: Government Printing Office, 1944); and *Seventy-seventh Division: Summary of Operations in the World War* (Washington, D.C.: Government Printing Office, 1944).

4. The best accounts of the Yankee Division and the 102nd Regiment are: Emerson Taylor, *New England in France* (Boston, Mass.: Houghton-Mifflin, 1920); Daniel Strickland, *Connecticut Fights* (New Haven, Conn.: Quinnipiack Press, 1930); and Connell Albertine, *Yankee Doughboy* (Boston, Mass.: Braden Press, 1968).

5. Robert Alexander, *Memories of the World War* (New York: MacMillan Co, 1930), 156. See especially: Julius O. Adler, ed., *History of the Seventy-seventh Division* (New York: W. H. Crawford Printers, 1919); L. Wardlaw Miles, *History of the 308th Infantry* (New York: Putnam's 1927); W. Kerr Rainsford, *From Upton to the Meuse* (New York: Appleton, 1920); and Frank Tiebout, *History of the 305th* (New York: 305th Infantry Auxiliary, 1919).

6. James H. Hallas, *Squandered Victory: The American First Army at St. Mihiel* (Westport, Conn.: Praeger, 1995); Paul F. Braim, *Test of Battle: The American Expeditionary Forces in the Meuse-Argonne Campaign* (Newark: University of Delaware Press, 1987); Rainsford, *From Upton to the Meuse*, 240.

7. The commander of the Seventy-seventh Division, General Robert Alexander, fully agreed with Pershing. Long after the war, he still criticized the heavy emphasis on trench training. Alexander, *Memories of the Great War* (New York: Macmillan, 1931), 188.

8. Christian Blumenstein, *Whiz Bang!* (Buffalo, N.Y. privately printed, 1927), 17. A captain in the Seventy-seventh Division describes the average *poilu* in almost the complete opposite terms. "Perhaps the most noticeable feature of the French soldier's daily life, both officer and man, was the lack of all haste. . . . Four years of realistic war had worn off all non-essentials (if they had previously existed) and only the fundamental was left, namely common sense." Miles, *308th Infantry*, 69.

9. Rainsford, *From Upton to the Meuse*, 156–157, 180–181; Braim, *Test of Battle*, 184; and Frank Freidel, *Over There* (Philadelphia Pa.: Temple University Press, 1990), 176.

10. Strickland, *Connecticut Fights*, 133–135; Frank Sibley, *With the Yankee Division* (Boston: Little, Brown, 1919), 138–158; Benwell, *History of the Yankee Division* (Boston:

Cornhill, 1919), 71–76; and John H. Parker, "Action Front!" (Unpublished manuscript), 201–214, Parker Papers, USMAL.

11. Hills, *War History* (Hartford, Conn.: Privately printed, 1924), 14–15; Parker, "Action Front!" 209, 211–212, Parker Papers; Strickland, *Connecticut Fights*, 133–147; and Louis Popolizio, Military Service Questionnaire—New Haven, CSL.

12. *New Haven Union*, 24 Apr. 1918; *New Haven Times Leader*, 30 Apr. 1918; Edward M. Coffman, *War to End All Wars* (New York: Oxford University Press, 1968), 147–149; James J. Cooke, *Pershing and His Generals: Command and Staff in the AEF* (Westport, Conn.: Praeger, 1997), 66, 79–80; and Donald Smythe, *Pershing: General of the Armies* (Bloomington: Indiana University Press, 1986), 107–108.

13. Strickland, *Connecticut Fights*, 135.

14. An intelligence officer interviewed well after the war was extremely critical of the YD leadership. "Now, the Yankee Division [the Twenty-sixth] had this old fool, Clarence Edwards, in charge. He'd been a cavalry man and didn't know anything about modern war. And one of his colonels, 'Gatling Gun' Parker, was just as bad. He was supposed to know everything about machine guns, but he didn't know anything about trench warfare." Quoted in Henry Berry, *Make the Kaiser Dance* (Garden City, N.Y.: Doubleday, 1978), 32–33.

15. Miles, *308th Infantry*, 239–254, 270–278; Johnson and Pratt, *Lost Battalion;* and Merion and Susie Harries, *The Last Days of Innocence: America at War, 1917–1918* (New York: Random House, 1997), 370–372, 375–379.

16. American Battle Monuments Commission, *Armies and Battlefields in Europe: A History, Guide and Reference Book,* (Washington, D.C.: Government Printing Office, 1938), 337, 362–365; and Johnson and Pratt, *Lost Battalion.*

17. Miles, *308th Infantry*, 164–171; Henry O. Swindler, "The So-Called Lost Battalion," *American Mercury* 15 (Nov. 1928), 257–265; and Julius Klausner, *Company B, 307th Infantry* (New York: American Legion, Burke–Kelly Post No. 172, 1920), 18–19.

18. Liner, in letter printed in *American Hebrew*, 10 Jan. 1919; Alexander, *Memories of the World War*, 231; Fletcher and Pratt, *Lost Battalion*, 250–252; *New York Times*, 19 Dec. 1918; *JWB Sentinel*, Aug. 1919; and Irving Goldberg, AJC War Records Questionnaire, AJHS.

19. Siegel, "Measure of Life," (unpublished manuscript) AJA, 18–19.

20. *New York Tribune*, 9–11 Oct. 1918; and *New York Times*, 11, 12 Oct. 1918.

21. Smythe, *Pershing: General of the Armies*, 236–237; Braim, *Test of Battle;* and Kennedy, *Over There*, 204.

22. Ruby Hughes, entry for 9 November 1918, Wartime Diary, Ruby Hughes Papers, Special Collections Division, University of Arkansas Libraries, Fayetteville, Ark. See also Charles F. Minder, *This Man's War: The Day-by-Day Record of an American Private on the Western Front* (New York: Pevensey Press, 1931), 361.

23. Minder, *This Man's War*, 149, 152; Morton Greenwald questionnaire, box 6, folder 7f, AJC War Records, AJHS; and Strickland, *Connecticut Fights*, 83, 100, 323.

24. Miles, *308th Infantry*, 54; Minder, *This Man's War*, 187; and Siegel, "Measure of Life" 20.

25. Adler, *History of the Seventy-seventh Division*, 43; Blumenstein, *Whiz Bang!* 3; Minder, *This Man's War*, 24; and Keegan, *Face of Battle* (New York: Vintage, 1977), 264.

26. Miles, *308th Infantry*, 96; Minder, *This Man's War*, 164; Lee J. Levinger, *A Jewish Chaplain in France* (New York: Macmillan, 1921), 156–157; Siegel, "Measure of

Life," 16, 20; and Harry Weisburg questionnaire, Box 9, Folder 17a, AJC War Records Collection, AJHS.

27. Minder, *This Man's War*, 225, 234; Adler, ed., *History of the Seventy-seventh Division*, 43; Miles, *308th Infantry*, 98; and Blumenstein, *Whiz Bang!* 15.

28. Minder, *This Man's War*, 218, 306; John Ellis, *Eye Deep in Hell* (Baltimore, Md.: Johns Hopkins University Press, 1976), 125; Blumenstein, *Whiz Bang!* 26; and Adler, *History of the 306th*, 103.

29. Minder, *This Man's War*, 323–324, 342, 357; and Weisburg questionnaire, AJC War Records.

30. Henry W. Smith, *305th Machine Gun Battalion* (New York: Modern Composing Room, 1944), 60, 66; and Blumenstein, *Whiz Bang!* 17.

31. Minder, *This Man's War*, 234, 244, 277, 323; and Zirinsky questionnaire, box 9, folder 18, AJC War Records, AJHS.

32. Lieutenant Robert K. Haas to Parents, 6 Nov. 1918, Haas Papers; Arthur Wolff to Mother, 31 Aug. 1918, Wolff Papers, National Museum of American Jewish Military History; Minder, *This Man's War*, 175, 179, 194–197; and Lieutenant Harold P. Stokes to Mother, 30 Sept. 1918, Stokes Papers, YMA.

33. Alexander, *Memories of the World War*, 197–198; Minder, *This Man's War*, 225, 358; Smith, *305th Machine Gun Battalion*, 65; Blumenstein, *Whiz Bang!* 15, 22–23; and Strickland, *Connecticut Fights*, 137.

34. Miles, *308th Infantry*, 99; and Siegel, "Measure of Life," 21.

35. Soldier in 305th quoted in Freidel, *Over There*, 171–172; Rainsford, *From Upton to the Meuse*, 191; Blumenstein, *Whiz Bang!* 29; Minder, *This Man's War*, 356, 365–366, 368; and Smith, *305th Machine Gun Battalion*, 71.

36. Minder, *This Man's War*, 52, 231; Smith, *305th Machine Gun Battalion*, 62; Strickland, *Connecticut Fights*, 166–167; Schaffer, *America in the Great War*, 199–212; Keegan, *Face of Battle*, 270; and Herman Kleinfeld questionnaire, box 5 "Wounded—Straight Citations" folder, AJC War Records, AJHS.

37. Minder, *This Man's War*, 70, 203, 140–141, 208–209; and Lieutenant Samuel S. Nash to mother, 23 February 1919, Samuel S. Nash Papers, Southern History Collection, University of North Carolina Library, Chapel Hill, N.C. See also letter of Lieutenant Robert Haas to parents, 30 Aug. 1918, Haas Papers, USMAL.

38. Minder, *This Man's War*, 317. See also the comments of General Robert Alexander, *Memories of the World War*, 201; and the grotesque minstrel humor of Private "Buck" McCollum, *History and Rhymes of the Lost Battalion* (New York: Bucklee Publishers, 1919).

39. Anastasio letter printed in *New Haven Journal Courier*, 29 Apr. 1918; and Louis Popolizio, NHCHS War Records File.

40. Currano letter printed in *New Haven Times Leader*, 20 Mar. 1918; and Bove letter in *New Haven Register*, 3 Nov. 1918.

41. *New Haven Register*, 4, 21 Sept., 3 Nov. 1918; Rosa Ponselle and James A. Drake, *Ponselle: A Singer's Life* (New York: Doubleday, 1982) 67; Parker, "Action Front!" 215, 241–243; Philip H. English Diary (unpublished manuscript) NHCHS, 98; and Strickland, *Connecticut Fights*, 202–203, 260, 282–283, 323.

42. Popolizio, Miranda, Aiello, and Spinaci Military Service Questionnaires—New Haven, CSL; and *New Haven Register*, 30 July 1922; Collection of 102nd Machine Gun Company obituaries, dating from the 1950s through the 1980s, in author's possession.

43. *New Haven Journal Courier*, 5 Nov. 1918.

44. Ibid.

45. Albert I. Slomovitz, *The Fighting Rabbis: Jewish Military Chaplains and American History* (New York: New York University Press, 1999), 43–62.

46. Benjamin Friedman file—Biographies—Small Collections, AJA; and Levinger, *Jewish Chaplain*, 83–85. Rabbi Harry Davidowitz, a chaplain in the Eighty-second Division, described the many nonreligious services he performed for the soldiers. "They asked me to do for them the little tasks which they find no time or chance to do for themselves; they give me money to send to their folks at home; they come to me to make wills; they tell me all their troubles and difficulties. . . . Of what value a Jewish Chaplain may become when his Division goes into action, I can surmise only by multiplying the present effects one hundred fold and more." Davidowitz, in *JWB Sentinel*, Dec. 1919.

47. *New York Times*, 12 Oct. 1919; Miles, *308th Infantry*, 64; Friedman file—Small Collections; Levinger, *Jewish Chaplain*, 15, 139; and Voorsanger, notes for undated service, Box 2 File 11, Voorsanger Papers, AJA.

48. Howard, War Diary, 64, Howard Papers, YMA. He describes the rabbi as "a real Jew, with a forward thrust to his head, and heavy, soft features and glasses." In his editorial comments, written in 1969, Howard notes: "I regret finding this attitude toward Jews in my Diary."

49. Ibid., 89–91, 162; and James Howard, *The Autobiography of a Regiment: A History of the 304th Field Artillery in the World War* (New York: Privately printed, 1920), 109–110, 112.

50. Lieutenant Louis Egelson to Chester Teller, 18 Dec. 1918; and to Harry Cutler, 20 Mar. 1919, Louis Egelson Papers; Cyrus Adler, *I Have Considered the Days* (Philadelphia, Pa.: Jewish Publication Society, 1941), 320–321; and Levinger, *Jewish Chaplain*, 92–113.

51. Marcus, "Lost: Judaism in the A.E.F.," *American Hebrew*, 21 Mar. 1919. See also Marcus's influential article, "The Jewish Soldier," in *Hebrew Union College Monthly* (Jan. 1918).

52. Levinger, *Jewish Chaplain*, 149–150.

53. Ibid., 153–158, 205, 206–213.

54. Kaplan, AJC War Records Questionnaire, AJHS; Rabbi Benjamin Friedman, "But Weinstein" (typed manuscript), Friedman Nearprint file, AJA; Levinger, *Jewish Chaplain*, 110–111; and Slomovitz, *Fighting Rabbis*, 64–65.

55. See also the comments of Chaplain Louis I. Egelson to L. Joel, 26 Dec. 1918, Egelson Papers; and Sidney Linker to parents of Irwin Small, 31 Dec. 1918, Irwin Small Correspondence File, AJA.

56. Entries for 13 Sept., 14 Oct., 19 Nov., and 3, 7 Dec. 1917 in Jacob Marcus, "Diary for 1917–1918," Marcus Papers, AJA.

57. Entries for 17 Dec. 1917, 21 Aug., and 6 Dec. 1918, "Diary for 1917–1918," Marcus Papers.

58. Louis Marshall to Victor Rosewater, 19 Dec. 1917; to Stanley King, 12 Sept. 1918; to Leo Wise, 14 Nov. 1919; and to Harry Schneiderman, 23 Oct. 1918, Marshall Papers, AJA.

59. *JWB Sentinel*, Nov. 1918; *New York Times Magazine*, 4 May 1919; and Levinger, *Jewish Chaplain*, 117, 219.

60. "To Hester Street," reprinted from the *New York Herald*, in the *JWB Sentinel* (Jan. 1919).

61. Sibley, *With the Yankee Division*, 325; Strickland, *Connecticut Fights*, 285–289; and *Seventy-seventh Division: Summary of Operations*, 104.

62. Smith, *305th Machine Gun Battalion*, 80; Anonymous, *Through the War with Company D* (New York: Privately printed, 1919), 19; Adler, *History of the 306th*, 103; Tiebout, *History of the 305th*, 192; Hills, *War History*, 31; and English, *Diary*, 135.

63. Smith, *305th Machine Gun Battalion*, 82–83; Miles, *History of the 308th*, 206; and Blumenstein, *Whiz Bang!* 28.

64. Tiebout, *History of the 305th*, 193–221; Mark Meigs, "Crash–Course Americanism: The AEF University, 1919," *History Today* 44 (8 Aug. 1994), 36–43; Meigs, *Optimism at Armaggedon*, 69–107, 188–220; Alfred E. Cornebise, *Soldier-Scholars: Higher Education in the AEF, 1917–1919* (Philadelphia, Pa.: American Philosophical Society, 1997); Levinger, *Jewish Chaplain*, 102–103; Frank Antonio letter in *New Haven Union*, 1 Nov. 1918; and requests of Jewish soldiers for early discharges and permission to visit Eastern Europe cited in Diary Folders, Nov. 1918–Aug. 1919, Jewish Welfare Board—New York City Branch Collection, AJA.

65. Haas to parents, 30 Oct. 1918; and Miles, *308th Infantry*, 226.

66. Salvatore Liguore, Military Service Questionnaire—New Haven, CSL; English, *Diary*, 123–124; and Tiebout, *History of the 305th*, 225.

67. Hills, *War History*, 32–33; *New Haven Journal-Courier*, 23 June 1919; *New Haven Register*, 22, 23 June 1919; *Corriere del Connecticut*, 24 May, 28 June 1919; and Antonio Cannelli, *Colonia Italiana di New Haven* (New Haven, Conn.: privately printed, 1921), 302.

68. *Yiddishes Tageblatt*, 7 May 1919; *The Day*, 7 May 1919; *The Big Stick*, 9 May 1919; *New York Herald*, 7 May 1919; *New York Times*, 7 May 1919; and R. M. Flynn and Alexander T. Hussey, *Company E* (New York: Knickerbocker, 1919), 123–128.

69. *New York Times*, 26 Apr. 1919. See also Diary Folders, November 1918 to August 1919, NYJWB Collection, AJA; *Hebrew Standard*, 9 May 1919; *YMHA Bulletin*, 16, 23, 30 May 1919; and *American Jewish Year Book, 1920* (Philadelphia, Pa: American Jewish Committee, 1920), 433–447.

70. Tiebout, *History of the 305th*, 226; and Dixon Wecter, *When Johnny Comes Marching Home* (Cambridge, Mass.: Riverside Press, 1944), 310–311.

71. Naturalization Certificates for Darrico (#1959), Faiella (#1952), and Tinelli (#1948), NARA—Waltham; *New York Times*, 10 May 1919.

72. Siegel, "Measure of Life,"12, 22.

Epilogue

1. Alfred W. Crosby, Jr., *Epidemic and Peace, 1918* (Westport, Conn.: Greenwood Press, 1976), 60–61; *American Jewish Weekly News*, 23 May 1919; *New York Times*, 9, 22 May 1919; and *Corriere del Connecticut*, 22 Feb., 24 May 1919.

2. *New York Times*, 22 May 1919.

3. Cecilia O'Leary, *To Die For* (Princeton: Princeton University Press, 1999), 7.

4. For the increase of new immigrant participation in American politics during the 1920s, David Burner, *The Politics of Provincialism: The Democratic Party in Transition, 1918–1932* (New York: Alfred Knopf, 1968), 23; Irving Bernstein, *The Lean Years* (Boston, Mass.: Houghton Mifflin, 1960), 75–80; and Carl Degler, "American Political Parties and the Rise of the City: An Interpretation," *Journal of American History* 51 (June 1964), 44–67.

5. *New Haven Union,* 25–28 May 1919; *New Haven Register,* 25, 28 May 1919; and *New Haven Times Leader,* 24–28 May 1919.

6. *New Haven Union,* 28 May 1919; and *New Haven Times Leader,* 28, 29 May 1919.

7. *New Haven Union,* 28 May 1919.

8. *Corriere del Connecticut,* 31 May 1919; and *New Haven Times Leader,* 28 May 1919.

9. *New Haven Union,* 28 May 1919; *New Haven Times Leader,* 29 May 1919; and *New Haven City Directory, 1920.*

10. *New Haven Register,* 28, 29 May and 15 June 1919; *New Haven Union,* 28, 29 May 1919; and *New Haven Times Leader,* 29 May 1919.

11. Rollin G. Osterweis, *Three Centuries of New Haven* (New Haven, Conn.: Yale University Press, 1975), 410–420; Jerome Myers, "Assimilation to the Ecological and Social Systems of a Community," *American Sociological Review* 15 (1950), 367–372; and Myers, "Assimilation in the Political Community," *Sociology and Social Research* 35 (1951), 175–182.

12. Osterweis, *Three Centuries of New Haven,* 410–420; Samuel Koenig, *Immigrant Settlements in Connecticut* (Hartford: Connecticut WPA Federal Writers' Project, 1938), 53–57; Almeda King, "A Study of the Diet of a Group of Italian Families" (M.A. thesis, Yale University, 1935); *Corriere del Connecticut,* March–June 1919; and John W. Jeffries, *Testing the Roosevelt Coalition: Connecticut Society and Politics in the Era of World War II* (Knoxville: University of Tennessee Press, 1979), 123.

13. DiCenzo, *History of the Church of St. Anthony* (New Haven, Conn.: n.p., 1954).

14. Myers, "Assimilation in the Political Community," 177–182.

15. *New Haven Register,* 28 May and 25 June 1922.

16. *New York Times,* 9 Aug. 1926; Jeffries, *Testing the Roosevelt Coalition,* 3–50; and Robert Dahl, *Who Governs?* (New Haven, Conn.: Yale University Press, 1961), 48–51.

17. *Maccabaean,* Dec. 1919; and Elias Heifitz, *The Slaughter of the Jews in the Ukraine in 1919* (New York: Thomas Seltzer, 1921).

18. *New York Times,* 22 May 1919; *Yiddishes Tageblatt,* 22 May 1919; *The Big Stick,* 16, 23 May 1919; *Jewish Daily Forward,* 21 May 1919; and *American Jewish Weekly News,* 23 May 1919.

19. *New York Times,* 22 May 1919; *Yiddishes Tageblatt,* 22 May 1919; and *Hebrew Standard,* 30 May 1919.

20. Quoted in the *Maccabaean,* June 1919; Maurice Samuel, *Little Did I Know* (New York: Alfred A. Knopf, 1963), 252; and *American Jewish Weekly News,* 23 May 1919.

21. Harry Raymond, *Reminiscences of the Early Days of the Jewish War Veterans of the U.S.A.* (New York: pamphlet, n.d.), 11–13; *New York World,* 25 Nov. 1919; *New York Herald,* 25 Nov. 1919; *American Hebrew,* 25 Nov. 1919; Louis Marshall to Murray Rothenberg, 25 Nov. 1919; and Marshall to Aaron Cohen, 28 Nov. 1919, Marshall Papers, AJA.

22. Siegel, "Measure of Life" (unpublished manuscript) AJA, 27–28.

23. See Julian Jaffe, *Crusade Against Radicalism: New York during the Red Scare* (Port Washington, N.Y.: Kennikat Press, 1972).

24. Louis Eisenstein, *Stripe of Tammany's Tiger* (New York: R. Speller, 1966), 26–27; and Vladeck Memoirs, 99–100, 109–110.

25. Deborah Dash Moore, *At Home in America* (New York: Columbia University,

1981), 23; Harry L. Feingold, *Time for Searching* (Baltimore, Md.: Johns Hopkins, University Press, 1992), 55; and Wenger, *New York Jews and the Great Depression*, 15.

26. Moore, *At Home in America;* and Wenger, *New York Jews and the Great Depression.* See also Michael Alexander's important new interpretation of Jewish prosperity and anxiety during the period, *Jazz Age Jews* (Princeton, N.J.: Princeton University Press, 2001).

27. Nathan Glazer and Daniel Patrick Moynihan, *Beyond the Melting Pot* (Cambridge, Mass.: MIT Press, 1995), 166–171; and Moore, *At Home in America*, 201–230.

28. Ronald Takaki sums up this work in his synthesis *A Different Mirror:* "Throughout our past of oppressions and struggles for equality, Americans of different races and ethnicities have been 'singing with open mouths their strong melodious songs' in the textile mills of Lowell, the cotton fields of Mississippi, on the Indian reservations of South Dakota, the railroad tracks high in the Sierras of California, in the garment factories of the Lower East Side, the canefields of Hawaii, and a thousand other places across the country." Conflict, labor, and regional and ethnic specificity are the dominant subjects of this scholarship. Takaki, *Different Mirror* (Boston, Mass.: Little, Brown, 1993), 428.

Selected Bibliography

Manuscript Collections

American Jewish Archives [AJA], Cincinnati, Ohio
    Jacob Billikopf Papers
    Robert H. Bondy Papers
    David A. Brown Papers
    Louis I. Egelson Papers
    Jewish Welfare Board—New York City Branch Papers
    Jacob Rader Marcus Papers
    Louis Marshall Papers
    Jacob Schiff Papers
    Union of American Hebrew Congregations Papers
    Samuel Untermyer Papers
    Elkan and Henrietta Voorsanger Papers
    Felix Warburg Papers
    Leon L. Watters Papers
    Women of Reform Judaism Collection
American Jewish Historical Society [AJHS], Waltham, Massachusetts and
      New York City
    American Jewish Committee—Office of War Records Collection
    Jewish War Veterans of America Collection
    Jewish Welfare Board Papers
    Phi Epsilon Pi Papers
    Seligman Solomon Society Papers
    Isaac Siegel Papers
    Abraham Strauss Papers
    Milton Weill Papers
Archives of the Diocese of Hartford, Connecticut
    Parish Historical Files, Parish Statements
Center for Migration Studies, Staten Island, New York
    St. Anthony's Parish, New Haven, Conn., Papers
    St. Michael's Parish, New Haven, Conn., Papers

Connecticut State Library and Archives [CSL], Hartford, Connecticut
    Governor Marcus Holcomb Papers
    Connecticut National Guard Enlistment Papers, 2nd Regiment
    Connecticut State Council of Defense Records
    Women's Division Classified File, 1917–1919
    Veterans' Necrology Index
    War Records Department—Military Service Questionnaires, 1913–1920
Hoover Institution Archives [HIA], Stanford, California
    United States Food Administration Records
National Archives [NARA—Waltham], New England Division, Waltham,
    Massachusetts
    Naturalization Papers Collections
    New Haven Pleas Court, City Court
    United States District Court—New Haven, Conn.
    Camp Devens, Ayer, Mass.
National Archives, Washington, D.C.
    Records of the Selective Service System, 1917–1919
    Historical File, 1917–1919
    Local Board Experience File, 1917–1919
    Newspaper Clippings, 1917–1919
National Museum of American Jewish Military History, Washington, D.C.
    Captain Arthur M. Wolff Papers
    World War I Veterans' Files
New Haven Colony Historical Society, [NHCHS], New Haven, Connecticut
    New Haven Military Collection, 1712–1980—World War I Service
    Philip H. English Diary
    Jones Family Papers
New Haven Free Public Library [NHFPL], Local History Room
    European War Collection
    Industrial Clippings Collection
New York Public Library
    Victory Hall Association Correspondence Collection
United States Military Academy Library [USMAL]
    Lieutenant Robert K. Haas Papers
    Colonel John Henry Parker Papers
United States Military History Institute Archives [USMHIA], Carlisle, Pennsylvania
    World War I Survey
University of Arkansas Libraries, Special Collections Division, Fayetteville, Arkansas
    Ruby V. Hughes Papers
University of North Carolina, Southern Historical Collection, Chapel Hill, North
    Carolina
    Samuel Simpson Nash Papers
Western Connecticut State University, Ruth Haas Library, Danbury, Connecticut
    George Hawley Papers
Yale University Manuscripts and Archives [YMA], New Haven, Connecticut
    James Merriam Howard Papers
    Harold Phelps Stokes Papers
    Socialist Party of New Haven, Conn., Papers

Young Men's Hebrew Association, 92nd Street Y, New York City
Historical Files

Periodicals

Advance
American Jewish Chronicle
American Jewish Weekly News
American Jewish Year Book
American Labor Year Book
The Big Stick
Brooklyn Daily Eagle
Connecticut State Council of Defense Americanizer
Connecticut State Council of Defense Bulletin
Corriere del Connecticut
La Forche Caudine
Hebrew American
Hebrew Standard
L'Indipendente
Jewish Welfare Board Sentinel
Ladies Garment Worker
Maccabaean
The Masses
Mother Earth
New Haven City Year Book
New Haven Cut
New Haven Journal–Courier
New Haven Register
New Haven Times Leader
New Haven Union
New York Call
New York Herald
New York Journal American
New York Times
New York Tribune
New York World
Stars and Stripes
Trench and Camp (Upton)
Yiddishes Tageblatt
YMHA Bulletin

Memoirs and Regimental Histories

Adams, John W., and Lee C. McCollum. *"Our Company" by Two Bucks*. Seattle, Wash.: Lumberman Printing, 1919.
Adler, Julius O., ed. *History of the Seventy-seventh Division, August 25, 1917–November 11, 1918*. New York: W. H. Crawford Printers, 1919.
———. *History of the 306th Infantry*. New York: 306th Infantry Association, 1935.
Albertine, Connell. *The Yankee Doughboy*. Boston, Mass.: Braden Press, 1968.
Alexander, Robert. *Memories of the World War*. New York: Macmillan, 1931.

Anonymous. *Through the War with Company D, 307th Infantry, 77th Division*. New York: privately printed, 1919.

———. *"C" Battery Book, 306th F. A., 77th Division, 1917–1919*. Brooklyn, N.Y.: Braunworth, 1920.

Antin, Mary. *The Promised Land*. 2d ed. Boston, Mass.: Houghton Mifflin, 1969.

Bakewell, Charles M. *The Story of the American Red Cross in Italy*. New York: Macmillan, 1920.

Benwell, Harry. *History of the Yankee Division*. Boston, Mass.: Cornhill, 1919.

Bogen, Boris. *Born a Jew*. New York: Macmillan, 1930.

Blumenstein, Christian. *Whiz Bang!* Buffalo: Privately printed, 1927.

Camp, Charles W. *History of the 305th Field Artillery*. Garden City, N.Y.: Country Life Press, 1919.

Cannelli, Antonio. *La Colonia Italiana di New Haven*. New Haven: Privately printed, 1921.

Claessens, August. *Didn't We Have Fun*. New York: Rand School Press, 1953.

Crawford, Gilbert H., et al. *The 302nd Engineers: A History*. New York: privately printed, 1919.

Crowder, Enoch. *The Spirit of Selective Service*. New York: Century, 1920.

Crump, Irving. *Conscript 2989: Experiences of a Drafted Man*. New York: Dodd, Mead, 1918.

Eisenstein, Louis, and Elliot Rosenberg. *A Stripe of Tammany's Tiger*. New York: R. Speller, 1966.

Field, Francis, and G. H. Rishcards, eds. *The Battery Book: A History of Battery "A," 306 F. A.* New York: De Vinne Press, 1921.

Fischer, Ben B. comp. *"Hände Hoch! Hands High! An American Hero's Tale of the Great War: The Story of James F. Carty, D.S.C."* McLean, Va.: Privately printed, 1995.

Freeman, Joseph. *An American Testament: A Narrative of Rebels and Romantics*. New York: Farrar and Rinehart, 1936.

Gitlow, Benjamin. *I Confess: The Truth about American Communism*. New York: E. P. Dutton, 1940.

Goldman, Emma. *Living My Life*. 2 vols. New York: Alfred Knopf, 1931.

Havlin, Arthur C. *The History of Company A, 102d Machine Gun Battalion Twenty-sixth Division, A.E.F.* Boston: H. C. Rodd, 1928.

Hillquit, Morris. *Loose Leaves from a Busy Life*. New York: Da Capo Press, 1944.

Hills, Ratcliffe M. *The War History of the 102d Regiment, United States Infantry*. Hartford, Conn.: privately printed, 1924.

Howard, James M. *The Autobiography of a Regiment: A History of the 304th Field Artillery in the World War*. New York: Privately printed, 1920.

Hussey, Alexander T., and R. M. Flynn. *The History of Company E, 308th Infantry (1917–1919)*. New York: Knickerbocker, 1919.

Jastrow, Marie. *Looking Back: The American Dream Through Immigrant Eyes*. New York: W. W. Norton, 1986.

Johnson, Thomas, and Fletcher Pratt. *The Lost Battalion*. Indianapolis, Ind.: Bobbs-Merrill, 1938.

Kehillah of New York City. *The Jewish Communal Register, 1917–1918*. New York: Kehillah (Jewish Community) of New York, 1918.

King, Moses. *Company "I", Three Hundred and Fifth Infantry, 1917–1918*. New York: Privately printed, 1919.

Klausner, Julius. *Company B, 307th Infantry*. New York: American Legion, Burke-Kelly Post No. 172, 1920.

Levinger, Lee J. *A Jewish Chaplain in France*. New York: Macmillan, 1921.

McAdoo, William G. *Crowded Years*. Boston, Mass.: Houghton Mifflin, 1931.

McCarthy, Robert J. *A History of Troop A, Cavalry, Connecticut National Guard and Its Service in the Great War as Company D, 102d Machine Gun Battalion*. New Haven, Conn.: Tuttle, Morehouse, and Taylor, 1919.

McCollum, Lee C. *History and Rhymes of the Lost Battalion*. New York: Bucklee, 1919.

McKeogh, Arthur. *The Victorious 77th Division (New York's Own) in the Argonne Fight*. New York: Eggers, 1919.

Miles, L. Wardlaw. *History of the 308th Infantry, 1917–1919*. New York: Putnam's, 1927.

Minder, Charles F. *This Man's War: The Day-by-Day Record of an American Private on the Western Front*. New York: Pevensey, 1931.

Pershing, John J. *My Experiences in the World War*. New York: Frederick A. Stokes, 1931.

Rainsford, Walter Kerr. *From Upton to the Meuse with the Three Hundred and Seventh Infantry*. New York: Appleton, 1920.

Ranlett, Louis. *Let's Go! The Story of A.S. No. 2448602*. Boston, Mass.: Houghton Mifflin, 1927.

Roskolenko, Harry. *The Time That Was Then: The Lower East Side, 1900–1914, An Intimate Chronicle*. New York: Dial Press, 1971.

Sibley, Frank. *With the Yankee Division in France*. Boston: Little, Brown, 1919.

Smith, Henry W. *A Story of the 305th Machine Gun Battalion, 77th Division, A.E.F.* New York: Modern Composing Room, 1941.

Spitz, Leon. *The Memoirs of a Camp Rabbi*. New York: Bloch, 1927.

Strickland, Daniel W. *Connecticut Fights: The Story of the 102nd Regiment*. New Haven: Quinnipiack Press, 1930.

Taylor, Emerson G. *New England in France, 1917–1919: A History of the Twenty-sixth Division, U.S.A.* Boston, Mass.: Houghton Mifflin, 1920.

Tiebout, Frank. *A History of the 305th Infantry*. New York: 305th Infantry Auxiliary, 1919.

Wainwright, Philip S. *History of the 101st Machine Gun Battalion*. Hartford: 101st Machine Gun Battalion Association, 1922.

Waldman, Louis. *Labor Lawyer*. New York: E. P. Dutton, 1944.

Westbrook, Stillman F. *Those Eighteen Months: October 9, 1917–April 8, 1919*. Hartford, Conn.: Case, Lockwood, and Brainard, 1934.

Secondary Sources

Alexander, Michael. *Jazz Age Jews*. Princeton, N.J.: Princeton University Press, 2001.

American Jewish Committee. *The War Record of American Jews*. New York: American Jewish Committee, 1919.

Anderson, Benedict. *Imagined Communities: Reflections on the Origin and Spread of Nationalism*. London: Verso Books, 1991.

Armstrong, David A. *Bullets and Bureaucrats: The Machine Gun and the United States Army, 1861–1916*. Westport, Conn.: Greenwood Press, 1982.

Ashworth, Tony. *Trench Warfare, 1914–1918: The Live and Let Live System*. New York: Holmes and Meier, 1980.

Barbeau, Arthur E., and Henri Florette. *The Unknown Soldiers: Black American Troops in World War I*. Philadelphia, Pa.: Temple University Press, 1974.

Baron, Salo. *The Russian Jew Under Tsars and Soviets*. New York: Macmillan, 1976.

Barrett, James R. "Americanization from the Bottom Up: Immigration and the Remaking of the Working Class in the United States, 1880–1930." *Journal of American History* 79 (December 1992): 996–1020.

Barrett, James R., and David Roediger. "In-between Peoples: Race, Nationality, and the 'New Immigrant' Working Class." *Journal of American Ethnic History* 16 (spring 1997): 3–44.

Barton, Josef. *Peasants and Strangers: Italians, Rumanians and Slovaks in an American City, 1890–1950.* Cambridge, Mass.: Harvard University Press, 1975.

Baum, Charlotte, et al. *The Jewish Woman in America.* New York: Dial Press, 1976.

Beaver, Daniel. *Newton D. Baker and the American War Effort, 1917–1919.* Lincoln: University of Nebraska Press, 1966.

Berger, David, ed. *The Legacy of Jewish Migration: 1881 and Its Impact.* New York: Brooklyn College Press, 1983.

Berkowitz, Michael. *Western Jewry and the Zionist Project, 1914–1933.* Cambridge: Cambridge University Press, 1997.

Bernstein, Iver. *The New York City Draft Riots: Their Significance in American Society and Politics in the Era of the Civil War.* New York: Oxford University Press, 1990.

Berry, Henry. *Make the Kaiser Dance.* New York: Doubleday, 1978.

Bodnar, John, ed. *Bonds of Affection: Americans Define Their Patriotism.* Princeton, N.J.: Princeton University Press, 1996.

————. *The Transplanted: A History of Immigrants in Urban America.* Bloomington: Indiana University Press, 1986.

Brandt, Allan M. *No Magic Bullet: A Social History of Venereal Disease in the United States since 1880.* New York: Oxford University Press, 1985.

Breen, William J. *Uncle Sam at Home: Civilian Mobilization, Wartime Federalism, and the Council of National Defense, 1917–1919.* Westport, Conn.: Greenwood Press, 1984.

Briggs, John. *An Italian Passage: Immigrants in Three American Cities.* New Haven, Conn.: Yale University Press, 1978.

Bristow, Nancy K. *Making Men Moral: Social Engineering during the Great War.* New York: New York University Press, 1996.

Britten, Thomas A. *American Indians in World War I: At Home and at War.* Albuquerque: University of New Mexico Press, 1997.

Brumberg, Stephen K. *Going to America, Going to School: The Jewish Immigrant Public School Encounter in Turn-of-the-Century New York City.* New York: Praeger, 1986.

Burner, David. *The Politics of Provincialism: The Democratic Party in Transition, 1918–1932.* Cambridge, Mass.: Harvard University Press, 1986.

Carlevale, Joseph. *Who's Who Among Americans of Italian Descent in Connecticut.* New Haven, Conn.: Carlevale, 1942.

Caroli, Betty Boyd, et al. *The Italian Immigrant Woman in North America.* Toronto: Multicultural Society of Ontario, 1978.

Carroll, F. M. *American Opinion and the Irish Question, 1910–1923: A Study in Opinion and Policy.* New York: St. Martin's, 1978.

Chambers, Frank P. *The War Behind the War, 1914–1918: A History of the Political and Civilian Fronts.* New York: Arno Press, 1972.

Chambers, John Whiteclay II. *To Raise an Army: The Draft Comes to Modern America.* New York: Free Press, 1987.

Child, Irvin. *Italian or American? The Second Generation in Conflict.* New Haven, Conn.: Yale University Press, 1943.

Coben, Stanley H. "A Study of Nativism: The American Red Scare of 1919–1920." *Political Science Quarterly* 79 (March 1964): 52–75.

Coffman, Edward M. *The War to End All Wars: The American Military Experience in World War I.* New York: Oxford University Press, 1968.

Cohen, Lizabeth. *Making a New Deal: Industrial Workers in Chicago, 1919–1939.* New York: Cambridge University Press, 1990.

Cohen, Naomi. *American Jews and the Zionist Idea.* New York: KTAV, 1975.

Conner, Valerie Jean. *The National War Labor Board: Stability, Social Justice, and the Voluntary State in World War I.* Chapel Hill: University of North Carolina Press, 1983.

Crowell, Benedict, and Robert Wilson. *Demobilization: Our Industrial and Military De-mobilization After the Armistice, 1918–1920.* New Haven, Conn.: Yale University Press, 1921.

Cuff, Robert D. *The War Industries Board: Business-Government Relations During World War I.* Baltimore, Md: Johns Hopkins University Press, 1973.

Davidowicz, Lucy S. "Louis Marshall and the Jewish *Daily Forward*: An Episode in Wartime Censorship, 1917–1918," in *For Max Weinreich on His 70th Birthday.* The Hague: Mouton, 1964.

Davis, Allen F. "Welfare, Reform, and World War I." *American Quarterly* 19 (1967): 516–533.

Diggins, John P. *Mussolini and Fascism: The View from America.* Princeton, N.J.: Princeton University Press, 1972.

Diner, Hasia. *A Time for Gathering: The Second Migration, 1820–1880.* Baltimore, Md.: Johns Hopkins University Press, 1992.

Dinnerstein, Leonard. *Anti-Semitism in America.* New York: Oxford University Press, 1994.

Dubnow, S. M. *History of the Jews in Russia and Poland.* 2 vols. 1918. Reprint. New York: KTAV, 1975.

Dubofsky, Melvyn. "Organized Labor in New York City and the First World War, 1914–1918." *New York History* (October 1961): 380–401.

———. *We Shall Be All: A History of the Industrial Workers of the World.* Chicago: Quadrangle, 1969.

———. *When Workers Organize: New York City in the Progressive Era.* Amherst: University of Massachusetts Press, 1968.

Early, Frances H. *A World without War: How U.S. Feminists and Pacifists Resisted World War I.* Syracuse, N.Y.: Syracuse University Press, 1997.

Ellis, John. *Eye-Deep in Hell: Trench Warfare in World War I.* Baltimore, Md.: Johns Hopkins University Press, 1976.

Enloe, Cynthia. *Ethnic Soldiers: State Security in Divided Societies.* Athens: University of Georgia Press, 1980.

Epstein, Melech. *Jewish Labor in U.S.A.: An Industrial, Political, And Cultural History of the Jewish Labor Movement, 1914–1952.* New York: KTAV, 1969.

Ewen, Elizabeth. *Immigrant Women in the Land of Dollars: Life and Culture on the Lower East Side, 1890–1925.* New York: Monthly Review Press, 1985.

Farwell, Byron. *Over There: The United States in the Great War, 1917–1918.* New York: W. W. Norton, 1999.

Feingold, Henry L. *A Time for Searching: Entering the Mainstream, 1920–1945.* Baltimore, Md.: Johns Hopkins University Press, 1992.

Ferguson, Niall. *The Pity of War: Explaining World War I*. London: Penguin Press, 1998.

Ferrell, Robert H. *Woodrow Wilson and World War I, 1921–1921*. New York: Harper and Row, 1985.

Finnegan, John P. *Against the Specter of a Dragon: The Campaign for American Military Preparedness, 1914–1917*. Westport, Conn.: Greenwood Press, 1975.

Fischer, David H. *Albion's Seed: Four British Folkways in America*. New York: Oxford University Press, 1989.

Foerster, Robert. *The Italian Emigration of Our Times*. Cambridge, Mass.: Harvard University Press, 1919.

Ford, Nancy Gentile. "Mindful of the Traditions of His Race: Dual Identity and Foreign-born Soldiers in the First World War American Army." *Journal of American Ethnic History* 16 (winter 1997): 35–57.

Frank, Dana. "Housewives, Socialists, and the Politics of Food: The 1917 New York Cost-of-Living Protests." *Feminist Studies* 11 (summer 1985): 255–286.

Frankel, Jonathan. *Prophecy and Politics: Socialism, Nationalism, and the Russian Jew, 1862–1917*. Cambridge: Cambridge University Press, 1981.

Fraser, Steve. *Labor Will Rule: Sidney Hillman and the Rise of American Labor*. New York: Free Press, 1991.

Freiburger, William. "War Prosperity and Hunger: The New York Food Riots of 1917." *Labor History* 25 (spring 1984): 217–239.

Freidel, Frank. *Over There: The Story of America's First Great Overseas Crusade*. New York: 1990.

Fuchs, Lawrence. *The American Kaleidoscope: Race, Ethnicity, and the Civic Culture*. Hanover, N.H.: University Press of New England, 1990.

———. *The Political Behavior of American Jews*. Glencoe, Ill.: Free Press, 1956.

Fussell, Paul. *The Great War and Modern Memory*. New York: Oxford University, 1975.

Gabaccia, Donna R. *From Sicily to Elizabeth Street: Housing and Social Change Among Italian Immigrants, 1880–1930*. Albany: State University of New York Press, 1984.

Gambino, Richard. *Blood of My Blood: The Dilemma of the Italian-Americans*. Garden City, N.Y.: Doubleday, 1974.

Gastwirt, Harold. *Fraud, Corruption, and Holiness: The Controversy over the Supervision of the Jewish Dietary Practices in New York City, 1881–1940*. Port Washington, N.Y.: Kennikat Press, 1974.

Genthe, Charles V. *American War Narratives, 1917–1918: A Study and Bibliography*. New York: David Lewis, 1969.

Gerstle, Gary, et al. "People in Motion, Nation in Question: The Case of Twentieth-century America." *Journal of American History* 84 (September 1997): 524–580.

Glenn, Susan A. *Daughters of the Shtetl: Life and Labor in the Immigrant Generation*. Ithaca, N.Y.: Cornell University Press, 1990.

Goren, Arthur. *New York Jews and the Quest for Community: The Kehillah Experiment, 1908–1922*. New York: Columbia University Press, 1970.

Greene, Victor. *American Immigrant Leaders, 1800–1910: Marginality and Identity*. Baltimore, Md.: Johns Hopkins University Press, 1987.

Greenwald, Maurine. *Women, War, and Work: The Impact of World War I on Women Workers in the United States*. Westport, Conn.: Greenwood Press, 1980.

Grubbs, Frank L. *The Struggle for Labor Loyalty: Gompers, the A. F. of L., and the Pacifists, 1917–1920*. Durham, N.C.: Duke University Press, 1968.

Gurock, Jeffrey. *When Harlem Was Jewish, 1870–1930*. New York: Columbia University Press, 1979.

Halperin, Samuel. *The Political World of American Zionism*. Detroit, Mich.: Wayne State University Press, 1961.

Handlin, Oscar. *The Uprooted*. Boston, Mass.: Little, Brown, 1951.

Harries, Meirion, and Susie Harries. *The Last Days of Innocence: America at War, 1917–1918*. New York: Random House, 1997.

Hartmann, Edward G. *The Movement to Americanize the Immigrant*. New York: AMS Press, 1967.

Hawley, Ellis W. *The Great War and the Search for a Modern Order: A History of the American People and Their Institutions, 1917–1933*. New York: St. Martin's Press, 1979.

Heinz, Andrew R. *Adapting to Abundance: Jewish Immigrants, Mass Consumption, and the Search for American Identity*. New York: Columbia University Press, 1990.

Henderson, Thomas. *Tammany Hall and the New Immigrants: The Progressive Years*. New York: Arno Press, 1976.

Higham, John. *Send These to Me: Jews and Other Immigrants in Urban America*. New York: Atheneum, 1975.

———. *Strangers in the Land: Patterns of American Nativism, 1860–1925*. New York: Atheneum, 1963.

Hill, Everett G. *A Modern History of New Haven and Eastern New Haven County*. New York: S. J. Clarke, 1918.

Hirschfeld, Charles. "Nationalist Progressivism and World War I." *Mid-America* 45 (1963): 139–156.

Horne, Alistair. *The Price of Glory: Verdun, 1916*. London: Penguin Books, 1979.

Howe, Irving. *World of Our Fathers: The Journey of the East European Jews to America and the Life They Found and Made*. New York: Simon and Schuster, 1976.

Hyman, Paula. "Immigrant Women and Consumer Protest: The New York City Kosher Meat Boycott of 1902." *American Jewish History* 70 (1980): 91–105.

Jacobs, James B., and Leslie Anne Hays. "Aliens in the U.S. Armed Forces: A Historico-Legal Analysis." *Armed Forces and Society* 7 (winter 1980): 187–208.

Jacobson, Matthew. *Special Sorrows: The Diasporic Imagination of Irish, Polish, and Jewish Immigrants in the United States*. Cambridge, Mass.: Harvard University Press, 1995.

Jaffe, Julian. *Crusade Against Radicalism: New York during the Red Scare*. Port Washington, N.Y.: Kennikat Press, 1972.

Johnson, Donald. *The Challenge to American Freedoms: World War I and the Rise of the American Civil Liberties Union*. Lexington: University of Kentucky Press, 1963.

Johnson, James P. "The Wilsonians as War Managers: Coal and the 1917–18 Winter Crisis." *Prologue* 9 (1977): 193–208.

Jones, Jacqueline. *American Work: Four Centuries of Black and White Labor*. New York: W. W. Norton, 1998.

Joselit, Jenna Weissman. *The Wonders of America: Reinventing Jewish Culture, 1880–1950*. New York: Hill and Wang, 1994.

Katz, Jacob. *Out of the Ghetto: The Social Background of Jewish Emancipation, 1770–1870*. New York: Schocken Books, 1978.

Keegan, John. *The Face of Battle: A Study of Agincourt, Waterloo, and the Somme*. New York: Vintage, 1977.

———. *The First World War*. London: Hutchinson, 1998.

Keller, Morton. *Regulating a New Society: Public Policy and Social Change in America, 1900–1933*. Cambridge, Mass.: Harvard University Press, 1994.

Keller, Phyllis. *States of Belonging: German–American Intellectuals and the First World War*. Cambridge, Mass.: Harvard University Press, 1979.

Kennedy, David. *Over Here: The First World War and American Society*. New York: Oxford University Press, 1980.

Kennett, Lee. "The A.E.F. Through French Eyes." *Military Review* 52 (November 1972): 3–11.

Kessner, Thomas. *The Golden Door: Italian and Jewish Immigrant Mobility in New York City, 1880–1915*. New York: Oxford University Press, 1975.

Klier, John Doyle. *Imperial Russia's Jewish Question, 1855–1881*. Cambridge: Cambridge University Press, 1990.

Koistenen, Paul. *Mobilizing for Modern War: The Political Economy of American Warfare, 1865–1919*. Lawrence: University of Kansas Press, 1997.

Kreidberg, Marvin A., and Merton G. Henry. *History of Military Mobilization in the U.S. Army, 1775–1945*. Washington, D.C.: Government Printing Office, 1955.

Lasch, Christopher. *The American Liberals and the Russian Revolution*. New York: Columbia University Press, 1962.

Leeds, Eric. *No Man's Land: Combat and Identity in World War I*. New York: Cambridge University Press, 1979.

Leibman, Arthur. *Jews and the Left*. New York: John Wiley, 1979.

Leuchtenberg, William E. "The New Deal and the Analogue of War." In John Braeman et al., eds. *Change and Continuity in Twentieth-century America*. New York: Harper and Row, 1966.

Leviatin, David. *Followers of the Trail: Jewish Working-class Radicals in America*. New Haven, Conn.: Yale University Press, 1989.

Lighter, Jonathan. "The Slang of the American Expeditionary Forces in Europe, 1917–1919: An Historical Glossary." *American Speech* 47 (spring–summer 1972): 5–143.

Livermore, Seward W. *Politics Is Adjourned: Woodrow Wilson and the War Congress, 1916–1918*. Middletown, Conn.: Wesleyan University Press, 1966.

Luebke, Frederick. *Bonds of Loyalty: German-Americans and World War I*. DeKalb.: Northern Illinois University Press, 1974.

Marchand, Roland. *The American Peace Movement and Social Reform, 1898–1918*. Princeton, N.J.: Princeton University Press, 1973.

Marwick, Arthur. *The Deluge: British Society and the First World War*. New York: W. W. Norton, 1970.

May, Henry F. *The End of American Innocence: A Study of the First Years of Our Own Time, 1912–1917*. Chicago, Ill.: Quadrangle, 1964.

Meigs, Mark. "Crash-course Americanism: The AEF University, 1919." *History Today* 44, 8 (August 1994): 36–43.

———. *Optimism at Armageddon: Voices of American Participants in the World War*. New York: New York University Press, 1997.

Mendelsohn, Ezra. *Class Struggle in the Pale: The Formative Years of the Jewish Workers' Movement in Tsarist Russia*. Cambridge: Cambridge University Press, 1970.

Milford, Lewis, and Richard Severo. *Wages of War: When American Soldiers Came Home, from Valley Forge to Vietnam*. New York: Simon and Schuster, 1989.

Montgomery, David. "Nationalism, American Patriotism, and Class Consciousness among Immigrant Workers in the United States in the Epoch of World War I." In Dirk Hoerder, ed. *"Struggle a Hard Battle": Essays on Working Class Immigrants*. DeKalb.: Northern Illinois University Press, 1986.

Moore, Deborah Dash. *At Home in America: Second Generation New York Jews*. New York: Columbia University Press, 1981.

———. *When Jews Were G.I.'s: How World War II Changed a Generation and Remade American Jewry*. Ann Arbor, Mich.: Jean and Samuel Frankel Center for Judaic Studies, University of Michigan Press, 1994.

Mormino, Gary Ross. *Immigrants on the Hill: Italian Americans in St. Louis, 1882–1982*. Urbana: Illinois University Press, 1986.

Nelli, Humbert. *Italians in Chicago, 1880–1930: A Study in Ethnic Mobility*. New York: Oxford University Press, 1970.

Nettleton, George H., ed. *Yale in the World War*. 2 vols. New Haven, Conn.: Yale University Press, 1925.

Neuringer, Sheldon Morris. *American Jewry and United States Immigration Policy, 1881–1953*. New York: Arno Press, 1980.

O'Grady, Joseph, ed. *The Immigrants' Influence on Wilson's Peace Policies*. Lexington: University of Kentucky Press, 1967.

O'Keefe, Kevin J. *A Thousand Deadlines: The New York City Press and American Neutrality*. The Hague: Martinus Nijhoff, 1972.

O'Leary, Cecilia. *To Die For: The Paradox of American Patriotism*. Princeton, N.J.: Princeton University Press, 1999.

Orsi, Robert. *The Madonna of 115th Street: Faith and Community in Italian Harlem, 1880–1950*. New Haven, Conn.: Yale University Press, 1985.

O'Shea, Stephen. *Back to the Front: An Accidental Historian Walks the Trenches of World War I*. New York: Avon Books, 1996.

Osterweiss, Rollin G. *Three Centuries of New Haven, 1638–1938*. New Haven, Conn.: Yale University Press, 1975.

Paxson, Frederick L. *American Democracy and the World War*. 3 vols. Boston, Mass.: Houghton Mifflin, 1936–1948.

Peterson, H. C., and Gilbert C. Fite. *Opponents of War, 1917–1918*. Seattle: University of Washington Press, 1968.

Pohlenberg, Richard. *Fighting Faiths: The Abrams Case, the Supreme Court, and Free Speech*. New York: Oxford University Press, 1987.

Pozzetta, George. "Immigrants and Ethnics: The State of Italian-American Historiography." *Journal of American Ethnic History* (fall 1989): 67–95.

Preston, William, Jr. *Aliens and Dissenters: Federal Suppression of Radicals, 1903–1933*. New York: Harper and Row, 1966.

Rischin, Moses. *The Promised City: New York's Jews, 1870–1914*. Cambridge, Mass.: Harvard University Press, 1962.

Roskies, David, and Diane Roskies. *The Shtetl Book*. New York: KTAV, 1979.

Sarna, Jonathan, ed. *The American Jewish Experience*. New York: Holmes and Meier, 1986.

Schaffer, Ronald. *America in the Great War: The Rise of the War Welfare State*. New York: Oxford University Press, 1991.

Shapiro, Yonathan. *Leadership of the American Zionist Organization, 1897–1930*. Urbana: University of Illinois Press, 1971.

Sklar, Martin. J. *The United States as a Developing Country: Studies in U.S. History in the Progressive Era and the 1920s*. Cambridge: Cambridge University Press, 1992.

Sklare, Marshall. *Conservative Judaism: An American Religious Movement*. Glencoe, Ill.: Free Press, 1955.

Skowronek, Stephen. *Building a New American State: The Expansion of National Administrative Capacities, 1877–1920.* New York: Cambridge University Press, 1982.

Smith, Judith E. *Family Connections: A History of Italian and Jewish Immigrant Lives in Providence, Rhode Island, 1900–1940.* Albany: State University of New York Press, 1985.

Sorin, Gerald. *The Prophetic Minority: American Jewish Immigrant Radicals, 1880–1920.* Bloomington, Ind.: Indiana University Press, 1985.

———. *A Time for Building: The Third Migration, 1880–1920.* Baltimore, Md.: Johns Hopkins University Press, 1992.

Soyer, Daniel. *Jewish Immigrant Associations and American Identity in New York, 1880–1939.* Cambridge, Mass.: Harvard University Press, 1997.

Stallings, Laurence. *The Doughboys: The Story of the AEF, 1917–1918.* New York: Harper and Row, 1963.

Stanislavsky, Michael. *Tsar Nicholas I and the Jews: The Transformation of Jewish Society in Russia, 1825–1855.* Philadelphia, Pa.: Jewish Publication Society, 1983.

Sterba, Christopher M. " 'More Than Ever, We Feel Proud to be Italians': World War I and the New Haven *Colonia,* 1917–1918." *Journal of American Ethnic History* 20 (winter 2001): 70–106.

———. " 'Your Country Wants You': New Haven's Italian Machine Gun Company Enters World War I." *The New England Quarterly* 74 (June 2001): 179–209.

———. "Family, Work, and Nation: Hazleton, Pennsylvania, and the 1934 General Strike in Textiles." *Pennsylvania Magazine of History and Biography* 120 (January/April 1996): 3–35.

Stone, Norman. *The Eastern Front, 1914–1917.* London: Hodder and Stoughton, 1975.

Sullivan, Mark. *Our Times: The United States, 1900–1925.* 5 vols. New York: Scribner's, 1926–1935.

Szajkowski, Zosa. *Jews, Wars, and Communism.* New York: KTAV, 1972.

Takaki, Ronald. *A Different Mirror: A History of Multicultural America.* Boston, Mass.: Little, Brown, 1993.

Tenenbaum, Shelly. *A Credit to Their Community: Jewish Loan Societies in the United States, 1880–1945.* Detroit, Mich.: Wayne State University Press, 1993.

Urofsky, Melvin I. *American Zionism from Herzl to the Holocaust.* Garden City, N.Y.: Anchor Press, 1975.

Vaughn, Stephen L. *Holding Fast the Inner Lines: Democracy, Nationalism and the Committee on Public Information.* Chapel Hill: University of North Carolina Press, 1979.

Vecoli, Rudolph. "Contadini in Chicago: A Critique of the Uprooted." *Journal of American History* 51 (Dec. 1964): 404–417.

———. "Peasants and Prelates: Italian Immigrants and the Catholic Church." *Journal of Social History* 2 (spring 1969): 217–268.

Ward, Robert D. "The Origin and Activities of the National Security League, 1914–1919." *Mississippi Valley Historical Review* 47 (1960): 51–65.

Weber, Eugen. *Peasants Into Frenchmen: The Modernization of Rural France, 1870–1914.* Stanford, Calif.: Stanford University Press, 1976.

Wecter, Dixon. *When Johnny Comes Marching Home.* Cambridge, Mass.: Riverside Press, 1944.

Weigley, Russell. *History of the United States Army.* New York: Macmillan, 1967.

———. *Towards an American Army: Military Thought from Washington to Marshall.* New York: Columbia University Press, 1962.

Weinberg, Sydney Stahl. *The World of Our Mothers: The Lives of Jewish Immigrant Women*. Chapel Hill: University of North Carolina Press, 1988.

Weinstein, James. *The Decline of Socialism in America, 1912–1925*. New York: Vintage, 1969.

Wenger, Beth S. *New York Jews and the Great Depression: Uncertain Promise*. New Haven, Conn.: Yale University Press, 1996.

Wiebe, Robert. *The Search for Order, 1877–1920*. New York: Hill and Wang, 1967.

Williams, Phyllis. *South Italian Folkways in Europe and America*. New Haven, Conn.: Yale University Press, 1938.

Yans-McLaughlin, Virginia. *Family and Community: Italian Immigrants in Buffalo, 1880–1920*. Ithaca, N.Y.: Cornell University Press, 1978.

Unpublished Papers and Dissertations

Baldwin, Fred D. "The American Enlisted Man in World War I." Ph.D. diss., Princeton University, 1964.

Child, Irvin. "A Psychological Study of Second-generation Italians." Ph.D. diss., Yale University, 1939.

Conolly–Smith, Peter. "The Translated Community: New York City's German–Language Press as an Agent of Cultural Resistance and Integration, 1910–1918." Ph.D. diss., Yale University, 1996.

Ford, Nancy Gentile. "War and Ethnicity: Foreign-born Soldiers and United States Military Policy During World War I." Ph.D. diss., Temple University, 1994.

Fraser, Bruce. "Yankees at War: Social Mobilization on the Connecticut Home Front, 1917–1918." Ph.D. diss., Columbia University, 1976.

Johnston, William. "On the Outside Looking In: Irish, Italian, and Black Ethnic Politics in an American City." Ph.D. diss., Yale University, 1978.

Keene, Jennifer. "Civilians in Uniform: Building an American Mass Army for the Great War." Ph.D. diss., Carnegie–Mellon University, 1991.

King, Almeda. "A Study of the Italian Diet in a Group of New Haven Families." M.A. thesis, Yale University, 1935.

Lassonde, Stephen. "Learning to Forget: Schooling and Family Life in New Haven's Working Class, 1870–1940." Ph.D. diss., Yale University, 1994.

Miller, Morty. "New Haven: The Italian Community." B.A. thesis, Yale University, 1969.

Myers, Jerome K. "Time Differential Factor in Assimilation: A Study of the Aspects and Processes of Assimilation among the Italians of New Haven." Ph.D. diss., Yale University, 1949.

Oberdeck, Kathryn. "Labor's Vicar and the Variety Show: Popular Religion, Popular Theatre, and Cultural Class Conflict in Turn-of-the-Century America." Ph.D. diss., Yale University, 1991.

Rappaport, Joseph. "Jewish Immigrants and World War I: A Study of Yiddish Press Attitudes." Ph.D. diss., Columbia University, 1951.

Sterba, Christopher M. "The Melting Pot Goes to War: Italian and Jewish Immigrants in America's Great Crusade, 1917–1919." Ph.D. diss., Brandeis University, 1999.

Victory, James. "Soldier Making: The Forces that Shaped the Infantry Training of White Soldiers in the United States Army in World War I." Ph.D. diss., Kansas State University, 1990.

White, Bruce. "The Military and the Melting Pot: The American Army and Minority Groups, 1865–1924." Ph.D. diss., University of Wisconsin–Madison, 1968.

Index